Major Crises
in Contemporary American
Foreign Policy

D0146873

MAJOR CRISES IN CONTEMPORARY AMERICAN FOREIGN POLICY

A Documentary History

Edited by RUSSELL D. BUHITE

Primary Documents in American History and Contemporary Issues

GREENWOOD PRESS
Westport, Connecticut • London

Library of Congress Cataloging-in-Publication Data

Major crises in contemporary American foreign policy : a documentary
history / edited by Russell D. Buhite.
p.   cm.—(Primary documents in American history and
contemporary issues, ISSN 1069–5605)
Includes bibliographical references and index.
ISBN 0–313–29468–2 (alk. paper)
1. United States—Foreign relations—1945–1989—Sources.
2. United States—Foreign relations—1989– —Sources.   I. Buhite,
Russell D.   II. Series: Primary documents in American history and
contemporary issues series.
E744.M24   1997
327.73—dc20   96–32415

British Library Cataloguing in Publication Data is available.

Library of Congress Catalog Card Number: 96–32415
ISBN: 0–313–29468–2
ISSN: 1069–5605

First published in 1997

Greenwood Press, 88 Post Road West, Westport, CT 06881
An imprint of Greenwood Publishing Group, Inc.

Printed in the United States of America

The paper used in this book complies with the
Permanent Paper Standard issued by the National
Information Standards Organization (Z39.48–1984).

10   9   8   7   6   5   4   3   2   1

Copyright Acknowledgments

Contents

Contents

Contents

Series Foreword

This series is designed to meet the research needs of high school and college students by making available in one volume the key primary documents on a given historical event or contemporary issue. Documents include speeches and letters, congressional testimony, Supreme Court and lower court decisions, government reports, biographical accounts, position papers, statutes, and news stories.

The purpose of the series is twofold: (1) to provide substantive and background material on an event or issue through the text of primary documents that shaped policy or law, raised controversy, or influenced the course of events; and (2) to trace the controversial aspects of the event or issue through documents that represent a variety of viewpoints. Documents for each volume have been selected by a recognized specialist in that subject with the advice of a board of other subject specialists, school librarians, and teachers.

To place the subject in historical perspective, the volume editor has prepared an introductory overview and a chronology of events. Documents are organized either chronologically or topically. The documents are full text or, if unusually long, have been excerpted by the volume editor. To facilitate understanding, each document is accompanied by an explanatory introduction. Suggestions for further reading follow the document or the chapter.

It is the hope of Greenwood Press that this series will enable students and other readers to use primary documents more easily in their research, to exercise critical thinking skills by examining the key documents in American history and public policy, and to critique the variety of viewpoints represented by this selection of documents.

Introduction

During its early history the United States experienced a multitude of crises. Some crises, such as the secession of the southern states in 1860 and 1861, threatened the country's very existence. Other periods of international tension, such as the neutrality crises between 1794 and 1812 with Great Britain and France, provided crucial tests of the ability of the United States to maneuver in the world arena. Between 1800 and 1941, the United States fought five wars—for territorial acquisition, balance of power, and, to some degree, for principle. These wars were interspersed between several peacetime disputes: with Spain over Florida, with Great Britain over Canada and Oregon, and over British support of the Confederacy. Tensions with the great powers of Europe also erupted as the U.S. government attempted to apply the Monroe Doctrine during the French intervention in Mexico in the 1860s and during the British and German creditor demands on Venezuela in 1902. There was conflict with the fledgling Soviet Union in 1918–1919. There were also major differences with Japanese expansion in Asia as well as continuing U.S. interventions in Latin America.

All of these conflicts constituted crises of one sort or another, as did the panics, depressions, episodes of labor and farm unrest, and other domestic disturbances of the late nineteenth and early twentieth centuries. But only in the twentieth century, and particularly after World War II, did foreign relations issues bring great trauma, cost, and sacrifice: chronic crisis, serious military/diplomatic disputes of a regular, recurring nature in which the United States became a major player, and catastrophic war loomed on the horizon following America's involvement in World War II.

Indeed, World War II represents a dramatic watershed in the history of American foreign relations, and the differences in American international behavior before and after World War II are clear and striking. For one thing, from the close of the eighteenth century until the mid-twentieth century, the United States entered no peacetime alliances with other states. Not until 1949, when it joined the North Atlantic Treaty Organization (NATO), did the United States depart from the nonentangled position it had achieved in the convention of 1800, the Franco-American agreement that terminated the Revolutionary War treaties of 1778 between the two countries. The NATO alliance was only the beginning. During the Cold War era the United States established over forty security arrangements around the world. Most of these security arrangements included American economic assistance programs as well—a feature of foreign policy also nearly unheard of in the prewar period.

If the United States abjured political entanglements prior to World War II, it likewise adopted an essentially nonmilitarized foreign policy. The nation mobilized for war on six different occasions, not counting the conflicts with Native American tribes, but when war ended American armies generally evaporated. Seldom did military expenditures approach more than 1 percent of the gross national product; seldom did military spending account for more than a small fraction of the national budget; only a minuscule segment of the male population was ever called upon—except during war—for military service. American security, if not free, came about as close to being free as possible for any modern state. Following World War II, the United States demobilized rapidly but then soon undertook the building of a gigantic infrastructure of world power—a huge army, navy, and air force, bases around the world, industry geared to military production—and in a thousand other ways made itself into a national security colossus.

Prewar U.S. foreign policy was also neither assisted nor encumbered by a formal intelligence establishment. Spies provided information about enemies in the nation's wars. During World War I a primitive intelligence agency came into existence; in the interwar period American agents succeeded in some code breaking efforts; and in World War II the Office of Strategic Services (OSS) engaged in a variety of cloak and dagger activities. Not until 1947, however, with the passage of the National Security Act, did the nation get its first formal intelligence body, the Central Intelligence Agency. The budget of this agency alone would account for the inauguration of an era of relatively expensive security following World War II.

A further departure of postwar foreign policy was the country's association with the United Nations. Although President Woodrow Wilson after World War I had insisted on tying the League of Nations to the Treaty of Versailles and a majority of his countrymen probably would have favored joining the League, a combination of the president's political opponents and his own obstinacy made League membership impossible. Between 1920 and the mid-1930s, several attempts to achieve limited international cooperation through association with the World Court likewise failed. After 1943 President Franklin D. Roosevelt worked assiduously to secure allied agreement to create the United Nations. Then he moved carefully to avoid Wilson's failures. In the years immediately following World War II the United States used the UN as an agency of its foreign policy; during the 1960s the UN became increasingly a propaganda organization for communist and developing nations. But it was always a presence in U.S. policy.

From the early nineteenth century until World War I the United States never experienced a significant external threat, and in the two decades after that many Americans, including some in high office, came to believe that U.S. intervention in World War I had been a mistake, that imperial Germany had never directly challenged American interests. Until 1939, the notion of conflict as the essence of international relations probably seemed as foreign to the public and many U.S. policymakers as European cabinet diplomacy and reinsurance treaties. The experience of World War II and the Cold War changed all that, making Americans conscious of ever-present conflict and bringing recurring crises.

This book is a documentary history of eight major crises in contemporary—that is to say, post-1945—U.S. foreign relations: the crisis of 1945–1947 with the Soviet Union, the Berlin Blockade of 1948–1949, the Korean War, the Berlin crises of 1958 and 1961, the Cuban missile crisis, the Vietnam War, the Iranian hostage crisis, and the Gulf War with Iraq. Six of these are crises of the Cold War, and the conflict with Iran over the seizure of the U.S. Embassy occurred in the Cold War context. Three are actual, though undeclared, wars.

An informal operating definition of crisis proved relatively easy to achieve for this work. All of the episodes chosen are either generally agreed upon crises of a highly explosive nature or wars of major consequence. Some serious crises, like the Taiwan Straits dispute with the People's Republic of China in 1954–1955 and 1958, and the Suez crisis of 1956, are omitted not because of their lack of significance but because of word and scope limitations.

The documents printed herein obviously are not the only ones available; for most of these episodes primary sources are accessible and plentiful. For five of the Cold War crises many of the pertinent State and Defense Department records have been published in the U.S. State Department's series *Foreign Relations of the United States*. There are also a multitude of memoirs and diaries by participants in the events of the period. The objective of the work has always been to present a variety of documents and some semblance of balance, and to convey the drama of this most important period of American foreign policy.

Part I

Soviet-American Relations and the Origins of the Cold War, 1945–1947

Between 1945 and 1947, the world witnessed the onset of the Cold War, a struggle between the Soviet Union and the United States that would continue for more than four decades. Although this conflict was by no means inevitable, a number of long-standing issues in the Soviet-American relationship made it eminently predictable; nothing that had occurred prior to or during their Second World War "marriage of convenience" against the Axis powers should have led to much hope for lasting cooperation.

The mutual hostility between the Soviet Union and the United States originated with the Bolshevik Revolution of November 1917. Because the Bolsheviks immediately challenged the norms of international behavior and called for the overthrow of capitalist governments around the world, President Woodrow Wilson refused to extend diplomatic recognition to the Soviet Union, and in 1918–1919 the United States participated in an international effort with the British, French, and Japanese to overthrow the new regime.

In the period between the two world wars, neither diplomatic relations, which began in 1933, nor the initiation of trade served to ameliorate the animosity. The Soviets stepped up their propaganda campaign and promoted the American Communist Party during the Great Depression, while U.S. credit restrictions prevented much in the way of Soviet commercial expansion. Soviet Premier Josef Stalin's purges of the late 1930s reinforced the view held by the American public and policymakers alike that his regime was evil and oppressive, while the Nazi-Soviet Pact of August 1939 seemed to demonstrate the regime's hostile intentions. Only the judgment that Nazi Germany, which invaded the Soviet Union in June 1941, posed a greater immediate danger to Western civilization accounted for the submerging of American fears and the granting of Lend-Lease assistance to the Soviets.

Despite the best intentions of President Franklin D. Roosevelt to bring the Soviets into a formalized détente with the United States, World War II did little to improve the relationship. The Soviets proved secretive, refused to cooperate in stating their economic priorities, did not inform their public of the Western contribution to the victory over Nazi Germany, and openly expressed their expansionist aspirations. The United States and its ally, Great Britain, delayed opening a second front, did not share the atomic secret with the Soviets, and maintained tight control over the Italian peace negotiations. The United States, moreover, resolutely refused Soviet entreaties for a share in the occupation of Japan.

Differences over Eastern Europe and Germany occasioned the first major postwar conflict. The Yalta Agreements (February 1945) signed by the Big Three (Soviet Union, United Kingdom, and United States), provided the USSR with a sphere of influence in Soviet-occupied Poland. The United States and the United Kingdom insisted, however, that Yalta assured them a measure of access to Poland and all the newly liberated countries of Eastern Europe. Later, at the Potsdam (Berlin) Conference (July–August 1945), Josef Stalin, British Prime Minister Winston Churchill (followed by Clement Attlee), and Harry Truman would attempt to resolve their disputes over their joint occupation of Germany, and would plan their mutual effort against the military forces of Imperial Japan.

Conflicting Soviet and American world-views, not to mention objectives, soon led to increasing tension between the victorious allies. The ultimate suspicion in Western Europe and the United States was that Stalin was seeking to maximize Soviet security by undermining their own. The Soviets' brutality in imposing their will over the countries of Eastern Europe further alarmed the Western allies, as did Soviet control over Western Europe's communist parties. Soviet aspirations, rooted in an aggressive, messianic ideology and in historic Russian imperialism, seemed truly unlimited.

Containment became the strategic response of the United States toward this perceived Soviet threat. The documents presented in this part analyze some of the major issues of the early years of the Cold War and trace the implementation of the U.S. containment policy.

CHRONOLOGY

1945
January. Red Army advances across Eastern Europe
February 4. Yalta Conference begins

March 7. Western allies cross the Rhine into Germany

March. Roosevelt-Stalin cables on liberated American POWs

April 12. Roosevelt's death/Truman becomes president

April. United Nations Charter signed

April 23. Truman meets Molotov in Washington

May 7. Nazi Germany surrenders

July 16. U.S. tests atomic device at Alamogordo, New Mexico

July 25. Potsdam Conference and Declaration to Japan

August 6, 9. U.S. drops atomic bombs on Japan

August 8. Soviet Union declares war on Japan

August 14. Japan announces surrender

September 2. Japan formally surrenders on USS *Missouri* in Tokyo Bay

September. Sec. of War Stimson's memo on U.S.-USSR relations

September. Council of Foreign Ministers Meeting in London

December. UN debate of Soviet troop withdrawal from Iran

1946

February 9. Stalin's speech to Moscow voters

February 22. Kennan's "Long Telegram"

March 2. Soviet troops near Tehran spark crisis in Iran

March 5. Churchill's "Iron Curtain" speech

September. Clifford-Elsey Report to Truman

1947

March 12. Truman Doctrine provides aid to Greece and Turkey

June 5. Marshall Plan announced

July 26. National Security Act signed

September. COMINFORM established

1948

February. Communist coup in Czechoslovakia

March. Western zones of Germany unified

April 1. Soviet blockade of Berlin begins

June 23. Western allies begin airlift into Berlin

November. Truman elected president

1949

April. U.S. joins North Atlantic Treaty Organization (NATO)

AGREEMENTS AND PERSONALITIES AT YALTA

Roosevelt, Churchill, and Stalin met at Yalta in the Soviet Crimea (February 4–11, 1945) to make military arrangements for the conclusion of the war and to resolve major political/diplomatic issues for the postwar period. The primary matters addressed were the boundaries and composition of the government of Poland, what to do about liberated Europe generally, treatment to be accorded a defeated Germany, the establishment of the United Nations organization, and the terms under which the Soviet Union would enter the Allied war against Japan.

DOCUMENT 1: The Yalta Conference Protocol and Agreements (February 1945)

I. WORLD ORGANIZATION

It was decided:

(1) that a United Nations Conference on the proposed world organization should be summoned for Wednesday, 25th April, 1945, and should be held in the United States of America. . . .

II. DECLARATION ON LIBERATED EUROPE

The Premier of the Union of Soviet Socialist Republics, the Prime Minister of the United Kingdom, and the President of the United States of America have consulted with each other in the common interests of the peoples of their countries and those of liberated Europe. They jointly declare their mutual agreement to concert during the temporary period of instability in liberated Europe the policies of their three governments in assisting the peoples liberated from the domination of Nazi Germany and the peoples of the former Axis satellite states of Europe to solve by democratic means their pressing political and economic problems.

The establishment of order in Europe and the rebuilding of national economic life must be achieved by processes which will enable the liberated peoples to destroy the last vestiges of Nazism and Fascism and to creat[e] democratic institutions of their own choice. This is a principle of the Atlantic Charter—the right of all peoples to choose the form of government under which they will live—the restoration of sovereign rights and self-government to those peoples who have been forcibly deprived of them by the aggressor nations. . . .

The three governments will consult the other United Nations and provisional authorities or other governments in Europe when matters of direct interest to them are under consideration.

When, in the opinion of the three governments, conditions in any European liberated state or any former Axis satellite state in Europe make such action necessary, they will immediately consult together on the measures necessary to discharge the joint responsibilities set forth in this declaration. . . .

VII. POLAND

The following Declaration on Poland was agreed by the Conference:

A new situation has been created in Poland as a result of her complete liberation by the Red Army. This calls for the establishment of a Polish Provisional Government which can be more broadly based than was possible before the recent liberation of the Western part of Poland. The Provisional Government which is now functioning in Poland should therefore be reorganized on a broader democratic basis with the inclusion of democratic leaders from Poland itself and from Poles abroad. This new Government should then be called the Polish Provisional Government of National Unity.

Mr. [Vyacheslav M.] Molotov, Mr. [W. Averell] Harriman and Sir A. Clark Kerr are authorized as a commission to consult in the first instance in Moscow with members of the present Provisional Government and with other Polish democratic leaders from within Poland and from abroad, with a view to the reorganization of the present Government along the above lines. This Polish Provisional Government of National Unity shall be pledged to the holding of free and unfettered elections as soon as possible on the basis of universal suffrage and secret ballot. In these elections all democratic and anti-Nazi parties shall have the right to take part and to put forward candidates.

When a Polish Provisional Government of National Unity bas been properly formed in conformity with the above, the Government of the USSR, which now maintains diplomatic relations with the present Provisional Government of Poland, and the Government of the United Kingdom and the Government of the U.S.A. will establish diplomatic relations with the new Polish Provisional Government of National Unity, and will exchange Ambassadors by whose reports the respective Governments will be kept informed about the situation in Poland.

The three Heads of Government consider that the Eastern frontier of Poland should follow the Curzon Line with digressions from it in some regions of five to eight kilometers in favour of Poland. They recognize that Poland must receive substantial accessions of territory in the North and West. They feel that the opinion of the new Polish Provisional Government of National Unity should be sought in due course on the extent of these accessions and that the final delimitation of the Western frontier of Poland should thereafter await the Peace Conference.

Source: U.S. Department of State, *Foreign Relations of the United States, The Conferences at Malta and Yalta, 1945* (Washington: GPO, 1955), 975–80.

DOCUMENT 2: Soviet Diplomat Andrei Gromyko Recalls the Stalin-Roosevelt Meeting at Yalta, and the Issue of Soviet Forces in the Pacific (February 1945)

During the Yalta conference, Stalin was living . . . a short distance from the Livadia Palace. There he had his study where he received delegation members and held meetings. . . .

One morning, before leaving for Livadia, I was in my room and got a call to report to Stalin at once.

He was alone when I arrived in his study. . . . I realized he was worrying about other things than the state of his [FDR's] health. A special messenger had just delivered an urgent letter in English for him, and he handed it to me.

"This is from Roosevelt [and] I want to know what he says before the session begins."

I gave him an impromptu translation and he occasionally asked me to repeat a phrase. The letter was about the Kurile Islands and Sakhalin. Roosevelt reported that the U.S. government recognized the USSR's right to the half of the islands of Sakhalin and the Kuriles under Japanese occupation.

Stalin was very pleased. He paced the room, repeating, "Good, very good!" . . . After a few seconds, as he pondered the contents of the letter, he spoke his thoughts: "This is an important letter. The Americans recognize the justice of our position on Sakhalin and the Kuriles. Now in return they will try to insist on our participation in the war against Japan." . . .

He suddenly shot a question at me: "Tell me, what do you think of Roosevelt? Is he clever?" . . .

I knew from the many letters from Stalin I had passed to Roosevelt that even when Stalin did not take the same position as the President, he held him in high regard.

I replied: "Comrade Stalin, Roosevelt is a highly intelligent, very capable man. Just the fact that he got himself elected President for a third and then a fourth term speaks for itself. Of course, he was helped by the international situation. And a lot of it was also due to the capable job the Democrats did in popularizing his name. But his talks on the radio, his 'Fireside Chats', also made a big impact on millions of Americans."

Stalin remarked laconically: "That was smart of him. Yes, he got every-thing right."

He had what I would call a smile of solid satisfaction on his face. It was an expression I had noticed when he was feeling good, when the discussion was about someone to whom he was well disposed. As I left him, I had the feeling that his positive response to Roosevelt's letter would have an influence on the session that was to start in about an hour's time.

Certain significant events had led up to the letter. Already, back in Tehran, Roosevelt had asked Stalin about Soviet help in the war against Japan. It became apparent then that the opening of a second front by the Allies was being linked to the USSR's willingness to help the USA in the East. The USA and USSR reached an understanding in principle on that occasion, but it was not regarded as a firm agreement, and the final word on the question was not given until after Roosevelt's letter about Sakha-lin and the Kuriles. That was why, in my opinion, Stalin was so pleased by Roosevelt's letter. Several times he walked across the room with it, as if he didn't want to let go of it, and he was still holding it when I left him.

Source: Andrei Gromyko, *Memories*, translated by Harold Shukman (London: Hutchinson, 1989), 88–90.

DOCUMENT 3: Soviet "Spymaster" Compares Soviet Geopolitical Gains from the 1939 Nazi-Soviet Pact with Stalin's Expansionist Motives at Yalta (Spring 1945)

The fate of the Baltic states [agreed upon in the Molotov-Ribbentrop Pact between the Soviet Union and Nazi Germany in August 1939] . . . was similar to the fate of the East European states decided at Yalta. There are striking similarities: the preliminary agreement was to set up coali-tion governments friendly to both sides. We needed a buffer between us and the spheres of influence of the other world powers, and we were willing to face harsh confrontations in those areas where the Red Army remained in place at war's end. Once again, for the Kremlin, the mission of communism was primarily to consolidate the might of the Soviet state. Only military strength and domination of the countries on our borders could ensure us a superpower role. The idea of propagating world Com-munist revolution was an ideological screen to hide our desire for world domination. Although originally this concept was ideological in nature, it acquired the dimensions of real-politik. This possibility arose for the Soviet Union only after the Molotov-Ribbentrop Pact was signed. In the secret protocols the Soviet Union's geopolitical interests . . . for the enlargement of its frontiers were for the first time formally accepted by one of the leading powers in the world. . . .

[C]onfrontation with the Western allies had begun when the Red Army liberated Eastern Europe. . . . The principle agreed upon with Roosevelt at Yalta, providing for multiparty elections, was acceptable to us only for the transition period after the defeat of Germany, while the fate of Eastern Europe was in the balance.

Source: Pavel Sudoplatov and Anatoli Sudoplatov, with Jerrold and Leona Schecter, *Special Tasks: The Memoirs of an Unwanted Witness—A Soviet Spymaster* (Boston: Little, Brown, 1994), 102, 221.

REPATRIATION AND POLAND

In seeking U.S. acceptance of the Soviet-communist dominated government of Poland, Stalin used American ex-prisoners of war as pawns and in the process added to American disquiet over his intentions for Poland and the rest of Eastern Europe.

DOCUMENT 4: Army Chief of Staff General George C. Marshall's Instructions to General John Deane to Investigate the Treatment of American Servicemen Behind Russian Lines (3 March 1945)

Please deliver the following message from the President to Marshal Stalin at once. . . .

I [General Marshall] have reliable information regarding the difficulties which are being encountered in collecting, supplying and evacuating American ex-prisoners of war and American aircraft crews who are stranded east of the Russian lines. It is urgently requested that instructions be issued authorizing ten American aircraft with American crews to operate between Poltava and places in Poland where American ex-prisoners of war and stranded airmen may be located. This authority is requested for the purpose of providing supplementary clothing, medical and food supplies for all American soldiers, to evacuate stranded aircraft crews and liberated prisoners of war, and especially to transfer the injured and sick to the American hospital at Poltava. I regard this request to be of the greatest importance not only for humanitarian reasons but also by reason of the intense interest of the American public in the welfare of our ex-prisoners of war and stranded aircraft crews. Secondly on the general matter of prisoners of war in Germany I feel that we ought to do something quickly. The number of these prisoners of war, Russian, British and U.S., is very large. In view of your disapproval of the plan we submitted what do you suggest in place of it?

Source: U.S. Department of State, *Foreign Relations of the United States, 1945,* Vol. 5, *The Soviet Union* (hereafter *FRUS, 1945*) (Washington: GPO, 1967), 1072–73.

DOCUMENT 5: American Ambassador to the Soviet Union Cables State Department that Soviets Using U.S. Servicemen "as a Club" in Negotiations (14 March 1945)

I [Ambassador W. Averell Harriman] assume the Department has been informed by the War Department of the great difficulties General Deane and I have been having with the Soviet Government in regard to the care and repatriation of our liberated prisoners of war. In the beginning it appeared that the Soviet authorities were going to interpret our agreement substantially as we did, namely that we be allowed to send our contact officers to several points within Poland to which our prisoners first find their way, to fly in emergency supplies and to evacuate our wounded on the returning trips of the planes, although in Soviet planes rather than United States planes. We obtained authority for one contact team of an officer and doctor to go to Lublin with one plane load of supplies and they have done extremely useful work there. No other teams or supplies have since been permitted and authority for the Lublin team to remain has recently been withdrawn. The Soviets have now contended that Odessa is the only present "camps and points of concentration" referred to in the agreement to which our contact officers are to be permitted. The Soviets are, however, planning also to establish camps at Lwow, Bronnitz and Volkoivisk which are just east of the present Polish border and will be accessible to our officers, but even these camps are a long way from the original points of liberation.

Our prisoners have suffered serious hardships from lack of food, clothing, medical attention, et cetera, in finding their way to concentration points in Poland and on the long rail trip to Odessa because we have been stopped from sending in our contact teams and emergency supplies. A considerable number of sick and wounded are still hospitalized in Poland. I have been urging for the last 2 weeks that General Deane be permitted to survey the situation with a Red Army officer. This was first approved in writing with the qualification that arrangements must be made with the Polish authorities. An officer of our Military Mission informally approached the Polish Embassy here and was advised that no Polish authorization was necessary as it was entirely within the competence of the Red Army. We have been unable, however, to get authorization for Deane's trip.

It seems clear that the Soviets have changed their point of view during the last several weeks and are now rigidly determined that none of our officers shall be permitted in Poland. . . .

I feel that the Soviet Government is trying to use our liberated prisoners of war as a club to induce us to give increased prestige to the Provisional Polish Government by dealing with it in this connection as the Soviets are doing in other cases. General Deane and I have not been able to find a way to force the Soviet authorities to live up to our interpretation of our agreement. We have used every argument to no avail. Unless some steps can be taken to bring direct pressure on the Soviets our liberated prisoners will continue to suffer hardships, particularly the wounded and sick. I recommend that the Department consult with the War Department with a view of determining what further steps might be taken here or elsewhere to induce the Soviets to change their present uncooperative attitude. . . .

Consideration might be given to such actions as, or combination thereof: (1) That General [Dwight D.] Eisenhower issue orders to restrict the movements of Soviet contact officers in France to several camps or points of concentration of their citizens far removed from the points of liberation, comparable to Lwow and Odessa; (2) that Lend-Lease refuse to consider requests of Soviet Government additional to our Fourth Protocol commitments for such items as sugar, industrial equipment or other items that are not immediately essential for the Red Army and the Russian war effort; (3) that consideration be given to allowing our prisoners of war en route to Naples to give stories to the newspapers of the hardships they have been subjected to between point of liberation and arrival at Odessa and that in answer to questions of correspondents, the War Department explain the provisions of our agreement and the Soviet Government's failure to carry out the provisions of the agreement according to any reasonable interpretation.

I request urgent consideration of this question and the Department's preliminary reaction. General Deane requests that this cable be shown to General Marshall.

Source: FRUS, 1945, 1079–81.

DOCUMENT 6: President Franklin Roosevelt's Letter to Josef Stalin on Evacuation and Treatment of Liberated U.S. Servicemen in Eastern Europe (17 March 1945)

With reference to the question of evacuation of American prisoners from Poland I have been informed that the arrangement for General Deane with a Soviet Army officer to make a survey of the U.S. prisoners of war situation has been cancelled. In your last message to me you stated that there was no need to accede to my request that American aircraft be allowed to carry supplies to Poland and to evacuate the sick. I have information that I consider positive and reliable that there are a very considerable number of sick and injured Americans in hospitals in Poland and also numbers of liberated U.S. prisoners in good health who are awaiting entrainment in Poland to transit camps in Odessa, or are at large in small groups that have not yet made contact with Soviet authorities.

Frankly I cannot understand your reluctance to permit American officers and means to assist their own people in this matter. This Government has done everything to meet each of your requests. I now request you to meet mine in this particular matter.

Source: FRUS, 1945, 1082.

DOCUMENT 7: Stalin's Reply to President Roosevelt's Cable [Document 6] on the Evacuation of American POWs from Liberated Eastern Europe (22 March 1945)

In regard to the information which you have about a seemingly great number of sick and wounded Americans who are in Poland, and also those who are waiting for departure for Odessa or who did not get in touch with Soviet authorities, I must say that that information is not exact. In reality, on the territory of Poland by March 16 there were only 17 sick Americans, except a number of Americans who are on the way to Odessa. Today I have received a report that very soon they (17 persons) will be taken to Odessa by planes.

In regard to a request contained in your message I must say that if that request concerned me personally I would readily agree even to the prejudice of my interests. But in this case the matter concerns the interests of the Soviet armies at the front and Soviet commanders, who do not want to have extra officers with them, having no relation to military operations but at the same time requiring care for their accommodation, for the organization of meetings and all kinds of connections for them, for their guard from possible diversions on the part of German agents who have not yet been caught, and other measures diverting commanders and officers under their command from their direct duties.

Our commanders pay with their lives for the state of matters at the front and in the immediate rear and I do not consider it possible to limit their rights in any degree.

In addition to this I have to say that former American prisoners of war liberated by the Red Army are in Soviet prisoner-of-war camps in good conditions, at any rate in better conditions than former Soviet prisoners of war in American camps where they have been partially placed together with German prisoners of war and where some of them were subjected to unfair treatment and unlawful inconveniences up to beating as it was reported to the American Government more than once.

Source: FRUS, 1945, 1082–83.

DOCUMENT 8: Ambassador Harriman Reports the Unsatisfactory Conditions for Liberated American Servicemen in Soviet Camps (24 March 1945)

[Soviet Foreign Minister V. M.] Molotov has given me a copy of Stalin's answer to your message regarding American liberated prisoners of war in Poland. No doubt the Red Army has reported that on March 16th there were no more of our liberated prisoners in Poland except the 17 sick to which he refers. On the other hand General Deane and I believe that there are a number of our ex-prisoners, including sick, still at large in Poland. Since February 26th we have had continual definite statements from the Foreign Office and the Red Army Staff to the effect that there are no prisoners left in Poland and each time these statements have been proved to be wrong. The American Red Cross representative recently returned from Poland tells me that on the day he left Praga [suburb of Warsaw], March 18th, he talked to one American officer in the street.

Stalin's statement that our liberated prisoners are in Soviet camps under good conditions is far from the truth. Soviet facilities in Odessa meet the barest minimum needs but are improved as a result of the work of our contact officers and the American food, clothing and medical supplies that we have been able to furnish. Until arrival at Odessa the hardships undergone have been inexcusable. No effort whatsoever has been made by the Red Army to do anything until our men drifted into camps at Warsaw, Lodz, Lublin, or Wrzesnia which the Red Army advertised as points of assembly. These are some hundreds of miles from points of liberation and our men would have starved if it had not been for the generosity and hospitality of the Polish people. Individual headquarters of the Red Army have sometimes given a meal to our men. On the other hand reports indicate that in other places not only was nothing done but Red Army soldiers have taken wrist watches, clothing, and other articles at the point of a gun.

The unsatisfactory conditions existing in these camps have been ameliorated at several points by the activities of the Polish Red Cross. Conditions at the Rembertow camp at Warsaw were unbelievable. Our men were mixed with civilian refugees of all kinds, sleeping on floors, utterly no sanitary or washing facilities. Food was served twice a day at irregular intervals and consisted of barley soup, bread, potatoes, or kasha, and tea or coffee. There were no delousing facilities. I believe as a result of your cables to Stalin, and General Deane's and my pressure, our liberated prisoners have been moved to Odessa somewhat more rapidly than would otherwise have been the case. It may be there are only a relatively few of our men still in Poland, but on the other hand additional numbers may be liberated at any time and there is no reason to believe that their care will be any better than that experienced so far. Reports from our liberated prisoners when they arrive home will show that they have great gratitude for the Polish people and Polish Red Cross but nothing but resentment for the treatment received from the Russians, despite the fact that upon liberation they were deeply grateful to the Russians. The only exceptions to this are the dozen who had the good luck to get through to Moscow quickly.

Stalin's statement that the Red Army command cannot be bothered with a dozen American officers in Poland to look after the welfare of our liberated prisoners is preposterous when we think of what the American people have done in supplying the Red Army with vehicles and food. There was no thought of having our contact officers in the combat zone but I understand from General Eisenhower that he is giving Soviet contact officers complete freedom of movement to visit Russian citizens wherever they may be.

When the story of the treatment accorded our liberated prisoners by the Russians leaks out I cannot help but feel that there will be great and lasting resentment on the part of the American people.

I suggest that you reply again to Marshal Stalin, expressing thanks for his promise to fly out the 17 sick but stating that you cannot accept his position. . . . I further recommend that since the Russians cannot do less than they are now doing for our men, General Eisenhower be instructed to limit the movements of the Russian contact officers in France to several camps where Russian citizens are collected, far to the rear. We should, of course, continue to give the best treatment possible to liberated Soviet citizens and all reasonable courtesies and assistance to their contact officers at these camps in the rear.

Source: FRUS, 1945, 1084–86.

DOCUMENT 9: President Harry Truman Meets with Soviet Foreign Minister Molotov in Washington (22–23 April 1945)

On the evening of 22 April and the morning of 23 April, President Truman met with Soviet Foreign Minister Molotov in Washington at Blair House. Secretary of State Edward Stettinius, Ambassador Harriman, and Charles Bohlen were in attendance for the evening session and were joined by President Truman's Chief of Staff, Admiral William Leahy, the next day. Ambassador Andrei Gromyko joined Minister Molotov during the second session with Alexandr Pavlov serving both days as the Foreign Minister's interpreter.

The Russian Foreign Minister expressed the belief that a good basis for agreement existed in the Dumbarton Oaks [Conference of September 1944 held in Washington, at which representatives from China, Britain, the USSR, and the United States drew up a blueprint for the charter of the United Nations] and the Crimea [Yalta Agreements] decisions, and I replied that I stood firmly by those decisions and intended to carry them out. I said that I wanted to bring up at this point that the most difficult question relating to the Crimea decision was the Polish matter. . . .

Molotov expressed his understanding of that point but contended that the matter was even more important for the Soviet Union. Poland, he said, was far from the United States but bordered on the Soviet Union. The Polish question was therefore vital to them. . . .

When Molotov arrived [the next day] . . . I went straight to the point. . . .

The United States Government . . . could not agree to be a party to the formation of a Polish government which was not representative of all Polish democratic elements. I said bluntly that I was deeply disappointed that the Soviet government had not held consultations with representatives of the Polish government other than the officials of the Warsaw regime. . . .

I explained to Molotov that . . . no policy in the United States, whether foreign or domestic, could succeed unless it has public confidence and support. This, I pointed out, applied in the field of economic as well as political collaboration. In this country, I said, legislative appropriations were required for any economic measures in the foreign field, and I had no hope of getting such measures through Congress unless there was public support for them. . . .

Mr. Molotov repeated that his government supported the Crimea decisions but that he could not agree that an abrogation of those decisions by others could be considered a violation by the Soviet government. He added that surely the Polish question, involving as it did a neighboring country, was of very great interest to the Soviet government.

Since Molotov insisted on avoiding the main issue, I said what I had said before—that the United States was prepared to carry out loyally all the agreements reached at Yalta, . . . but I wanted it clearly understood that this could be only on a basis of the mutual observation of agreements and not on the basis of a one-way street.

"I have never been talked to like that in my life," Molotov said.

I told him, "Carry out your agreements and you won't get talked to like that."

Source: Harry S. Truman, *Memoirs: Year of Decisions* (Garden City, N.Y.: Doubleday, 1955), 70–82.

ATOMIC DIPLOMACY AND POTSDAM

President Roosevelt and Prime Minister Churchill did not share with Stalin the secret of the Manhattan Project (the top-secret American plan to develop an atomic bomb). After the successful test of the bomb, President Truman informed Stalin at the Potsdam Conference (17 July– 2 August 1945) of the new weapon. Stalin was not surprised at Truman's disclosure because his intelligence service had kept him apprised of the progress of the U.S. project. On 6 and 9 August, the United States dropped atomic bombs on both Hiroshima and Nagasaki, Japan, leading quickly to the Japanese surrender on 14 August (formal surrender came on 2 September 1945); then the United States kept the Soviets out of the occupation of Japan.

DOCUMENT 10: Winston Churchill to Secretary of War Henry Stimson on "Tube Alloys" (18 July 1945)

MR. SECRETARY STIMSON[:] I enclose a photostat record of the Hyde Park Agreement on T. A., for which you asked the Chancellor of the Exchequer. . . .

Aide-Mémoire of Conversation Between the President and the Prime Minister at Hyde Park, September 18, 1944.

1. The suggestion that the world should be informed regarding TUBE ALLOYS, with a view to an international agreement regarding its control and use, is not accepted. The matter should continue to be regarded as of the utmost secrecy; but when a "bomb" is finally available, it might perhaps, after mature consideration, be used against the Japanese, who should be warned that this bombardment will be repeated until they surrender.

2. Full collaboration between the United States and the British Government in developing TUBE ALLOYS for military and commercial purposes should continue after the defeat of Japan unless and until terminated by joint agreement.

F[ranklin] D R[oosevelt]   W[inston] S C[hurchill]

Source: U.S. Department of State, *Foreign Relations of the United States, The Conference of Berlin (The Potsdam Conference), 1945,* Vol. 2 (Washington: GPO, 1960), 1370–71.

DOCUMENT 11: Soviet Foreign Minister Molotov Recalls the Soviets' Atomic Program and the Role of American Scientists Julius and Ethel Rosenberg (1943–1953)

We'd been working on th[e atomic bomb] since 1943. I [Vyacheslav M. Molotov] was ordered to take charge, find someone who could build an atomic bomb. The *Chekists* [secret police] gave me a list of reliable physicists. I made my choice and summoned [Pytor] Kapista, an Academician.

He indicated we weren't prepared, that the atomic bomb was a weapon not for this war but for the next. . . .

I decided to give him the material from our intelligence service—the agents had done something very important. . . . This was sometime after the Battle of Stalingrad in 1943. . . .

I myself didn't understand anything about the material, but I knew it had been obtained from good, reliable sources. . . .

This was a fine operation on the part of our *Chekists*. They did well in getting what we needed—at precisely the right time, when we had just begun this project. . . .

The Rosenberg couple . . . I tried not to ask any questions about that, but I think they were connected with [our] intelligence. . . . Somebody helped us a great deal with the atomic bomb. The secret service played a very big role. In America, the Rosenbergs paid for this. It's not excluded that they were involved in helping us.

Source: Woodford McClellan, "Molotov Remembers," *Cold War International History Project Bulletin* 1 (Spring 1992) (Washington: Wilson International Center for Scholars, 1992), 20.

DOCUMENT 12: Secretary of War Stimson's Memo to President Truman on the Effect of the U.S. Atomic Bomb on Relations with Russia (11 September 1945)

In handing you today my memorandum about our relations with Russia in respect to the atomic bomb, I am not unmindful of the fact that when in Potsdam I talked with you about the question whether we could be safe in sharing the atomic bomb with Russia while she was still a police state and before she put into effect provisions assuring personal rights of liberty to the individual citizen.

I still recognize the difficulty and am still convinced of the importance of the ultimate importance of a change in Russian attitude toward individual liberty but I have come to the conclusion that it would not be possible to use our possession of the atomic bomb as a direct lever to produce the change. I have become convinced that any demand by us for an internal change in Russia as a condition of sharing in the atomic weapon would be so resented that it would make the objective we have in view less probable.

I believe that the change in attitude toward the individual in Russia will come slowly and gradually and I am satisfied that we should not delay our approach to Russia in the matter of the atomic bomb until that process has been completed. My reasons are set forth in the memorandum I am handing you today. Furthermore, I believe that this long process of change in Russia is more likely to be expedited by the closer relationship in the matter of the atomic bomb which I suggest and the trust and confidence that I believe would be inspired by the method of approach which I have outlined. . . .

The advent of the atomic bomb has stimulated great military and probably even greater political interest throughout the civilized world. In a world atmosphere already extremely sensitive to power, the introduction of this weapon has profoundly affected political considerations in all sections of the globe.

In many quarters it has been interpreted as a substantial offset to the growth of Russian influence on the continent. We can be certain that the Soviet Government has sensed this tendency and the temptation will be strong for the Soviet political and military leaders to acquire this weapon in the shortest possible time. . . . Such a condition will almost certainly stimulate feverish activity on the part of the Soviets toward the development of this bomb in what will in effect be a secret armament race of a rather desperate character. There is evidence to indicate that such activity may have already commenced.

Source: FRUS, 1945, Vol. 2, 40–44.

DOCUMENT 13: Ambassador Gromyko Recalls How President Truman Notified Stalin that America Was Preparing to Use the Atomic Bomb Against Japan (24 July 1945)

Long before the [Potsdam] conference, the USA had been making intense efforts to develop the atom bomb, and later, when many facts pertaining to its invention were made public, the behavior of Truman and Churchill at Potsdam became clear. The U.S. Secretary for War, Stimson, wrote in his memoirs that Washington had thought it essential to delay deciding post-war European and other problems until the USA had the trump of the nuclear weapon in its hand.

Certainly, until the timetable for making the bomb had been met, the American president tried to delay the Potsdam meeting, and it was in fact postponed at his request from June to July. He waited impatiently for the results of the test and when he finally got them—on 16 July 1945, secretly, just one day before the opening of the conference—he obviously felt he would be able to take a tough line in the talks.

This was immediately apparent in the initial discussions on Eastern Europe. Truman loudly made the unsubstantiated claim that the Soviet side had not fulfilled the obligations agreed by the three powers in the

Crimea. We firmly rejected this assertion, as well as Washington's attempts to interfere in Eastern Europe which reflected its expansionist ambitions there and in other areas of the world.

The U.S. side was therefore compelled to recognize that, without the bomb as an open political factor, in effect as blackmail, nothing would come of their tough stand. Accordingly, a few days later, on 24 July, as Stalin was making his exit after the session, the president held him back and said: "I have something to tell you in confidence." Stalin stopped and waited. Truman said, "The United States has built a new weapon of great destructive power which we intend to use against Japan."

Stalin took the news calmly, showing no emotion—a reaction which apparently disappointed Truman.

Very soon afterwards, however, a meeting took place in Stalin's residence at Potsdam which has etched itself in my mind. Only Stalin, Molotov, [Soviet Ambassador to Britain] Gusev and I were present. . . .

Stalin then raised the matter which turned out to be the main point of our meeting.

"Our allies have told us that the USA has a new weapon, the atom bomb. I spoke with our own physicist, Kurchatov, as soon as Truman told me they had tested it successfully. We will no doubt have our own bomb before long. But its possession places a huge responsibility on any state. The real question is, should the countries which have the bomb simply compete with each other in its production, or should they, and any other countries that acquire it later, seek a solution that would mean the prohibition of its production and use? It's hard at this moment to see what sort of agreement there could be, but one thing is clear: nuclear energy should only be allowed to be used for peaceful purposes."

Molotov agreed and added: "And the Americans have been doing all this work on the atom bomb without telling us."

Stalin said tersely: "Roosevelt clearly felt no need to put us in the picture. He could have done it at Yalta. He could simply have told me the atom bomb was going through its experimental stages. We were supposed to be allies."

It was noticeable that, even though Stalin was annoyed, he spoke calmly. He continued: "No doubt Washington and London are hoping we won't be able to develop the bomb ourselves for some time. And meanwhile, using America's monopoly, in fact America's and Britain's, they want to force us to accept their plans on questions affecting Europe and the world. Well, that's not going to happen!" And now, for once, he cursed in ripe language. A broad grin appeared on the face of my good friend Gusev.

Of course, Stalin did not touch on the scientific or technical aspects of the problem. But it is widely known that, while in Potsdam, he contacted Moscow several times to give instructions to the experts on this matter.

Source: Gromyko, *Memories*, 107–10.

DOCUMENT 14: The Potsdam Conference's Protocol of Proceedings (1 August 1945)

1. ESTABLISHMENT OF A COUNCIL OF FOREIGN MINISTERS

The Conference reached the following agreement for the establishment of a Council of Foreign Ministers to do the necessary preparatory work for the peace settlements:

(1) There shall be established a Council composed of the Foreign Ministers of the United Kingdom, the Union of Soviet Socialist Republics, China, France and the United States.

(2) (i) The Council shall normally meet in London, which shall be the permanent seat of the joint Secretariat which the Council will form. Each of the Foreign Ministers will be accompanied by a high-ranking Deputy, duly authorized to carry on the work of the Council in the absence of his Foreign Minister, and by a small staff of technical advisers.

(ii) The first meeting of the Council shall be held in London not later than September 1st 1945. Meetings may be held by common agreement in other capitals as may be agreed from time to time.

(3) (i) As its immediate important task, the Council shall be authorized to draw up, with a view to their submission to the United Nations, treaties of peace with Italy, Rumania, Bulgaria, Hungary and Finland, and to propose settlements of territorial questions outstanding on the termination of the war in Europe. The Council shall be utilized for the preparation of a peace settlement for Germany to be accepted by the Government of Germany when a government adequate for the purpose is established.

(ii) For the discharge of each of these tasks the Council will be composed of the Members representing those States which were signatory to the terms of surrender imposed upon the enemy State concerned. For the purposes of the peace settlement for Italy, France shall be regarded as a signatory to the terms of surrender for Italy. Other Members will be invited to participate when matters directly concerning them are under discussion.

(iii) Other matters may from time to time be referred to the Council by agreement between the Member Governments.

Source: The Conference of Berlin (Potsdam), Vol. 1, 1478–98.

DOCUMENT 15: Soviet General Recounts Stalin's Cancellation of Soviet Landing on the Japanese Island of Hokkaido (August 1945)

On the eve of the Soviet campaign against Japan, Stalin ordered [Marshal Alexander Mikhailovich] Vasilievsky, commander of Soviet forces in the Far East, not only to liberate the southern half of the island of Sakhalin and the Kurile Islands, but also to occupy half the island of Hokkaido to the north of a line between the towns of Kusiro and Rumoi, deploying two infantry divisions, one fighter and one bomber wing. When Soviet forces had reached the southern half of Sakhalin, on 23 August 1945 Stalin ordered the embarkation of the 87th Infantry Corps for a landing on Hokkaido. This order had not yet been carried out when, on the 25th, southern Sakhalin was already liberated. Stalin paused: what would he gain by a landing? It would probably spoil his already deteriorating relations with the Allies. He cancelled the order for the landing on Hokkaido. The Far East chief of headquarters staff, General S. P. Ivanov, passed on his instructions: "In order to avoid conflict and misunderstanding with our Allies, the launching of any ships or aircraft in the direction of Hokkaido is strictly forbidden."

Source: Dmitri Volkogonov, *Stalin: Triumph and Tragedy*, translated by Harold Shukman (London: Weidenfeld & Nicolson, 1991), 502 nn. 13, 14.

DOCUMENT 16: Soviet Intelligence Officer Reveals that an American Scientist Informed Soviets of America's Inability to Conduct a Nuclear War Against the USSR (Late 1940s)

[Klaus] Fuchs revealed that American production was one hundred kilograms of U-235 a month and twenty kilos of plutonium per month. This was of the highest importance, because from this information we could calculate the number of atomic bombs possessed by the Americans. Thus, we were able to determine that the United States was not prepared for a nuclear war with us at the end of the 1940s or even in the early 1950s. . . .

Stalin pursued a tough policy of confrontation against the United States when the Cold War started; he knew he did not have to be afraid of the American nuclear threat, at least until the end of the 1940s. Only by 1955 did we estimate the stockpile of American and British nuclear weapons to be sufficient to destroy the Soviet Union.

Source: Sudoplatov and Sudoplatov, *Special Tasks*, 210.

THE COUNCIL OF FOREIGN MINISTERS: TRIPOLITANIA, JAPAN, AND IRAN

The six-month period after the conclusion of the war was a critical time in American-Soviet relations. The failure of the Foreign Ministers' Conferences at London and Moscow satisfactorily to resolve differences over Eastern Europe, Soviet interest in Japan and in the Middle East, and Stalin's seeming declaration of ideological warfare in February 1946 seriously troubled American policymakers.

DOCUMENT 17: Secretary of State James Byrnes Remembers the Council of Foreign Ministers Meeting in London (September 1945)

I [James F. Byrnes] had been Secretary of State two months when we boarded the Queen Elizabeth on September 5, 1945, for London and the first meeting of the Council of Foreign Ministers. . . .

One of the things that gave us particular concern in these talks was the unmistakable evidence of Russian expansion. I had secured the Yalta agreement on the Kuriles, Sakhalin, Dairen and Port Arthur from the Map Room, in the White House. At Potsdam we had encountered the Soviet demands that Poland be given a large portion of eastern Germany to compensate for the Polish territory east of the Curzon Line taken over by the Soviets; her demands for Koenigsberg; for a share in the administration of the Ruhr; and for control of the Dardanelles. Her determination to dominate the Balkan states had become apparent, and at Potsdam she had made a bid for control of one of Italy's North African colonies, preferably Tripolitania.

This last request was especially disturbing because events had convinced me that the Soviets' interest in this territory was primarily military. Throughout the war they had shown a tendency to enter into multilateral arrangements when they were economic in character and demonstrably of direct benefit to them, but to prefer unilateral action where military and security considerations were involved. . . .

Mr. Molotov was precise and specific. He wanted to discuss Tripolitania. The Soviet Union had a sea outlet in the north, he asserted, and in view of its vast territory should have one also in the south, "especially so since we now have the right to use Dairen and Port Arthur in the Far East."

"The Soviet Union should take the place that is due it," he said, "and therefore should have bases in the Mediterranean for its merchant fleet. We do not propose to introduce the Soviet system into this territory apart from the democratic order that is desired by the people." And then, he added, "This will not be done along the lines that have been used in Greece."

In a private conversation with Mr. Molotov it became apparent that another difficult misunderstanding in language had arisen between ourselves and the Russians. At the San Francisco Conference when the question of establishing a trusteeship system within the United Nations was being considered, the Soviet delegation had asked Mr. Stettinius what the American attitude would be toward the assumption by the Soviet Union of a trusteeship. Mr. Stettinius replied in general terms, expressing the opinion that the Soviet Union was "eligible" to receive a territory for administration under trusteeship. Mr. Molotov took this to mean we would support a Soviet request for a trusteeship. He told me he was surprised that we were opposing his request for Tripolitania. He admitted the letter contained no specific commitment as to the Italian colonies, but asserted that these colonies provided the only opportunity that the Soviet Union would have to acquire a trusteeship, and therefore a commitment was certainly implied.

Source: James F. Byrnes, *Speaking Frankly* (New York: Harper and Brothers, 1947), 92, 96–97, 102.

DOCUMENT 18: Secretary Byrnes Recalls Ambassador Harriman's Report of Stalin's Keen Interest in the Allied Occupation of Japan (November 1945)

[After the London Conference] I had asked Ambassador Harriman to request an interview with Generalissimo Stalin who was then on vacation in the Crimea. I wanted him to present to Stalin directly an amended proposal for a peace conference. . . .

The result was a revelation. When the Ambassador started to present our views on European questions, Stalin interrupted to say that what he wanted to hear about was our view on the control of Japan. Mr. Harriman was as surprised as he was unprepared, and my surprise was even greater.

At London when Mr. Molotov had raised the question of Japan at the same time that he was killing days discussing procedural questions, we had concluded it was simply part of his war of nerves. Ambassador Harriman, who was present at London, agreed with me that the Balkan issue was the crucial one. Now, we suddenly realized we had been wrong. The remarkable performance that had led to the breakdown of the London Conference had been stimulated by the Russians' belief that they were not being consulted adequately by our officials in Japan.

Source: Byrnes, *Speaking Frankly*, 108.

DOCUMENT 19: Secretary Byrnes at the Council of Foreign Ministers Meeting in Moscow and His Discussion with Stalin about Iran (December 1945)

My talks with the Generalissimo . . . were marked by their encouraging combination of frankness and cordiality. One of the issues on which I placed particular emphasis was the situation in Iran.

At our first meeting on December 19, I told him we were concerned about the events in Iran because of the pledge President Roosevelt had entered into with him and Prime Minister Churchill at Teheran in 1943. In that pledge, the three leaders recognized "the assistance which Iran has given in the prosecution of the war against the common enemy, particularly by facilitating transportation of supplies from overseas to the Soviet Union." The declaration promised that "any economic problem confronting Iran at the close of hostilities should receive full consideration" along with those of other members of the United Nations. It expressly declared that they were "at one with the Government of Iran in their desire for the maintenance of the independence, sovereignty and territorial integrity of Iran."

Developments within Iran prior to the Moscow meeting indicated that the pledge was in danger of being broken. The Iranian Government had protested that when it dispatched 1,500 troops toward the province of Azerbaijan to quell what the Iranians said was an insurrection encouraged by foreign sources, the force had been stopped en route and ordered by the Red army to turn back. The Iranian Government thereupon asked for the withdrawal of all foreign troops. We promptly issued an order to the remaining American troops to evacuate and I sent a message to the Soviet Union and the United Kingdom urging that they take similar action.

The Iranian protest was still pending and I told the Generalissimo that, unless we fulfilled the Teheran Declaration, Iran very likely would place its complaint before the forthcoming meeting of the United Nations in London. As a signatory of the declaration, the United States would feel obliged to support Iran's right to be heard. We felt it would be difficult to explain how the Soviet Army of 30,000 would have been endangered, as they had asserted, by the presence of 1,500 Iranian soldiers.

Stalin outlined what he termed "the pertinent facts" in the matter. The Baku oil fields in the south of Russia lay close to the border and this created a special problem. These fields had to be safeguarded against any possible hostile action by Iran against the Soviet Union, and no confidence could be placed in the Iranian Government. Saboteurs might be sent to the Baku oil fields to set them on fire, he continued. Since the Soviet Union had a right, by treaty, to maintain troops in Iran until March 15, it did not want to withdraw before that date. At that time, he said, it would be necessary to examine the situation and see whether or not it was possible to evacuate the soldiers. The decision would depend upon the conduct of the Iranian Government. He pointed out that a 1921 treaty with Iran gave the Soviet Union the right to send troops into northern Iran if there was a possible danger from an outside source.

I told him I was greatly surprised to learn that he considered the Iranian Government hostile in view of his declaration at Teheran, and in view of the report made to me by General Connolly, the commanding general of our forces in Iran, that the Government had co-operated well with both the Red Army and the American forces in moving supplies through to the Soviet Union. While he had a right to maintain his troops in Iran until March, I pointed out that he was not required to do so. The United States, incidentally, had always regarded March 2 as the deadline date rather than March 15, as cited by Stalin.

Stalin told me that the Soviet Union had no designs, territorial or otherwise, against Iran and would withdraw its troops as soon as they felt secure about the Baku oil fields.

Source: Byrnes, *Speaking Frankly,* 118–19.

DOCUMENT 20: Stalin's Speech that the Western Powers Initially Assessed as "The Declaration of World War III" (9 February 1946)

Eight years have elapsed since the last elections to the Supreme Soviet. This was a period rich in events of a decisive nature. . . .

It would be wrong to believe that the Second World War broke out accidentally or as a result of the mistakes of some or other statesmen, though mistakes certainly were made. In reality, the war broke out as an inevitable result of the development of world economic and political forces on the basis of modern monopoly capitalism.

Marxists have stated more than once that the capitalist system of world economy conceals in itself the elements of general crisis and military clashes, that in view of this in our time the development of world capitalism takes place not as a smooth and even advance but through crises and war catastrophes.

The reason is that the unevenness of the development of capitalist countries usually results, as time passes, in an abrupt disruption of the equilibrium within the world system of capitalism, and that a group of capitalist countries which believes itself to be less supplied with raw materials and markets usually attempts to alter the situation and re-divide the "spheres of influence" in its own favour by means of armed force.

This results in the splitting of the capitalist world into two hostile camps in war between them.

Perhaps the catastrophes of war could be avoided if there existed possibility of re-distributing periodically raw materials and markets among countries in accordance with their economic weight—by means of adopting coordinated and peaceful decisions. This, however, cannot be accomplished under present capitalist conditions of the development of world economy.

Thus the first crisis of the capitalist system of world economy resulted in the First World War, and the second crisis resulted in the Second World War. . . .

And so, what are the results of the war?

There is one main result which served as a basis for all other results. This result is that at the end of the war the enemies suffered defeat and we, together with our Allies, emerged as victors. We ended the war in complete victory over the enemy—this is the principal result of the war. . . .

Our victory means, in the first place, that our Soviet social system has won, that the Soviet social system successfully withstood the trial in the flames of war and proved its perfect viability.

Source: J. V. Stalin, "Speech Delivered by J. V. Stalin at a Meeting of Voters of the Stalin Electoral Area of Moscow, February 9, 1946" (Washington: Embassy of the U.S.S.R., March 1946).

THE LONG TELEGRAM, THE IRON CURTAIN SPEECH, AND THE CLIFFORD REPORT

From February to September 1946 the United States began firming up its opposition to Soviet behavior. First came Chargé d'Affaires George Kennan's Long Telegram from Moscow discussing the sources of Soviet conduct and his prescription for dealing with that conduct; then came—with President Truman's blessing—Prime Minister Churchill's enunciation of the Iron Curtain speech at Westminster College, and finally presidential aide Clark Clifford's report on the need for a tough new American policy toward the Soviet Union.

DOCUMENT 21: East-West Tension Ascribed to Kremlin's Ideological Conception of Inevitability of Conflict Between Communist-Capitalist Camps (June 1946)

Columbia Broadcasting correspondent [Richard C.] Hottelet interviewed [Maxim] Litvinov, [former Soviet Foreign Minister then out of any position of power] June 18 in latter's office. As Litvinov was very outspoken, Hottelet has not used material from interview. He has reported it to us for Dept's and our information and requests that its substance be conveyed to [Edward R.] Murrow of CBS for his background information only. Report follows should obviously be handled with great discretion.

Discussing international situation, Litvinov said outlook was bad and it seemed to him differences between East and West have gone too far to be reconciled. Asked cause of this he said that as far as he was concerned root cause was ideological conception prevailing here [Moscow] of inevitability of conflict between Communist and capitalist worlds. It seemed to him that there had once been chance that two worlds would be able to exist side by side but that was obvious[ly] no longer case.

There has now been return in USSR to outmoded concept of geographical security.

In discussing principles being explored now to find basis of cooperation, Litvinov said basis of cooperation must be agreement among great powers. Obviously Haiti or Denmark could not threaten world peace and it is not unreasonable for USSR to be suspicious of any forum in which she would constantly be outvoted. Hottelet asked how this present chasm could be bridged. Litvinov answered, I won't say until they call on me and they certainly will not call on me. Hottelet asked him if he was sure he would not be called upon and he replied, I am positive. He said I am an observer and I am glad to be out of it. His whole attitude in this part of the conversation was one of passive resignation. Hottelet asked what chances would be of postponing any conflict between East and West long enough to allow new and younger men to grow up and take over. His answer was, what difference does it make if the young men are educated intensively in precise spirit of the old.

Hottelet asked if he had heard of [Bernard] Baruch's suggestion to turn atomic secrets over to International Control Board and said that this seemed to him to be a most dramatic crystallization of the world's current dilemma, and asked what would USSR do—whether she would accept international control or refuse it. Litvinov reflected for a moment and said there was a vast difference between subscribing to principle of international control and actually subjecting oneself to rigid inspection. Hottelet asked him specifically whether USSR was likely to go whole way. He said he thought USSR was unlikely to submit to inspection. Hottelet asked him if suspicion which seems to be large motivating force in Soviet policy would be mitigated if West were suddenly to give in and grant all Russian demands, like Trieste, Italian colonies, et cetera—whether that would lead to easing of situation. He said it would lead to West being faced after period of time with next series of demands.

Discussing question of mutual suspicion, topic of genuine security versus imperialist aggression was dwelt on. Litvinov said Hitler probably genuinely felt that his demands were justified, that he wanted *Lebensraum*. Hitler was probably genuinely convinced that his actions were preventive and forced on him by external circumstance. Advantages that accrue to any totalitarian govt through its possibility of ignoring its public opinion were discussed. Litvinov volunteered that there was nothing one could do inside a totalitarian state to change it. He said that Italian and German people did not revolt even in face of most dreadful punishment. In 1792 French people could storm arsenals, grab muskets and make revolution, but today people would need artillery, tanks, radio stations, printing presses, all of which are held tightly in the hands of any totalitarian state. That is why it would be terribly difficult, for instance, to dislodge [Spain's fascist dictator Francisco] Franco. Even for a palace revolution one would need support of army and police.

Switching back to atomic bomb, Hottelet asked whether since gas was outlawed and not used during World War II, what he thought chances were of atomic bomb not being used in event of another war. Litvinov said that depends on attitude of people who have an atomic bomb. If one side thinks it can bring about quick victory by use of atomic bombs then temptation will be great. If evenly matched and if one side feels that its immense area and manpower, resources and dispersed industry safeguard it to large extent, it will not be too loath to use it. This would be especially true where public opinion has no weight, where state leadership has completely conditioned public mind. Hottelet asked why present leaders who are after all astute and capable men cling to a patently outworn idea that a river or mountain range or 1,000 kilometers of ground would provide security. Litvinov answered, because they are conservative in their thinking and still follow old lines.

Germany was discussed. It was Litvinov's opinion that it would obviously be broken up into two parts. Since all Allies professed to want unified Germany Hottelet asked would it not somehow be possible to find single solution. Litvinov answered each side wants unified Germany under its control. It was his opinion that of all single problems in world today, Germany was greatest problem.

At end of conversation Litvinov underscored that he was a private citizen speaking his own individual ideas.

Source: Foreign Relations of the United States, 1946, Vol. 6, Eastern Europe; The Soviet Union (Washington: GPO, 1969), 763–65.

DOCUMENT 22: Chargé George F. Kennan's "Long Telegram" (22 February 1946)

I apologize in advance for this burdening of telegraphic channel; but questions involved are of such urgent importance, particularly in view of recent events, that our answers to them ... deserve attention ... at once. ...

At bottom of Kremlin's neurotic view of world affairs is traditional and instinctive Russian sense of insecurity. Originally, this was insecurity of a peaceful agricultural people trying to live on vast exposed plain in neighborhood of fierce nomadic peoples. To this was added, as Russia came into contact with economically advanced West, fear of more competent, more powerful, more highly organized societies in that area. But this latter type of insecurity was one which afflicted rather Russian rulers than Russian people; for Russian rulers have invariably sensed that their rule was relatively archaic in form, fragile and artificial in its psychological foundation, unable to stand comparison or contact with political systems of Western countries. For this reason they have always feared foreign penetration, feared direct contact between Western world and their own, feared what would happen if Russians learned truth about world without or if foreigners learned truth about world within. And they had learned to seek security only in patient but deadly struggle for total destruction of rival power, never in compacts and compromises with it.

It was no coincidence that Marxism, which had smouldered ineffectively for half a century in Western Europe, caught hold and blazed for first time in Russia. Only in this land which had never known a friendly neighbor or indeed any tolerant equilibrium of separate powers, either internal or international, could a doctrine thrive which viewed economic conflicts of society as insoluble by peaceful means. After establishment of Bolshevist regime, Marxist dogma, rendered even more truculent and intolerant by Lenin's interpretation, became a perfect vehicle for sense of insecurity with which Bolsheviks, even more than previous Russian rulers, were afflicted. In this dogma, with its basic altruism of purpose, they found justification for their instinctive fear of outside world, for the dictatorship without which they did not know how to rule, for cruelties they did not dare not to inflict, for sacrifices they felt bound to demand. In the name of Marxism they sacrificed every single ethical value in their methods and tactics. Today they cannot dispense with it. It is fig leaf of their moral and intellectual respectability. Without it they would stand before history, at best, as only the last of that long succession of cruel and wasteful Russian rulers who have relentlessly forced [the] country on to ever new heights of military power in order to guarantee external security of their internally weak regimes. This is why Soviet purposes must always be solemnly clothed in trappings of Marxism, and why no one should underrate importance of dogma in Soviet affairs. Thus Soviet leaders are driven [by] necessities of their own past and present position to put forward a dogma which [appears to the] outside world as evil, hostile and menacing, but as bearing within itself germs of creeping disease and destined to be wracked with growing internal convulsions until it is given final coup de grace by rising power of socialism and yields to new and better world. This thesis provides justification for that increase of military and police power of Russian state, for that isolation of Russian population from outside world, and for that fluid and constant pressure to extend limits of Russian police power which are together the natural and instinctive urges of Russian rulers. Basically this is only the steady advance of uneasy Russian nationalism, a centuries old movement in which conceptions of offense and defense are inextricably confused. But in new guise of international Marxism, with its honeyed promises to a desperate and war torn outside world, it is more dangerous and insidious than ever before.

It should not be thought from above that Soviet party line is necessarily disingenuous and insincere on part of all those who put it forward. Many of them are too ignorant of outside world and mentally too dependent to question [this] self-hypnotism, and who have no difficulty making themselves believe what they find it comforting and convenient to believe. Finally we have the unsolved mystery as to who, if anyone, in this great land actually receives accurate and unbiased information about outside world. In atmosphere of oriental secretiveness and conspiracy which pervades this Government, possibilities for distorting or poisoning sources and currents of information are infinite. The very disrespect of Russians for objective truth—indeed, their disbelief in its existence—leads them to view all stated facts as instruments for furtherance of one ulterior purpose or another. There is good reason to suspect that this Government is actually a conspiracy within a conspiracy; and I for one am reluctant to believe that Stalin himself receives anything like an objective picture of outside world. Here there is ample scope for the type of subtle intrigue at which Russians are past masters. Inability of foreign governments to place their case squarely before Russian policy makers—extent to which they are delivered up in their relations with Russia to good graces of obscure and unknown advisers who they never see and cannot influence—this to my mind is most disquieting feature of diplomacy in Moscow, and one which Western statesmen would do well to keep in mind if they would understand nature of difficulties encountered here. . . .

In summary, we have here a political force committed fanatically to the belief that with US there can be no permanent modus vivendi, that it is desirable and necessary that the internal harmony of our society be disrupted, our traditional way of life be destroyed, the international authority of our state be broken, if Soviet power is to be secure. This political force has complete power of disposition over energies of one of world's greatest peoples and resources of world's richest national territory, and is borne along by deep and powerful currents of Russian nationalism. In addition, it has an elaborate and far flung apparatus for exertion of its influence in other countries, an apparatus of amazing flexibility and versatility, managed by people whose experience and skill in underground methods are presumably without parallel in history. Finally, it is seemingly inaccessible to considerations of reality in its basic reactions. For it, the vast fund of objective fact about human society is not, as with us, the measure against which outlook is constantly being tested and re-formed, but a grab bag from which individual items are selected arbitrarily and tendentiously to bolster an outlook already pre-conceived. This is admittedly not a pleasant picture. Problem of how to cope with this force [is] undoubtedly greatest task our diplomacy has ever faced and probably greatest it will ever have to face. It should be point of departure from which our political general staff work at present juncture should proceed. It should be approached with same thorough-ness and care as solution of major strategic problem in war, and if nec-essary, with no smaller outlay in planning effort. I cannot attempt to suggest all answers here. But I would like to record my conviction that problem is within our power to solve—and that without recourse to any general military conflict. And in support of this conviction there are cer-tain observations of a more encouraging nature I should like to make:

1. Soviet power, unlike that of Hitlerite Germany, is neither schematic nor adventuristic. It does not work by fixed plans. It does not take un-necessary risks. Impervious to logic of reason, and it is highly sensitive to logic of force. For this reason it can easily withdraw—and usually does—when strong resistance is encountered at any point. Thus, if the adversary has sufficient force and makes clear his readiness to use it, he rarely has to do so. If situations are properly handled there need be no prestige-engaging showdowns.

2. Gauged against Western World as a whole, Soviets are still by far the weaker force. Thus, their success will really depend on degree of cohesion, firmness and vigor which Western World can muster. And this is factor which it is within our power to influence.

3. Success of Soviet system, as form of internal power, is not yet finally proven. It has yet to be demonstrated that it can survive supreme test of successive transfer of power from one individual or group to another. Lenin's death was first such transfer, and its effects wracked Soviet state for 15 years. After Stalin's death or retirement will be second. But even this will not be final test. Soviet internal system will now be subjected, by virtue of recent territorial expansions, to series of additional strains which once proved severe tax on Tsardom. We here are convinced that never since termination of civil war have mass of Russian people been emotionally farther removed from doctrines of Communist Party than they are today. In Russia, party has now become a great and—for the moment—highly successful apparatus of dictatorial administration, but it has ceased to be a source of emotional inspiration. Thus, internal soundness and permanence of movement need not yet be regarded as assured.

4. All Soviet propaganda beyond Soviet security sphere is basically negative and destructive. It should therefore be relatively easy to combat it by any intelligent and really constructive program.

For these reasons I think we may approach calmly and with good heart problem of how to deal with Russia. As to how this approach should be made, I only wish to advance, by way of conclusion, following comments:

1. Our first step must be to apprehend, and recognize for what it is, the nature of the movement with which we are dealing. We must study it with same courage, detachment, objectivity, and same determination not to be emotionally provoked or unseated by it, with which doctor studies unruly and unreasonable individual.

2. We must see that our public is educated to realities of Russian situation. I cannot over-emphasize importance of this. Press cannot do this alone. It must be done mainly by Government, which is necessarily more experienced and better informed on practical problems involved. In this we need not be deterred by [the magnitude] of picture. I am convinced that there would be far less hysterical anti-Sovietism in our country today if realities of this situation were better understood by our people. There is nothing as dangerous or as terrifying as the unknown. It may also be argued that to reveal more information on our difficulties with Russia would reflect unfavorably on Russian-American relations. I feel that if there is any real risk here involved, it is one which we should have courage to face, and sooner the better. But I cannot see what we would be risking. Our stake in this country, even coming on heels of tremendous demonstrations of our friendship for Russian people, is remarkably small. We have here no investments to guard, no actual trade to lose, virtually no citizens to protect, few cultural contacts to preserve. Our only stake lies in what we hope rather than what we have; and I am convinced we have better chance of realizing those hopes if our public is enlightened and if our dealings with Russians are placed entirely on realistic and matter-of-fact basis.

3. Much depends on health and vigor of our own society. World communism is like malignant parasite which feeds only on diseased tissue. This is point at which domestic and foreign policies meet. Every courageous and incisive measure to solve internal problems of our own society, to improve self-confidence, discipline, morale and community spirit of our own people, is a diplomatic victory over Moscow worth a thousand diplomatic notes and joint communiques. If we cannot abandon fatalism and indifference in face of deficiencies of our own society, Moscow will profit—Moscow cannot help profiting by them in its foreign policies.

4. We must formulate and put forward for other nations a much more positive and constructive picture of sort of world we would like to see than we have put forward in past. It is not enough to urge people to develop political processes similar to our own. Many foreign peoples, in Europe at least, are tired and frightened by experiences of past, and are less interested in abstract freedom than in security. They are seeking

guidance rather than responsibilities. We should be better able than Russians to give them this. And unless we do, Russians certainly will.

5. Finally we must have courage and self-confidence to cling to our own methods and conceptions of human society. After all, the greatest danger that can befall us in coping with this problem of Soviet communism, is that we shall allow ourselves to become like those with whom we are coping.

Source: Cable from Kennan to U.S. State Department, in U.S. Department of State, *Foreign Relations of the United States, 1946*, Vol. 6, *The Soviet Union* (Washington: GPO, 1969), 696–709.

DOCUMENT 23: Winston Churchill's "Iron Curtain" Speech (5 March 1946)

A shadow has fallen upon the scenes so lately lighted by the Allied victory. Nobody knows what Soviet Russia and its Communist international organization intends to do in the immediate future, or what are the limits, if any, to their expansive and proselytizing tendencies. I have a strong admiration and regard for the valiant Russian people and for my wartime comrade, Marshal Stalin. There is sympathy and good will in Britain—and I doubt not here also—toward the peoples of all the Russias and a resolve to persevere through many differences and rebuffs in establishing lasting friendships.

We understand the Russian need to be secure on her western frontiers from all renewal of German aggression. We welcome her to her rightful place among the leading nations of the world. Above all, we welcome constant, frequent, and growing contacts between Russian people and our own people on both sides of the Atlantic. It is my duty, however, to place before you certain facts about the present position in Europe.

From Stettin in the Baltic to Trieste in the Adriatic, an iron curtain has descended across the continent. Behind that line lie all the capitals of the ancient states of central and eastern Europe. Warsaw, Berlin, Prague, Vienna, Budapest, Belgrade, Bucharest, and Sofia, all these famous cities and the populations around them lie in the Soviet sphere and all are subject, in one form or another, not only to Soviet influence but to a very high and increasing measure of control from Moscow. Athens alone, with its immortal glories, is free to decide its future at an election under British, American, and French observation.

The Russian-dominated Polish government has been encouraged to make enormous and wrongful inroads upon Germany, and mass expulsions of millions of Germans on a scale grievous and undreamed of are now taking place. The Communist parties, which were very small in all these eastern states of Europe, have been raised to preeminence and power far beyond their numbers and are seeking everywhere to obtain totalitarian control. Police governments are prevailing in nearly every case, and so far, except in Czechoslovakia, there is no true democracy.

Turkey and Persia are both profoundly alarmed and disturbed at the claims which are made upon them and at the pressure being exerted by the Moscow government. An attempt is being made by the Russians in Berlin to build up a quasi-Communist party in their zone of occupied Germany by showing special favors to groups of left-wing German leaders. At the end of the fighting last June, the American and British Armies withdrew westward, in accordance with an earlier agreement, to a depth at some points of 150 miles on a front of nearly 400 miles, to allow the Russians to occupy this vast expanse of territory which the western democracies had conquered.

If now the Soviet government tries, by separate action, to build up a pro-Communist Germany in their areas, this will cause new serious difficulties in the British and American zones, and will give the defeated Germans the power of putting themselves up to auction between the Soviets and the western democracies. Whatever conclusions may be drawn from these facts—and facts they are—this is certainly not the liberated Europe we fought to build up. Nor is it one which contains the essentials of permanent peace.

In front of the iron curtain which lies across Europe are other causes for anxiety. In Italy the Communist party is seriously hampered by having to support the Communist-trained Marshal Tito's claims to former Italian territory at the head of the Adriatic. Nevertheless, the future of Italy hangs in the balance. . . .

However, in a great number of countries, far from the Russian frontiers and throughout the world, Communist fifth columns are established and work in complete unity and absolute obedience to the directions they receive from the Communist center. Except in the British Commonwealth, and in the United States, where communism is in its infancy, the Communist parties or fifth columns constitute a growing challenge and peril to Christian civilization. These are somber facts for anyone to have to recite on the morrow of a victory gained by so much splendid comradeship in arms and in the cause of freedom and democracy, and we should be most unwise not to face them squarely while time remains.

The outlook is also anxious in the Far East and especially in Manchuria. The agreement which was made at Yalta, to which I was a party, was extremely favorable to Soviet Russia, but it was made at a time when no one could say that the German war might not extend all through the summer and autumn of 1945 and when the Japanese war was expected to last for a further eighteen months from the end of the German war. . . .

Our difficulties and dangers will not be removed by closing our eyes to them; they will not be removed by mere waiting to see what happens; nor will they be relieved by a policy of appeasement. What is needed is a settlement, and the longer this is delayed, the more difficult it will be and the greater our dangers will become. From what I have seen of our Russian friends and allies during the war, I am convinced that there is nothing they admire so much as strength, and there is nothing for which they have less respect than for military weakness. For that reason the old doctrine of a balance of power is unsound. We cannot afford, if we can help it, to work on narrow margins, offering temptations to a trial of strength. If the Western democracies stand together in strict adherence to the principles of the United Nations Charter, their influence for fur-thering these principles will be immense and no one is likely to molest them. If, however, they become divided or falter in their duty, and if these all-important years are allowed to slip away, then indeed catastro-phe may overwhelm us all. . . .

There never was a war in all history easier to prevent by timely action than the one which has just desolated such great areas of the globe. It could have been prevented without the firing of a single shot, and Ger-many might be powerful, prosperous, and honored today, but no one would listen and one by one we were all sucked into the awful whirl-pool.

We surely must not let that happen again. This can only be achieved by reaching now, in 1946, a good understanding on all points with Rus-sia under the general authority of the United Nations and by the main-tenance of that good understanding through many peaceful years, by the world instrument, supported by the whole strength of the English-speaking world and all its connections.

Source: Congressional Record (1946), 79th Congress, 2nd session, A1145–47.

DOCUMENT 24: The "Monumental Top-Secret" Clifford-Elsey Report Prepared for President Truman (24 September 1946)

The primary objective of United States policy toward the Soviet Union is to convince Soviet leaders that it is in their interest to participate in a system of world cooperation, that there are no fundamental causes for war between our two nations, and that the security and prosperity of the Soviet Union, and that of the rest of the world as well, is being jeopardized by aggressive militaristic imperialism such as that in which the Soviet Union is now engaged.

However, these same leaders with whom we hope to achieve an understanding on the principles of international peace appear to believe that a war with the United States and the other leading capitalistic nations is inevitable. They are increasing their military power and the sphere of Soviet influence in preparation for the "inevitable" conflict, and they are trying to weaken and subvert their potential opponents by every means at their disposal. So long as these men adhere to these beliefs, it is highly dangerous to conclude that hope of international peace lies only in "accord," "mutual understanding," or "solidarity" with the Soviet Union.

Adoption of such a policy would impel the United States to make sacrifices for the sake of Soviet-U.S. relations, which would only have the effect of raising Soviet hopes and increasing Soviet demands, and to ignore alternative lines of policy, which might be much more compatible with our own national and international interests.

The Soviet Government will never be easy to "get along with." The American people must accustom themselves to this thought, not as a cause for despair, but as a fact to be faced objectively and courageously. If we find it impossible to enlist Soviet cooperation in the solution of world problems, we should be prepared to join with the British and other Western countries in an attempt to build up a world of our own which will pursue its own objectives and will recognize the Soviet orbit as a distinct entity with which conflict is not predestined but with which we cannot pursue common aims.

As long as the Soviet Government maintains its present foreign policy based upon the theory of an ultimate struggle between Communism and Capitalism, the United States must assume that the U.S.S.R. might fight any time for the twofold purpose of expanding the territory under communist control and weakening its potential capitalist opponents. The Soviet Union was able to flow into the political vacuum of the Balkans, Eastern Europe, the Near East, Manchuria and Korea because no other nation was both willing and able to prevent it. Soviet leaders were encouraged by easy success and they are now preparing to take over new areas in the same way. The Soviet Union, as Stalin euphemistically phrased it, is preparing "for any eventuality."

Unless the United States is willing to sacrifice its future security for the sake of "accord" with the U.S.S.R. now, this government must, as a first step toward world stabilization, seek to prevent additional Soviet aggression. The greater the area controlled by the Soviet Union, the greater the military requirements of this country will be. Our present military plans are based on the assumption that, for the next few years at least, Western Europe, Middle East, China and Japan will remain outside the Soviet sphere. If the Soviet Union acquires control of one or more of these areas, the military forces required to hold in check those of the U.S.S.R. and prevent still [further] acquisitions will be substantially enlarged. That will also be true if any of the naval and air bases in the Atlantic and Pacific, upon which our present plans rest, are given up. This government should be prepared, while scrupulously avoiding any act which would be an excuse for the Soviets to begin a war, to resist vigorously and successfully any efforts of the U.S.S.R. to expand into areas vital to American security.

The language of military power is the only language which disciples of power politics understand. The United States must use that language in order that Soviet leaders will realize that our government is determined to uphold the interests of its citizens and the rights of small nations. Compromise and concessions are considered, by the Soviets, to be evidences of weakness and they are encouraged by our "retreats" to make new and greater demands.

The main deterrent to Soviet attack on the United States, or to attack on areas of the world which are vital to our security, will be the military power of this country. It must be made apparent to the Soviet Government that our strength will be sufficient to repel any attack and sufficient to defeat the U.S.S.R. decisively if a war should start. The prospect of defeat is the only sure means of deterring the Soviet Union.

The Soviet Union's vulnerability is limited due to the vast area over which its key industries and natural resources are widely dispersed, but it is vulnerable to atomic weapons, biological warfare, and long-range air power. Therefore, in order to maintain our strength at a level which will be effective in restraining the Soviet Union, the United States must be prepared to wage atomic and biological warfare. A highly mechanized army, which can be moved either by sea or by air, capable of seizing and holding strategic areas, must be supported by powerful naval and air forces. A war with the U.S.S.R. would be "total" in a more horrible sense than any previous war and there must be constant research for both offensive and defensive weapons. . . .

Comparable to our caution in agreeing to arms limitation, the United States should avoid premature disclosure of scientific and technological information relating to war materiel until we are assured of either a change in Soviet policies or workable international controls. Any disclosure would decrease the advantage the United States now has in technological fields and diminish our strength in relation to that of the U.S.S.R.

In addition to maintaining our own strength, the United States should support and assist all democratic countries which are in any way menaced or endangered by the U.S.S.R. Providing military support in case of attack is a last resort; a more effective barrier to communism is strong economic support. Trade agreements, loans and technical missions strengthen our ties with friendly nations and are effective demonstrations that capitalism is at least the equal of communism. The United States can do much to ensure that economic opportunities, personal freedom and social equality are made possible in countries outside the Soviet sphere by generous financial assistance. Our policy on reparations should be directed toward strengthening the areas we are endeavoring to keep outside the Soviet sphere. Our efforts to break down trade barriers, open up rivers and international waterways, and bring about economic unification of countries, now divided by occupation armies, are also directed toward the re-establishment of vigorous and healthy noncommunist economies.

The Soviet Union recognizes the effectiveness of American economic assistance to small nations and denounces it bitterly by constant propaganda. The United States should realize that Soviet propaganda is dangerous (especially when American "imperialism" is emphasized) and should avoid any actions which give an appearance of truth to the Soviet charges. A determined effort should be made to expose the fallacies of such propaganda.

There are some trouble-spots which will require diligent and considered effort on the part of the United States if Soviet penetration and eventual domination is to be prevented. In the Far East, for example, this country should continue to strive for a unified and economically stable China, a reconstructed and democratic Japan, and a unified and independent Korea. We must ensure Philippine prosperity and we should assist in the peaceful solution, along noncommunistic lines, of the political problems of Southeast Asia and India.

With respect to the United Nations, we are faced with the fact that the U.S.S.R. uses the United Nations as a means of achieving its own ends. We should support the United Nations and all other organizations contributing to international understanding, but if the Soviet Union should threaten to resign at any time because it fails to have its own way, the United States should not oppose Soviet departure. It would be better to continue the United Nations as an association of democratic states than to sacrifice our principles to Soviet threats.

Since our difficulties with the Soviet Union are due primarily to the doctrines and actions of a small ruling clique and not the Soviet people, the United States should strive energetically to bring about a better understanding of the United States among influential Soviets and to counteract the anti-American propaganda which the Kremlin feeds to the Soviet people. To the greatest extent tolerated by the Soviet Government, we should distribute books, magazines, newspapers and movies among the Soviets, beam radio broadcasts to the U.S.S.R., and press for an exchange of tourists, students and educators. We should aim, through intellectual and cultural contacts, to convince Soviet leaders that the United States has no aggressive intentions and that the nature of our society is such that peaceful coexistence of capitalistic and communistic states is possible. . . .

Our best chances of influencing Soviet leaders consist in making it unmistakably clear that action contrary to our conception of a decent world order will redound to the disadvantage of the Soviet regime whereas friendly and cooperative action will pay dividends. If this position can be maintained firmly enough and long enough, the logic of it must permeate eventually into the Soviet system. . . .

Our policies must also be global in scope. By time-honored custom, we have regarded "European Policy," "Near Eastern Policy," "Indian Policy" and "Chinese Policy" as separate problems to be handled by experts in each field. But the areas involved, far removed from each other by our conventional standards, all border on the Soviet Union and our actions with respect to each must be considered in the light of overall Soviet objectives.

Only a well-informed public will support the stern policies which Soviet activities make imperative and which the United States Government must adopt. The American people should be fully informed about the difficulties in getting along with the Soviet Union, and the record of Soviet evasion, misrepresentation, aggression and militarism should be made public.

In conclusion, as long as the Soviet Government adheres to its present policy, the United States should maintain military forces powerful enough to restrain the Soviet Union and to confine Soviet influence to its present area. All nations not now within the Soviet sphere should be given generous economic assistance and political support in their opposition to Soviet penetration.

Source: Thomas Etzold and John Gaddis, eds., *Containment: Documents on American Policy and Strategy, 1945–1950* (New York: Columbia University Press, 1978), 64–71.

THE TRUMAN DOCTRINE AND THE NATIONAL SECURITY ACT

The first major implementation of containment came in the Truman Doctrine of 1947, which promised American funds for Greece to help stem a communist (but not Soviet) rebellion in that country, and support for Turkey to help the latter resist Soviet pressures. Along with the new

American approach came a military reorganization, which "unified" the armed forces, created the Central Intelligence Agency, and established the National Security Council to help (it was hoped) coordinate military and foreign policy.

DOCUMENT 25: President Truman Reveals Plan to Aid Greece and Turkey as Crucial Element of His Doctrine to Contain Communist Expansion (12 March 1947)

The gravity of the situation which confronts the world today necessitates my appearance before a joint session of the Congress.

The foreign policy and the national security of this country are involved.

One aspect of the present situation, which I wish to present to you at this time for your consideration and decision, concerns Greece and Turkey.

The United States has received from the Greek Government an urgent appeal for financial and economic assistance. Preliminary reports from the American economic mission now in Greece and reports from the American ambassador in Greece corroborate the statement of the Greek Government that assistance is imperative if Greece is to survive as a free nation. . . .

I do not believe that the American people and the Congress wish to turn a deaf ear to the appeal of the Greek Government. . . .

Greece's neighbor, Turkey, also deserves our attention. . . .

The British Government has informed us that, owing to its own difficulties, it can no longer extend financial or economic aid to Turkey.

As in the case of Greece, if Turkey is to have the assistance it needs, the United States must supply it. We are the only country able to provide that help.

I am fully aware of the broad implications involved if the United States extends assistance to Greece and Turkey, and I shall discuss these implications with you at this time.

One of the primary objectives of the foreign policy of the United States is the creation of conditions in which we and other nations will be able to work out a way of life free from coercion. This was a fundamental issue in the war with Germany and Japan. Our victory was won over countries which sought to impose their will, and their way of life, upon other nations.

To ensure the peaceful development of nations, free from coercion, the

United States has taken a leading part in establishing the United Nations. The United Nations is designed to make possible lasting freedom and independence for all its members. We shall not realize our objectives, however, unless we are willing to help free peoples to maintain their free institutions and their national integrity against aggressive movements that seek to impose upon them totalitarian regimes. This is no more than a frank recognition that totalitarian regimes imposed upon free peoples, by direct or indirect aggression, undermine the foundations of international peace and hence the security of the United States.

The peoples of a number of countries of the world have recently had totalitarian regimes forced upon them against their will. The Government of the United States has made frequent protests against coercion and intimidation, in violation of the Yalta agreement, in Poland, Rumania, and Bulgaria. I must also state that in a number of other countries there have been similar developments.

At the present moment in world history nearly every nation must choose between alternative ways of life. The choice is too often not a free one.

One way of life is based upon the will of the majority, and is distinguished by free institutions, representative government, free elections, guarantees of individual liberty, freedom of speech and religion, and freedom from political oppression.

The second way of life is based upon the will of a minority forcibly imposed upon the majority. It relies upon terror and oppression, a controlled press and radio, fixed elections, and the suppression of personal freedoms.

I believe that it must be the policy of the United States to support free peoples who are resisting attempted subjugation by armed minorities or by outside pressures.

I believe that we must assist free peoples to work out their own destinies in their own way.

I believe that our help should be primarily through economic and financial aid which is essential to economic stability and orderly political processes.

The world is not static, and the status quo is not sacred. But we cannot allow changes in the status quo in violation of the Charter of the United Nations by such methods as coercion, or by such subterfuges as political infiltration. In helping free and independent nations to maintain their freedom, the United States will be giving effect to the principles of the Charter of the United Nations.

It is necessary only to glance at a map to realize that the survival and integrity of the Greek nation are of grave importance in a much wider situation. If Greece should fall under the control of an armed minority, the effect upon its neighbor, Turkey, would be immediate and serious.

Confusion and disorder might well spread throughout the entire Middle East.

Moreover, the disappearance of Greece as an independent state would have a profound effect upon those countries in Europe whose peoples are struggling against great difficulties to maintain their freedoms and their independence while they repair the damages of war.

It would be an unspeakable tragedy if these countries, which have struggled so long against overwhelming odds, should lose that victory for which they sacrificed so much. Collapse of free institutions and loss of independence would be disastrous not only for them but for the world. Discouragement and possibly failure would quickly be the lot of neighboring peoples striving to maintain their freedom and independence.

Should we fail to aid Greece and Turkey in this fateful hour, the effect will be far reaching to the West as well as to the East.

We must take immediate and resolute action.

I therefore ask the Congress to provide authority for assistance to Greece and Turkey in the amount of $400,000,000 for the period ending June 30, 1948. In requesting these funds, I have taken into consideration the maximum amount of relief assistance which would be furnished to Greece out of the $350,000,000 which I recently requested that the Congress authorize for the prevention of starvation and suffering in countries devastated by the war.

In addition to funds, I ask the Congress to authorize the detail of American civilian and military personnel to Greece and Turkey, at the request of those countries, to assist in the tasks of reconstruction, and for the purpose of supervising the use of such financial and material assistance as may be furnished. I recommend that authority also be provided for the instruction and training of selected Greek and Turkish personnel.

Finally, I ask that the Congress provide authority which will permit the speediest and most effective use, in terms of needed commodities, supplies, and equipment, of such funds as may be authorized.

If further funds, or further authority, should be needed for the purposes indicated in this message, I shall not hesitate to bring the situation before the Congress. On this subject the executive and legislative branches of the Government must work together.

This is a serious course upon which we embark.

I would not recommend it except that the alternative is much more serious.

The United States contributed $341,000,000,000 toward winning World War II. This is an investment in world freedom and world peace.

The assistance that I am recommending for Greece and Turkey amounts to little more than one-tenth of 1 percent of this investment. It is only common sense that we should safeguard this investment and make sure that it was not in vain.

The seeds of totalitarian regimes are nurtured by misery and want. They spread and grow in the evil soil of poverty and strife. They reach their full growth when the hope of a people for a better life has died.

We must keep that hope alive.

The free peoples of the world look to us for support in maintaining their freedoms.

If we falter in our leadership, we may endanger the peace of the world—and we shall surely endanger the welfare of our own Nation.

Great responsibilities have been placed upon us by the swift movement of events.

I am confident that the Congress will face these responsibilities squarely.

Source: Public Papers of the Presidents, Harry S Truman, 1947 (Washington: GPO, 1963), 176–80.

DOCUMENT 26: National Security Act of 1947 . . . the NSC, the CIA, the JCS, and the National Military Establishment (26 July 1947)

Be it enacted by the Senate and House of Representatives of the United States of America in Congress assembled,

That this Act may be cited as the "National Security Act of 1947".

SEC. 2. In enacting this legislation, it is the intent of Congress to provide a comprehensive program for the future security of the United States; to provide for the establishment of integrated policies and procedures for the departments, agencies, and functions of the Government relating to the national security; to provide three military departments for the operation and administration of the Army, the Navy (including naval aviation and the United States Marine Corps), and the Air Force, with their assigned combat and service components; to provide for their authoritative coordination and unified direction under civilian control but not to merge them; to provide for the effective strategic direction of the armed forces and for their operation under unified control and for their integration into an efficient team of land, naval, and air forces.

TITLE 1—COORDINATION FOR NATIONAL SECURITY
NATIONAL SECURITY COUNCIL

SEC. 101. (a) There is hereby established a council to be known as the National Security Council.

The President of the United States shall preside over meetings of the Council: *Provided*, That in his absence he may designate a member of the Council to preside in his place.

The function of the Council shall be to advise the President with respect to the integration of domestic, foreign, and military policies relating to the national security so as to enable the military services and the other departments and agencies of the Government to cooperate more effectively in matters involving the national security. . . .

CENTRAL INTELLIGENCE AGENCY

SEC. 102. (a) There is hereby established under the National Security Council a Central Intelligence Agency with a Director of Central Intelligence, who shall be the head thereof. The Director shall be appointed by the President, by and with the advice and consent of the Senate, from among the commissioned officers of the armed services or from among individuals in civilian life. . . .

[2](d) For the purpose of coordinating the intelligence activities of the several Government departments and agencies in the interest of national security, it shall be the duty of the Agency, under the direction of the National Security Council, [to]

(1) advise the National Security Council in matters concerning such intelligence activities of the Government departments and agencies as relate to national security; (2) make recommendations to the National Security Council for the coordination of such intelligence activities of the departments and agencies of the Government as relate to the national security; (3) correlate and evaluate intelligence relating to the national security, and provide for the appropriate dissemination of such intelligence within the Government using where appropriate existing agencies and facilities: *Provided*, That the Agency shall have no police, subpoena, law enforcement powers, or internal-security functions: *Provided further*, That the departments and other agencies of the Government shall continue to collect, evaluate, correlate, and disseminate departmental intelligence: *And provided further*, That the Director of Central Intelligence shall be responsible for protecting intelligence sources and methods from unauthorized disclosure; (4) perform, for the benefit of the existing intelligence agencies, such additional services of common concern as the National Security Council determines can be more efficiently accomplished centrally; [and] (5) perform such other functions and duties related to intelligence affecting the national security as the National Security Council may from time to time direct.

NATIONAL SECURITY RESOURCES BOARD

SEC. 103. (a) There is hereby established a National Security Resources Board to be composed of the Chairman of the Board and such heads or representatives of the various executive departments and independent agencies as may from time to time be designated by the President to be members of the Board. . . .

(c) It shall be the function of the Board to advise the President concerning the coordination of military, industrial, and civilian mobilization[.] . . .

TITLE 2—THE NATIONAL MILITARY ESTABLISHMENT

NATIONAL MILITARY ESTABLISHMENT

SEC. 201. (a) There is hereby established the National Military Establishment, and the Secretary of Defense shall be the head thereof.

(b) The National Military Establishment shall consist of the Department of the Army, the Department of the Navy, and the Department of the Air Force, together with all other agencies created under title 2 of this Act. . . .

JOINT CHIEFS OF STAFF

SEC. 211. (a) There is hereby established within the National Military Establishment the Joint Chiefs of Staff, which shall consist of the Chief of Staff, United States Army; the Chief of Naval Operations; the Chief of Staff, United States Air Force; and the Chief of Staff to the Commander in Chief, if there be one.

(b) Subject to the authority and direction of the President and the Secretary of Defense, it shall be the duty of the Joint Chiefs of Staff [to]

(1) prepare strategic plans and to provide for the strategic direction of the military forces; (2) prepare joint logistic plans and to assign to the military services logistic responsibilities in accordance with such plans; (3) establish unified commands in strategic areas when such unified commands are in the interest of national security; (4) formulate policies for joint training of the military forces; (5) formulate policies for coordinating the education of members of the military forces; (6) review major material and personnel requirements of the military forces, in accordance with strategic and logistic plans; and (7) provide United States representation on the Military Staff Committee of the United Nations in accordance with the provisions of the Charter of the United Nations. . . .

(e) The Joint Chiefs of Staff shall act as the principal military advisers to the President and the Secretary of Defense and shall perform such other duties as the President and the Secretary of Defense may direct or as may be prescribed by law.

Source: Public Law 253 (1947), 80th Congress, 1st session.

THE MARSHALL PLAN AND COMINFORM

Because Western Europe was economically shattered by the war and had not begun to recover sufficiently, and possessed, at least in France and Italy, strong communist parties, the United States moved in 1947–1948 to provide massive financial assistance through the Marshall Plan. The United States invited Soviet participation but was genuinely relieved at the Soviets' refusal to participate in the recovery program.

DOCUMENT 27: American Diplomat George Kennan Explains the Functions of the State Department's Policy Planning Staff and Its Recommendations to Secretary of State George Marshall of Plan for the Economic Reconstruction of Europe (24 May 1947)

On 24 May 1947 Secretary of State George Marshall had a meeting in his office at which State Department officers Dean Acheson, Will Clayton, Benjamin Cohen, Chip Bohlen, and George Kennan reviewed plans for the economic reconstruction of Europe. Secretary Marshall asked his aides for comments and supporting arguments for their 23 May Planning Staff Report that became known as the "Marshall Plan."

The function of the Planning Staff was primarily to bring together the knowledge and views of all these people, to cull out of them a workable recommendation for the principles on which our approach to this problem might be based and for the procedure that might best be followed, and to accept formal responsibility before the Secretary of State for this recommendation. . . .

Our principal contributions consisted:

(a) in establishing the principle that the Europeans should themselves take the initiative in drawing up a program and should assume central responsibility for its terms;

(b) in the insistence that the offer should be made to all of Europe—that if anyone was to divide the European continent, it should be the Russians, with their response, not we with our offer; and

(c) in the decisive emphasis placed on the rehabilitation of the

German economy and the introduction of the concept of German recovery as a vital component of the recovery of Europe as a whole.

Source: George F. Kennan, *Memoirs, 1925–1950* (Boston: Little, Brown, 1967), 342–
43.

DOCUMENT 28: Soviet General Stresses that COMINFORM Was Stalin's Response to Truman's Doctrine of Containment (September 1947)

Stalin was prepared to use any means, including the international labour and Communist movements and the emerging peace movement, if
it gained ground for the Soviet Union in its competitive struggle with
the transatlantic colossus. After prolonged discussion with Molotov and
[Andrei] Zhdanov, he decided on a move that was bound to be seen by
the West in an extremely negative light. He resolved to establish an
agency to coordinate the activities of the Communist Parties. . . .

On 22–27 September 1947, the Polish Communists, encouraged by Stalin, organized a meeting of nine European Communist parties in the
Polish town of Szklarska Poreba. On the eve of the meeting, Zhdanov,
who had been deputed by Stalin to represent the Soviet Communist
Party, sent a coded telegram to Moscow outlining the preliminary results
of a working party:

It was proposed to start with informational reports from all the participating Communist parties. Then to work out an agenda. We will suggest 1) the international situation, the speech to be made by us, 2)
coordinating the parties' activities. The outcome should be a coordinating centre with its residence in Warsaw. . . . [later became the Warsaw
Pact]

Stalin gave his approval. As a result of the Szklarska meeting, and
four years after the dissolution of Comintern, the Information Bureau of
the Communist and Labour Parties came into being as Informburo, or
Cominform in Western parlance. . . . Zhdanov's speech on the international situation contained the thesis that would become virtually the cor-
nerstone of Soviet propaganda, namely the division of the world into
two opposing camps, in effect the response to the Truman Doctrine.

Source: Volkogonov, *Stalin: Triumph and Tragedy*, 533–34 n. 64.

FURTHER READING

Buhite, Russell D. *Decisions at Yalta* (1987).
Gaddis, John Lewis. *The Long Peace* (1987).
———. *Strategies of Containment* (1982).
Herkin, Gregg. *The Winning Weapon* (1987).
Hogan, Michael J. *The Marshall Plan* (1987).
LaFeber, Walter. *America, Russia and the Cold War*, 7th ed. (1993).
Larson, Deborah W. *Origins of Containment: A Psychological Explanation* (1985).
Leffler, Melvyn P. *A Preponderance of Power* (1992).
Mayers, David. *George Kennan and the Dilemmas of U.S. Foreign Policy* (1988).
Messer, Robert L. *The End of an Alliance* (1982).
Pollard, Robert A. *Economic Security and the Origins of the Cold War* (1986).
Rhodes, Richard. *The Making of the Atomic Bomb* (1987).
Woods, Randall, and Howard Jones. *Dawning of the Cold War* (1990).

Part II

The Berlin Blockade and Airlift, 1948–1949

The Berlin crisis of 1948–1949 originated in World War II decisions about the occupation of Germany and imprecision about Western access to the city of Berlin, as well as in political/economic differences over Germany between 1948 and 1949. At the Moscow Foreign Ministers' Conference of October 1943 the Big Three powers (Great Britain, the Soviet Union, and the United States) agreed to establish the European Advisory Commission to recommend zones for the postwar allied occupation of Germany. Before the commission had had a chance to meet, the British came forward with a proposal that gave the United States territory in southwestern Germany, the British a zone in the northwest, and the Soviets control of the eastern sector of the country. The advisory commission soon put its imprimatur on the plan. The Soviets accepted this proposal in early 1944, and the Americans, who had not given the matter concerted attention at the official level, soon did likewise. At the Yalta Conference France was given a zone to be carved out of territory controlled by the Western allies.

Until the war ended no one gave much thought to access to Berlin, which was to lie approximately one hundred fifty miles within the Soviet sector and was to be divided into occupation zones like the rest of the country. Only on 29 June 1945 did the Soviet commander in Germany, Marshal G. K. Zhukov, verbally grant the allies access via one air corridor, one highway, and one rail line.

At the Potsdam Conference the allies agreed to treat Germany as one political and economic unit, but therein lay the genesis of difficulty over Berlin. The Soviets, who had suffered massive destruction and death at the hands of the Germans, refused to ship agricultural products from their sector to the West even though they continued to extract reparations from the western zones. In May 1946 the United States and Britain stopped the shipments of reparations and soon began the process of merging their zones, an effort that the French joined at the end of 1947. In 1948 the Western allies moved toward the creation of a separate West German state integrated into the Western economic community.

The Soviets responded as they were capable of responding: by holding Berlin hostage—or, in other words, by imposing a blockade on Western access to the city. The United States then led its allies in a decision to impose a counter-blockade which, among other things, shut off the supply of coal from the Ruhr to the East; and it began a massive airlift of supplies into Berlin. The latter move eventually proved so successful that by the spring of 1949 the Soviets agreed to lift the blockade. They had obviously chosen not to push the United States into war over this issue, though their tactics of harassing American supply planes led to some terribly tense moments, and they realized that the West would not be expelled from the city or deterred in its plans for West Germany. The major consequence of this crisis was that the United States, by standing firm, had achieved its first significant victory in a Cold War confrontation with the Soviet Union.

CHRONOLOGY

1944
September. Lancaster House Protocol on Zones of Occupation

1945
February. Yalta Conference Protocol on Defeated Germany

May 7. Nazi Germany surrenders

August 2. Potsdam Conference Protocol on Zones of Occupation

September 2. Japan formally surrenders on USS *Missouri* in Tokyo Bay

November 30. Allied Control Council approves air corridors

1946
September 6. Sec. of State Byrnes' speech on postwar Germany

1947
March 12. Truman Doctrine of military aid against communists

June 5. Marshall Plan announced

July 26. National Security Act signed

1948
February. Communist coup in Czechoslovakia

March. Western zones of Germany unified

April 1. Soviet blockade of Berlin begins

June 23. Western allies begin airlift into Berlin

July 6. U.S. diplomatic note to USSR

July. Secretary Forrestal sends B-29s to Britain

September 26. Western foreign ministers refer crisis to UN

November. Truman elected president

1949

February 2. Stalin's interview with Kingsbury Smith

April. North Atlantic Treaty Organization created

March–May. Ambassador Jessup's "Park Avenue diplomacy"

May 4. Blockade ends with Four Power Agreement on Berlin

August. Soviet Union explodes atomic bomb

September–October. Communist forces win civil war in China

1950

January. State Department's Hiss convicted of perjury

February. Sen. McCarthy questions loyalty of diplomatic corps

April 25. NSC-68 as basis of U.S. policy toward containing Soviet and Chinese communist expansion

June 25. North Koreans invade South Korea; Korean War begins

November 26. China enters Korean War

THE ALLIES' GERMANY AND BERLIN DILEMMA

The documents in this section refer to the establishment of occupation zones in Germany and Berlin, the breakdown of the Potsdam Agreement, the termination of reparations shipments from the western zones of Germany to the Soviet sector, and the creation of a West German state. The final document raises a question about Stalin's motives: Did he impose the blockade in part as a way of assisting the Chinese communists?

DOCUMENT 29: Lancaster House Protocol on the Zones of Occupation in Germany and the Administration of "Greater Berlin" (12 September 1944)

The Governments of the United States of America, the United Kingdom of Great Britain and Northern Ireland, and the Union of Soviet

Socialist Republics have reached the following agreement with regard to the execution of Article 11 of the Instrument of Unconditional Surrender of Germany:

1. Germany, within her frontiers as they were on the 31st December, 1937, will, for the purposes of occupation, be divided into three zones, one of which will be allotted to each of the three Powers, and a special Berlin area, which will be under joint occupation by the three Powers.

2. The boundaries of the three zones and of [the] Berlin area, and the allocation of the three zones as between U.S.A., the U.K., and the U.S.S.R. will be as follows: Eastern Zone . . . North-Western Zone . . . South-Western Zone . . . Berlin Area.

The Berlin area (by which expression is understood the territory of "Greater Berlin" as defined by the Law of the 27th April, 1920) will be jointly occupied by armed forces of the U.S.A., U.K., and U.S.S.R., assigned by the respective Commanders-in-Chief. For this purpose the territory of "Greater Berlin" will be divided into the following three parts:

North-Eastern part of "Greater Berlin" . . . will be occupied by the forces of the U.S.S.R. . . . North-Western part of "Greater Berlin" will be occupied by the forces of the U.K. . . . Southern part of "Greater Berlin" will be occupied by the forces of the U.S.A. . . .

3. The occupying forces in each of the three zones into which Germany is divided will be under a Commander-in-Chief designated by the Government of the country whose forces occupy that zone.

4. Each of the three Powers may, at its discretion, include among the forces assigned to occupation duties under the command of its Commander-in-Chief, auxiliary contingents from the forces of any other Allied Power which has participated in military operations against Germany.

5. An Inter-Allied Governing Authority (Komendatura) consisting of three Commandants, appointed by their respective Commanders-in-Chief, will be established to direct jointly the administration of the "Greater Berlin" Area.

6. This Protocol has been drawn up in triplicate in the English and Russian languages. Both texts are authentic. The Protocol will come into force on the signature by Germany of the Instrument of Unconditional Surrender.

Source: U.S. Department of State, Documents on Germany, 1944–1985 (Washington: GPO, 1985), 1–3.

DOCUMENT 30: Protocol on Germany at the Yalta Conference (February 1945)

It was agreed that Article 12 (a) of the Surrender Terms for Germany should be amended to read as follows:

"The United Kingdom, the United States of America and the Union of the Soviet Socialist Republics shall possess supreme authority with respect to Germany. In the exercise of such authority they will take such steps, including the complete disarmament, demilitarization and the dismemberment of Germany as they deem requisite for future peace and security."

The study of the procedure for the dismemberment of Germany was referred to a committee, consisting of Mr. Eden [U.K.] (Chairman), Mr. Winant [U.S.A.] and Mr. Gousev [U.S.S.R.]. This body would consider the desirability of associating with it a French representative.

Source: U.S. Department of State, *Foreign Relations of the United States, The Conferences at Malta and Yalta, 1945* (Washington: GPO, 1955), 978.

DOCUMENT 31: U.S. General Lucius Clay and Soviet General Georgi Zhukov Discuss Lines of Communication Between Germany and Berlin (29 June 1945)

We had explained our intent to move into Berlin utilizing three rail lines and two highways and such air space as we needed. Zhukov would not recognize that these routes were essential and pointed out that the demobilization of Soviet forces was taxing existing facilities. I countered that we were not demanding exclusive use of these routes but merely access over them without restrictions other than the normal traffic control and regulations which the Soviet administration would establish for its own use. [British] General [Anthony] Weeks supported my contention strongly. We both knew there was no provision covering access to Berlin in the agreement reached by the European Advisory Commission. We did not wish to accept specific routes which might be interpreted as a denial of our right of access over all routes but there was merit to the Soviet contention that existing routes were needed for demobilization purposes. We had already found transport a bottleneck to our own redeployment. Therefore Weeks and I accepted as a temporary arrangement the allocation of a main highway and rail line and two air corridors, reserving the right to reopen the question in the Allied Control Council. I must admit that we did not then fully realize that the requirement of unanimous consent would enable a Soviet veto in the Allied Control Council to block all of our future efforts. While no record was kept at this meeting, I dictated my notes that evening and they include the following:

"It was agreed that all traffic—air, road and rail, . . . would be free from border search or control by customs or military authorities." I had no way of knowing that Soviet insistence on border and customs control would serve as the excuse for the initial imposition of the blockade of Berlin. . . .

The die had been cast and for better or worse the Western Allies were now committed to withdraw to their separate zones of occupation and to start the move into Berlin on July 1. The first step toward four-power government had been taken.

Source: Lucius D. Clay, *Decision in Germany* (Garden City, N.Y.: Doubleday, 1950), 25–27.

DOCUMENT 32: The Berlin (Potsdam) Conference Protocol (2 August 1945)

The Berlin Conference of the Three Heads of Government of the USSR, USA, and UK, which took place from July 17 to August 2, 1945, came to the following conclusions: . . .

II. *The Principles to Govern the Treatment of Germany in the Initial Control Period.*

A. Political Principles

1. In accordance with the Agreement on Control Machinery in Germany, supreme authority in Germany is exercised, on instructions from their respective Governments, by the Commanders-in-Chief of the armed forces of the United States of America, the United Kingdom, the Union of Soviet Socialist Republics, and the French Republic, each in his own zone of occupation, and also jointly, in matters affecting Germany as a whole, in their capacity as members of the Control Council.

2. So far as is practicable, there shall be uniformity of treatment of the German population throughout Germany. . . .

B. Economic Principles

11. In order to eliminate Germany's war potential, the production of

arms, ammunition and implements of war as well as all types of aircraft and sea-going ships shall be prohibited and prevented. Production of metals, chemicals, machinery and other items that are directly necessary to a war economy shall be rigidly controlled and restricted to Germany's approved post-war peacetime needs to meet the objectives stated in Paragraph 15. . . .

14. During the period of occupation Germany shall be treated as a single economic unit. . . .

15. Allied controls shall be imposed upon the German economy but only

(a) to carry out programs of industrial disarmament and demilitarization, of reparations, and of approved exports and imports; (b) to assure the production and maintenance of goods and services required to meet the needs of the occupying forces and displaced persons in Germany and essential to maintain in Germany average living standards not exceeding the average of standards of living of European countries. (European countries means all European countries excluding the United Kingdom and the Union of Soviet Socialist Republics); (c) to ensure in the manner determined by the Control Council the equitable distribution of essential commodities between the several zones so as to produce a balanced economy throughout Germany and reduce the need for imports; (d) to control German industry and all economic and financial international transactions, including exports and imports, with the aim of preventing Germany from developing a war potential and of achieving the other objectives named herein; [and] (e) to control all German public or private scientific bodies, research and experimental institutions, laboratories, et cetera, connected with economic activities.

Source: U.S. Department of State, *Foreign Relations of the United States, The Conference of Berlin (The Potsdam Conference), 1945*, Vol. 2 (Washington: GPO, 1960), 1478–98.

DOCUMENT 33: General Clay Recalls the Allied Control Council's Decision to Approve Air Corridors to and from Berlin (30 November 1945)

Marshal Zhukov recalled that the Coordinating Committee had approved the establishing of three air corridors, namely, Berlin-Hamburg, Berlin-Bueckeburg and Berlin–Frankfurt-on-Main. . . .

Marshal Zhukov expressed himself confident that in due course the other air corridors would be opened. He added that he would like to make a proposal on this paper. He assumed that his colleagues would give the Soviet military authorities the right to fly along these air corridors into the Western zones and would consent to put at their disposal appropriate airfields for landing Soviet aircraft, or at least allow Soviet ground staffs on terminal and intermediate airfields along the proposed air corridors to facilitate the servicing of Soviet aircraft. The reason which Marshal Zhukov gave for the necessity of establishing Soviet airfields in the Western zones was the work of dismantling plants for deliveries on account of reparations when it comes to sending Soviet experts to organize that work. . . .

Marshal Zhukov said that he would like to clarify his declaration: namely, he proposed that appropriate airfields should be placed at the disposal of the Soviet authorities in the Western zones, or that permission should be given for Soviet ground crews for the servicing of Soviet aircraft to be stationed at these airfields.

Field Marshal Montgomery proposed to refer the proposal made by the head of the Soviet delegation to the Air Directorate for examination. He asked whether his understanding was correct that the question of the three air corridors from the Western zones to Berlin was settled and that the organization of these air corridors could be started immediately, without awaiting the results of the examination of the Soviet proposal.

Marshal Zhukov observed that he considered the paper accepted and expressed the hope that the proposal of the Soviet delegation on placing airfields in the Western zones at the disposal of the Soviet authorities would meet with full sympathy on the part of his colleagues.

The Meeting

(a) approved the establishment of three air corridors from Berlin to the Western zones. . . . (b) agreed to refer proposal of the Soviet delegation on the placing of airfields at the disposal of the Soviet authorities or the setting up of Soviet ground crews in the Western zones to the Air Directorate for study.

Source: U.S. Department of State, *Documents on Germany, 1944–1985,* 72–74.

DOCUMENT 34: Secretary of State James Byrnes' Speech at Stuttgart Concerning U.S. Relations with Postwar Germany (6 September 1946)

I have come to Germany to learn at firsthand the problems involved in the reconstruction of Germany and to discuss with our representatives the views of the United States Government as to some of the problems confronting us. . . .

In agreeing at Potsdam that Germany should be disarmed and demilitarized and in proposing that the four major powers should by treaty jointly undertake to see that Germany is kept disarmed and demilitarized for a generation, the United States was not unmindful of the responsibility resting upon it and its major Allies to maintain and enforce peace under the law. . . .

The United States, therefore, is prepared to carry out fully the principles outlined in the Potsdam Agreement on demilitarization and reparations. However, there should be changes in the levels of industry agreed upon by the Allied Control Commission if Germany is not to be administered as an economic unit as the Potsdam Agreement contemplates and requires.

The basis of the Potsdam Agreement was that, as part of a combined program of demilitarization and reparations, Germany's war potential should be reduced by elimination and removal of her war industries and the reduction and removal of heavy industrial plants. It was contemplated this should be done to the point that Germany would be left with levels of industry capable of maintaining in Germany average European living standards without assistance from other countries.

The plants so to be removed were to be delivered as reparations to the Allies. The plants to be removed from the Soviet zone would go to the Soviet Union and Poland and the plants to be removed from the western zones would go in part to the Soviet Union but in the main to the western Allies. Provision was also made for the distribution of Germany's foreign assets among the Allies.

After considerable discussion the Allies agreed upon levels to which the principal German industries should be reduced in order to carry out the Potsdam Agreement. These levels were agreed to upon the assumption that the indigenous resources of Germany were to be available for distribution on an equitable basis for all of the Germans in Germany and that products not necessary for use in Germany would be available for export in order to pay for necessary imports.

In fixing the levels of industry no allowance was made for reparations from current production. Reparations from current production would be wholly incompatible with the levels of industry now established under the Potsdam Agreement.

Obviously, higher levels of industry would have had to be fixed if reparations from current production were contemplated. The levels of industry fixed are only sufficient to enable the German people to become self-supporting and to maintain living standards approximating the average European living conditions.

That principle involves serious hardships for the German people, but it only requires them to share the hardships which Nazi aggression imposed on the average European. . . .

That was the principle of reparation to which President Truman agreed at Potsdam. And the United States will not agree to the taking from Germany of greater reparations than was provided by the Potsdam Agreement.

The carrying out of the Potsdam Agreement has, however, been obstructed by the failure of the Allied Control Council to take the necessary steps to enable the German economy to function as an economic unit. Essential central German administrative departments have not been established, although they are expressly required by the Potsdam Agreement.

The equitable distribution of essential commodities between the several zones so as to produce a balanced economy throughout Germany and reduce the need for imports has not been arranged, although that too is expressly required by the Potsdam Agreement.

The working out of a balanced economy throughout Germany to provide the necessary means to pay for approved imports has not been accomplished, although that too is expressly required by the Potsdam Agreement.

The United States is firmly of the belief that Germany should be administered as an economic unit and that zonal barriers should be completely obliterated so far as the economic life and activity in Germany are concerned.

The conditions which now exist in Germany make it impossible for industrial production to reach the levels which the occupying powers agreed were essential for a minimum German peacetime economy. Obviously, if the agreed levels of industry are to be reached, we can not continue to restrict the free exchange of commodities, persons, and ideas throughout Germany. The barriers between the four zones of Germany are far more difficult to surmount than those between normal independent states.

The time has come when the zonal boundaries should be regarded as defining only the areas to be occupied for security purposes by the armed forces of the occupying powers and not as self-contained economic or political units.

That was the course of development envisaged by the Potsdam Agreement, and that is the course of development which the American Government intends to follow to the full limit of its authority. It has formally announced that it is its intention to unify the economy of its own zone with any or all of the other zones willing to participate in the unification.

So far only the British Government has agreed to let its zone participate. We deeply appreciate their cooperation. Of course, this policy of unification is not intended to exclude the governments not now willing to join. The unification will be open to them at any time they wish to join.

Source: U.S. Department of State, Documents on Germany, 1944–1985, 91–99.

DOCUMENT 35: The London Conference Communiqué on Germany (7 June 1948)

1. ASSOCIATION OF BENELUX COUNTRIES IN POLICY REGARD-
ING GERMANY

The recommendations include specific provisions for a close association between military governments and Benelux representatives in Germany on matters affecting Benelux interests. Moreover full opportunities
will be given the Benelux representatives to be kept informed of developments in the western zones.

2. ROLE OF THE GERMAN ECONOMY IN THE EUROPEAN ECON-
OMY AND CONTROL OF THE RUHR

(A) It ha[s] been agreed that for the political and economic well-being
of the countries of Western Europe and of a democratic Germany, there
must be a close association of their economic life. This close association,
which will enable Germany to contribute to and participate in European
recovery, has been ensured by the inclusion on April 16 of the combined
zone and French zone in the organization for European economic cooperation as full members.

(B) It was agreed to recommend the establishment of an international
authority for the control of the Ruhr in which United States, United Kingdom, France, Benelux countries and Germany would participate, and
which does not involve the political separation of the Ruhr area from
Germany. It does, however, contemplate control of distribution of coal,
coke and steel of Ruhr in order that on the one hand industrial concentration in that area shall not become an instrument of aggression, and
on the other will be able to make its contribution to all countries participating in a European cooperative economic program, including of
course, Germany itself. . . .

(C) Arising out of the discussions on the Ruhr it has been recommended that the principle of non-discrimination against foreign interests
in Germany be reaffirmed, and that each government should promptly
study the problem of safeguarding foreign interests in order that there
may be subsequently established as soon as possible an intergovernmen-

tal group to review the question and make recommendations to their governments.

3. EVOLUTION OF POLITICAL AND ECONOMIC ORGANIZATION OF GERMANY

(A) Further consideration has been given by all delegates to the problem of the evolution of the political and economic organization of Germany. They recognize, taking into account the present situation, that it is necessary to give the German people the opportunity to achieve on the basis of a free and democratic form of government the eventual reestablishment of German unity at present disrupted. In these circumstances they have reached the conclusion that it would be desirable that the German people in the different states should now be free to establish for themselves the political organization and institutions which will enable them to assume those governmental responsibilities which are compatible with the minimum requirements of occupation and control and which ultimately will enable them to assume full governmental responsibility. The delegates consider that the people in the States will wish to establish a constitution with provisions which will allow all the German states to subscribe as soon as circumstances permit.

Therefore the delegates have agreed to recommend to their governments that the military governors should hold a joint meeting with the Ministers-President of the western zone in Germany. At that meeting the Ministers-President will be authorized to convene a Constituent Assembly in order to prepare a constitution for the approval of the participating states.

Delegates to this Constituent Assembly will be chosen in each of the states in accordance with procedure and regulations to be determined by the legislative bodies of the individual states.

The constitution should be such as to enable the Germans to play their part in bringing to an end the present division of Germany not by the reconstitution of a centralized Reich but by means of a federal form of government which adequately protects the rights of the respective states, and which at the same time provides for adequate central authority and which guarantees the rights and freedoms of the individual.

If the constitution as prepared by the Constituent Assembly does not conflict with these general principles the military governors will authorize its submissions for ratification by the people in the respective states.

At the meeting with the military governors the Ministers-President will also be authorized to examine the boundaries of the several states in order to determine which modifications might be proposed to the military governors for the purpose of creating a definitive system which is satisfactory to the peoples concerned.

(B) Further discussions have taken place between the United States,

United Kingdom and French delegations on measures for coordinating economic policies and practices in the combined zone and the French zone. Agreed recommendations have been reached on the joint conduct and control of the external trade of the whole area. It has been recognized that a complete economic merger of the two areas cannot effectively take place until further progress has been made in establishing the necessary German institutions common to the entire area.

4. PROVISIONAL TERRITORIAL ARRANGEMENTS

The delegations have agreed to submit for the consideration of their governments proposals for dealing with certain minor provisional territorial adjustments in connection with the western frontiers of Germany.

5. SECURITY . . .

General Provision. The United States, United Kingdom and French Delegates reiterated the firm views of their governments that there could not be any general withdrawal of their forces from Germany until the peace of Europe is secured and without prior consultation. During this period there should be no general withdrawal of the forces of occupation of the United States, France or the United Kingdom without prior consultation. It was further recommended that the governments concerned should consult if any of them should consider that there was a danger of resurgence of German military power or of the adoption by Germany of a policy of aggression.

Source: U.S. Department of State, *Foreign Relations of the United States, 1948*, Vol. 2, *Germany and Austria* (hereafter *FRUS, 1948*) (Washington: GPO, 1973), 313–17.

DOCUMENT 36: Soviet Intelligence Officer Pavel Sudoplatov Asserts that Stalin Initiated the Crisis to Assure Communist Victory in China (1994)

The Soviet leadership's knowledge that the United States and Britain had a low nuclear stockpile of atomic weapons eased Stalin in deciding to initiate the blockade of Berlin. Later assertions by Soviet officials hint that Stalin's actions in Berlin were also intended to assure a communist victory in China's civil war in 1947–1948.

We were aware that President Harry Truman was seriously considering the use of nuclear weapons to prevent a Chinese Communist victory. Then Stalin initiated the Berlin crisis, blockading the Western-controlled sectors of the city in 1948. . . . The American government overestimated our threat in Berlin and lost the opportunity to use the nuclear threat to support the Chinese nationalists.

Stalin provoked the Berlin crisis deliberately to divert attention from the crucial struggle for power in China. In 1951, when we were discussing plans for military operations against American bases, Molotov told me that our position in Berlin helped the Chinese Communists. For Stalin, the Chinese Communist victory supported his policy of confrontation with America. He was preoccupied with the idea of a Sino-Soviet axis against the Western world.

Source: Pavel Sudoplatov and Anatoli Sudoplatov, with Jerrold and Leona Schecter, *Special Tasks: The Memoirs of an Unwanted Witness—A Soviet Spymaster* (Boston: Little, Brown, 1994), 210–11.

OPERATION VITTLES

These documents reveal the American reaction to the Soviet imposition of the blockade and the gravity of the crisis from the U.S. perspective. Students will note the discussion of the atomic bomb and the "implication" intended in sending B-29 bombers to England, as well as the care exercised in drafting the diplomatic messages conveyed to Moscow.

DOCUMENT 37: General Clay's Cable to Army General Omar Bradley (1 April 1948)

Three of our trains entered Soviet zone at midnight. One train commandant now under investigation apparently lost his nerve and permitted Soviet representatives to board train, and this train passed through Soviet zone. Remaining two trains were stopped and Soviet representatives insisted on boarding train. They were denied access and did not attempt to force access. However, the trains could not have proceeded forward except by use of force, and with traffic control in Soviet hands could not have proceeded very far even with force. Two British trains entered Soviet zone stocked with rations for several days. These trains were likewise stopped and Soviet representatives refused entry. At present these two British trains remain in the Soviet zone. Our two trains have been backed out of the Soviet zone.

For the present we have cancelled military trains and have laid on airlift which I believe will meet our needs for some days. British and

French are desirous that a Control Council meeting be called to discuss problem. However, since Soviet broke up last meeting and did not call successive meeting, I propose to weigh this for several days before making a decision as to its advisability. I am giving some thought to sending a guarded truck convoy through, since this could force the issue whereas rail traffic cannot be moved with others controlling the signal system. Obviously I will not take this action without consultation with you.

I do think it advisable for our Government to give some consideration to possible retaliatory measures such as the enactment of stringent regulations which would make Soviet use of ocean canals, bunkering facilities, and other facilities under our and British control, difficult if not impossible. A careful examination has indicated little if anything that can be done here in Germany in retaliation. In any event, I propose to depend upon airlift for next several days before taking any further specific action.

Source: Jean Edward Smith, ed., *The Papers of General Lucius D. Clay: Germany, 1945–1949*, Vol. 2 (Bloomington: Indiana University Press, 1974), 607–8.

DOCUMENT 38: Teleconference Between General Clay, Army Secretary Royall, and Army Chief of Staff General Bradley over Evacuation from Berlin (2 April 1948)

OMAR BRADLEY: We are receiving many inquiries from Members of Congress as to why we do not evacuate dependents from Berlin. Evacuation now might be plausible because it would reduce number to be supplied by air.

Such evacuation might be interpreted as either start of withdrawal from Berlin entirely, or on the other hand as a clearing of decks for action if necessary. What is your thinking on this subject in view of new situation?

CLAY: Please read my message prepared prior to start of telecon which I believe will answer your question. Message follows: To: Dept of Army

1. Highway and air traffic conditions are normal today. Civil freight for Germans moving normally. Military freight into Berlin appears to be moving normally so far free from attempted search. Passenger trains not moving in view of Soviet action. Also, no outward movement by rail of military freight as no loadings can be made without Soviet permission and this we will not ask.

2. Compromise believed impossible to attain now as in my view

this is only Soviet first step. British deputy [Maj. Gen. N.C.D. Brownjohn] visited Soviet deputy [Lt. Gen. M. I. Dratvin] last evening to find opening and found none.

3. We can continue under present conditions indefinitely and in my opinion should do so although this will require substantial increase in air passenger lift. British wish to propose compromise but I cannot agree that such an offer would serve any useful purpose except humiliating rebuff.

4. I do not believe we should evacuate now. In emergency, we can evacuate quickly. However, evacuation now would play into Soviet hands and frighten rest of Europe.

5. I propose (A) to sit tight, spending most of my time in Berlin for immediate future. (B) To let dependents who are nervous go home. (C) To speed up planned transfer of employees to Frankfurt. (D) To gradually move unessential employees. This will be done over weeks rather than days so that each additional aggravation will find our support problem lessened. In general, in spite of some imaginative correspondents' reports our people are calm and continuing their everyday life normally.

6. While Soviets won train victory in success in stopping move, I am sure our position has stopped for time being further interference with air and highway movements which would require force to implement.

7. I anticipate in next few weeks Soviet demand for our withdrawal because of failure of A[llied] C[ontrol] C[ouncil] to govern Germany. I think we should await such demand before making any decision to evacuate non-combatants.

8. While British would like to find a compromise, [Gen. Sir Brian] Robertson assured me today he would stick with us. French are firm now but not wholly reliable.

9. Finally, there are few dependents here who have any thought of leaving unless required to do so. I do wish to emphasize there is little nervousness among them here. Our stake is too high and evacuation would deceive no one as to military intent.

KENNETH ROYALL: Do you think situation has reached stage where it should be taken up with Moscow by Washington? Or should we await further conference by you in Berlin?

CLAY: I think we should await further clarification here. Robertson and I will make joint recommendation to US/UK Governments when [we] believe Government action timely.

ROYALL: We have been studying in connection with State and Commerce what general retaliatory commercial measures we could adopt against Russia, but have not yet received a report. If we found it possible to adopt measures which might adversely affect Russia to a material extent, what effect would such course have on your situation in Berlin?

CLAY: I think retaliatory measures would be very effective particularly in shipping. Have Soviet ship loading in Bremen now and am having great difficulty in finding fuel. However, if measures are not substantial, effect can be bad. I would appreciate knowing if effective measures are found but would recommend withholding application until you have further word from us. Measures would be an ace in the hole to us if there are such.

ROYALL: With the strong feeling about evacuation of dependents in Congress and elsewhere we will have to consider further what course to follow. However, Bradley and I are inclined to support your views as are the J[oint] C[hiefs of] S[taff].

CLAY: Evacuation in face of Italian elections and European situation is to me almost unthinkable. Our women and children can take it and they appreciate import. I cannot overemphasize my fear of consequences. Your support in this greatly appreciated.

Source: Smith, *Papers of General Lucius D. Clay: Germany, 1945–1949,* Vol. 2, 613–15.

DOCUMENT 39: General Clay Orders Airlift Phase of Operation Vittles (June 1948)

When the order of the Soviet Military Administration to close all rail traffic from the western zones went into effect at 6:00 A.M. on the morning of June 24, 1948, the three western sectors of Berlin, with a civilian population of about 2,500,000 people, became dependent on reserve stocks and airlift replacements. It was one of the most ruthless efforts in modern times to use mass starvation for political coercion. Our food stocks on hand were sufficient to last for thirty-six days and our coal stocks for forty-five. These stocks had been built up with considerable difficulty as our transportation into Berlin was never adequate. We had foreseen the Soviet action for some months. We could sustain a minimum economy with an average daily airlift of 4000 tons for the German population and 500 tons for the Allied occupation forces. This minimum would not maintain industrial output or provide for domestic heating and normal consumer requirements. . . . Electricity from the Soviet Zone was cut off when the blockade was imposed. The capacity which remained could provide electricity for essential purposes only a few hours each day, and even these hours of use had to be staggered for the various parts of western Berlin. Despite these conditions, we had confidence that its people were prepared to face severe physical suffering rather than live again under totalitarian government, that they would endure much hardship to retain their freedom.

The resources which we had within the theater to defeat the blockade were limited. Our transport and troop carrier planes, although more than 100 in number, were C-47s, twin-engine planes of about two and a half tons cargo capacity, and many of them had seen hard war service. The British resources were even more limited. There were no French transport planes to be made available.

Nevertheless, I felt that full use of our available C-47s would prove that the job could be done. I called General [Curtis] LeMay on the telephone on the morning of June 24 and asked him to drop all other uses of our transport aircraft so that his entire fleet of C-47s could be placed on the Berlin run. . . . At the same time arrangements were made for the movement of food to our airports and on the morning of June 25 the first C-47s arrived in Berlin with food for its people. . . .

On the next day, June 26, the airlift became an organized operation.

Source: Clay, *Decision in Germany,* 362–67.

DOCUMENT 40: The Importance of Transatlantic Teleconference Communication, and General Clay's Request to Upgrade the Airlift with C-54s (July 1948)

The co-ordination of American thinking and the exchange of information during these somewhat trying days were superb. Our officials in Berlin, London, and Washington were in daily communication through the use of the teleconference, and each move was discussed in detail with Secretary Royall, Under Secretary [Robert] Lovett, and Ambassador [Lewis] Douglas. While Ambassador [Walter Bedell] Smith was not in the teleconference circuit, he was kept informed so that he could transmit his opinion by cable. It was more difficult to reconcile our views with those of the British and French governments, which was largely Douglas' assignment in London. The necessity for the co-ordination of three positions prior to each move and the time required for their reconciliation proved a major handicap to the progress of the discussions. Almost a month was to pass before the three ambassadors in Moscow received their instructions to protest. Thereafter they were delayed frequently for the same reason.

During this crisis General Clay was summoned to Washington to report to the National Security Council. On July 21, General Clay reported to President Truman, Secretaries Marshall and Forrestal, and the Joint Chiefs of Staff.

I asserted my confidence that, given the planes, we could remain in Berlin indefinitely without war and that our departure would be a serious if not disastrous blow to the maintenance of freedom in Europe. I asked for 160 C-54s, a plane which would carry ten tons of cargo as compared to the two and a half tons carried by the C-47. [Secretary of the Air Force Stuart] Symington and [Air Force] General Hoyt Vandenberg . . . said they could deliver these planes in a relatively short time. There was no dissent to my recommendations, which were approved by the National Security Council. When the Council adjourned, President Truman honored me by asking me to remain with him for further discussion, during which I told him that I was sure that the Berlin population would stand fast through the coming winter if it proved necessary. I left his office inspired by the understanding and confidence I received from him.

Source: Clay, *Decision in Germany,* 368.

DOCUMENT 41: General Bradley Remembers the Airlift as the Cold War's "Single Greatest Triumph" (1983)

We were very, very lucky in the Berlin Blockade. Clay's brainchild, the airlift, worked out far better than anyone dared hope. . . . The common effort created a close bond between us and the West German people, who, in time, became staunch allies. Thus the airlift turned out to be our single greatest triumph in the Cold War.

Source: Omar N. Bradley and Clay Blair, *A General's Life: An Autobiography* (New York: Simon and Schuster, 1983), 477–81.

DOCUMENT 42: Secretary of Defense James Forrestal's Diary with Comments on the Blockade, B-29s to Britain, and the Atomic Bomb (June–July 1948)

Several cabinet meetings during the summer of 1948 discussed the option of sending American B-29 aircraft to Europe. Secretary Forrestal's diary does not explain the implications of this option. The B-29 was known throughout the world as the atomic bomber, and to put a strong force of them on British bases would be to bring them within striking distance of Moscow. The sudden escalation of the Berlin crisis was to compel much serious reappraisal of the bomb and of its real place in American policy and strategy.

2 July 1948 . . . Cabinet

General Marshall discussed the situation in Berlin.

He read a copy of a message which the State Department had drawn and proposes to send to Stalin. It recites both the legal and moral considerations for the Western Allies remaining in Berlin and reaffirms the determination of the Allies to stay there. . . .

The French and British both agree that a meeting of the Council of Foreign Ministers is not desirable at this time—that it would only lead to protracted discussions with probably the same sterile results of previous meetings of these personalities.

He reported the beefing up of the B-29 strength in Germany from one squadron to a group. He said that the British had been asked whether they would like to have two additional B-29 groups proceed to Britain and that Bevin had replied in the affirmative. Douglas had been instructed to ask Bevin whether he had fully explored and considered the effect of the arrival of these two groups in Britain upon British public opinion, and he (Marshall) had to weigh the effect (a) on the Russians, and (b) of the implications and inferences to be derived from sending these groups to Britain. He said the effect on the Russians had to be balanced against the appearance to our own people of what might be construed as a provocative action. . . .

15 July 1948 . . . Sending of B-29s to Britain

Summary of considerations affecting the decision to send B-29s to England:

1. It would be an action which would underline to the American people how seriously the government of the United States views the current sequence of events.

2. It would give the Air Force experience in this kind of operation; it would accustom the British to the necessary habits and routines that go into the accommodation of an alien, even though an allied, power.

3. We have the opportunity now of sending these planes, and once sent they would become somewhat of an accepted fixture, whereas a deterioration of the situation in Europe might lead to a condition of mind under which the British would be compelled to reverse their present attitude.

15 July 1948 . . . Meeting—the President and
Secretary Marshall . . . Atomic Bomb

. . . The President was chipper and in very good form and obviously pleased with the results of his speech at the [Democratic National] Convention last night. . . .

I informed the President this morning that I asked for a meeting with him for the next week to discuss the question of custody of atomic weapons. I said I did not propose to ask him for a decision on their use because I felt confident his decision would be the right one whenever the circumstances developed that required a decision. He then remarked he wanted to go into this matter very carefully and he proposed to keep, in his own hands, the decision as to the use of the bomb, and did not propose "to have some dashing lieutenant colonel decide when would be the proper time to drop one."

I said I had found in the military no thought of denying him freedom of action on this subject but that there was a very serious question as to the wisdom of relying upon an agency other than the user of such a weapon, to assure the integrity and usability of such a weapon. I said, however, I did not think it appropriate to argue the merits of the case unilaterally but that I thought it needed a decision at an early date.

21 July 1948 . . . Meeting at the White House

Meeting at the White House today with the President, members of the Atomic Energy Commission, Secretary Royall, Secretary Symington and Mr. Carpenter [Donald F. Carpenter, an executive of the Remington Arms Company], the latter the chairman of the Military Liaison Committee of the National Military Establishment (liaison with the Atomic Energy Commission), David Lilienthal, chairman of the AEC, and his four other associates.

Subject of the meeting was the presentation of a formal request of the National Military Establishment for an executive order from the President turning over custody of the atomic bomb to the Military Establishment, the chief reasons being (1) that the user of the bomb, who would ultimately be responsible for its delivery, should have custody of it with the accompanying advantages and familiarity, etc., which this would bring, and (2) concentration of authority-unified command.

Lilienthal based his objection to the transfer of the bomb on the broad general theory that the atomic bomb was not simply another weapon but an instrument of destruction which carried the widest kind of international and diplomatic implications; that the law which created the AEC dealt with certain constitutional relationships of the President; that actually greater efficiency in terms of surveillance, further developments, etc., could be had by leaving custody with the AEC.

The President made the observation that the responsibility for the use of the bomb was his and that was the responsibility he proposed to keep. He said he would reserve decision.

Source: James V. Forrestal, *The Forrestal Diaries,* edited by Walter Millis (New York: Viking Press, 1951), 451–62.

DOCUMENT 43: Secretary Forrestal to Secretary of State Marshall on U.S. Preparation for Global Conflict (28 July 1948)

In accordance with recommendations by the Joint Chiefs of Staff, in which I concur, it is requested that the British and French Governments be approached by your Department with strong requests for maximum air support for the present supply operation for Berlin.

It is also requested that discussion be initiated with the British and French Governments with a view toward developing preliminary plans for the use of composite (British, French and United States) armed convoys for the supply of Berlin. In this connection and for your information only, the Joint Chiefs of Staff do not recommend supply to Berlin by armed convoy in view of the risk of war involved and the inadequacy of United States preparation for global conflict. They believe it prudent, however, to plan for such an operation in the event that:

(a) Every other possible solution to the Berlin problem has first failed or been discarded. (b) Current evaluation indicates that the effort is likely to succeed. (c) The United States has first determined that risk of war in the near future and for the Berlin cause is acceptable, and (d) All possible time shall first have been gained and used for adequate preparation for the attempt to supply by force and for full-out major war action in support thereof if war results.

It should be impressed upon the British and French Governments that these discussions for the development of preliminary plans do not in any way represent a decision by the United States Government that these armed convoys should be used at the present time, but that the United States Government reserves its decision in this matter pending further developments in the Berlin situation.

Source: FRUS, 1948, 994–95.

DOCUMENT 44: U.S. Diplomatic Note to the Soviet Government (6 July 1948)

The United States Government wishes to call to the attention of the Soviet Government the extremely serious international situation which has been brought about by the actions of the Soviet Government in imposing restrictive measures on transport which amount now to a blockade against the sectors in Berlin occupied by the United States, United Kingdom and France. The United States Government regards these measures of blockade as a clear violation of existing agreements concerning the administration of Berlin by the four occupying powers.

The rights of the United States as a joint occupying power in Berlin derive from the total defeat and unconditional surrender of Germany. The international agreements undertaken in connection therewith by the Governments of the United States, United Kingdom, France and the Soviet Union defined the zones in Germany and the sectors in Berlin which are occupied by these powers. They established the quadripartite control of Berlin on a basis of friendly cooperation which the Government of the United States earnestly desires to continue to pursue.

These agreements implied the right of free access to Berlin. This right has long been confirmed by usage. It was directly specified in a message sent by President Truman to Premier Stalin on June 14, 1945, which agreed to the withdrawal of United States forces to the zonal boundaries, provided satisfactory arrangement could be entered into between the military commanders, which would give access by rail, road and air to United States forces in Berlin. Premier Stalin replied on June 16 suggesting a change in date but no other alteration in the plan proposed by the President. Premier Stalin then gave assurances that all necessary measures would be taken in accordance with the plan. Correspondence in a similar sense took place between Premier Stalin and Mr. Churchill. In accordance with this understanding, the United States, whose armies had penetrated deep into Saxony and Thuringia, parts of the Soviet zone, withdrew its forces to its own area of occupation in Germany and took up its position in its own sector in Berlin. Thereupon the agreements in regard to the occupation of Germany and Berlin went into effect. The United States would not have so withdrawn its troops from a large area now occupied by the Soviet Union had there been any doubt whatsoever about the observance of its agreed right of free access to its sector of Berlin. The right of the United States to its position in Berlin thus stems from precisely the same source as the right of the Soviet Union. It is impossible to assert the latter and deny the former.

It clearly results from these undertakings that Berlin is not a part of the Soviet zone, but is an international zone of occupation. Commitments entered into in good faith by the zone commanders, and subsequently confirmed by the Allied Control Authority, as well as practices sanctioned by usage, guarantee the United States together with other powers, free access to Berlin for the purpose of fulfilling its responsibilities as an occupying power. The facts are plain. Their meaning is clear. Any other interpretation would offend all the rules of comity and reason.

In order that there should be no misunderstanding whatsoever on this point, the United States Government categorically asserts that it is in occupation of its sector in Berlin with free access thereto as a matter of established right deriving from the defeat and surrender of Germany and confirmed by formal agreements among the principal Allies. It further declares that it will not be induced by threats, pressures or other actions to abandon these rights. It is hoped that the Soviet Government entertains no doubts whatsoever on this point.

This Government now shares with the Governments of France and the United Kingdom the responsibility initially undertaken at Soviet request on July 7, 1945, for the physical well-being of 2,400,000 persons in the western sectors of Berlin.

Source: U.S. Department of State, *Documents on Germany, 1944–1985*, 156–58.

DOCUMENT 45: Note from the Soviet Union to the United States (14 July 1948)

1. The Soviet Government has familiarized itself with the note of the Government of the United States of America of July 6, 1948 in which the situation which has been created at the present time in Berlin is described as a result of measures taken by the Soviet side. The Soviet Government cannot agree with this statement of the Government of the United States and considers that the situation which has been created in Berlin has arisen as a result of violation by the Governments of the United States of America, Great Britain, and France of agreed decisions taken by the four powers in regard to Germany and Berlin which [violation] has found its expression in the carrying out of a separate currency reform, in the introduction of a special currency for the western sectors of Berlin and in the policy of the dismemberment of Germany. The Soviet Government has more than once warned the Governments of the United

States of America, Great Britain, and France in regard to the responsibility which they would take upon themselves in following along the path of the violation of agreed decisions previously adopted by the four powers in regard to Germany. The decisions adopted at the Yalta and Potsdam Conferences and also the agreement of the four powers concerning the control mechanism in Germany have as their aim the demilitarization and democratization of Germany, the removal of the base itself of Germany [sic] militarism and the prevention of the revival of Germany as an aggressive power and thereby the transformation of Germany into a peace-loving and democratic state. These agreements envisage the obligation of Germany to pay reparations and thereby to make at least partial compensation for the damage to those countries which suffered from German aggression. In accordance with these agreements the Governments of the four powers took upon themselves the responsibility for the administration of Germany and bound themselves jointly to draw up a statute for Germany or for any areas including Berlin which were part of German territory and to conclude with Germany a peace treaty which should be signed by a Government of a democratic Germany adequate for that purpose.

These most important agreements of the four powers in regard to Germany have been violated by the Governments of the United States of America, Great Britain, and France. Measures for the demilitarization of Germany have not been completed and such a very important center of German military industry as the Ruhr district has been taken out from under the control of the four powers. The execution of decisions concerning reparations from the western zones of occupation of Germany has been interrupted by the Governments of the U.S.A., the U.K., and France. By the separate actions of the Government of the U.S.A., Great Britain, and France the four power control mechanism in Germany has been destroyed and the Control Council as a result thereof has ceased its activity.

Following the London meeting of the three powers with the participation of Benelux, measures have been undertaken by the governments of the U.S.A., Great Britain, and France directed towards the division and dismemberment of Germany including preparations which are now in progress for the designation of a separate Government for the western zones of Germany and the separate currency reform for the western zones of occupation carried out on June 18th of this year.

In as much as the situation created in Berlin as well as in all Germany is the direct result of the systematic violation by the Governments of the U.S.A., Great Britain, and France of the decisions of the Potsdam Conference and also of the agreement of the four powers concerning the control mechanism in Germany, the Soviet Government must reject as completely unfounded the statement of the Government of the U.S. to the effect that the measures for the restriction of transport communications between Berlin and the western zones of occupation of Germany introduced by the Soviet command for the defense of the economy of the Soviet zone against its disorganization are allegedly in violation of the existing agreements concerning the administration of Berlin.

2. The Government of the U.S. declares that it is occupying its sector in Berlin by right arising out of the defeat and capitulation of Germany, referring in this connection to agreements between the four powers in regard to Germany and Berlin. This merely confirms the fact that the exercise of the above mentioned right in regard to Berlin is linked to the obligatory execution by the powers occupying Germany of the four power agreements concluded among themselves in regard to Germany as a whole. In conformity with these agreements Berlin was envisaged as the seat of the supreme authority of the four powers occupying Germany, in which connection the agreement concerning the administration of "Greater Berlin" under the direction of the Control Council was reached.

Source: U.S. Department of State, *Documents on Germany, 1944–1985*, 158–62.

DOCUMENT 46: Secretary Marshall to U.S. Ambassador Lewis Douglas on the Allied Approach Toward Stalin (20 July 1948)

High-level conferences over the weekend and today, including discussions with Foster Dulles and ending with confirmation by the President himself, have resulted in a firm determination of U.S. policy in the Berlin matter. It is that the United States is resolved to maintain its position in Berlin and to take all measures necessary for the exercise of its rights, including the fulfillment of supply of the population of its sector.

In the pursuit of the foregoing policy, this Government is prepared to use any means that may be necessary. However, careful analysis of the Soviet note does not support the view that the Politburo is definitely determined upon a course of action leading to war. We do not feel, up to the present, that the Soviet Government has committed itself so irretrievably to maintain the blockade as to preclude the possibility of some face-saving retreat on their part. In these circumstances, precisely because we are firm in our determination to carry this matter through to the end, we feel we should explore every possibility which might lead to an agreed solution.

We therefore believe that prior to the dispatch of a formal note, which might elevate the matter further into the realms of prestige considerations, an effort should be made to approach Stalin directly. This, however, could only be done on an agreed three-power basis with the senior Ambassador in Moscow speaking for the three Governments, and on the understanding that the French and British Governments share our determination in this matter.

If the idea of an approach to Stalin, in accordance with the above procedure, would be acceptable to the British and French Governments, the Ambassador representing the three powers might be instructed along the following lines:

1. The Ambassador on behalf of the three Governments should inform Stalin of the extremely serious view which the three countries take of the situation created in Berlin as a result of the restrictions on communications between the western zones and the western sectors of Berlin. The reasons given in the Soviet note justify action of this nature and therefore cannot as such be accepted.

2. The U.S., U.K. and France are in Berlin as a matter of unquestioned right. Under no circumstances will they withdraw from Berlin under duress, whatever methods may be employed by the Soviet Military Commander.

3. The Governments of the U.S., U.K. and France consider that by international agreement they have an occupational duty with respect to the supply of the western sectors of Berlin and that they will take all measures which may prove necessary to assure the supply of their forces in Berlin and the discharge of their responsibilities towards the civilian population of these sectors.

4. The three Governments do not wish for war and assume that the Soviet Government holds the same view. However, the three governments cannot tolerate indefinitely actions of the Soviet military authorities which constitute a grave encroachment upon the military positions of the three Governments and an attempt to prevent their military forces from performing occupational duties laid upon them by an international agreement to which the Soviet Government is a party. Methods of coercion, irrespective of their motivation, obviously can lead to war if the Government applying such methods continues to pursue them to the end.

5. In so far as negotiations are concerned, the three Governments have never refused to discuss German matters in the appropriate place and in the appropriate manner. In fact, the three Governments are entirely prepared to discuss any question affecting Germany or any matter in dispute concerning the European settlements which fall within the agreed competence of the Council of Foreign Ministers.

6. The question of negotiation is therefore not the issue. The difficulty

lies in the measures still in force in Berlin which restrict the right of communication between the western zones and the western sectors of Berlin. The Soviet Government must understand that, irrespective of any questions of negotiations, we cannot tolerate the continuation of this situation with respect to the supply of Berlin.

7. The Ambassador should state that it is not clear to the Governments of U.S., U.K. and France exactly why the admitted restrictions on communications between Berlin and the western zones have been put into effect by the Soviet Government and would appreciate clarification on the following points:

(a) If as indicated in the note these measures are genuinely caused by the currency problem or by any technical difficulties, they are obviously insufficient to justify the nature of the Soviet counter action since such causes could have been and can be adjusted by the representatives of the four powers in Berlin.

(b) If these measures are designed to bring about negotiations with the three western powers, they are entirely unnecessary since at no time did these countries refuse a straight-forward proposal to negotiate on any subject within the competence of the four powers.

(c) If, however, the real but undisclosed purpose of the blockade is either (a) an attempt to force the western powers to withdraw from Berlin, or (b) an attempt to compel them to abandon the measures they have been forced to take in the administration of the western zones in the absence of general German settlement, then Stalin must understand that these efforts cannot and will not succeed.

8. The Ambassador should state that on the assumption that it is not in the interest of the Soviet Union any more than it is in those of the three western powers to allow this situation to move in the direction of war, it should be possible for the four Governments to find some way of getting around the difficulties in order to bring to an end the highly dangerous situation that has developed in Berlin as a result of the Soviet measures.

9. In the event that Stalin's reply to this inquiry should indicate that the measures in Berlin are caused by either "a" or 'b" of 7, the Ambassador should invite his views as to the means of overcoming the difficulties and would be prepared to discuss with Stalin some practical arrangement which would provide a resolution of the Berlin situation without loss of prestige to either side, possibly along the lines of reopening of the communications by rail, road and water to Berlin with a simultaneous announcement of an agreement to resume negotiations in Berlin at an agreed later date or an announcement of a four-power meeting to consider broader questions. *End.*

Source: FRUS, 1948, 971–73.

DOCUMENT 47: Foreign Ministers' Communiqué Refers the Crisis to the UN Security Council (26 September 1948)

The Governments of France, the United States and the United Kingdom are in agreement that the Soviet note of September 25 is unsatisfactory. The Soviet Government fails to provide the assurance requested in the notes from the three governments of September 22, 1948, that the illegal blockade measures be removed. In addition it demands that commercial and passenger traffic between the Western Zones and Berlin, by air as well as by rail, water and road be controlled by the Soviet Command in Germany. This demand of the Soviet Government is restated with emphasis in the official communique issued in Moscow. Moreover, in regard to currency, the Soviet note is evasive and does not answer the clear position stated by the three governments.

Accordingly, the three governments are transmitting a note to the Soviet Government fully setting out their position and informing it that in view of the insistence of the Soviet Government upon maintaining the blockade and upon the institution of restrictions on air communications they are compelled in compliance with their obligations under the Charter of the United Nations, to refer the matter to the Security Council.

Source: U.S. Department of State, *Documents on Germany, 1944–1985*, 177–78.

DOCUMENT 48: Dean Acheson on the State Department's Reaction to Stalin's Interview with Kingsbury Smith (February 1949)

In January 1949, Kingsbury Smith, the European General Manager of the International News Service, filed with the Soviet Foreign Office four questions addressed to Stalin. This was common procedure. Smith's questions were answered within a few days; Stalin's answers created a press sensation. On the day Stalin's replies were published, State Department officers discussed them and Secretary of State Dean Acheson took their conclusions to President Truman.

We judged the episode to be a cautious signal from Moscow. The significant fact was that in answering a question on ending the blockade,

Stalin had not mentioned the stated Russian reason for it—the new West German currency. The signal, we thought, told us that Moscow was ready to raise the blockade for a price. The price would be too high if it required abandonment of tripartite plans for the allied zones of Germany, in which case the maneuver could be changed into a propaganda offensive against hard-won allied unity on German policy. I asked permission to signal back through a bland and relaxed press conference that we had gotten the message and then to follow this with a secret inquiry into just what Moscow was prepared to do. The President agreed, and agreed further that our purpose and operation should be kept as close and secret as his intention to nominate me to be Secretary had been.

The press conference took place on February 2, on its regular day of the week, Wednesday, to rob it of any atmosphere of unusual significance. My remarks, though carefully thought out, were an "extemporaneous," patient examination of a press stunt built up out of all proportion to its intrinsic importance. . . .

Finally we came to the only question Mr. Smith had asked relating to an issue between the Soviet Union and the allies: Would the USSR be willing to remove restrictions on traffic to Berlin if the United States, Britain, and France agreed not to establish a separate western German state pending a Council of Foreign Ministers meeting to discuss the German problem as a whole? Stalin answered that it would, upon acceptance by the allies of the condition stated in the question and upon their removing their counter-restrictions against traffic to the Soviet zone.

Stalin's second point, I said, raised no problem since the allies had "always stated that if the Soviet Government permits normal communications with and within Berlin their counter measures will, of course, be lifted." The important point, however, was that the very terms of the question made the answer unresponsive to the facts. The reasons given for the blockade had been technical transportation difficulties and the currency reform. At one time the question of postponing German governmental arrangements had been raised but had been abandoned by the Soviet Union as a condition to raising the blockade. The Western governments, I said, "have stressed, repeated again and again to the Soviet Union, that their agreements in regard to Western Germany do not in any sense preclude agreements on Germany as a whole . . . [and] are . . . purely provisional pending such agreement on Germany as a whole." For months, I continued, the "Western powers have tried patiently and persistently to solve the difficulties . . . put forward . . . as the reasons for the blockade," but Soviet authorities would not discuss them.

Then I signaled our message: "There are many ways in which a serious proposal by the Soviet Government . . . could be made. . . . I hope you [the press] will not take it amiss if I point out that if I on my part were seeking to give assurance of seriousness of purpose I would choose some other channel than the channel of a press interview."

This press conference aptly illustrates the difficulties faced by an open society in conducting diplomatic interchanges with a closed one through the press. Stalin need answer only such written questions as he chose to answer. He permitted no cross-examination. Whatever the correspondent cabled home went through a censor. The Secretary, however, spoke and was cross-examined *viva voce*. In this case I had two purposes—to play down Stalin's initiative in order to avoid premature hardening of the Russian position and to signal the Russians that if they wanted serious discussion they should use a more private channel. Continuation of a public one would be interpreted as an indication of propaganda purposes only.

Source: Dean Acheson, *Present at the Creation: My Years in the State Department* (New York: Norton, 1969), 267–69.

DOCUMENT 49: Ambassador Philip Jessup's "Park Avenue Diplomacy—Ending the Berlin Blockade" (March–May 1949)

On March 2, 1949, I [Philip Jessup] was confirmed by the Senate as United States ambassador at large. My base shifted to Washington but I still dealt with some United Nations matters in New York. On March 14, the United States mission to the UN in New York received a telephone message from the Soviet delegation, saying that Ambassador Malik would like to see me the next time I was in New York. I sent word that the following day, March 15, would be a convenient time for me.

The Soviet mission then occupied the handsome house on the corner of 68th Street and Park Avenue, the former Pyne residence, just across the street from the Council on Foreign Relations. I was led up to Malik's office on the second floor and greeted cordially. . . .

We sat on opposite sides of a small table with the Russian interpreter between us. Malik's English is excellent, but he spoke in Russian, partly reading from a prepared statement. The fact that his interpreter took down all that was said made it the more natural for me to scribble down both Malik's remarks and my own.

Malik said that he had received a message from Moscow in response to his reporting the question I had put to him; Moscow informed him that Marshal Stalin's omission of any reference to the currency question was "not accidental." Moscow said that the currency question could be discussed at the meeting of the foreign ministers when Berlin and the whole German question were discussed. I inquired whether this meant that Moscow attributed more or less importance to the currency question; Malik said the statement had no bearing on either the importance or the unimportance of that question. I asked whether Moscow meant that the blockade would continue during a meeting of the foreign ministers. Malik said that I had not previously asked that question and he had no instructions about it. He said if I had other questions we could have further discussions later. I said that I was not suggesting that we have any negotiations but that I would be glad to learn any more information he received. . . .

Amid this badinage, Malik asked if I had any views about other points made by Marshal Stalin in his statement of January 31. I asked if he were referring to the question of the so called establishment of a West German government. Malik said that was one of the points. I remarked that it was not necessary to urge the postponement of those steps as a precondition to a meeting of the CFM if one were held soon, since no West German government was actually in existence. As will be seen, this was a point on which later difficulties arose. We talked about reciprocity in the lifting of restrictions on access to Berlin; Malik said the Soviet Union's measures were adopted in response to those of the West and I replied that reciprocally I could make that same speech to him. I said I came to New York from time to time and would always be glad to talk with him if he received further information.

When I reported to the small group in the State Department, we agreed that here were opportunities to be exploited and dangers to be avoided. If we immediately told the British and French, the danger of leaks was increased. But if Moscow decided to exaggerate the talks as proof that the West had surrendered and that the United States was negotiating for a settlement of the Berlin question, we would be in deep trouble with our Allies just at the time when the final negotiation of the NATO treaty was being completed—the pact was to be signed in Washington on April 4. It was decided that I should tell the British and French UN representatives in New York, which I did on Monday, March 21, the same day that I had a second talk with Malik. . . .

Malik said that he had told Vishinsky about our previous talk and that Vishinsky had said that if there should be an affirmative agreement on a date for a meeting of the CFM, there could be a reciprocal lifting of restrictions on traffic and trade to Berlin. I pressed him to state whether the lifting of the blockade would precede the meeting; for example, if there were a meeting on April 15, would the blockade be lifted on April 10, April 5, or April 1? Malik said the date for lifting the blockade could be prior to the date of the meeting. He asked how soon such a meeting could be held since Vishinsky believed it should be in the near future. I said I had no instructions on that point but would let him know; we agreed the arrangements would take some time. . . .

We then turned to what was for the Russians the key issue, one on which Vishinsky was intent on getting a commitment. Malik said that Vishinsky attributed importance to my statement at our previous meeting that no West German government was now in existence. At this point there was trouble with the interpretation, but the indication was that I had said that we would "call off" the formation of a West German government if there were a CFM. I interrupted to remind Malik that I had made no such promise; I had pointed out merely that since no West German government existed at the moment, if there were a CFM now, it would meet in the absence of such a government. Malik confirmed my recollection and corrected the interpreter. He did not ask for any promise from me on this point. . . .

At our talk on April 5, again at the Soviet headquarters, Malik had a very good interpreter; we talked for an hour and forty minutes. I began by telling Malik that I was authorized to speak for the three governments and I read him the agreed statement. Malik asked for clarification of the relative dates for lifting the blockade and for the holding of the CFM; I explained that when we fixed the date for the meeting we would have to fix an earlier date for the end of the blockade.

Most of the conversation related to what was, for the Russians, the key question—would the Western powers delay or postpone the preparations for the establishment of a West German government? Malik gave a fair summary of what I had said at our last conversation, and I underscored the fact that the West was making no promise about postponement and that, as the statement I had just read explained, if the CFM were held in the near future, it would be held before the West German government was established. Malik then read from typed notes which he had in front of him, recalling Stalin's reply to Kingsbury Smith and what I had said at our last meeting. Malik also read from his notes a summary of the points Vishinsky had made and to which I had previously responded. The argument went back and forth; when I said that in mentioning "the reasonably near future," I took into account that it would probably take five or six weeks to complete the preparations for a CFM, Malik asked if that meant we would suspend the preparations for a West German government for five or six weeks. Again I had to explain that the steps necessary for the establishment of the West German government could not be completed in five or six weeks, but that we made no promise at all about that date and did not agree to any interruption or suspension of the preparations for establishing that government. . . .

We then agreed that our conversations were in no way binding and

Malik said he would report to Vishinsky. I said I would await word about meeting him again. . . .

The communiqué was duly issued on May 5. The restrictions were removed and the CFM met in Paris as scheduled.

Source: Philip C. Jessup, "Park Avenue Diplomacy—Ending the Berlin Blockade," *Political Science Quarterly* 87, no. 3 (September 1972), 377–400.

DOCUMENT 50: Communiqué of Agreement on Berlin from the French, British, and United States Representatives to the United Nations (4 May 1949)

We, the Representatives of France, the United Kingdom and the United States on the Security Council, have the honor to request that you bring to the attention of the Members of the Security Council the fact that our Governments have concluded an agreement with the Government of the Union of Soviet Socialist Republics providing for the lifting of the restrictions which have been imposed on communications, transportation and trade with Berlin. A copy of the communiqué indicating the agreement reached between us is enclosed. . . .

COMMUNIQUÉ

The Governments of France, the Union of Soviet Socialist Republics, the United Kingdom, and the United States have reached the following agreement:

1. All the restrictions imposed since March 1, 1948, by the Government of the Union of Soviet Socialist Republics on communications, transportation, and trade between Berlin and the Western zones of Germany and between the Eastern zone and the Western zones will be removed on May 12, 1949.

2. All the restrictions imposed since March 1, 1948, by the Governments of France, the United Kingdom, and the United States, or any one of them, on communications, transportation, and trade between Berlin and the Eastern zone and between the Western and Eastern zones of Germany will also be removed on May 12, 1949.

3. Eleven days subsequent to the removal of the restrictions referred to in paragraphs one and two, namely, on May 23, 1949, a meeting of the Council of Foreign Ministers will be convened in Paris to consider questions relating to Germany and problems arising out of the situation in Berlin, including also the question of currency in Berlin.

Source: U.S. Department of State, *Documents on Germany, 1944–1985*, 221.

FURTHER READING

Ferrell, Robert H. *Harry S. Truman: A Life* (1994).

Isaacson, Walter, and Evan Thomas. *The Wise Men* (1986).

Jonas, Manfred. *The U.S. and Germany* (1984).

Milward, Alan S. *The Reconstruction of Western Europe, 1945–1951* (1984).

Miscamble, Wilson D. *George F. Kennan and the Making of American Foreign Policy, 1947–1950* (1992).

Ninkovich, Frank. *Germany and the United States* (1988).

Shlaim, Avi. *The U.S. and the Berlin Blockade* (1983).

Part III

The Korean War, 1950–1953

Until the end of World War II American interest in Korea had been peripheral. As a colony of Japan since 1910 and before that an area of competition between Czarist Russia and Japan, Korea simply did not attract much U.S. attention. During World War II the United States, as the major prosecutor of the war against Japan, promoted the objective of divesting Japan of all territory it had seized from China, Korea, and other Asian nations. At the Cairo Conference of 1943, in which the British, U.S., and Chinese governments participated, it was decided among other things, that upon war's end Korea should become free and independent.

American involvement in the Korean War had its basis in conflicting post–World War II Soviet-American objectives for Korea and in the differing ideologies and aspirations of their respective client regimes on the peninsula. The Soviet Union, which bordered Korea, desired either control over the entire peninsula or domination of a sector of it as a way of extending and protecting its empire. If neither of these goals was possible to achieve, projection of Soviet influence through the Korean communist party would constitute a backup strategy. The United States wanted a free and independent Korea consistent with the provisions of the Cairo Declaration (Document 51), one that would not be an irritant in American relations with any other nation or pose a threat to a U.S.-occupied Japan.

Soviet entrance into the war against Japanese forces in Manchuria on 8 August 1945 allowed the Red Army to get to Korea about a month before the American arrival and led American officials on 10 August to propose a division of the country at the 38th parallel for purposes of accepting the Japanese surrender. By the time U.S. forces arrived in early September, the Soviets had established a communist regime in power north of the 38th parallel and had begun the process of putting communist committees in strategic political positions in the South. American officials dissolved these units and began an occupation that eventually resulted in control of the region by noncommunist Korean nationalists.

Between 1945 and the end of 1947, the United States and the Soviet Union tried negotiations to secure a unified Korea. When it became apparent to U.S. policymakers that these negotiations could not result in a unified noncommunist country, they decided to take the issue to the United Nations to gain a settlement that would allow the United States to remove its troops and put first priority on containment of Soviet power in Europe. Ideally the UN would conduct elections in both North and South Korea preparatory to the establishment of a unified government, after which all U.S. and Soviet troops would leave. Actually, as most everyone at the United Nations was well aware, the elections would occur only in the South, given the closed Soviet system in place in the North and, while the UN-sponsored government of the South might pretend to be the legitimate power in the peninsula, nothing would really change.

The United States had never placed Korea in a vital interest category and did not see the peninsula as an appropriate spot to challenge its Soviet adversary. The UN solution (dividing Korea at the 38th parallel and withdrawal of American and Soviet troops from North and South Korea) gave the United States a way to extricate itself from the peninsula, but it also hardened the positions of both northern and southern regimes and led to debate in U.S. policy circles—a continuing debate, actually—about what the United States should do in the event of a communist drive to unify the country by force. Until 25 June 1950 the official U.S. policy was that the United States would consider Korea as lying outside the American defense perimeter in Asia, a view given public expression by Secretary of State Dean Acheson in a National Press Club speech in early January 1950. In the Soviet decision to support a North Korean invasion of the South, this American definition of Korea's value almost certainly played an important part.

During a visit to Moscow in late 1949 North Korean leader Kim Il-Sung convinced Josef Stalin that a military campaign to unify the country would be successful, that in fact it was necessary to move quickly before South Korea, under President Syngman Rhee, invaded North Korea. Stalin gave his approval on the assumption that the United States would not intervene. What Stalin did not know was that a powerful contending line of thought existed in the Truman Administration that argued the United States could not allow South Korea to fall to the communists if it wished to maintain the credibility of America's global commitments to contain communism. In other words, while the prevailing policy opinion held that Korea lay outside the U.S. defense perimeter, a number of American policymakers had argued convincingly that it was essential for the United States to defend South Korea as a way of demonstrating its credibility to friends and foes alike that it was a strong and trustworthy ally.

With the shock of the Soviet-backed North Korean invasion of the South on 25 June 1950, this came to the fore. The United States quickly sent air and naval forces to Korean waters and a couple of days later ground troops to South Korea. This resulted in American participation in a large-scale war in an area not considered vital and against a surrogate enemy. The conflict lasted until July 1953 and is arguably the most important event in the history of the Cold War. It was costly monetarily; it led to over 30,000 American deaths; it brought war with China, a vitalized North Atlantic Treaty Organization, approval of a vastly increased U.S. military capability, and a political quarrel in the United States of nearly unprecedented proportions. Because the war was fought under a UN mandate, it also tended to strengthen the prestige of that institution, at least temporarily.

CHRONOLOGY

1943

December 1. Cairo Conference Declaration on postwar Korea

1945

August 14. Japan announces surrender

August. Decision to divide Korea at 38th parallel

September 2. Japan formally surrenders on USS *Missouri* in Tokyo Bay

December 16. Gen. MacArthur recommends withdrawal from Korea

1947

September. U.S. refers Korean question to UN

September. U.S. military assesses national interests in Korea

1949

August. Soviet Union explodes atomic bomb

1950

January 12. Sec. of State Acheson's "Defense Perimeter" speech

April 25. NSC-68 as basis of U.S. policy toward containing Soviet and Chinese communist expansion

June 25. North Koreans invade South Korea; Korean War begins

September. U.S. launches major amphibious landing at Inchon

October. North Korean forces retreat from South

October. Truman and MacArthur meet on Wake Island

October 7. U.S. forces cross into North Korea

November 24. UN forces reach Yalu River along China's border

November 26. China enters Korean War

1951

April 10. MacArthur relieved of command

April. Korean War armistice talks begin

April. Australian–New Zealand–United States (ANZUS) Treaty

1952

July. U.S. hydrogen bomb tested

November. Eisenhower elected president

December. Eisenhower visits Korea

1953

February 11. NSC discusses use of atomic weapons in Korea

March 5. Stalin dies; Malenkov and Khrushchev share power

March 30. China's Zhou En-lai's cable on repatriation of POWs

April. Eisenhower-Rhee correspondence on Korean armistice

July 26. Korean armistice signed at Panmunjom

PRIOR TO 25 JUNE 1950

The documents in this section illustrate U.S. policy in Korea between 1945 and 1950, showing, in particular, the nature of American interests, how and why the country was divided at the 38th parallel, and why the United States experienced tension between its need to demonstrate credibility and its desire to avoid a military commitment in the region.

DOCUMENT 51: The Cairo Declaration by President Roosevelt, Prime Minister Churchill, and Generalissimo Jiang (1 December 1943)

The several military missions have agreed upon future military operations against Japan. The Three Great Allies expressed their resolve to bring unrelenting pressure against their brutal enemies by sea, land, and air. This pressure is already rising.

The Three Great Allies are fighting this war to restrain and punish the aggression of Japan. They covet no gain for themselves and have no thought of territorial expansion. It is their purpose that Japan shall be stripped of all the islands in the Pacific which she has seized or occupied since the beginning of the first World War in 1914, and that all the territories Japan has stolen from the Chinese, such as Manchuria, Formosa, and the Pescadores, shall be restored to the Republic of China. Japan will also be expelled from all other territories which she has taken by violence and greed. The aforesaid three great powers, mindful of the enslavement of the people of Korea, are determined that in due course Korea shall become free and independent.

With these objects in view the three Allies, in harmony with those of the United Nations at war with Japan, will continue to persevere in the serious and prolonged operations necessary to procure the unconditional surrender of Japan.

Source: United States Senate, Committee on Foreign Relations, *The United States and the Korean Problem: Documents, 1943–1953*, edited by Alexander Wiley (Washington: GPO, 1953), 1.

DOCUMENT 52: Dean Rusk Recalls How "Two Tired Colonels" Divided Korea at the 38th Parallel (14 August 1945)

One episode had greater significance than we realized at the time. Widely scattered Japanese forces had to surrender, and the State and War Departments differed over where and when American forces should accept their surrender. The State Department wanted us to accept the surrender as far north on the mainland of China as possible, including key points in Manchuria. But the U.S. Army, concerned about the future, did not want responsibility for areas where it had no or few forces. In fact, the Army did not want to go onto the mainland at all.

We finally reached a compromise that would keep at least some U.S. forces on the Asian mainland, a sort of toehold on the Korean peninsula for symbolic purposes. During a SWINK [the State/War/Navy Coordinating Committee] meeting on August 14, 1945, the same day of the Japanese surrender, Colonel Charles Bonesteel and I retired to an adjacent room late at night and studied intently a map of the Korean peninsula. Working in haste and under great pressure, we had a formidable task: to pick a zone for the American occupation. Neither Tic nor I was a Korea expert, but it seemed to us that Seoul, the capital, should be in the American sector. We also knew that the U.S. Army opposed an extensive area of occupation. Using a National Geographic map, we looked just north of Seoul for a convenient dividing line but could not find a natural geographical line. We saw instead the thirty-eighth parallel and decided to recommend that.

SWINK accepted it without too much haggling, and surprisingly, so did the Soviets. I had thought they might insist on a line farther south in view of our respective military positions. No one present at our meeting, including two young American colonels, was aware that at the turn of the century the Russians and Japanese had discussed spheres of influence in Korea, divided along the thirty-eighth parallel. Had we known that, we almost surely would have chosen another line of demarcation. Remembering those earlier discussions, the Russians might have interpreted our action as acknowledgment of their sphere of influence in Korea north of the thirty-eighth parallel. Any future talk about the agreed-upon reunification of Korea would be seen as mere show. But we were ignorant of all this, and SWINK'S choice of the thirty-eighth parallel, recommended by two tired colonels working late at night, proved fateful.

Source: Dean Rusk as Told to Richard Rusk. Edited by Daniel S. Papp, *As I Saw It* (New York: Norton, 1990), 120–24.

DOCUMENT 53: As Commander of U.S. Forces in the Pacific, General Douglas MacArthur Recommends to the War Department that Both American and Russian Forces Be Withdrawn from Korea (16 December 1945)

After 3 months in occupation of south Korea I have reached the following definite conclusions. These are considered a further crystallization of previous reports.

The dual occupation of Korea with Russia north and US south of the 38th degree parallel imposes an impossible condition upon our occupation missions of establishing sound economy and preparing Korea for future independence. In South Korea the US [is] blamed for the partition and [there] is growing resentment against all Americans in the area including passive resistance to constructive efforts we make here. . . . Every Korean knows full well that under the dual occupation any talk of real freedom and independence is purely academic. It will be extremely difficult, if not impossible, ever to accomplish unity of spirit in the Koreans until they see the present 38th parallel barrier removed. Every day of delay fosters further and permanent division of the people. . . .

The Russian methods of occupation north of the 38th degree are not understandable to Americans. There is evidence that they have constructed and maintain an effective field works system of defense against invasion just north of 38 degree. . . . Although outwardly friendly relations between troops of the two nations exist, persistent reports come from the north that Russians repeatedly speak of war with US. There are also rumors south of 38 degree that US and Russia are preparing for war. Under current conditions, border incidents of a dangerous character could easily occur. Russian Consulate is maintained in Seoul with large staff with no legitimate reasons. The Consul General and ranking members of his staff are making increasingly frequent trips across the occupational boundary and are conferring with local Koreans. Despite the Russian border control there is a daily flow southward of 5,000 to 6,000 destitute refugees, both Japs and Koreans, giving strong indication that the control valve is open for southward movement of undesirables. Koreans well know that the Russians have a force locally of about 4 to 1 to Americans and with the usual oriental slant are willing to do homage and are doing homage to the man with the largest weapon. On the part of the masses there is an increasing tendency to look to Russia, for the future.

In summary, the U.S. occupation of Korea, under present condition and policies is surely drifting to the edge of a political-economic abyss from which it can never be retrieved with any credit to United States prestige in the Far East. Positive action on the international level or the seizure of complete initiative in South Korea by the U.S. in the very near future is absolutely essential to stop this drift. Specifically and urgently needed are:

(1) Clarification and removal of 38th degree barrier so as to unify Korea.

(2) Clear-cut statement abandoning "Trusteeship".

(3) Positive statement of policy regarding status of former Japanese property in Korea and reparations as applied to any such property.

(4) Reiteration of Allied promise of Korean independence accompanying foregoing acts.

(5) Establish complete separation of Korea from Japan in the minds of the press, the public, the State and War Depts and Allied Nations.

Under present conditions with no corrective action forthcoming I would go so far as to recommend we give serious consideration to an agreement with Russia that both the U.S. and Russia withdraw forces from Korea simultaneously and leave Korea to its devices and an inevitable internal upheaval for its self purification.

Source: U.S. Department of State, *Foreign Relations of the United States, 1945* (Washington: GPO, 1969), 6:1144–48.

DOCUMENT 54: U.S. Notification to Soviets of Intent to Refer the Korean Question to the UN (7 September 1947)

The decision of the Soviet Government as conveyed in your letter of September 4, not to participate in Four Power discussions of proposals of the United States Government designed to achieve the speedy realization of the aims of the Moscow Agreement on Korea is deeply regretted. For almost two years the United States Government has been faithfully endeavoring to reach agreement with the Soviet Government to carry out the terms of the Moscow Agreement but with no appreciable success. It has even proved impossible for the Soviet and United States Delegations on the Joint Commission in Korea to agree upon a joint report of the status of their deliberations up to the present. There is no sign of the early setting up of a Korean Provisional Government. Korea remains divided and her promised independence unrealized.

The United States Government believes that this situation must not be permitted to continue indefinitely. In view of the fact that bilateral negotiations have not advanced Korean independence and that the Soviet Government does not agree to discussions among the powers adhering to the Moscow Agreement, there is but one course remaining. It is the intention, therefore, of my Government to refer the problem of Korean independence to the forthcoming session of the General Assembly of the United Nations. It is suggested that the members of the Joint Commission hold themselves in readiness to give such aid and assistance to the General Assembly as may be required during the Assembly's consideration of this problem.

Source: Acting Secretary of State Robert Lovett to Soviet Foreign Minister Molotov, September 7, 1947, in U.S. Department of State, *Bulletin* 17, no. 430 (September 28, 1947), 623–24.

DOCUMENT 55: Joint Chiefs of Staff's Assessment of America's National Interest in Korea (September 1947)

15 September 1947

[T]he State Department requests, as a matter of urgency, the views of the Joint Chiefs of Staff regarding the interest of the U.S. in military occupation of South Korea from the point of view of the military security of the United States. . . .

26 [29] September, 1947

From Secretary of Defense Forrestal to Secretary of State Marshall.

The Joint Chiefs of Staff consider that, from the standpoint of military security, the United States has little strategic interest in maintaining the present troops and bases in Korea for the reasons hereafter stated.

In the event of hostilities in the Far East, our present forces in Korea would be a military liability and could not be maintained there without substantial reinforcement prior to the initiation of hostilities. Moreover, any offensive operation the United States might wish to conduct on the Asiatic continent most probably would by-pass the Korean peninsula.

If, on the other hand, an enemy were able to establish and maintain strong air and naval bases in the Korean peninsula, he might be able to interfere with United States communications and operations in East China, Manchuria, the Yellow Sea, Sea of Japan and adjacent islands. Such interference would require an enemy to maintain substantial air and naval forces in an area where they would be subject to neutralization by air action. Neutralization by air action would be more feasible and less costly than large scale ground operations.

In light of the present severe shortage of military manpower, the corps of two divisions, totaling some 45,000 men, now maintained in south Korea, could well be used elsewhere, the withdrawal of these forces from Korea would not impair the military position of the Far East Command unless, in consequence, the Soviets establish military strength in south Korea capable of mounting an assault in Japan.

At the present time, the occupation of Korea is requiring very large expenditures for the primary purpose of preventing disease and disorder which might endanger our occupation forces with little, if any, lasting benefit to the security of the United States.

Source: U.S. Department of State, *Foreign Relations of the United States, 1947* (Washington: GPO, 1972), 6:789, 817–18.

DOCUMENT 56: Soviet Ambassador to North Korea Reports to Stalin of Kim Il-Sung's Increasing Preparations to Attack South Korea (19 January 1950)

In mid-1994 Russian President Boris Yeltsin presented to South Korean President Kim Young-Sam previously classified Soviet documents on the origins of the war. Historian Kathryn Weathersby has translated several of these ciphered telegrams relating to Kim Il-Sung's March 1949 meeting with Stalin and to later critical discussions between Kim and Soviet diplomats in Pyongyang. In an 11 September 1949 cable sent by then-Deputy Soviet Foreign Minister Andrei Gromyko to the Soviet Embassy in the North Korean capital, mention is made that Kim had again raised on 12 August 1949 the question of a military campaign against South Korea. Initially reluctant to agree to Kim's invasion plans, Stalin appears to have warmed to the idea of a military campaign against the South Koreans after the victory of the communist forces in China in the fall of 1949. In a 19 January 1950 telegram, Soviet Ambassador T. F. Shtykov in Pyongyang refers to Kim's understanding with Mao Zedong and the importance of the changing "international situation" (withdrawal of U.S. military forces from Korea) in Asia.

Kim . . . began to speak about how now, when China is completing its liberation, the liberation of the Korean people in the south . . . is next in line. In conjunction with this he said:

"The people of the southern portion of Korea trust me and rely on our armed might. Partisans will not decide the question. . . . If the matter of the liberation of the people of the southern portion of Korea and the unification of the whole country is drawn out, then I can lose the trust of the people of Korea." Further Kim stated that when he was in Moscow, Comrade Stalin said to him that it was not necessary to attack the south, in case of an attack on the north of the country by the army of Rhee Syngmann, then it is possible to go on the counteroffensive to the south of Korea. . . . Kim said that he himself cannot begin an attack, because he is a communist, a disciplined person and for him the order of Comrade Stalin is law. Then [Kim] stated that if it is now possible to meet with Comrade Stalin, then he will meet with Mao Zedong, after his return from Moscow. Kim underscored that Mao promised to render him assistance after the conclusion of the war in China. . . . Kim . . . also questioned the possibility of the creation of an eastern [Asian] bureau of the COMINFORM. . . .

Then Kim Il Sung placed before me the question, why don't I allow him to attack the Ongjin peninsula [around the South Korean capital of Seoul], which the [North Korean] People's Army could take in three days, and with a general attack the People's Army could be in Seoul in several days.

Source: Kathryn Weathersby, "To Attack, or Not to Attack? Stalin, Kim Il Sung, and the Prelude to War," *Cold War International History Bulletin* 5 (Spring 1995), 1–9.

DOCUMENT 57: Secretary of State Dean Acheson's "Defensive Perimeter of the Pacific" Speech During a Meeting of the U.S. Press Club (12 January 1950)

What is the situation in regard to the military security of the Pacific area, and what is our policy in regard to it?

In the first place, the defeat and the disarmament of Japan has placed upon the United States the necessity of assuming the military defense of Japan so long as that is required, both in the interest of our security and in the interests of the security of the entire Pacific area and, in all honor, in the interest of Japanese security. We have American—and there are Australian—troops in Japan. I am not in a position to speak for the Australians, but I can assure you that there is no intention of any sort of abandoning or weakening the defenses of Japan and that whatever arrangements are to be made either through permanent settlement or otherwise, that defense must and shall be maintained.

This defensive perimeter runs along the Aleutians to Japan and then goes to the Ryukyus. We hold important defense positions in the Ryukyu Islands, and those we will continue to hold. In the interest of the population of the Ryukyu Islands, we will at an appropriate time offer to hold these islands under trusteeship of the United Nations. But they are essential parts of the defensive perimeter of the Pacific, and they must and will be held.

The defensive perimeter runs from the Ryukyus to the Philippine Islands. Our relations, our defensive relations with the Philippines are contained in agreements between us. Those agreements are being loyally carried out and will be loyally carried out. Both peoples have learned by bitter experience the vital connections between our mutual defense requirements. We are in no doubt about that, and it is hardly necessary for me to say an attack on the Philippines could not and would not be tolerated by the United States. But I hasten to add that no one perceives the imminence of any such attack.

So far as the military security of other areas in the Pacific is concerned, it must be clear that no person can guarantee these areas against military attack. But it must also be clear that such a guarantee is hardly sensible or necessary within the realm of practical relationship.

Should such an attack occur—one hesitates to say where such an armed attack could come from—the initial reliance must be on the people attacked to resist it and then upon the commitments of the entire civilized world under the Charter of the United Nations which so far has not proved a weak reed to lean on by any people who are determined to protect their independence against outside aggression. But it is a mistake, I think, in considering Pacific and Far Eastern problems to become obsessed with military considerations. Important as they are, there are other problems that press, and these other problems are not capable of solution through military means. These other problems arise out of the susceptibility of many areas, and many countries in the Pacific area, to subversion and penetration. That cannot be stopped by military means.

Source: U.S. Department of State, Bulletin 22, no. 551 (January 23, 1950), 111–18.

DOCUMENT 58: Acheson Recalls His Speech and the Defeat of an Aid Package (1950)

The speech was another effort to get the self-styled formulators of public opinion to think before they wrote, and do more than report as news the emotional or political utterances of political gladiators. On the preceding day [11 January 1950], one of these, Senator [Robert] Taft, had been widely quoted charging in the Senate that the State Department had "been guided by a left-wing group who obviously have wanted to get rid of Chiang and were willing at least to turn China over to the Communists for that purpose." Senator [Arthur] Vandenberg had rebuked him for saying this. At the time, Mao Tse-tung was in Moscow negotiating with Stalin what proved to be the Sino-Soviet Treaty of February 14, 1950. It was a supercharged moment to be speaking on Asian matters. . . .

Later it was argued that my speech "gave the green light" to the attack on South Korea by not including it within the "defensive perimeter." This was specious, for Australia and New Zealand were not included either, and the first of all our mutual defense agreements was made with Korea. If the Russians were watching the United States for signs of our intentions in the Far East, they would have been more impressed by the two years' agitation for withdrawal of combat forces from Korea, the defeat in Congress of a minor aid bill for it, and the increasing discussion of a peace treaty with Japan.

Source: Dean Acheson, Present at the Creation (New York: Norton, 1969), 355–58.

DOCUMENT 59: National Security Council Paper #68 (25 April 1950)

CONCLUSIONS

16. The risk of war with the U.S.S.R. is sufficient to warrant, in common prudence, timely and adequate preparation by the United States.

a. Even though present estimates indicate that the Soviet leaders probably do not intend deliberate armed action involving the United States at this time, the possibility of such deliberate resort to war cannot be ruled out.

b. Now and for the foreseeable future there is a continuing danger that war will arise either through Soviet miscalculation of the determination of the United States to use all the means at its command to safeguard its security, through Soviet misinterpretation of our intentions, or through U.S. miscalculation of Soviet reactions to measures which we might take.

17. Soviet domination of the potential power of Eurasia, whether achieved by armed aggression or by political and subversive means, would be strategically and politically unacceptable to the United States.

18. The capability of the United States either in peace or in the event of war to cope with threats to its security or to gain its objectives would be severely weakened by internal developments, important among which are:

a. Serious espionage, subversion and sabotage, particularly by concerted and well-directed communist activity.

b. Prolonged or exaggerated economic instability.

c. Internal political and social disunity.

d. Inadequate or excessive armament or foreign aid expenditures.

e An excessive or wasteful usage of our resources in time of peace.

f. Lessening of U.S. prestige and influence through vacillation or appeasement or lack of skill and imagination in the conduct of its foreign policy or by shirking world responsibilities.

g. Development of a false sense of security through a deceptive change in Soviet tactics. . . .

19. Our current security programs and strategic plans are based upon these objectives, aims, and measures:

a. To reduce the power and influence of the U.S.S.R. to limits which no longer constitute a threat to the peace, national independence and stability of the world family of nations.

b. To bring about a basic change in the conduct of international relations by the government in power in Russia, to conform with the purposes and principles set forth in the U.N. Charter.

In pursuing these objectives, due care must be taken to avoid permanently impairing our economy and the fundamental values and institutions inherent in our way of life.

20. We should endeavor to achieve our general objectives by methods short of war through the pursuit of the following aims:

a. To encourage and promote the gradual retraction of undue Russian power and influence from the present perimeter areas around traditional Russian boundaries and the emergence of the satellite countries as entities independent of the U.S.S.R.

b. To encourage the development among the Russian peoples of attitudes which may help to modify current Soviet behavior and permit a revival of the national life of groups evidencing the ability and determination to achieve and maintain national independence.

c. To eradicate the myth by which people remote from Soviet military influence are held in a position of subservience to Moscow and to cause the world at large to see and understand the true nature of the U.S.S.R. and the Soviet-directed world communist party, and to adopt a logical and realistic attitude toward them.

d. To create situations which will compel the Soviet Government to recognize the practical undesirability of acting on the basis of its present concepts and the necessity of behaving in accordance with precepts of international conduct, as set forth in the purposes and principles of the U.N. Charter.

21. Attainment of these aims requires that the United States:

a. Develop a level of military readiness which can be maintained as long as necessary as a deterrent to Soviet aggression, as indispensable support to our political attitude toward the U.S.S.R., as a source of encouragement to nations resisting Soviet political aggression, and as an adequate basis for immediate military commitments and for rapid mobilization should war prove unavoidable.

b. Assure the internal security of the United States against dangers of sabotage, subversion, and espionage.

c. Maximize our economic potential, including the strengthening of our peacetime economy and the establishment of essential reserves readily available in the event of war.

d. Strengthen the orientation toward the United States of the non-Soviet nations; and help such of those nations as are able and willing to make an important contribution to U.S. security, to increase their economic and political stability and their military capability.

e. Place the maximum strain on the Soviet structure of power and particularly on the relationships between Moscow and the satellite countries.

f. Keep the U.S. public fully informed and cognizant of the threats to our national security so that it will be prepared to support the measures which we must accordingly adopt. . . .

In summary, we must, by means of a rapid and sustained build-up of the political, economic, and military strength of the free world, and by means of an affirmative program intended to wrest the initiative from the Soviet Union, confront it with convincing evidence of the determination and ability of the free world to frustrate the Kremlin design of a world dominated by its will. Such evidence is the only means short of war which eventually may force the Kremlin to abandon its present course of action and to negotiate acceptable agreements on issues of major importance.

The whole success of the proposed program hangs ultimately on recognition by this Government, the American people, and all free peoples, that the cold war is in fact a real war in which the survival of the free world is at stake.

Source: U.S. Department of State, *Foreign Relations of the United States, 1950* (hereafter *FRUS, 1950*) (Washington: GPO, 1976), 1:237–92.

THE 38TH PARALLEL

Crossing the 38th parallel in the Korean War may well have been the major American military/diplomatic mistake of the mid-twentieth century. These documents reveal the nature of the initial decision to intervene and then show how and why U.S. policymakers escalated the primary objectives by deciding to push north of the dividing line between North and South Korea.

DOCUMENT 60: President Truman Responds to the North Korean Attack (25 June 1950)

President Truman was at his home in Independence, Missouri, when he received a late evening call from Secretary of State Acheson reporting the North Korean invasion of South Korea. Truman agreed with Secretary Acheson's initial recommendation to immediately call for an emergency meeting of the UN Security Council and to declare that an act of aggression had been committed against the Republic of Korea. Acheson's next call came the following (Sunday) morning. Acheson reported that the Security Council had been called into emergency session but that a call for a cease-fire would probably be ignored by the North Koreans and "their big allies." Truman understood that he had to make some decision at once as to the degree of aid which the United States was willing to extend to South Korea.

The [presidential] plane left Kansas City . . . and it took just a little over three hours to make the trip to Washington. I had time to think aboard the plane. In my generation, this was not the first occasion when the strong had attacked the weak. I recalled some earlier instances: Manchuria, Ethiopia, Austria. I remembered how each time that the democracies failed to act it had encouraged the aggressors to keep going ahead. Communism was acting in Korea just as Hitler, Mussolini, and the Japanese had acted ten, fifteen, and twenty years earlier. I felt certain that if South Korea was allowed to fall Communist leaders would be emboldened to override nations closer to our own shores. If the Communists were permitted to force their way into the Republic of Korea without opposition from the free world, no small nation would have the courage to resist threats and aggression by stronger Communist neighbors. If this was allowed to go unchallenged it would mean a third world war, just as similar incidents had brought on the second world war. It was also clear to me that the foundations and the principles of the United Nations were at stake unless this unprovoked attack on Korea could be stopped.

Back in Washington at a Blair House meeting with his top advisers, President Truman called on Secretary Acheson to give a detailed picture of the situation and to present the recommendations of the State and Defense Departments. Secretary Acheson presented President Truman with the following recommendations for immediate action:

1. That MacArthur should evacuate the Americans from Korea—including the dependents of the Military Mission—and, in order to do so, should keep open the Kimpo and other airports, repelling all hostile attacks thereon. In doing this, his air forces should stay south of the 38th parallel.
2. That MacArthur should be instructed to get ammunition and supplies to the Korean army by airdrop.
3. That the Seventh Fleet should be ordered into the Formosa Straits to prevent the conflict from spreading to that area. . . . We should make a statement that the fleet would repel any attack on Formosa and that no attacks should be made from Formosa on the mainland.
At this point I interrupted to say that the Seventh Fleet should be ordered north [from the Philippines] at once but that I wanted to withhold making any statement until the fleet was in position.

Source: Harry S. Truman, *Memoirs: Years of Trial and Hope* (New York: Doubleday, 1956), 332–35.

DOCUMENT 61: President Truman's Military Response to Attack (27 June 1950)

The attack upon Korea makes it plain beyond all doubt that communism has passed beyond the use of subversion to conquer independent nations and will now use armed invasion and war. It has defied the orders of the Security Council of the United Nations issued to preserve peace and security. In these circumstances the occupation of Formosa by Communist forces would be a direct threat to the security of the Pacific area and to United States forces performing their lawful and necessary functions in that area.

Accordingly I have ordered the Seventh Fleet to prevent any attack on Formosa. As a corollary of this action I am calling upon the Chinese Government on Formosa to cease all air and sea operations against the mainland. The Seventh Fleet will see that this is done. The determination of the future status of Formosa must await the restoration of security in the Pacific, a peace settlement with Japan, or consideration by the United Nations.

Source: United States Senate, Hearings Before the Committee on Armed Services and the Committee on Foreign Relations, 82d Congress, "To Conduct an Inquiry into the Military Situation in the Far East and the Facts Surrounding the Relief of General MacArthur," *Military Situation in the Far East, 1951*, Pt. 5 (Washington: GPO, 1951), 3369.

DOCUMENT 62: President Truman on Military Action in Korea (30 June 1950)

At a meeting with congressional leaders at the White House this morning the President, together with the Secretary of Defense, the Secretary of State, and the Joint Chiefs of Staff, reviewed with them the latest developments of the situation in Korea.

The congressional leaders were given a full review of the intensified military activities.

In keeping with the United Nations Security Council's request for support to the Republic of Korea in repelling the North Korean invaders and restoring peace in Korea, the President announced that he had authorized the United States Air Force to conduct missions on specific military targets in Northern Korea wherever militarily necessary, and had ordered a naval blockade of the entire Korean coast.

General MacArthur has been authorized to use certain supporting ground units.

Source: Military Situation in the Far East, 1951, Pt. 5, 3372.

DOCUMENT 63: American Diplomat George Kennan Recalls Discussions at the State Department to Restore 38th Parallel as the *Status Quo Ante* (June–July 1950)

During those uncertain days immediately following the North Korean invasion, American strategists advocated a vigorous and determined military reaction to the North Korean attack. The American counteroffensive was initially directed at repelling the attack, and then expelling North Korean forces from the area south of the 38th parallel. No plan was then contemplated to push the conflict on north of the 38th. However, on June 27, just two days after the attack, State Department officer George Kennan found himself briefing several NATO ambassadors in Washington on what U.S. policy would be after the defeat of the North Korean invasion. Kennan assured the assembled diplomats that the U.S. government's sole intention was to restore the *status quo ante.*

Only one day later, however—June 28—the Air Force was already pushing for authorization to operate beyond the parallel. This was discussed that same day in the Secretary of State's office; and I find in my own notes the following account of my part in the discussion:

I said I thought we might consider an alteration of our position about the 38th parallel, to the following effect: that while we would continue to state it as our purpose not to reoccupy any territory north of the parallel, we would not limit our forces to operation south of the parallel but would say that they would operate anywhere in Korea where their operations might promote the achievement of [their] missions.

Source: George F. Kennan, *Memoirs, 1925–1950* (Boston: Little, Brown, 1967), 487–89.

DOCUMENT 64: Internal State Department Memorandum Outlining U.S. Policy Concerning the 38th Parallel (1 July 1950)

Subject: Korean Speech for President Truman [Given on 19 July]

I understand that there has been some suggestion that in the speech which is being prepared for President Truman to make on the Korean situation there should be included a statement to the effect that United States forces and presumably South Korean forces will only attempt to drive the North Koreans back to the 38th parallel and will not go any farther. I most strongly urge that no such statement be included in the speech. In my opinion it would be fatal to what may be left of South Korean morale if such a statement were made. It would also appear to me to be most unrealistic in the present situation. I believe there is ample justification in the last part of the second Resolution of the Security Council for any action which may be deemed appropriate at the time which will contribute to the permanent restoration of peace and stability in that area. I am convinced that there will be no permanent peace and stability in Korea as long as the artificial division at the 38th parallel continues. I believe the time has come when we must be bold and willing to take even more risks than we have already and, while I certainly would not advocate saying in the speech that we would proceed beyond the 38th parallel, nevertheless we should not commit ourselves at this time not to do so.

I personally feel that if we can, and I am not at all certain we can, we should continue right on up to the Manchurian and Siberian border, and, having done so, call for a UN-supervised election for all of Korea. Any action on our part now which would inhibit such action in the future would, I think, be most unwise.

Source: Director of Northeast Asian Affairs, John M. Allison, to Assistant Secretary of State Dean Rusk, July 1, 1950, in *FRUS, 1950*, 7:272.

DOCUMENT 65: John Foster Dulles' 38th Parallel Memorandum (14 July 1950)

Since I understand thought is being given in the Policy Planning Staff to the desirability of a present public commitment on the part of the U.S.

to permit the North Koreans anytime they wish to retreat in good order and re-form behind the 38th Parallel, I give you briefly my views as follows:

1. The 38th Parallel was never intended to be, and never ought to be, a political line. The United Nations has, from the beginning, insisted that equity and justice require a united Korea. The 38th Parallel, if perpetuated as a political line and as providing asylum to the aggressor, is bound to perpetuate friction and ever-present danger of new war. If we have the opportunity to obliterate the line as a political division, certainly we should do so in the interest of "peace and security in the area". (U.N. Resolution)

2. I would think that, from a national standpoint, it would be folly to allow the North Korean army to retire in good order with its armor and equipment and re-form behind the 38th Parallel from whence it could attack again the now ravaged and weakened Republic of Korea. To permit that would mean either the exposure of the Republic of Korea to greater peril than preceded the June 25th attack or the maintenance by the United States of a large military establishment to contain the North Korean Army at the 38th Parallel. The North Korean Army should be destroyed, if we have the power to destroy it, even if this requires pursuit beyond the 38th Parallel. That is the only way to remove the menace.

3. Neither equity nor good sense dictates that an unprovoked act of aggression should occur without risk of loss to the aggressor. If there can be armed aggression under conditions such that failure involves no permanent loss, then that puts a premium on aggression. There must be a penalty to such wrong-doing unless we want to encourage its repetition.

4. I do not suggest that we should at this time make any public declaration of intention. Perhaps expediency would make it wise to stop at the 38th Parallel. But I believe strongly that we should not now tie our hands by a public statement precluding the possibility of our forces, if victorious, being used to forge a new Korea which would include at least most of the area north of the 38th Parallel.

We should preserve our freedom to act in the way that seems best at the time when a decision is practically needed. That may be months hence and no one can now know the then surrounding circumstances.

5. I would not suppose that a united Korea would necessarily include the North Kankyo [North Hamgyong] Province, which runs up to the neighborhood of Vladivostok or the North Heian [North Pyangan] Province, which borders on the Yalu River. But most of Korea could be, and should be, united without this involving any territorial threat to the Soviet Union. Also, any reuniting should involve U.N. auspices, not merely U.S. unilateral action.

Source: John Foster Dulles to Director of Policy Planning Staff, Paul Nitze, July 14, 1950, in *FRUS, 1950,* 7:386–87.

DOCUMENT 66: Secretary of Defense George Marshall to General MacArthur to Cross the 38th Parallel (29 September 1950)

Top Secret. Flash. From JCS to personal for Genl of the Army Douglas MacArthur, SecDef sends. For his eyes only. Reference present report of supposed announcement by Eighth Army that ROK [Republic of Korea] Divisions would halt on 38th parallel for regrouping: We want you to feel unhampered tactically and strategically to proceed north of 38th parallel. Announcement above referred to may precipitate embarrassment in UN where evident desire is not to be confronted with necessity of a vote on passage of 38th parallel, rather to find you have found it militarily necessary to do so.

Source: Secretary Marshall to General MacArthur, 29 September 1950, in *FRUS, 1950,* 7:826.

DOCUMENT 67: General MacArthur's Rationale for Amphibious Landing at Inchon (23 August 1950)

I was now finally ready for the last great stroke to bring my plan into fruition . . . a turning movement deep into the flank and rear of the enemy that would sever his supply lines and encircle all his forces south of Seoul. I had made similar decisions in past campaigns, but none more fraught with danger, none that promised to be more vitally conclusive if successful.

The target I selected was Inchon, 20 miles west of Seoul and the second largest port in South Korea. The target date, because of the great tides at Inchon, had to be the middle of September. This meant that the staging for the landing at Inchon would have to be accomplished more rapidly than that of any other large amphibious operation in modern warfare.

Source: Douglas MacArthur, *Reminiscences* (New York: McGraw-Hill, 1964), 348–49.

TRUMAN-MacARTHUR CONTROVERSY

One of the major stories of the Korean conflict was the struggle over policy and authority that developed between General Douglas Mac-Arthur and President Truman. As demonstrated below, Truman's commitment to avoid a wider war and his belief in American vulnerability to Soviet attack in Europe, as well as his ultimate unwillingness to tolerate MacArthur's defiant insubordination, led to his dismissal of the popular general.

DOCUMENT 68: General MacArthur's Proposed Message to the Chicago Convention of Veterans of Foreign Wars (28 August 1950)

The geographic location of Formosa is such that in the hand of a power unfriendly to the United States it constitutes an enemy salient in the very center of this defensive perimeter, 100 to 150 miles closer to the adjacent friendly segments—Okinawa and the Philippines—than any point in continental Asia.

At the present time there is on Formosa a concentration of operational air and naval bases which is potentially greater than any similar concentration of the Asiatic mainland between the Yellow Sea and the Strait of Malacca. Additional bases can be developed in a relatively short time by an aggressive exploitation of all World War II Japanese facilities.

An enemy force utilizing those installations currently available could increase by 100 per cent the air effort which could be directed against Okinawa as compared to operations based on the mainland and at the same time could direct damaging air attacks with fighter-type aircraft against friendly installations in the Philippines, which are currently beyond the range of fighters based on the mainland. Our air supremacy at once would become doubtful.

As a result of its geographic location and base potential, utilization of Formosa by a military power hostile to the United States may either counter-balance or overshadow the strategic importance of the central and southern flank of the United States front line position.

Formosa in the hands of such a hostile power could be compared to an unsinkable aircraft carrier and submarine tender ideally located to accomplish offensive strategy and at the same time checkmate defensive or counter-offensive operations by friendly forces based on Okinawa and the Philippines.

This unsinkable carrier-tender has the capacity to operate from ten to twenty air groups of types ranging from jet fighters to B-29 type bombers as well as to provide forward operating facilities for short-range coastal submarines.

In acquiring this forward submarine base, the efficacy of the short-range submarine would be so enormously increased by the additional radius of activity as to threaten completely sea traffic from the south and interdict all sea lanes in the Western Pacific. Submarine blockade by the enemy with all its destructive ramifications would thereby become a virtual certainty.

Should Formosa fall and bases thereafter come into the hands of a potential enemy of the United States, the latter will have acquired an additional "fleet" which will have been obtained and can be maintained at an incomparably lower cost than could its equivalent in aircraft carriers and submarine tenders.

Current estimates of air and submarine resources in the Far East indicate the capability of such a potential enemy to extend his forces southward and still maintain an imposing degree of military strength for employment elsewhere in the Pacific area.

Historically, Formosa has been used as a springboard for just such military aggression directed against areas to the south. The most notable and recent example was the utilization of it by the Japanese in World War II. At the outbreak of the Pacific War in 1941, it played an important part as a staging area and supporting base for the various Japanese invasion convoys. The supporting air forces of Japan's Army and Navy were based on fields situated along southern Formosa.

From 1942 through 1944 Formosa was a vital link in the transportation and communication chain which stretched from Japan through Okinawa and the Philippines to Southeast Asia. As the United States carrier forces advanced into the Western Pacific, the bases on Formosa assumed an increasingly greater role in the Japanese defense scheme.

Should Formosa fall into the hands of a hostile power, history would repeat itself. Its military potential would again be fully exploited as the means to breach and neutralize our Western Pacific defense system and mount a war of conquest against the free nations of the Pacific basin.

Nothing could be more fallacious than the threadbare argument by those who advocate appeasement and defeatism in the Pacific that if we defend Formosa we alienate continental Asia.

Those who speak thus do not understand the Orient. They do not grant that it is in the pattern of the Oriental psychology to respect and follow aggressive, resolute and dynamic leadership and to quickly turn on a leadership characterized by timidity or vacillation—and they underestimate the Oriental mentality. Nothing in the last five years has so inspired the Far East as the American determination to preserve the bulwarks of our Pacific Ocean strategic position from future encroachment, for few of its people fail accurately to appraise the safeguard such determination brings to their free institutions.

Source: Military Situation in the Far East, 1951, Pt. 5, 3477–80.

DOCUMENT 69: Secretary of Defense Louis Johnson and President Truman's Responses to MacArthur's VFW Message (August 1950)

26 August 1950

The President of the United States directs that you withdraw your message for National Encampment of Veterans of Foreign Wars, because various features with respect to Formosa are in conflict with the policy of the United States and its position in the United Nations.

The White House—29 August 1950

I am sending you for your information the text of a letter which I sent to Ambassador Austin dated Aug 27. I am sure that when you examine this letter, and the letter which Ambassador Austin addressed to Trygve Lie on Aug. 25 (a copy of which I am told was sent to your headquarters that night), you will understand why my action of the 26th in directing the withdrawal of your message to the Veterans of Foreign Wars was necessary.

Source: Military Situation in the Far East, 1951, Pt. 5, 3480.

DOCUMENT 70: President Truman Recalls Policy Differences with General MacArthur (August 1950)

General MacArthur's visit to Formosa on July 31 had raised much speculation in the world press. Chiang Kai-shek's aides let it be known that the Far East commander was in fullest agreement with their chief on the course of action to be taken. The implication was—and quite a few of our newspapers said so—that MacArthur rejected my policy of neutralizing Formosa and that he favored a more aggressive method. . . . [O]n August 14 the Joint Chiefs of Staff informed General MacArthur, with my approval, that the intent of the directive to him to defend Formosa was to limit United States action there to such support operations as would be practicable without committing any forces to the island itself. No commitments were to be made to the National Government for the basing of fighter squadrons on Formosa, and no United States forces of any kind were to be based ashore on Formosa except with the specific approval of the Joint Chiefs of Staff.

I assumed that this would be the last of it and that General MacArthur would accept the Formosa policy laid down by his Commander in Chief. But I was mistaken. Before the month ended—on August 26—the White House Press Room brought me a copy of a statement which General MacArthur had sent to the commander in chief of the Veterans of Foreign Wars. This document was not to be read until August 28, but MacArthur's public relations office in Tokyo had handed it to the papers several days in advance, and when I first heard about it, on the morning of August 26, a weekly magazine was already in the mails with the full text. . . .

It was my opinion that this statement could only serve to confuse the world as to just what our Formosa policy was, for it was at odds with my announcement of June 27, and it also contradicted what I had told the Congress.

Source: Truman, *Memoirs: Years of Trial and Hope*, 354–55.

DOCUMENT 71: President Truman's Meeting at Wake Island with General MacArthur (October 1950)

The general assured me that the victory was won in Korea. He also informed me that the Chinese Communists would not attack and that Japan was ready for a peace treaty.

Then he brought up the subject of his statement about Formosa to the Veterans of Foreign Wars. He said that he was sorry if he had caused any embarrassment. I told him that I considered the incident closed. He said he wanted me to understand that he was not in politics in any way—that he had allowed the politicians to make a "chump" (his word) of him in 1948 and that it would not happen again.

I told him something of our plans for the strengthening of Europe, and he said he understood and that he was sure it would be possible to send one division from Korea to Europe in January 1951. He repeated that the Korean conflict was won and that there was little possibility of the Chinese Communists coming in. . . .

General MacArthur stated his firm belief that all resistance would end, in both North and South Korea, by Thanksgiving. This, he said, would enable him to withdraw the Eighth Army to Japan by Christmas. He would leave two divisions and the detachments of the other United Nations in Korea until elections had been held there. He thought this might be done as early as January and that it would then be possible to take all non-Korean troops out of the country. . . .

"What are the chances," I asked, "for Chinese or Soviet interference?"

The general's answer was really in two parts. First he talked about the Chinese. He thought, he said, that there was very little chance that they would come in. At the most they might be able to get fifty or sixty thousand men into Korea, but, since they had no air force, "if the Chinese tried to get down to Pyongyang, there would be the greatest slaughter."

Then he referred to the possibilities of Russian intervention. He referred to the Russian air strength, but he was certain that their planes and pilots were inferior to ours. He saw no way for the Russians to bring in any sizable number of ground troops before the onset of winter. This would leave the possibility of combined Chinese-Russian intervention, he observed, with Russian planes supporting Chinese ground units. This, he thought, would be no danger. "It just wouldn't work," he added, "with Chinese Communist ground and Russian air."

Source: Truman, *Memoirs: Years of Trial and Hope,* 364–65.

DOCUMENT 72: General MacArthur Remembers Wake Island Meeting with President Truman (October 1950)

The conference itself was innocuous enough. The sketchy agenda contained nothing upon which Washington did not already have my fullest views as they affected my responsibilities either as supreme commander for the Allied powers in Japan or as commander-in-chief for the United Nations in Korea. . . . Formosa was not on the agenda.

Near the end of the conference, the possibility of Chinese intervention was brought up almost casually. It was the general consensus of all present that Red China had no intention of intervening. . . .

My views were asked as to the chance of Red China's intervention. I replied that the answer could only be speculative; that neither the State Department through its diplomatic listening posts abroad, nor the Central Intelligence Agency to whom a field commander must look for guidance as to a foreign nation's intention to move from peace to war, reported any evidence of intent by the Peiping government to intervene with major forces; that my own local intelligence, which I regarded as unsurpassed anywhere, reported heavy concentrations near the Yalu border in Manchuria whose movements were indeterminate; that my own military estimate was that with our largely unopposed air forces, with their potential capability of destroying, at will, bases of attack and lines of supply north as well as south of the Yalu, no Chinese military commander would hazard the commitment of large forces upon the devastated Korean peninsula. The risk of their utter destruction through lack of supply would be too great. There was no disagreement from anyone. This episode was later completely misrepresented to the public through an alleged but spurious report in an effort to pervert the position taken by me. It was an ingeniously fostered implication that I flatly and unequivocally predicted that under no circumstances would the Chinese Communists enter the Korean War. This is prevarication.

Source: MacArthur, *Reminiscences,* 360–61.

DOCUMENT 73: General MacArthur's "My Authority as Field Commander" Statement (24 March 1951)

Operations continue according to schedule and plan. We have now substantially cleared South Korea of organized Communist forces. It is becoming increasingly evident that the heavy destruction along the enemy's lines of supply, caused by our round-the-clock massive air and naval bombardment, has left his troops in the forward battle area deficient in requirements to sustain his operations.

This weakness is being brilliantly exploited by our ground forces. The enemy's human wave tactics definitely failed him as our own forces became seasoned to this form of warfare; his tactics of infiltration are but contributing to his piecemeal losses, and he is showing less stamina than our own troops under rigors of climate, terrain, and battle. . . .

The enemy therefore must by now be painfully aware that a decision of the United Nations to depart from its tolerant effort to contain the war to the area of Korea through expansion of our military operations to his coastal areas and interior bases would doom Red China to the risk of imminent military collapse. . . .

Within the area of my authority as military commander, however, it should be needless to say I stand ready at any time to confer in the field with the commander in chief of the enemy forces in an earnest effort to find any military means whereby the realization of the political objectives of the United Nations in Korea, to which no nation may justly take exception, might be accomplished without further bloodshed.

Source: Military Situation in the Far East, 1951, Pt. 5, 3181.

DOCUMENT 74: Joint Chiefs of Staff Message to General MacArthur (24 March 1951)

The President has directed that your attention be called to his order as transmitted 6 December 1950. In view of the information given you 20 March 1951 any further statements by you must be coordinated as prescribed in the order of 6 December.

The President has also directed that in the event Communist military leaders request an armistice in the field, you immediately report that fact to the JCS for instructions.

Source: Military Situation in the Far East, 1951, Pt. 5, 3181–82.

DOCUMENT 75: The Open Letters Between Minority Leader Congressman Joseph Martin and General MacArthur Discussing U.S. Policy in Asia and Europe (March 1951)

Office of the Minority Leader, House of Representatives, Washington, D.C., March 8, 1951

General of the Army Douglas MacArthur,

My Dear General: In the current discussions of foreign policy and over-all strategy many of us have been distressed that, although the European aspects have been heavily emphasized, we have been without the views of yourself as Commander in Chief of the Far Eastern Command.

I think it is imperative to the security of our Nation and for the safety of the world that policies of the United States embrace the broadest possible strategy and that in our earnest desire to protect Europe we not weaken our position in Asia.

Enclosed is a copy of an address I delivered in Brooklyn, N.Y., February 12, stressing this vital point and suggesting that the forces of Generalissimo Chiang Kai-shek on Formosa might be employed in the opening of a second Asiatic front to relieve the pressure on our forces in Korea.

I have since repeated the essence of this thesis in other speeches, and intend to do so again on March 21, when I will be on a radio hook-up.

I would deem it a great help if I could have your views on this point, either on a confidential basis or otherwise. Your admirers are legion, and the respect you command is enormous. May success be yours in the gigantic undertaking which you direct.

Sincerely yours. *Joseph W. Martin, Jr.*

* * * * *

General Headquarters, Supreme Commander for the Allied Powers, Tokyo, Japan, March 20, 1951

Hon. Joseph W. Martin, Jr.,

Dear Congressman Martin: I am most grateful for your note of the 8th forwarding me a copy of your address of February 12. The latter I have read with much interest, and find that with the passage of years you have certainly lost none of your old-time punch.

My views and recommendations with respect to the situation created by Red China's entry into war against us in Korea have been submitted to Washington in most complete detail. Generally these views are well known and clearly understood, as they follow the conventional pattern of meeting force with maximum counterforce, as we have never failed to do in the past. Your view with respect to the utilization of the Chinese forces on Formosa is in conflict with neither logic nor this tradition.

It seems strangely difficult for some to realize that here in Asia is where the Communist conspirators have elected to make their play for global conquest, and that we have joined the issue thus raised on the battlefield; that here we fight Europe's war with arms while the diplomats there still fight it with words; that if we lose the war to communism in Asia the fall of Europe is inevitable, win it and Europe most probably would avoid war and yet preserve freedom. As you pointed out, we must win. There is no substitute for victory.

With renewed thanks and expressions of most cordial regard, I am

Faithfully yours, *Douglas MacArthur*

Source: Military Situation in the Far East, 1951, Pt. 5, 3182.

DOCUMENT 76: President Truman's Dismissal of General MacArthur (April 1951)

The time had come to draw the line. MacArthur's letter to Congressman Martin showed that the general was not only in disagreement with the policy of the government but was challenging this policy in open insubordination to his Commander in Chief.

I asked Acheson, Marshall, Bradley, and Harriman to meet with me on Friday morning, April 6, to discuss MacArthur's action. I put the matter squarely before them. What should be done about General Mac-Arthur? We discussed the question for an hour. Everyone thought that the government faced a serious situation.

Averell Harriman was of the opinion that I should have fired Mac-Arthur two years ago. In the spring of 1949, as in 1948, MacArthur had pleaded that he could not come home because of the press of business in Tokyo. . . .

Secretary of Defense Marshall advised caution, saying he wished to reflect further. He observed that if I relieved MacArthur it might be difficult to get the military appropriations through Congress.

General Bradley approached the question entirely from the point of view of military discipline. As he saw it, there was a clear case of insubordination and the general deserved to be relieved of command. He did wish, however, to consult with the Chiefs of Staff before making a final recommendation.

Acheson said that he believed that General MacArthur should be relieved, but he thought it essential to have the unanimous advice of the Joint Chiefs of Staff before I acted. He counseled that the most careful consideration be given to this matter since it was of the utmost seriousness. He added, "If you relieve MacArthur, you will have the biggest fight of your administration."

. . . I was careful not to disclose that I had already reached a decision. Before the meeting adjourned, I suggested to Marshall that he go over all the messages in the Pentagon files that had been exchanged with General MacArthur in the past two years. Then I asked all four to return the following day at 9 A.M.

The next morning, Saturday, April 7, we met again in my office. This meeting was short. General Marshall stated that he had read the messages and that he had now concluded that MacArthur should have been fired two years ago. . . .

At nine o'clock Monday morning I again met with Marshall, Bradley, Acheson, and Harriman. General Bradley reported that the Joint Chiefs of Staff had met with him on Sunday, and it was his and their unanimous judgment that General MacArthur should be relieved.

Source: Truman, *Memoirs: Years of Trial and Hope,* 332–35.

DOCUMENT 77: President Truman Replaces General MacArthur (10 April 1951)

I deeply regret that it becomes my duty as President and Commander in Chief of the United States military forces to replace you as Supreme Commander, Allied Powers; Commander in Chief, United Nations Command; Commander in Chief, Far East; and Commanding General, United States Army Far East.

You will turn over your commands, effective at once, to Lt. Gen. Matthew B. Ridgway. You are authorized to have issued such orders as are necessary to complete desired travel to such place as you select.

My reasons for your replacement will be made public concurrently with the delivery to you of the foregoing order, and are contained in the next following message.

*STATEMENT OF THE PRESIDENT
RELATIVE TO THE RELIEF OF GENERAL MacARTHUR*

With deep regret I have concluded that General of the Army Douglas MacArthur is unable to give his wholehearted support to the policies of the United States Government and of the United Nations in matters pertaining to his official duties. In view of the specific responsibilities imposed upon me by the Constitution of the United States and the added responsibility which has been entrusted to me by the United Nations, I have decided that I must make a change of command in the Far East. I have, therefore, relieved General MacArthur of his commands and have designated Lt. Gen. Matthew B. Ridgway as his successor.

Full and vigorous debate on matters of national policy is a vital element in the constitutional system of our free democracy. It is fundamental, however, that military commanders must be governed by the policies and directives issued to them in the manner provided by our laws and Constitution. In time of crisis, this consideration is particularly compelling.

General MacArthur's place in history as one of our greatest commanders is fully established. The Nation owes him a debt of gratitude for the distinguished and exceptional service which he has rendered his country in posts of great responsibility. For that reason I repeat my regret at the necessity for the action I feel compelled to take in his case.

Source: Military Situation in the Far East, 1951, Pt. 5, 3179–80.

COMBAT AND ESPIONAGE

Chinese intervention, triggered by the crossing of the 38th parallel, changed the nature of the Korean conflict. These documents show how American officials failed to heed warnings of this development, how the decision was made to "slug it out" with Chinese forces, and how the war progressed as it did through early 1951.

DOCUMENT 78: Indian Diplomat K. M. Panikkar Warns Western Governments from Post in Beijing of Impending Intervention in Korea by Communist China (October 1950)

At midnight on the 2nd of October . . . I was awakened . . . with the news that Chen Chia-kang, the Director of Asian Affairs for the [People's Republic of China's] Foreign Ministry, was waiting for me in the drawing-room. I hastily [dressed] and went downstairs, not knowing what it could be which had brought so important an officer at midnight to my house. Chen was very apologetic about the lateness of the hour but added that the matter was most important and that the Prime Minister [Zhou En-lai] desired to see me immediately at his residence. . . .

I had guessed from the beginning that the reason for this sudden call was something connected with Korea. . . . At 12:30 I was with Premier [Z]hou En-lai at his official residence.

Though the occasion was the most serious I could imagine, . . . [Z]hou En-lai was as courteous . . . as ever and did not give the least impression of worry or nervousness. . . . Then he came to the point. He thanked Pandit Nehru for what he had been doing in the cause of peace, but there were occasions when peace could only be defended by determination to resist aggression. If the Americans crossed the 38th parallel China would be forced to intervene in Korea. Otherwise he was most anxious for a peaceful settlement. . . . I asked him whether he had already news of the Americans having crossed the borders. He replied in the affirmative but added that he did not know where they had crossed. I asked him whether China intended to intervene, if only the South Koreans crossed the parallel. He was emphatic: "The South Koreans did not matter but American intrusion into North Korea would encounter Chinese resistance."

I returned home at 1:30 where my first secretary and cypher assistant were waiting. A telegram conveying the gist of the conversation . . . went the same night to New Delhi.

Source: Kavalam M. Panikkar, *In Two Chinas: Memoirs of a Diplomat* (London: George Allen and Unwin, 1955), 109–11.

DOCUMENT 79: Commander of Chinese Forces in Korea, Marshal Peng Dehuai, Describes His Strategy of Protracted War Against the United States (1950–1951)

We employed the tactic of purposely showing ourselves to be weak, increasing the arrogance of the enemy, letting him run amuck, and luring him deep into our areas. While some small units of our army remained in contact with enemy troops, our main force . . . made use of the favorable terrain to build camouflaged positions.

This method of fighting, which the enemy troops had never experienced before, took them by surprise. . . .

The enemy plan was to do everything to lure our troops to attack his fortified positions, and then to mount a frontal attack against us and land his marines on our flank to cut off our retreat route.

The Chinese People's Volunteers had . . . neither an air force nor sufficient anti-aircraft guns to protect them from enemy bombers. Bombed by aircraft and shelled by long-range guns day and night, our troops could not move about in the daytime. . . .

In February 1951, Marshal Peng was recalled from the front to Beijing to report to Chairman Mao. Here he comments on his conversation with Mao and on the Chairman's orders to him in the conduct of the war against the American forces.

I explained that . . . the Korean War could not be won quickly. . . . The Chairman gave a clear instruction for conducting the War to Resist U.S. Aggression and Aid Korea: "Win a quick victory if you can; if you can't, win a slow one." That is a clear and flexible principle. . . .

Chairman Mao [later] sent a telegram instructing us not to try to annihilate large bodies of American troops at a time, but to decimate them piece-meal. This was an excellent method, but a transitional period was needed . . .

[O]ur forces had constructed a network of good fortifications. The surface defensive positions of our forces were giving way to fortifications built underground. A defence-in-depth tunnel system was taking shape gradually [the Chinese and North Koreans dug 1,250 km. of tunnels along 38th parallel]. The tunnel fortifications were so strong that no enemy troops could penetrate them [the tunnels of Sangkumryung Ridge]. As a result, the enemy's attacks were repulsed one after another.

Source: Peng Dehuai, *Memoirs of a Chinese Marshal: The Autobiographical Notes of Peng Dehuai, 1898–1974,* translated by Zheng Longpu (Beijing: Foreign Languages Printing, 1984), 472–84.

DOCUMENT 80: Chairman of Joint Chiefs of Staff General Omar Bradley Recalls Critical Decisions (November 1950)

The next sixty days—the months of November and December 1950—were among the most trying of my professional career.... The war in Korea abruptly turned from victory to humiliating defeat....

The JCS and NSC met in almost continuous session, weighing alternatives and options, drafting directives or discussing the unthinkable prospects of nuclear war....

Influenced by MacArthur's assessment, I now decided in my own mind that our "consensus" ... to order a pullback to the narrow waist of Korea would be premature and perhaps unwise.... There seemed to be ... a reasonable chance of success. It should not be abandoned by "timidity." ... We had to back the man on the scene.

Source: Omar N. Bradley and Clay Blair, *A General's Life: An Autobiography* (New York: Simon and Schuster, 1983), 581, 590–94.

DOCUMENT 81: An American Soldier's Letter from the Front to His Family Back Home (2 December 1950)

Dear Folks,

This letter is being written on a rifle butt in a field about ten miles south of Sunch'on. The roads are clogged with troops and vehicles and refugees. It's bitterly cold and my hands as I write this are freezing. They just served us noon chow but such a little amount it wouldn't fill a pigeon. Boy, how I wish I had some of Mom's cooking now.

I guess I told you I've been recommended for the Silver Star for my part in the attack on Armistice Day on that hill. I'd gladly give away all the medals and honors to be home with you. Those things don't seem important now.

We just received word that there was a major Communist breakthrough to the north and the whole UN Army is pulling back to avoid being trapped. I'm sure you know more about it than I do. I hope and pray to God that I'll get out of here alive so I'll be with you all again. Things look pretty grim now.

Source: Donald Knox, "Letter from PFC James Cardinal to Folks Back Home," in *The Korean War: Pusan to Chosin, An Oral History* (San Diego: Harcourt Brace Jovanovich, 1985), 652–53.

DOCUMENT 82: State Department Memorandum Chronicles Dean Rusk's Position that U.S. Make an Effective Stand in Korea (4 December 1950)

Mr. Rusk thought that we might talk to the Military about making the best possible effort to consolidate our position to one point or points in Korea. He thought we could at least force the Chinese Communists to make a really major effort at great cost to themselves if they were to get us out of Korea. He said that we do have, of course, to consider the welfare and protection of our troops but thought that within that range we might be able to consolidate and make a really effective stand. He mentioned the great difficulty which would result to our position in both Europe and the Far East if we were to simply bow out at this point. He referred to the some 23,000 replacements which were scheduled to move into Korea and asked whether these and possibly others might not be thrown in to help hold a position at some point.

Source: Memorandum by Lucius D. Battle, Special Assistant to the Secretary of State, December 4, 1950, in *FRUS, 1950,* 7:1345.

DOCUMENT 83: State Department Minutes of President Truman–British Prime Minister Clement Attlee Meeting to Discuss Allied Interests in Asia (December 1950)

THE PRIME MINISTER said that . . . he felt that they must take a broad view on a wide horizon. A first point was the maintenance of the prestige and authority of the United Nations. . . . This problem has now become very difficult with the Chinese Communists coming in. It is common to our thinking that we wish the Korean business to be limited to asserting the authority of the United Nations against aggression in Korea. We all realize that other forces might come in and might bring on another world war. We are very eager to avoid the extension of the conflict. If our forces become engaged in China, it will weaken us elsewhere.... [T]he United Kingdom and France have other Asian interests, but it would help the Russians if we were fully engaged in Asia. We do not have very great forces.... A few weeks ago we might have played those cards from a stronger hand. We now have a weak hand although we do have future potential strength. There is an obvious time factor....

If we become involved in war with the Chinese, we must consider what effect that would have on opinion in the United States, Europe and Asia. In his thinking, it was very, very difficult for any of us to contemplate this situation. It would seem to be handing the game over to the Russians....

THE PRIME MINISTER continued that their [British] appreciation of Chinese intentions differed from [that] of the United States. The United States thinks that the Chinese are completely subservient to the USSR and that they are not only Communists but Stalinists. There was a great difference here. They can be Marxists and yet not bow to Stalin.... There was a chance of Titoism. The case of Tito was of very great importance as Stalin himself thinks. Stalin had gone ahead with his imperialist policy believing that wherever a Communist nucleus was established they had a unit fully subservient to them. In every case where the country owed its delivery to the Soviet and not to its own efforts, as in Bulgaria, Czechoslovakia, and other satellites, this had been true but Yugoslavia was the one case where the people claimed that they had delivered themselves. Accordingly, Tito, while remaining a communist, was not a satellite. The Russians have not given very much help to China. The Chinese do not owe them very much. There is a strong mixture of Chinese nationalism in their communist attitude....

THE PRIME MINISTER said that ... it is not hopeless that the Chinese are not fully imbued with Soviet ideas. They will no doubt go quite a way in the communist direction as the only alternative to a rotten regime. But Chinese civilization is very old and is accustomed to absorbing new things. They may wear the Red flag with a difference. The question was what we could do to prevent the Chinese looking to the USSR as their only friend, as a result of which they would be completely absorbed in that huge land mass. If we say that China is just part of the USSR, we link them together and play the game of Russian imperialism. The longer we can hold out without a major war the more likely it is that people behind the Iron Curtain will object to Stalin's iron rule.

Source: Minutes of the First and Second Meetings of President Truman and Prime Minister Attlee, 4–5 December, 1950, in *FRUS, 1950,* 7:1361–69, 1392–99.

DOCUMENT 84: General Matthew Ridgway Assumes Command of U.S. 8th Army in Korea (26 December 1950)

My meeting with MacArthur began at nine-thirty [26 December 1950] in the Commander in Chief's office in the Dai-Ichi Building [in Tokyo]. ... I had known MacArthur since my days as a West Point instructor but, like nearly everyone who ever dealt with him, I was again deeply impressed by the force of his personality. To confer with him was an experience that could happen with few others. He was a great actor too, with an actor's instinct for the dramatic—in tone and gesture. Yet so lucid and so penetrating were his explanations and his analyses that it was his mind rather than his manner or his bodily presence that dominated his listeners. ...

His chief concern at this conference seemed to be the fact that we were then operating in a "mission vacuum," as he termed it, while diplomacy attempted to feel its way. "A military success," he said, "will strengthen our diplomacy."

He noted that Communist China was wide open in the south and that an attack by forces already on Formosa would greatly relieve pressure on our forces in Korea. He had already recommended such an attack, he told me, but Washington had not approved. Yet in telling me this he expressed no criticism whatever of Washington, nor was any implied. It was simply a decision by higher authority that he had accepted as a soldier.

He urged me especially not to underestimate the Chinese. "They constitute a dangerous foe," he warned me. "Walker reported that the Chinese avoid roads, using the ridges and hills as avenues of approach. They will attack in depth. Their firepower in the hands of their infantry is more extensively used than our own. The enemy moves and fights at night. The entire Chinese military establishment is in this fight."

Source: Matthew B. Ridgway, *The Korean War* (Garden City, N.Y.: Doubleday, 1967), 81–83.

DOCUMENT 85: Britain's Kim Philby and Soviet Espionage During the War (Autumn 1950)

By any reckoning, [Kim] Philby's decision to allow [Guy] Burgess to stay with him was extremely foolhardy. ... So the question becomes:

why did the Russian intelligence service allow Philby and Burgess to commit such an elementary breach of security?

There are several likely answers. There is the simple one: the Russians agreed with Philby's assessment of the situation, that Burgess was safer with him than roaming the streets of Washington. . . . And there is the conspiratorial theory. This is that far from Philby helping Burgess [as a friend], Burgess had come to Washington to help Philby. The Korean war was occupying a lot of Philby's attention. Indeed, his work for Moscow on the war may well have been more important than his information on CIA/SIS [UK Secret Intelligence Service] covert action operations. Harry Rositzke [a senior CIA officer working in the Soviet Bloc Division in the early 1950s] certainly thinks so.

"The positive value to Moscow came out of Philby's political reporting from Washington in the fall of 1950. That was a crucial period in terms of what was going to happen in Korea. Stalin was as cut off as he could be from what was going on in the West, but here was a bright, alert, politically aware intelligence officer who could tell him what was the American thinking on, for example, whether the UN forces would go up to, or cross, the Yalu River. And, obviously, Stalin could tell the North Koreans and the Chinese."

In the middle of this period, with Philby working day and night, Burgess gets a still unexplained posting to Washington and moves in with his fellow Russian agent. We cannot rule out the suggestion, therefore, that Burgess manoeuvered the posting to help Philby cope with his extra duties for Moscow caused by the Korean war.

Source: Phillip Knightley, *Philby: The Life and Views of the KGB Master Spy* (London: Andre Deutsch, 1984), 166. (Based on author's interview with Harry Rositzke in November 1981.)

DOCUMENT 86: UN General Assembly Resolution Declaring Communist China an Aggressor (1 February 1951)

The General Assembly,

Noting that the Security Council, because of lack of unanimity of the permanent members, has failed to exercise its primary responsibility for the maintenance of international peace and security in regard to Chinese Communist intervention in Korea,

Noting that the Central People's Government of the People's Republic of China has not accepted United Nations proposals to bring about a cessation of hostilities in Korea with a view to peaceful settlement, and that its armed forces continue their invasion of Korea and their large-scale attacks upon United Nations forces there,

1. Finds that the Central People's Government of the People's Republic of China, by giving direct aid and assistance to those who were already committing aggression in Korea and by engaging in hostilities against United Nations forces there, has itself engaged in aggression in Korea;

2. Calls upon the Central People's Government of the People's Republic of China to cause its forces and nationals in Korea to cease hostilities against the United Nations forces and to withdraw from Korea;

3. Affirms the determination of the United Nations to continue its action in Korea to meet the aggression;

4. Calls upon all States and authorities to continue to lend every assistance to the United Nations action in Korea;

5. Calls upon all States and authorities to refrain from giving any assistance to the aggressors in Korea;

6. Requests a Committee composed of the members of the Collective Measures Committee as a matter of urgency to consider additional measures to be employed to meet this aggression and to report thereon to the General Assembly, it being understood that the Committee is authorized to defer its report if the Good Offices Committee referred to in the following paragraph reports satisfactory progress in its efforts;

7. Affirms that it continues to be the policy of the United Nations to bring about a cessation of hostilities in Korea and the achievement of United Nations objectives in Korea by peaceful means, and requests the President of the General Assembly to designate forthwith two persons who would meet with him at any suitable opportunity to use their good offices to this end.

Source: Military Situation in the Far East, 1951, Pt. 5, 3513–14.

DOCUMENT 87: CIA Estimate on Communist Capabilities and Intentions in Korea (6 August 1951)

PROBABLE COMMUNIST MILITARY COURSES OF ACTION IN THE FAR EAST

1. If cease-fire negotiations should break down, we believe that Communist forces in Korea will continue large-scale military operations in

the area and may undertake offensive actions against UN troops at an early date. . . .

3. We believe . . . that in the event of a breakdown of cease-fire discussions and the continuance of large-scale military operations in Korea, the Communists will have to choose between two possible major courses of action: (a) to accept the continuation of a conflict of substantially the scale and nature that preceded the cease-fire negotiation or (b) to take more drastic measures to destroy or expel UN forces. . . . Whichever course of action is undertaken, the Communists will maintain military pressure in Korea, while probably trying to keep the door open for political negotiations at any time when the global interests of the USSR would make a diplomatic settlement of the Korean conflict advantageous. . . .

INDICATIONS OF CURRENT COMMUNIST INTENTIONS

10. There have been many indications of Communist preparations for a new offensive, including troop movements, logistic build-up and reinforcements. Efforts to build and maintain airfields in North Korea continue, and the gradual southward extension of enemy air activities indicates an enemy intention to extend air defense progressively over all Communist-controlled Korea. There are no reliable indications, however, of enemy intent to commit the entire air force available to the Chinese Communists. . . . However, there are indications that tanks and artillery are moving into Korea. . . . [R]eports of Soviet assistance in the organization of a modern Chinese Communist army in Manchuria continue. . . . There have also been unconfirmed reports of Soviet troop concentrations in Manchuria, including locations along the Korean border, but there are no reliable indications of Soviet preparation to move troops into Korea in the near future. . . .

11. There are no reliable indications of early Chinese Communist military action in other areas of the Far East beyond the scope of present efforts, although numerous reports state variously that invasions of Japan, Taiwan, and Indochina are planned within the next few months.

Source: The Declassified Document Reference System, 1982, "CIA Special Estimate: Probable Immediate Developments in the Far East Following a Failure in the Cease-Fire Negotiations in Korea" (SE-9), cit. 000009.

EISENHOWER-DULLES PLAN

The next three sections focus on Korea as an issue in American politics in the election of 1952 and show how President Dwight D. Eisenhower moved to end a war that he had determined as inimical to the U.S. interest. Particular focus is on the troublesome issue of the repatriation of prisoners of war in the armistice negotiations, and on Eisenhower's consideration of the use of atomic weapons. The final section deals with some of the political and social consequences of the Korean conflict.

DOCUMENT 88: John Foster Dulles to President-Elect Eisenhower on POWs, and the Advantages the Soviets Derive from the Korean War (26 November 1952)

PERSONAL AND PRIVATE

1. It is probable that the dominant will with which we have to deal is that of the Soviet Union. The Kremlin cannot impose its will on Communist China in the same arbitrary way that it imposes its will upon Poland, Rumania, etc. Nevertheless the Chinese Communist Party accepts the dominance of the Soviet Communist Party as leader of the world proletariat.

2. If this conclusion is sound, the considerations which determine whether or not the Communists will continue the war are global considerations and not considerations limited merely to the battle line in Korea or the desires of the North Koreans or Chinese Communists. There is no doubt that Moscow looks on the Korean war as only one of many fronts. What it does there will be determined not by local considerations alone, but by other situations in Asia, Europe and the Middle East.

3. From the Soviet standpoint the Korean war:

(a) holds a large part of the U.S. land forces on an Asian peninsula where in the case of general war they might be lost. (I do not think that the Soviet now plans a general war but the bad strategic disposition of U.S. land forces consequent on the Korean war is an advantage to Soviet Russia which no doubt they calculate weakens our resolution with respect to other actual and potential areas of conflict such, for example, as Iran.)

(b) absorbs large amounts of military equipment which slows down the rearming of Western Europe, of Chinese nationalists on Formosa and of native and French forces in Vietnam.

(c) provides an excuse for Soviet Russia to hold onto Port Arthur and to control Manchuria.

(d) provides a propaganda gold mine which is being exploited to the immense advantage of the Communist position throughout all of Asia.

(e) provides a source of serious friction between the U.S. and the other NATO powers.

(f) maintains a constant military threat to Japan, which builds up anxiety and neutralism there.

The foregoing factors could make the Soviet Union want to continue the war, irrespective of the prisoner-of-war issue, so long as it can get these advantages without the risks of a military defeat in Korea. That risk probably seems negligible under present circumstances because the United Nations side seems not to have the will, and perhaps not the capability, to win in Korea a victorious decision.

However, the prisoner-of-war issue is doubtless important, not primarily from the standpoint of the actual prisoners taken in the Korean war, but from the standpoint of the world-wide situation. If there is no forcible repatriation, that may encourage defections everywhere. If there is forcible repatriation, enabling the Communists to make an example of those who have been "disloyal", that will deter future desertions and facilitate consolidation of the Communist position.

Source: Memo by Dulles to Dwight D. Eisenhower, November 26, 1952, in U.S. Department of State, *Foreign Relations of the United States, 1952–54* (hereafter *FRUS, 1952–54*) (Washington: GPO, 1984), 15:692–93.

DOCUMENT 89: President-elect Dwight Eisenhower Visits Korea and Meets with South Korean President Syngman Rhee (December 1952)

In December 1952 President-elect Dwight D. Eisenhower went to Korea and met with U.S. Generals Mark Clark and James Van Fleet. In addition to speaking with American and UN military commanders during his three-day stay, Eisenhower also met with South Korea's President Rhee.

President Rhee, of course, was for all-out, full-scale attack to drive the invading forces up and off the peninsula. Such an attack would require an extension of the war across the Yalu River and attacks against the supporting bases of the invaders in China. At this time—December 1952—it had been tacitly accepted by both sides, including all of the Allied governments providing troops for the war, that we were fighting defensively and would take no risks of turning the conflict into a global war, which many feared would occur should we undertake offensive operations on a scale sufficient to win a decisive victory. We were also faced with the fact that negotiations between the two sides for an armistice had been going on for months. In our conversations, field commanders agreed that if these were not completed successfully within a reasonable time, our only recourse would eventually be to mount an all-out attack regardless of the risks. Under the circumstances of the moment, decisions of this kind could not even be made; but discussion was valuable. My conclusion as I left Korea was that we could not stand forever on a static front and continue to accept casualties without any visible results. Small attacks on small hills would not end this war.

Source: Dwight David Eisenhower, *Mandate for Change: The White House Years, 1953–56* (Garden City, N.Y.: Doubleday, 1963), 93–94.

DOCUMENT 90: President Eisenhower's Plan to End the War with Atomic Weapons (January 1953)

Of the manifold problems confronting me early in 1953 none required more urgent attention than the war in Korea. . . . To keep the attack from becoming overly costly, it was clear that we would have to use atomic weapons.

This necessity was suggested to me by General MacArthur while I, as President-elect, was still living in New York. The Joint Chiefs of Staff were pessimistic about the feasibility of using tactical atomic weapons on front-line positions, in view of the extensive underground fortifications which the Chinese Communists had been able to construct; but such weapons would obviously be effective for strategic targets in North Korea, Manchuria, and on the Chinese coast.

If we decided upon a major, new type of offensive, the present policies would have to be changed and the new ones agreed to by our allies. Foremost would be the proposed use of atomic weapons. In this respect American views have always differed somewhat from those of some of our allies. For the British, for example, the use of atomic weapons in war at that time would have been a decision of the gravest kind. My feeling was then, and still remains, that it would be impossible for the United States to maintain the military commitments which it now sustains around the world (without turning into a garrison state) did we not possess atomic weapons and the will to use them when necessary. But an American decision to use them at that time would have created strong disrupting feelings between ourselves and our allies. However, if an all-out offensive should be highly successful, I felt that the rifts so caused could, in time, be repaired.

Of course, there were other problems, not the least of which would be the possibility of the Soviet Union entering the war. In nuclear warfare the Chinese Communists would have been able to do little. But we knew that the Soviets had atomic weapons in quantity and estimated that they would soon explode a hydrogen device. Of all the Asian targets which might be subjected to Soviet bombing, I was most concerned about the unprotected cities of Japan.

Source: Eisenhower, *Mandate for Change*, 171–72.

DOCUMENT 91: President Eisenhower's Correspondence with South Korea's President Rhee (April 1953)

On 9 April 1953 Korean President Rhee wrote President Eisenhower a letter of protest criticizing the communists' recent offer for resumption of peace negotiations. Rhee wrote that if a peace agreement should be arranged that would allow the Chinese to remain in Korea, South Korea would feel justified in asking all its allies to get out of the country except those who would be willing to join in a drive northward to the Yalu. The Rhee letter was drastic in tone and extreme in its terms, and Eisenhower answered promptly in an effort to restrain and reassure him.

I expressed sympathy with his aspirations and those of the Korean people to bring an end to the artificial and unnatural division of their country, and with their desire to expel the Chinese invader. But I emphasized these points:

First, the action taken by the United Nations in Korea was to assist your valiant country in repelling the armed attack directed against it initially by the North Korean regime and subsequently by the Chinese Communists. This has successfully been accomplished.

Second, the task of repelling the armed attack having been accomplished, it would not be defensible to refuse to stop the fighting on an honorable basis as a prerequisite to working out the remaining issues by peaceful means.

Third, the United States and the United Nations have consistently supported the unification of Korea under conditions which would assure its freedom and independence. Neither the United States nor the United Nations has ever committed itself to resort to war to achieve this objective. To do so would be a complete negation of the basic tenets of this country and the United Nations.

Fourth, any agreement to stop the fighting on an honorable basis presupposes a willingness on the part of both sides to discuss the remaining issues and to make every reasonable effort to reach agreement thereon. As I said in my address of April 16 an honorable armistice "means the immediate cessation of hostilities and the prompt initiation of political discussions leading to the holding of free elections in a United Korea." . . .

The ink was scarcely dry on all this correspondence when a bombshell exploded. Twenty-five thousand North Korean non-Communist prisoners had somehow escaped from the stockades in which they were being held.

Shortly thereafter, Rhee's government admitted complicity in the incident.

Source: Eisenhower, *Mandate for Change,* 181–85.

PRISONERS OF WAR AND REPATRIATION DILEMMA

DOCUMENT 92: Kim Il-Sung Proposal on Repatriation of Prisoners (February 1953)

[To] *Gen Mark W. Clark, CINC, UNC.*

Concerning the ques[tion] of repatriating with priority seriously sick and seriously injured POW of both sides, the del[egation] for armistice negotiations of both sides had, as a matter of fact, reached agreement, in accordance with humanitarian principles, on Para 53 of the draft Korean Armistice Agreement. It was solely because the Korean armistice negotiations were suspended that there was no way to implement this agreed provision. In consequence, it has not been possible up to the present to repatriate seriously sick and seriously injured POW of both sides.

Since your side now expresses readiness to apply the provisions of the Geneva Convention to sick and injured POW in the custody of both sides, our side, as an expression of the similar intent, fully agrees to your side's proposal to exchange sick and injured POW of both sides during the period of hostilities. This proposal should be dealt with in accordance with the provisions of Article 109 of the Geneva Convention. At the same time, we consider that the reasonable settlement of the ques of exchanging sick and injured POW of both sides during the period of hostilities should be made to lead to the smooth settlement of the entire ques of

POW, thereby achieving an armistice in Korea for which people through-out the world are longing. Therefore our side proposes that the delegates for armistice negotiations of both sides immediately resume the negoti-ations at Panmunjom. Furthermore, our liaison off is prepared to meet your liaison off to discuss and decide on the date for resuming the ne-gotiations.

> Kim Il-Sung, Supreme Com of the Korean Peoples Army,
> Peng Teh-Huai, Com of the Chinese Peoples Volunteers.

Source: (Letter dated 22 February 1953), Commander in Chief, United Nations Command (Clark) to the Joint Chiefs of Staff, 28 March, 1953, in FRUS, 1952–54, 15:818–19.

DOCUMENT 93: Dulles and Eisenhower Discuss Chinese Premier Zhou En-lai's Cablegram on Role of Neutral States in Repatriation (30 March 1953)

The Secretary telephoned with reference to the statement by Chou En-lai on Korea. The Secretary said we think it is a little better than the Indian solution if we can get a really "neutral" party, the Indian required a committee of four, half of which was communist.

The President asked what we proposed to do, and the Secretary said we propose to do nothing, it was only a radio broadcast and while they have taken that way to speak to us in the past, the reply really should be addressed to Gen. Clark.

The President said that he had the papers on it and would see that they got to the staff.

Source: Memo of Telephone Conversation Between the President and the Secre-tary of State, 30 March, 1953, in FRUS, 1952–54, 15:824. For Zhou En-lai's state-ment, see the Department of State Bulletin, April 13, 1953, 526–27.

DOCUMENT 94: State Department Memo Notes U.S. Reaction to Zhou En-lai's Proposal for Repatriation (30 March 1953)

In connection with our consideration of this proposal, I think it inter-esting to recall that General Clark made a very similar suggestion in July, 1952. At that time he suggested that "upon signing the armistice the supervision, control, and responsibility for determination as to the ultimate disposition of all POWs of both sides who have not been previously repatriated or released would be passed to a group of neutral nations," both sides to abide by the decision of such group for disposition of non-repatriates.

Similar suggestions were also at various times informally considered within the Department and the Department of Defense but dismissed at the time because of the practical difficulties. However, some of these practical difficulties are, of course, lessened if there is agreement by both sides to such procedure. We are urgently working on all aspects of this matter and the foregoing is for background information only.

Source: Memorandum by the Assistant Secretary of State for Far Eastern Affairs (Allison) to Sec State, March 30, 1953, in *FRUS, 1952–54*, 15:825.

DOCUMENT 95: National Security Council's James Lay Notes the Relationship of POW Issue to Armistice Negotiations (2 April 1953)

Excluding resort to global war, or complete withdrawal from Korea, or yielding to the communist position on prisoners of war in the armistice negotiations, there appear to be two major alternative courses of action open to the United States in Korea. The first alternative maintains the current restrictions on military operations, the second removes these restrictions. . . .

Armistice Negotiations

8. Negotiations for an armistice were undertaken in June, 1951 and agreement has been reached on all major points except the question of non-forcible repatriation. A draft incorporating the agreed provisions of the armistice consisting of some 63 articles has been preliminarily approved by both sides. . . .

9. Discussions of the prisoner of war question were undertaken in December, 1951 and continued until October, 1952. It clearly demonstrated that under present conditions further search for a formula, agreeable to the Communists and ourselves, for the disposition of those Chinese and North Korean prisoners of war held by the United Nations Command opposed to repatriation is hopeless. The Communist rejection of the Indian resolution in the General Assembly, which was supported by virtually all non-Soviet bloc UN members, indicated that the Communists have been willing to face the maximum of free world political

pressure rather than recede from their position on the prisoner of war issue. Whatever the Communist basic attitude towards an armistice may be, the ability of the Communists to supply and reinforce their troop strength in Korea has unquestionably reinforced their unwillingness to concede in the POW question what is possibly to them an important matter of principle and prestige striking at the roots of their system. They may well consider that agreement to any form of non-forcible repatriation so admits to the right of individual self-determination as to endanger maintenance of their concept of relations between the individual and the state. It also directly involves the question of mass defections from their armed forces in any future conflict, a matter upon which they are undoubtedly very sensitive. It is a problem in which the ideological conflict between the free and Soviet worlds is finding a focus.

10. It is out of the question for the United States to consider any abandonment of the principle of non-forcible repatriation. This position has been strongly and publicly set forth in categorical terms by this Government and has received the overwhelming support of virtually every non-Soviet bloc member of the United Nations. As set forth in the preceding paragraph, it has implications for the struggle between the free and the Soviet worlds far transcending the importance of the individuals involved. Apart from problems that would arise from the spectacle of United States forces using force against very large numbers of prisoners violently resisting return to the Communists, any abandonment of principle in this regard would in the present context constitute appeasement of the most serious sort. As the prisoners have now been screened and thus declared their attitude towards the Communists, to return those opposing repatriation would be the grossest betrayal of trust and would undoubtedly subject them to most severe reprisals. It might well also lead the Soviets to the conclusion that our desire for an armistice was so strong that they could up their price in other regards and we would find ourselves facing increasing demands from the Soviets as the cost of an armistice.

Source: Note by the Executive Secretary (James Lay) to the National Security Council, April 2, 1953, in *FRUS, 1952–54,* 15:838–43.

DOCUMENT 96: American Diplomat Charles Bohlen Helps Draft State Department Formula Toward Prisoners-of-War Issue (1952–1953)

In the Department of State, I [Charles Bohlen] became directly involved in the trickiest and most involved question connected with the

Korean armistice negotiations—what to do about the prisoners of war. As the war raged on, the major sticking point to an armistice was the fact that the majority of prisoners captured by the United Nations forces did not wish to return to North Korea or China. They were definitely anti-Communist. The enemy refused to repatriate the prisoners they held unless we turned all in our hands over to them. The argument in Washington split along classic lines. The military, whose primary interest was the safety of our men, was inclined to be rather callous about forcing the enemy prisoners to return. The State Department argued that the humanitarian reputation of the United States would be damaged by forced repatriation. The State Department view reflected the American tradition of freedom of choice. In addition, the State Department warned that dissidents in Communist-controlled countries would be less likely to defect in the future if they thought they were going to be turned back like cattle. I was in the State Department group that tried to come up with a formula to break the impasse, but even though there was a tendency to minimize the anti-Communist feelings of the POWs in order to make it easier for our consciences to turn them back, we could not reach a satisfactory solution.

Source: Charles E. Bohlen, *Witness to History, 1929–1969* (New York: Norton, 1973), 300.

DOCUMENT 97: Prisoners of War and the U.S. Military Code of Conduct (1980)

The Code of Conduct consists of six articles and accompanying explanations. Soldiers cannot take it lightly; they should be familiar with it. The Code holds that as an American fighting soldier, you should be ready to give your life for your country. Never surrender your own free will. If captured, make every effort to escape. Make no agreements to obtain parole or accept special favors. You must keep faith with fellow prisoners. The senior prisoner eligible for command, whether officer or enlisted, assumes command (secretly, if necessary) within a PW camp or with a group of PWs, according to rank, without regard to service. Others obey the lawful orders of their superiors, regardless of service; they support superiors in every way.

To repeat for emphasis: prisoners when questioned must give *only name, rank, service number, and date of birth.* They must resist, avoid, or evade, to the best of their ability, all enemy efforts to secure statements or actions which further the enemy's cause. A prisoner who unwillingly

or accidentally discloses unauthorized information must regroup and renew resistance; he must use a fresh approach or an alternate line of
mental defense. Finally, never forget: you are an American fighting soldier responsible for your actions and dedicated to the principles that
made your country free.

Source: U.S. Department of the Army, *Prisoners of War* (Washington: Department
of the Army Training Circular 27-10-2, 1980), 30–32. Also see U.S. Department
of Defense, *Code of the U.S. Fighting Force* (Washington: American Forces Information Service, [DoD Gen-11A], 1979), 1–15.

ASSESSING THE USE OF ATOMIC WEAPONS IN KOREA

DOCUMENT 98: Indian Prime Minister Jawaharlal Nehru Fears U.S. Will Use Atomic Bomb Only Against Asiatics (3 December 1950)

Prime Minister [Nehru] says there is great anxiety about recent developments, [and] President Truman's mention [of] use of the atomic
bomb. [H]e is most anxious to help in any effort to avoid war [and] feels
that the best procedure would be for representatives of the great powers
to meet and to attempt to stop the rapid progressive deterioration. But
even a temporary solution must now be quickly sought. Any such discussion must include "China" (Peiping).

If we can obtain a cease-fire followed by a demarcation of a demilitarized zone the whole question of a settlement in Korea and later of
Formosa can be negotiated. Nehru is convinced that unless the question
of Formosa can be disposed of along the lines of the Cairo declaration
there is no hope for lasting peace in Asia.

Nehru wants to make clear he is not condoning Chinese intervention
in Korea but it is necessary to face reality. The Prime Minister thinks the
Chinese feel the United States has aggressive designs against them and
makes special reference to "non-recognition" policy.

Nehru believes that it is a matter of absolute necessity to avoid use of
the atomic bomb. Such use would make war inevitable. There is a widespread feeling in Asia that the atomic bomb is a weapon used only
against Asiatics.

Source: Memorandum by Assistant Secretary of State for United Nations Affairs,
3 December 1950, in *FRUS, 1950,* 7:1334.

DOCUMENT 99: National Security Council Discusses Use of Atomic Weapons (11 February 1953)

General Bradley's briefing on this subject was sharply pointed to two messages from General Clark. The first of these stated that the so-called "Kaesong sanctuary", which had been created through the armistice negotiations and had an area of approximately 28 square miles, was now chock full of troops and materiel. General Clark believed that the Communists were using this area to build up for an attack on the UN. He therefore was requesting permission himself to attack as soon as he believes that the Communist attack is imminent. He also desires that steps be taken to end the immunity which has thus far prevailed within the Kaesong area. General Bradley stated that the Joint Chiefs were not of the opinion that such permissions should be given.

Secretary Dulles inquired whether the others present did not believe that the time had come when we should indeed end those arrangements in Korea which had been originally designed to facilitate armistice negotiations which were now defunct. He pointed out, however, that we would need some time to prepare our friends for this step. In his view the sooner these arrangements were terminated the better. . . .

The President stated his desire that the Secretary of State begin prompt consideration of this matter with our friends and to determine their reaction to this proposal. He then expressed the view that we should consider the use of tactical atomic weapons on the Kaesong area, which provided a good target for this type of weapon. In any case, the President added, we could not go on the way we were indefinitely.

General Bradley thought it desirable to begin talking with our allies regarding an end of the sanctuary, but thought it unwise to broach the subject yet of possible use of atomic weapons.

Secretary Dulles discussed the moral problem and the inhibitions on the use of the A-bomb, and Soviet success to date in setting atomic weapons apart from all other weapons as being in a special category. It was his opinion that we should try to break down this false distinction.

The President added that we should certainly start on diplomatic negotiations with our allies. To him, it seemed that our self respect and theirs was involved, and if they objected to the use of atomic weapons we might well ask them to supply three or more divisions needed to drive the Communists back, in lieu of use of atomic weapons. In conclusion, however, the President ruled against any discussion with our allies of military plans or weapons of attack.

Source: Memorandum of Discussion at the 131st Meeting of the National Security Council, February 11, 1953, in *FRUS, 1952–54*, 15:769–70.

DOCUMENT 100: Joint Chiefs of Staff and State Department Meeting on the Use of Atomic Weapons (27 March 1953)

[Army Chief of Staff General J. Lawton] Collins: In the new paper on alternative courses of action in Korea that we have just sent forward, we had a section which indicated that consideration should be given to use of atomic weapons. Personally, I am very skeptical about the value of using atomic weapons tactically in Korea. The Communists are dug into positions in depth over a front of one hundred fifty miles, and they are very thoroughly dug in. Our tests last week proved that men can be very close to the explosion and not be hurt if they are well dug in. . . .

[State Department officer Paul] Nitze: The question of the use of atomic weapons in Korea was raised at length with us by the seven consultants. They seem to have the attitude that we had gone to great expense to develop these weapons, we have tested them only in such tests as we could conduct ourselves, and we could certainly test them better under combat conditions. Their question was why should the State Department object to their use in Korea. We replied that there was no unshakeable policy barrier to use of atomic weapons, but the real question was whether the advantages would outweigh the disadvantages. We had to assess whether or not atomic weapons could be effective under Korean conditions. If they were not effective, we would have to be concerned with the question as to whether this would not depreciate the value of our stockpile. We had to weigh the political difficulties with our allies, which would arise from employment of atomic weapons, and these difficulties would be magnified if the weapons were not in fact effective. And the further question had to be considered as to whether the U.S.S.R. would not be faced with a decision and whether or not in that case they might not decide to retaliate in kind.

General Bradley: I think the consultants reflect the thinking of a lot of our people. Because of the casualties that will be involved in any stepped up ground action, we may find that we will be forced to use every type of weapon that we have.

[Air Force Chief of Staff General Hoyt] Vandenberg: I hope that if we do use them, we use them in Manchuria against the bases. They would be effective there.

General Collins: Before we use them we had better look to our air defense. Right now we present ideal targets for atomic weapons in Pusan and Inchon. An atomic weapon in Pusan harbor could do serious damage to our military position in Korea. We would again present an ideal target if we should undertake a major amphibious operation. An amphibious landing fleet would be a perfect target for an atomic weapon at the time when it was putting the troops ashore. On the other hand, the Commies, scattered over one hundred fifty miles of front, and well dug in, don't present nearly as profitable a target to us as we do to them.

Source: Memorandum of Discussion at a Department of State–Joint Chiefs of Staff Meeting, 27 March 1953, in *FRUS, 1952–54*, 15:817–18.

DOCUMENT 101: President Eisenhower Weighs the Options of Using Atomic Weapons in Korea (31 March 1953)

On Tuesday, 31 March 1953, the National Security Council met informally with civilian consultants designated by NSC Action No. 726-c regarding basic national security policies and programs in relation to their costs.

The President then spoke his mind on the Korean problem. If, he said, we decide to go up to the strength which will be necessary to achieve a sound tactical victory in Korea—for example, to get to the waist—the Russians will very quickly realize what we are doing. They would respond by increasing the Communist strength in Korea, and, as a result, we would be forced ultimately into a situation very close to general mobilization in order to get such a victory in Korea. General Bradley expressed agreement with the President's thesis.

The President then raised the question of the use of atomic weapons in the Korean war. Admittedly, he said, there were not many good tactical targets, but he felt it would be worth the cost if, through use of atomic weapons, we could (1) achieve a substantial victory over the Communist forces and (2) get to a line at the waist of Korea.

Mr. Robertson expressed the opinion that the American people would, under the circumstances, support an all-out effort in Korea. . . .

Mr. [Deane] Malott argued that he nevertheless believed that we ought to use a couple of atomic weapons in Korea.

The President replied that perhaps we should, but we could not blind ourselves to the effects of such a move on our allies, which would be very serious since they feel that they will be the battleground in an atomic war between the United States and the Soviet Union. Nevertheless, the President and Secretary Dulles were in complete agreement that somehow or other the tabu which surrounds the use of atomic weapons would have to be destroyed. While Secretary Dulles admitted that in the present state of world opinion we could not use an A-bomb, we should make every effort now to dissipate this feeling.

Source: Memorandum of Discussion at a Special Meeting of the National Security Council on March 31, 1953, in *FRUS, 1952–54,* 15:825–27.

DOCUMENT 102: NSC Policy Statement on the Advantages and Disadvantages of Using Atomic Weapons in Korea (2 April 1953)

Use of Atomic Weapons

21. Each of the suggested courses of action . . . permits but does not require employment of atomic weapons. In each case . . . the use or non-use of such weapons is left open for future determination. This determination should be made only after a thorough study of the military, psychological and political implications of the use of atomic weapons has been completed, and considered by the National Security Council. A tentative statement of some of the military and political advantages and disadvantages of using atomic weapons follows.

22. *Military Advantages:*

a. Would considerably augment capabilities of U.S.-UN forces and somewhat offset the implications of developing a conventional capability to produce equivalent military effects outside Korea.

b. Would result in curtailment of Communist Chinese capability of continuing present hostilities, of threatening U.S.-UN security in Korea and Japan, or of initiating aggression elsewhere.

c. Might serve to increase the deterrent effect of our atomic capabilities on the USSR, as pertains to both global and limited war.

d. Threats to our military position in Korea could be eliminated more effectively, quickly and cheaply than by use of conventional weapons.

23. *Military Disadvantages:*

a. Unless the use of atomic weapons results in a decisive military victory, the deterrent effect might be reduced.

b. Any profitable strategic use requires extension of hostilities outside of Korea.

c. A precedent would be established, and UN forces and installations are, in general, better targets for atomic weapons than those of the enemy; for example, the ports of Inchon and Pusan, UN airfields and concentrations for amphibious operations.

d. Use of substantial numbers will reduce the U.S. stockpile and global atomic capabilities.

24. *Political Advantages:* There would be political advantages in the use of atomic weapons:

a. If their use in Korea alone was effective in achieving a military victory and thereby a political settlement in Korea, without encountering such enemy reaction as would lead to a spread of hostilities to Communist China.

b. If their use in Korea and against Communist China was effective in achieving a military victory in Korea and sufficient military results against Communist China to bring about a political settlement in Korea and a general political settlement with Communist China, without encountering such enemy reaction as would lead to a spread of hostilities to the USSR.

c. If their use in Korea or against Communist China was clearly required in order to avoid a U.S.-UN military disaster in Korea.

25. *Political Disadvantages:* There would be political disadvantages in the use of atomic weapons:

a. If other free world nations believe that

(i.) the net effectiveness of the use of atomic weapons in Korea would be insufficient for the achievement of our military objectives there.

(ii.) the net effectiveness of the use of atomic weapons in Korea and against Communist China would be insufficient to achieve decisive military results.

(iii.) such military results as could be achieved by the use of atomic weapons either in Korea or against Communist China would be insufficient to achieve our political objectives in Korea or a general settlement with Communist China.

(iv.) the use of atomic weapons in Korea would involve the West in general hostilities with Communist China or the use of atomic weapons against Communist China would involve the West in hostilities with the USSR.

(v.) the use of atomic weapons would lead to enemy retaliation in kind against vulnerable U.S.-UN targets.

(vi.) the use of atomic weapons is not required to avert military disaster and if they believe, particularly in the light of current Communist peace offers, that our military and political objectives in Korea can be achieved without their use.

b. If such action were taken without consultation with other free world governments and without the concurrence in advance of our major allies.

c. If merely raising the question of the use of atomic weapons in Korea or against Communist China resulted in a dissipation of the support we now have from other free nations for terms of a Korean settlement acceptable to us.

26. *Estimated Communist Reaction:* We believe that if atomic weapons were employed by U.S./UN forces in any of the above alternative courses of action, the Communists would recognize the employment of these weapons as indicative of Western determination to carry the Korean war to a successful conclusion. We are unable to estimate whether this recognition would by itself lead the Communists to make the concessions necessary to reach an armistice. We believe that the Communist reaction would be in large part determined by the extent of damage inflicted.

Source: Note by the Executive Secretary (Lay) to the National Security Council, April 2, 1953, in *FRUS, 1952–54*, 15:845–46.

CONSEQUENCES OF THE KOREAN CONFLICT

DOCUMENT 103: Prominent Diplomat Charles Bohlen Sees the Korean War as Juncture Where the U.S. Becomes a World Power (1973)

I have mentioned that [fellow diplomat George] Kennan and I concluded that Stalin's intention in Korea was simply to get control of the whole country, largely because he realized that there was very little chance of his playing the same type of sabotage role in Japan that he had played in Germany. [Secretary] Acheson, influenced . . . by those in the State Department who did not know Soviet Russia, felt that the Korean war represented a new Soviet foreign policy of military expansion and that all of the areas contiguous to the free nations in Europe were threatened by attack.

As the result of this erroneous judgment, the United States over-interpreted the Korean war and overextended our commitments. The government concluded that godless Communism had conspired to take over the world and that the United States was the knight in shining armor who would fight it everywhere. Before Korea, the United States had only one commitment of a political or military nature outside the Western Hemisphere. This was the North Atlantic Treaty. Our bases in

Germany and Japan were regarded as temporary, to be given up when the occupation ended. True, as a hangover from prewar days, we felt it necessary to retain bases in the Philippines, but there was no pledge on their use. The only other places we had military facilities were in England, where we had transit privileges, and Saudi Arabia, where we had an airfield. As a result of our overinterpretation of Communism's goal, we had by 1955 about 450 bases in thirty-six countries, and we were linked by political and military pacts with some twenty countries outside of Latin America. It was the Korean war and not World War II that made us a world military-political power.

Source: Bohlen, *Witness to History,* 303.

DOCUMENT 104: General Bradley's Assessment as to Why the Korean War Ended (March 1953)

Shortly after taking office, President Eisenhower and Secretary of State Dulles leaked to the Chinese that if they did not negotiate, the United States would not be limited by any worldwide "gentlemen's agreement," that it would move decisively without inhibition in its use of weapons, and that it would no longer be responsible for confining hostilities to the Korean peninsula.

In late March 1953, North Korean Premier Kim Il-Sung and China's Premier Zhou En-lai both agreed to a preliminary exchange of sick and wounded POWs. Zhou said the time was ripe for settling the "entire question" of POWs, to cease the hostilities in Korea, and to conclude an armistice agreement.

The JCS continued, however, with its plans to go "atomic."

After a hiatus of some six months, talks resumed at Panmunjom on 26 April. The armistice was signed on 27 July. The Korean War had cost America 142,091 casualties: 33,629 dead, 103,284 wounded, 5,178 captured or missing.

All during that spring [1953] the JCS . . . produced various studies on possible ways to end the Korean War. . . . In March, the JCS took the unprecedented step of recommending that "the timely use of atomic weapons should be considered against military targets affecting operations in Korea" [with] possible "direct action against Communist China and Manchuria." That same month, Joseph Stalin died. . . .

We recommended to the NSC that if the negotiations fell through again, we hit the communists with an all-out effort. This included "extensive strategical and tactical use of atomic bombs" against China and Manchuria, coordinated with a massive Eighth Army ground offensive to achieve a position along the "waist." The NSC voted to adopt our proposals "as a general guide" should conditions arise "requiring more positive action in Korea."

Source: Bradley and Blair, *A General's Life*, 660–61.

FURTHER READING

Ambrose, Stephen. *Eisenhower*. Vol. 2, *The President* (1984).

Chang, Gordon. *Friends and Enemies, 1948–1972* (1990).

Chen, Jian. *China's Road to the Korean War* (1994).

Cumings, Bruce. *The Origins of the Korean War*. 2 vols. (1981, 1990).

Donovan, Robert J. *Tumultuous Years: Harry Truman, 1949–1953* (1983).

Foot, Rosemary. *The Wrong War* (1985).

Goncharov, Sergei N., John W. Lewis, and Xue Litai. *Uncertain Partners: Stalin, Mao, and the Korean War* (1993).

Iriye, Akira, and Nagai Yonosuke, eds. *The Origins of the Cold War in Asia* (1977).

Kaufman, Burton I. *The Korean War: Challenges in Crisis, Credibility, and Command* (1986).

Matray, James I. *The Reluctant Crusade* (1986).

Reeves, Thomas C. *The Life and Times of Joe McCarthy* (1982).

Stueck, William W., Jr. *The Korean War: An International History* (1994).

Tucker, Nancy B. *Patterns in the Dust* (1983).

Weathersby, Kathryn. "Korea, 1949–50: To Attack, or Not to Attack? Stalin, Kim Il Sung, and the Prelude to War." *Cold War International History Project Bulletin* 5 (Spring 1995), 1–9.

Zhang Shuguang. *Deterrence and Strategic Culture* (1993).

Part IV

The Berlin Crises of 1958–1959 and 1961

After the Berlin crisis of 1948–1949 (see Part II), unease and concern in East Germany led to a mass exodus of Germans to the West, most of them emigrating through Berlin, many of them the most skilled, accomplished citizens of the German Democratic Republic (GDR). This development worried Soviet Premier Nikita Khrushchev, as did Western intelligence activity in the city. Not the least of his concerns, moreover, was the prosperity of West Germany and of West Berlin, with which the Soviet sector was always being compared. Berlin had become, he often stated, a bone in the throat of the Soviet Union.

In the fall of 1958 Khrushchev hit upon a way to solve the problem. In November he announced that the Soviets would insist on negotiations to address the Berlin issue. If the West refused to begin discussions within six months, Khrushchev said, he would sign a separate peace treaty with East Germany, which would take over responsibility for the city. In the meantime, if negotiations were held, Berlin could become a "free city."

All this sounded ominous to American officials, who were confident that East German control of Berlin would effectively end Western access to the city. They therefore refused to negotiate and prepared for the worst. Some of President Eisenhower's top military advisers and Secretary of State John Foster Dulles even recommended a direct military challenge to the Soviets. President Eisenhower, confident of U.S. military superiority and Soviet awareness of this superiority, decided on a policy of delay. The president's impulse proved correct, and the Soviets eventually dropped their ultimatum. In the spring of 1959 the crisis passed without incident, and Khrushchev met with Eisenhower in the United States later in the year.

Meanwhile, Berlin did not go away as an issue with the end of the Eisenhower Administration. In June 1961 President John F. Kennedy met with Khrushchev at a summit conference in Vienna, a rough and tumble session at which the Soviet premier once again announced his plans for Berlin. Kennedy, though pressed hard at this meeting, refused to relent and indeed later chose to make a major point of his defiance of the Soviets. In July he asked Congress for a major addition to the defense budget, indicated plans to call up military reserves, and urged the American people to build bomb shelters. The Soviets' response to this was to prevent emigration by erecting the hideous Berlin Wall in August 1961, which remained a symbol of the Cold War and communist repression until its dismantling in 1989.

CHRONOLOGY

1954
March. U.S. detonates hydrogen bomb at Bikini Island

March–May. Battle of Dienbienphu in Vietnam

July. Geneva Agreement (Vietnam)

September. Southeast Asia Treaty Organization (SEATO) created

November. Quemoy-Matsu/Taiwan Straits crisis with China

1955
May. Warsaw Pact created

1956
February. Khrushchev's 20th Party Congress speech

November. Eisenhower reelected

November. France and Britain join Israeli attack on Suez Canal

November. Soviets invade Hungary

1957
March. Eisenhower Doctrine

October 4. Soviets launch *Sputnik*

1958
February. Polish denuclearization plan for Central Europe

March. Soviet Union explodes hydrogen bomb

November 10. Khrushchev's "ultimatum" renews Berlin crisis

November 20. Chancellor Adenauer's letter to Sec. of State Dulles

November 27. Soviet diplomatic note on status of Berlin

December 31. U.S. diplomatic response to Soviet note

1959

February. Prime Minister Macmillan's "voyage" to Moscow
March 16. Eisenhower's radio-TV address to the nation
August 5. Communiqué agreeing to settlement of Berlin crisis
September. Khrushchev visits United States

1960

May 1. Soviets shoot down American U-2 and capture pilot
November. Kennedy elected president

1961

June 3–4. Vienna Summit between Kennedy and Khrushchev
July. Soviet Gen. Staff defector Penkovsky's debriefings to CIA
August 13. Berlin Wall erected
August 17. U.S. diplomatic note condemning the Berlin Wall

1963

June 26. Kennedy's "ich bin ein Berliner" speech

The Berlin Crisis of
1958–1959

KHRUSHCHEV MANEUVERS FOR GDR DIPLOMATIC
RECOGNITION

DOCUMENT 105: U.S. Embassy-Bonn Requests Policy Plan Regarding Western Access to Berlin and Authority of German Democratic Republic (GDR) (January 1958)

Even though we cannot anticipate nor be prepared for every possible Soviet move affecting access to Berlin, we must be prepared to deal quickly with any action impeding access and infringing upon our rights. While current policy provides for acceptance GDR personnel at checkpoints as "agents" of Soviets, planning for contingencies has not gone beyond assumption that such personnel in this capacity would merely look at documents and pass train. While such might well be the case initially, we would certainly be naive to think this procedure would go no further. It is certain that since acceptance of GDR "authority" by Western powers is underlying Soviet objective, continuous pressure to that end may be expected. The next step would logically and almost inevitably be demand for German translations, questioning status of travel, challenging right to move German mail car, insistence on GDR visas, etc. We can anticipate that protests to Soviets will encounter a referral to "Sovereign" GDR and we would reach an impasse. (While we are not predicting these events will occur, we would be remiss not to consider such assumptions in connection with policy planning.)

The above situation poses two problems:

(1) At what point beyond "showing" of documents is recognition of "authority" involved?

(2) What do we do when we turn back trains rather than recognize GDR "authority"?

On the first problem, I feel that acceptance at GDR request of any condition or procedure not in effect with Soviets would constitute recognizing GDR "authority." ...

The second problem involves the "self-imposed blockade," which raises visions of 1948 airlift, even though in assumed situation only consideration of Allied access (not German) involved. Our ability to take and hold a strong line with Soviets in this eventuality and to muster public opinion by dramatizing Soviets' actions blocking our access to Berlin depends upon how long we can accept cessation of military train service and official use of autobahn.

Source: U.S. Department of State, *Foreign Relations of the United States, 1958–1960,* Vol. 8, *Berlin Crisis* (hereafter *FRUS, 1958–60, Berlin*) (Washington: GPO, 1993), 1–2.

DOCUMENT 106: Polish Foreign Minister Adam Rapacki's Plan for Denuclearization of Central Europe (February 1958)

The threat of further complications, primarily in Central Europe, where the opposing military groupings come into a direct contact and the apparent danger of an increase in the international tension have prompted the Polish Government to initiate ... direct discussions through diplomatic channels on the Polish proposal submitted to the United Nations General Assembly on October 2, 1957, concerning the establishment of a denuclearized zone in Central Europe.

This proposal has evoked a wide interest in government and political circles as well as in the broad strata of public opinion in many countries.

Source: Polish Foreign Minister's (Adam Rapacki) Note to the U.S. Ambassador in Poland (Jacob D. Beam), on the Establishment of a Denuclearized Zone, 14 February 1958, in U.S. Department of State, *Documents on Germany, 1944–1985* (Washington: GPO, 1985), 518–21.

DOCUMENT 107: President Eisenhower's Diary on Not Being "Too Stiffnecked" about U.S. Recognition of German Democratic Republic (9 June 1958)

This morning I noted in the papers a report that an American helicopter was down in East Germany. Some difficulty was being incurred in our attempts to get the people back because of Soviet insistence that we deal with East Germany and our insistence that we wanted to deal with the Soviets because we do not recognize East Germany.

. . . About twelve noon, I called the secretary of state . . . to remind him that under somewhat similar circumstances we had dealt directly with Red China, which we do not recognize. When I had the secretary on the phone, he remarked that my call was a remarkable coincidence because he was just reaching for the phone to call his staff to remind them of the same circumstance and to express his opinion that we should not be too stiffnecked in our attitude. To do so might easily create a situation that could bring about a prolonged stalemate, such as we have had in China.

Source: Robert H. Ferrell, ed., *The Eisenhower Diaries* (New York: Norton, 1981), 355.

DOCUMENT 108: Chairman Khrushchev's "Ultimatum" Directing the Western Powers to Deal Directly with the GDR on Any Questions Concerning Berlin (10 November 1958)

If one were to speak of the four powers' undertakings with regard to Germany, one should speak of undertakings springing from the Potsdam Agreement. . . .

Whichever basic provisions of the Potsdam Agreement concerning the demilitarization of Germany and prevention of the resurgence of fascism we may consider, we shall arrive at the conclusion that these provisions, bearing the signatures of the United States, Britain and France, have been violated by them. What then is left of the Potsdam Agreement? One thing in effect: The so-called four-power status of Berlin, that is, a position in which the three western powers. . . . have the possibility of lording it in Western Berlin, turning that part of the city, which is the capital of the German Democratic Republic, into some kind of state within a state and, profiting by this, conducting subversive activities against the German Democratic Republic, against the Soviet Union and the other Warsaw Treaty countries. . . .

The question arises: Who stands to benefit from this situation and why have the United States, France and Britain not violated this part of the quadripartite agreement as well? The answer is clear: They have no intention of violating this part of the Potsdam Agreement. On the contrary, they cling to it, for the agreement on Berlin is advantageous to the western powers and to them alone. . . .

The time has obviously arrived for the signatories of the Potsdam Agreement to renounce the remnants of the occupation regime in Berlin and thereby make it possible to create a normal situation in the capital of German Democratic Republic. The Soviet Union, for its part, would hand over to the sovereign German Democratic Republic the functions in Berlin that are still exercised by Soviet agencies. . . .

Let the United States, France and Britain themselves build their relations with the German Democratic Republic, let them reach agreement with it themselves if they are interested in any questions concerning Berlin. As for the Soviet Union, we shall sacredly honour our obligations as an ally of the German Democratic Republic—obligations which stem from the Warsaw Treaty and which we have repeatedly reaffirmed to the German Democratic Republic. If any forces of aggression attack the German Democratic Republic, which is a full-fledged member of the Warsaw Treaty, we shall regard this as an attack on the Soviet Union, on all the Warsaw Treaty countries.

Source: Address by Chairman Khrushchev, in U.S. Department of State, *Documents on Germany, 1944–1985*, 542–46.

DOCUMENT 109: President Eisenhower Recalls the Physical and Psychological Symbolism of Berlin to Both Western Allies and Soviet Bloc (10 November 1958)

Soviet Premier Khrushchev's declaration on 10 November of the Soviets' intention of signing an early and separate "peace treaty" with East Germany transformed Berlin, which had remained relatively stable for more than nine years, into a tinderbox.

The physical and psychological condition of West Berlin had changed dramatically in the decade since the blockade, when the Allied airlift saved the city from starvation. No longer were West Berliners barely scraping along on subsistence amounts of food and fuel; they now had a fully-geared industrial economy. Its new prosperity required supplies and raw materials multiplied many times over those needed a decade before.

This thriving industrial metropolis was showing to the world, and to the East Germans in particular, the contrast between the Communist and free ways of life. West Berlin had long provided a haven for thousands upon thousands of unhappy, escaping East Germans of whom, to make matters even worse from Khrushchev's viewpoint, a considerable proportion were professionals and intellectuals. Small wonder he was to call the city a bone in his throat. An Allied retreat would remove it.

Source: Dwight D. Eisenhower, *The White House Years: Waging Peace, 1956–1961.* (Garden City, N.Y.: Doubleday, 1965), 329–30.

DOCUMENT 110: Nikita Khrushchev Remembers the Berlin Crisis of 1958–1959 (1974)

When we began to face up to the problem of West Berlin after Stalin's death, we realized that the agreement which had liquidated the blockade of West Berlin [1948–1949] was unfair. The West had managed to exploit the tension generated by the blockade and to impose conditions on East Germany which were even more constraining and one-sided than the ones set by the Potsdam agreement. The international situation throughout Europe was highly unstable. . . . Germany was a sort of barometer. The slightest fluctuation in the pressure of the world political atmosphere naturally registered at that point where the forces of the two sides were squared off against each other.

We wanted very much to relieve the tension which was building up dangerously over West Berlin, and we knew that the only way we could do it would be to conclude a peace treaty with the West. . . . It was already too late to talk about a treaty that would reunify Germany because neither East Germany nor West Germany wanted to accept the social-political system of the other side. . . . But we still wanted to find some workable and mutually beneficial terms for a treaty that would stabilize the situation. . . . It was clear that the existing situation was dangerous, and also that both sides wanted to avoid military confrontation. . . .

The Western powers rejected our proposal for the recognition of two German Republics. In response, we warned that we might have no choice but to initiate a peace treaty unilaterally, and we proposed a date for a meeting of all countries who wanted to sign the treaty. We warned that even if certain countries refused to sign, the rest of us would go ahead and conclude a treaty with the GDR [German Democratic Republic]. We would then be obliged to act according to the terms of the new treaty on various matters, including the matter of access to West Berlin.

Source: Nikita S. Khrushchev, *Khrushchev Remembers: The Last Testament*, translated by Strobe Talbott (Boston: Little, Brown, 1974), 452–54.

DOCUMENT 111: U.S. Ambassador Llewellyn Thompson Speculates from Moscow on Motives for Khrushchev's Ultimatum (11 November 1958)

Threat to end quadripartite status Berlin appears to have been deliberately stated in equivocal manner and may be only trial balloon. Difficult to see, however, how Soviets could simply let matter drop particularly in view coordinated action of East German note and memorandum. I therefore consider that speech represents a most dangerous move on part of Khrushchev. It is true that this is only one of a number of recent indications of hardening of Soviet policy which appears to be aiming at deliberate increase of tension and in that respect may be less serious than if German question alone were singled out for maximum pressure.

It is probable that Khrushchev has several motives in pursuing this general hard line. One may be that having failed to secure summit meeting by soft approach he intends to force meeting by building up tension to almost intolerable pitch. If this is primary motive, however, German problem is ill chosen since this is the one of two problems Soviets refuse to discuss with US. I believe that more likely explanation of general Soviet policy is that Khrushchev has concluded that he cannot achieve his objectives by top level negotiations with present American administration and that he intends to see what effect strong pressure and heightened tension will have on cohesion of Western powers. We may expect that such pressure will as usual alternate with friendly gestures and declarations of sweet reasonableness.

A further reason for deliberate heightening of tension may be that Khrushchev considers this will serve his personal objectives at 21st Party Congress. German Ambassador thinks this is so but that Khrushchev fails realize that other members of Presidium are already worried by his tendency to take unnecessary risks in field foreign affairs.

Source: FRUS, 1958–60, Berlin, 47–48.

DOCUMENT 112: American Diplomatic-Military Mission in Berlin Analyzes Khrushchev's Ultimatum (12 November 1958)

We see as most important point in this part of speech a warning directed primarily to US, UK and France to recognize GDR or face increasing pressure on access to Berlin. This theme is not new, but when Khrushchev says it, presumably Soviets have moved close to, and if not all the way to, a decision to implement it.

We think a key sentence re Berlin situation is that which reads: "For its part, Soviet Union will transfer to sovereign GDR those functions in Berlin which are now handled by Soviet organs." We interpret "will" to mean "are going to, whether other three powers do or not" rather than "I would if other three powers will." From other passages in speech we conclude that "Berlin" is intended to include access thereto. . . .

We have every reason believe Soviets take very seriously our security guarantee Berlin. We anticipate that turn over to GDR would be implemented gradually, and though GDR pressure would be applied in stages, avoid any action which Communists think would bring into force our security guarantee.

Source: FRUS, 1958–60, Berlin, 49–51.

DOCUMENT 113: State Department Circular to Diplomatic Missions (13 November 1958)

USSR may be pursuing one or more of following objectives:

1. Testing resolve and unity of will of US, UK and France to maintain their position in Berlin;

2. Forcing Western Powers into de facto recognition of East German regime through creation of situations on Allied access routes to Berlin calculated compel Western Powers deal with GDR officials;

3. Inhibiting emergence of West Germany as nuclear-capable power with strong influence in NATO;

4. Bringing about withdrawal of Western troops from Western Germany;

5. Bringing pressure for Four-Power talks on German peace treaty and talks between "two German states" on reunification;

6. In line with Communist pattern of behavior re Korea, Taiwan, and Vietnam, representing Western occupation of Berlin, special regime of Western Powers' access to Berlin, and influence exerted by Berlin on GDR as unjustified interference with internal German affairs;

7. Generating intensive and continuous pressures throughout world in order divide Western Powers. . . .

Khrushchev's basic argumentation re Berlin is not new and is essentially repetition line Soviets took as early as 1948. Most significant aspect is more explicit statement by highest Soviet official of threat Soviets have occasionally made by implication earlier, namely to relinquish and thus in effect cede to GDR remaining responsibilities re Berlin which Soviets continue exercise on basis quadripartite agreements and arrangements.

Source: FRUS, 1958–60, Berlin, 57–60.

DOCUMENT 114: Acting Secretary of State Christian Herter Reports to President Eisenhower Concerning Increased Tension over the Status of Berlin (13 November 1958)

In response to your request for information regarding the present Berlin situation resulting from the Khrushchev speech of November 10, I enclose a status report on this subject. . . .

Although there are a variety of speculations regarding Soviet motivation this action seems clearly related to a long-standing Soviet desire to force the Western Powers into de facto recognition of an East German regime through the creation of situations on allied access routes to Berlin calculated to compel the Western Powers to deal with East German officials.

The Department in public statements is emphasizing our quadripartite responsibilities in Berlin and the unacceptability of Soviet unilateral abrogation of specific quadrilateral agreements on Berlin (other than the Potsdam Agreement which is not pertinent to our position in Berlin).

Consideration is being given to the desirability of some tripartite reaffirmation of the Western position on Berlin. There is, however, some difference of view as to whether this would be useful at the present time. The British and Germans at the working level believe it would demonstrate our nervousness more than our determination and we think it advisable to wait at least a few days to see how the situation develops before issuing a tripartite statement. This is in line with our belief that our wisest course is to avoid actions which might over-dramatize the present situation.

Source: FRUS, 1958–60, Berlin, 60–62.

EISENHOWER-DULLES IN RESPONSE

DOCUMENT 115: President Eisenhower Recalls the Military and Diplomatic Options (20 November 1958)

On 14 November the Soviet troops detained three U.S. Army trucks for eight hours at a checkpoint on the Autobahn just outside Berlin. General Lauris Norstad, the Supreme Allied Commander in Europe, sent a message to his superiors in Washington that, in the absence of other instructions, he was planning to dispatch a test Berlin-Helmstedt convoy. If the Soviets were to detain it for more than three hours, he planned to extricate the convoy "by minimum force necessary."

Clearly, however, if such action were to be taken, it should first be made known to our allies. Therefore, even though the administration was generally sympathetic to Norstad's approach (the Chiefs of Staff thought we should move at once), his plan could not be put into effect immediately. To give time for consultation an order was sent temporarily suspending all convoys to Berlin.

Soon thereafter Foster Dulles informed me that the initial combativeness of the military had eased and the Chiefs of Staff and General Norstad now recognized the necessity for bringing our allies in line prior to taking drastic action. At a meeting a few days later—on the twentieth—Secretary Dulles observed that if Khrushchev should carry out his intention of transferring Soviet responsibilities to the East German government, he would create the most complicated situation in Berlin since the end of the 1949 blockade. Foster believed that Khrushchev would probably move soon to carry out his threat.

Source: Eisenhower, Waging Peace, 331.

DOCUMENT 116: President Eisenhower and Secretary Dulles Compare Tension over Berlin with Quemoy Crises of 1954 and 1958 with Communist China (18 November 1958)

I [Dulles] reported on the Berlin situation and that it had eased somewhat. . . .

The President reviewed at some length his recollection of the history of the Berlin arrangements; his feeling that we perhaps should not have committed ourselves as deeply as we had to Berlin, where the situation was basically untenable, as in the case of Quemoy and Matsu. However, he recognized that we were where we were and had to stand firm. The President emphasized, however, that we needed to have understanding with the British, the French and the Germans on this matter.

Source: FRUS, 1958–60, Berlin, 84–85.

DOCUMENT 117: West German Chancellor's Letter to Secretary Dulles (20 November 1958)

MY DEAR FRIEND MR. DULLES:

This morning Mr. [Andrei] Smirnov, the Ambassador of the Soviet Union, called on me to inform me officially that the Government of the Soviet Union intends in the next few days to denounce the "Occupation Statute" for the city of Berlin. The reason given for this is known to you from the statements of the Soviet Russian Prime Minister, Mr. Khrushchev. . . .

I am convinced that the Soviet Union will proceed astutely and warily. It will to begin with pretend [*sic*] that the transfer of the rights under the Four Power Agreement to the government of the so-called DDR will not in any way alter the present status. And it will, I believe, instruct the authorities of the DDR to keep up this pretense for the time being. If we acquiesce in this, a second step will follow. The DDR will, for example, take the position that free civilian traffic by air is no longer permissible but requires the consent of the authorities of the DDR. This would make it impossible for hundreds of thousands of people to find their way to freedom via the city of Berlin. At first the DDR will probably not cause any difficulties for the representatives of the three Western

Powers and the troops stationed in Berlin; it will restrict the freedom of traffic between Berlin and the Federal Republic and finally halt it, on the alleged grounds of its sovereignty.

The political, economic and in particular the psychological reactions in Berlin and in Germany are incalculable. But in other parts of the world as well, including the members of the Atlantic Community, the fear will arise that an initial concession will not be the last. In the historic world-wide conflict between communism and the free world the Soviet Union would thus easily win the first and perhaps decisive battle.

I consider it urgently necessary that we face these dangers with all frankness and seriousness. I am also writing to the British Prime Minister, Mr. Macmillan, to the same effect. As you know, I am meeting with the French Premier, General de Gaulle, this coming Wednesday; we have already placed this question on the agenda of the conversation. Furthermore, I consider it highly desirable, even necessary, that we come together immediately in a meeting of the four Governments when the Soviet Union announces its action.

Source: Konrad Adenauer Letter to Secretary Dulles, 20 November 1958, in *FRUS, 1958–60, Berlin*, 110–11.

DOCUMENT 118: U.S. Diplomatic and Pentagon Leaders Discuss Berlin (21 November 1958)

General [Chairman Joint Chiefs of Staff, Nathan F.] Twining opened the meeting with general remarks to the effect that the JCS were concerned that the U.S. would have to make a move very soon in connection with the Soviet intentions concerning Berlin. They did not want to be unprepared. With this in mind, they had prepared *draft instructions* to CINCUSAREUR [Commander of U.S. Army Forces in Europe] proposing the use of minimum force necessary to extricate any U.S. military truck convoy which might be detained by the Russians.

Mr. Murphy then referred to press items and other loose conversation regarding an airlift for Berlin, pointing out that evidence to date does not indicate that the USSR is thinking in terms of an immediate blockade of the civilian population of West Berlin. On the contrary, this would appear to be a more limited proposition designed to harass the Allied forces in Berlin with the ultimate intention of dislocating them from the city. There has been over-emphasis on the political reporting and press coverage on the question of the Russian intent to blockade the city. There does not appear to be a parallel with the 1948 blockade operation. However, the U.S. should remain flexible on the matter of an airlift which might conceivably be required by later developments, and no arbitrary decision should be taken now to exclude the possibility of an airlift.

General [of the Army Lyman] Lemnitzer discussed the factual situation and the *military risks* involved in pushing across 100 miles of hostile territory. He pointed out that our Berlin forces consist of two small battle groups opposed to 25 top-notch Russian divisions. He stated that the military facts of life in that situation are hard. He pointed out the ease with which bridges could be blown up and road-blocks established. Mr. Murphy indicated he was fully aware of these problems and risks as well as the Soviet military strength on the spot. Our military posture is, of course, unsatisfactory when viewed exclusively in those terms and we have faced this problem for a long time. There is much more involved, of course, in that the Russians are aware that an attack against our small force would bring into play a vastly different power situation. . . . Mr. Murphy pointed out at this time that we are initiating an *ad hoc working group* to consider the Berlin situation and to recommend contingency measures.

Source: FRUS, 1958–60, Berlin, 99–103.

DOCUMENT 119: Secretary Dulles' Controversial Press Conference (26 November 1958)

Q.: Mr. Secretary, what if, despite this responsibility, the Soviets go ahead and turn over to the East German authorities the check points on the autobahn and control to the land, sea, and air routes? Now the question would arise: Would we deal with the East German officials who would man the checkpoints, for example, even as—

A.: Well, we would certainly not deal with them in any way which involved our acceptance of the East German regime as a substitute for the Soviet Union in discharging the obligation of the Soviet Union and the responsibility of the Soviet Union.

Q.: Does that mean that we might deal with them as agents of the Soviet Union?

A.: We might, yes. There are certain respects now in which minor functionaries of the so-called G.D.R. are being dealt with by both the Western powers, the three allied powers, and also by the Federal Republic of Germany. It all depends upon the details of just how they act and how they function. You can't exclude that to a minor degree because it is going on at the present time and has been. On the other hand, if the character of the activity is such as to indicate that to accept this would involve acceptance of a substitution of the G.D.R. for the present obligation and responsibility of the Soviet Union, then that, I take it, we would not do.

Q.: Mr. Secretary, can you deal with them in such a way as to make a distinction between dealing with them as agents of the Soviet Union and dealing with them in such a way as to imply a kind of de facto recognition of their existence?

A.: I think that that certainly could be done. We often deal with people that we do not recognize diplomatically, deal with them on a practical basis. Of course, we do that with the Chinese Communists in a number of respects. And, as I pointed out, both the Federal Republic of Germany and the rest of us have, in certain practical matters, for many months been dealing with minor functionaries of the G.D.R. with respect to what might be called perfunctory, routine matters.

Q.: Mr. Secretary, you say we might deal with the East Germans as agents of the Soviet Union. Is that a matter of agreed policy between the three Western powers and the Federal Republic or only something that is possible?

A.: I think that it is agreed between us that we might. But, as I say, the question of whether we would or would not would have to depend upon the precise circumstances which surrounded the action, and that can't be anticipated in advance of knowing what, if anything, the Soviet Union is going to do.

Q.: Mr. Secretary, can you give us your view of why the Berlin crisis was reactivated at this time? I mean the Berlin situation between the East and the West. Do you have any idea of what the Communists had in mind?

A.: I was not surprised by it at all. I think that the Soviet Union and the Chinese Communists—what Khrushchev calls "the international Communist movement"—is disposed periodically to try to probe in different areas of the world to develop, if possible, weak spots—to develop, if possible, differences. I think that the probing that took place in the Taiwan area was one such effort. Now it is going on in Berlin and could go on at other places. The effort is, I think, periodically to try to find out whether they are up against firmness and strength and unity. If they find that, then I think the probing will cease. But we have got to expect these probes coming from time to time. As I say, I was not surprised that this Berlin probe took place. Indeed, I thought it probably would take place.

Source: FRUS, 1958–60, Berlin, 121–27.

DOCUMENT 120: U.S. Ambassador David Bruce Reports West German Reaction to Dulles' Remarks (26 November 1958)

About 7 o'clock tonight a storm broke out over remarks attributed to the Secretary at his press conference in Washington this morning. . . . As regards [their] effect on German public opinion, I [David Bruce] am thoroughly dissatisfied with it. The Secretary displayed his usual ability to state the alternatives clearly, but in recognizing the possibility of regarding GDR officials as agents of the Soviets he is certain to alarm governmental and private circles here to a high degree. In fact the excitement in Berlin is such that one of the Senators is flying down tonight to talk to [my staff] about it.

This is another instance of what has always seemed to me to be the folly of discussing publicly diplomatic crises and negotiations when, as almost any reputable newspaper correspondent will admit, an answer from an official that a response would not be in the public interest would be accepted. Moreover, if the Soviet proposal has not already been prepared, it might have some influence on its content. In a lesser degree, the Secretary's utterances some time ago comparing Quemoy and Matsu to Berlin had disturbing repercussions.

Source: FRUS, 1958–60, Berlin, 127–29.

DOCUMENT 121: Soviet Diplomatic Note to the United States (27 November 1958)

The policy of the USA, Britain, and France with respect West Germany has led to the violation of those provisions of the Potsdam Agreement designed to ensure the unity of Germany as a peace-loving and democratic state. And when a separate state, the Federal Republic of Germany, was set up independently [of the Soviet Union] in West Germany, which was occupied by the troops of the Three Powers, East Germany, where forces determined not to allow the German people to be plunged once again into disaster assumed the leadership, had no alternative but to create in its turn an independent State. . . .

Actually, of all the Allied agreements on Germany, only one is being carried out today. It is the agreement on the so-called quadripartite status of Berlin. On the basis of that status, the Three Western Powers are ruling the roost in West Berlin, turning it into a kind of state within a state and using it as a center from which to pursue subversive activity against the GDR, the Soviet Union, and the other parties of the Warsaw Treaty. The United States, Great Britain, and France are freely communicating with West Berlin through lines of communication passing through the territory and the airspace of the German Democratic Republic, which they do not even want to recognize. . . .

An obviously absurd situation has thus arisen, in which the Soviet Union seems to be supporting and maintaining favorable conditions for the Western Powers in their activities against the Soviet Union and its Allies under the Warsaw Treaty.

It is obvious that the Soviet Union, just as the other parties to the Warsaw Treaty, cannot tolerate such a situation any longer. . . .

In this connection, the Government of the USSR hereby notifies the United States Government that the Soviet Union regards as null and void the "Protocol of the Agreement between the Governments of the Union of Soviet Socialist Republics, the United States of America, and the United Kingdom on the zones of occupation in Germany and on the administration of Greater Berlin," of September 12, 1944, and the related supplementary agreements, including the agreement on the control machinery in Germany, concluded between the governments of the USSR, the USA, Great Britain, and France on May 1, 1945. . . .

Pursuant to the foregoing and proceeding from the principle of respect for the sovereignty of the German Democratic Republic, the Soviet Government will enter into negotiations with the Government of the GDR at an appropriate time with a view to transferring to the German Democratic Republic the functions temporarily performed by the Soviet authorities by virtue of the above-mentioned Allied agreements and under the agreement between the USSR and the GDR of September 20, 1955. . . .

One cannot of course fail to take into account the fact that the political and economic development of West Berlin during the period of its occupation by the three Western powers has progressed in a different direction from the development of East Berlin and the GDR, as a result of which the way of life in the two parts of Berlin are at the present time entirely different. The Soviet Government considers that when the foreign occupation is ended the population of West Berlin must be granted the right to have whatever way of life it wishes for itself. If the inhabitants of West Berlin desire to preserve the present way of life, based on private capitalistic ownership, that is up to them. The USSR, for its part, would respect any choice of the West Berliners in this matter.

In view of all these considerations, the Soviet Government on its part would consider it possible to solve the West Berlin question at the present time by the conversion of West Berlin into an independent political unit—a free city, without any state, including both existing German states, interfering in its life. Specifically, it might be possible to agree that the territory of the free city be demilitarized and that no armed forces be contained therein. The free city, West Berlin, could have its own government and run its own economic, administrative, and other affairs. . . .

The Soviet Government, guided by a desire to normalize the situation in Berlin in the interest of European peace and in the interest of a peaceful and independent development of Germany, has resolved to effect measures on its part designed to liquidate the occupation regime in Berlin. It hopes that the Government of the USA will show a proper understanding of these motives and make a realistic approach to the Berlin question. . . .

It should also be taken into consideration that the necessity may arise for talks between the municipal authorities of both parts of Berlin and also between the GDR and the FRG to settle any questions that may arise. In view of this, the Soviet Government proposes to make no changes in the present procedure for military traffic of the USA, Great Britain, and France from West Berlin to the FRG for half a year. . . .

If the above-mentioned period is not utilized to reach an adequate agreement, the Soviet Union will then carry out the planned measures through an agreement with the GDR.

Source: FRUS, 1958–60, Berlin, 552–59. Also see U.S. Department of State, *The Soviet Note on Berlin: An Analysis* (Washington: GPO [Publication 6757], 1958).

DOCUMENT 122: President Eisenhower's Perception that Khrushchev's Berlin Gambit Was an "Ultimatum" and "Showdown" to Divide the West (27 November 1958)

On 27 November the State Department received a note from Moscow that seemed to defer any move on Khrushchev's part for six months, during which time negotiations over Berlin should take place. Khrushchev also proposed that West Berlin become a "free city" under the United Nations, and that all occupying powers' military forces withdraw from Berlin.

We discussed the free city concept for a few moments. I would be willing to study the possibility of creating a free city, I said, if it included all of Berlin, East and West; if the avenues to the city from the West were placed also under the jurisdiction of the United Nations, and if the West German government approved. If the proposal applied to West Berlin only, I would have nothing to do with it. At the end of the conversation I asked Foster to urge a four-power conference of Western foreign ministers with a view of concerting the stand which the West would take.

At the conclusion of this conversation, I turned to John [Foster Dulles] and we speculated for a few moments. The immediate crisis was averted. But Khrushchev's latest pronouncement had, nevertheless, the tone of an ultimatum. At the end of six months, on May 27, 1959, to be exact, we presumably would be faced with a far more serious crisis—unless Khrushchev backed down or a solution satisfactory to all interested parties, not yet in sight, could be found. During the interim we could be sure that the Russians would use every weapon in their arsenal to divide the West and to play on the already taut nerves of some of its leaders. There seemed to be no avoiding a showdown because Khrushchev had apparently laid his prestige on the line.

Source: Eisenhower, *Waging Peace*, 333–34.

DOCUMENT 123: Khrushchev Describes Berlin as "a Bone in His Throat" (3 December 1958)

Khrushchev had mentioned Berlin as being thorn in relationships of four powers. He called it a cancer. I [Senator Hubert Humphrey] told him that I hoped USSR understands seriousness of our purpose in Berlin and that our position is firm and fully supported by both political parties and by our people. . . .

He wanted suggestions. "But if you try to talk about German reunification the answer is no. There are two German states and they will have to settle reunification by themselves." He will never agree to liquidation of socialist system in East Germany nor would West agree to liquidation of Federal German Republic and its system, so why should Four Powers use city of Berlin as bargaining point. Berlin ought to stand alone, separate from reunification. He stands for establishment of a free city. . . .

He talked at length about Austrian question and said Soviets had suggested withdrawal of troops and neutrality. He told me at length how Molotov had opposed this and he had responded to Council of Ministers and to Molotov that Russian troops in Austria were only worthwhile if Russia intended to expand westward and he didn't want to do that. He wanted peace, not war, so why troops in Austria? A neutral Austria was established and a source of conflict was removed. . . .

[Khrushchev continued] Some of your military men have made stupid statements lately—statements to effect that US will break through with tanks if East German Republic tries to get in the way. Soviets have tanks too, lots of them, and I warn you we will use them. We have rockets, too, and we don't even have to fire them from East Germany. We can send them from USSR. So don't threaten me by talking about breaking through with tanks. . . .

Khrushchev said "We are prepared to accept anything reasonable, what do you suggest?" I repeated my question, "What will you do to guarantee freedom of city—by this I mean access. We remember blockade of 1948 and airlift, and we don't want to see the city strangled." Khrushchev said we could enter into an agreement to guarantee access registered with UN. . . .

Khrushchev said that if we settle this question of Berlin everything will be better. "It is a bone in my throat."

Source: Meeting of Chairman Khrushchev and Senator Hubert H. Humphrey, in *FRUS, 1958–60, Berlin*, 148–52.

DOCUMENT 124: U.S. Embassy in Moscow Reports that Premier Khrushchev Worried over Intellectuals and Professionals Fleeing from Eastern Bloc (5 December 1958)

In my opinion both Soviet note and Khrushchev's remarks to Senator Humphrey tend to confirm that principal immediate explanation of Soviet action is desire to remove an impediment to further development of Communism in East Germany (and possibly Poland). The Soviets have never shown themselves capable of tolerating any deviation within their system and emphasis of past year in entire Communist Bloc has been toward orthodoxy and away from revisionism. I believe most important element for Soviets is the escape route for refugees. The flight of doctors and intellectuals has shown the difficulties of bringing East Germany into line so long as the Berlin escape route is open.

Khrushchev's long range objective is also clear, that is to absorb Berlin into GDR. Khrushchev has himself stated that our troops in Berlin serve no military purpose and he obviously would like to remove the guarantee they constitute of the continued freedom of West Berlin. I think it fair to state, however, that Khrushchev is also probably genuinely concerned at the threat to peace which could arise over the Berlin problem once Western Germany is fully armed.

Source: Ambassador Thompson to Secretary of State, in *FRUS, 1958–60, Berlin*, 153.

DOCUMENT 125: State Department Memo Expresses Concern that Premier Khrushchev May Lack Any Domestic Option for Flexibility over Berlin (8 December 1958)

Khrushchev probably has some flexibility in his position—he invited us through Senator Humphrey to make counter-proposals, and it would in any case be very un-Russian of him not to begin a maneuver with maximum demands. But a number of signs indicate that Khrushchev may be prepared to push his case to a really dangerous extreme, and therefore that his degree of flexibility is at present gravely short of any point to which contemplated proposals would reach from our side. We therefore seem to face a period in which risk of world war will rise to a very high point, perhaps higher than any so far. . . .

Khrushchev is by far the most "open" character yet to rule the USSR. Communication is more possible with him—on a thoroughly wary basis, of course. Moreover, he continues to show eager interest in communication—giving Humphrey eight hours of his time, for example, and again hinting that he would like to visit the U.S. Conversely, he reacts very negatively to indirect methods of persuasion or pressure, such as our summitry tactics or gestures of military threat—"Don't threaten me," he told Humphrey.

The conclusion to be drawn is that by far our best chance of avoiding war through some kind of acceptable modus vivendi is frank, direct talk with Khrushchev, by the President. Formal talks would hardly serve the purpose, and the effort to plan them would get bogged down in summitry anyway. The best device would be simply to invite Khrushchev over to see America.

Source: Memorandum from George Morgan of Policy Planning Staff to Assistant Secretary of State (Gerald Smith), in *FRUS, 1958–60, Berlin,* 158–59.

DOCUMENT 126: Former High Commissioner for Germany John McCloy Advises the State Department on Berlin Situation (10 December 1958)

After meeting with the former military commander for Germany, General Lucius Clay, McCloy made the following report to the Assistant Secretary of State for European Affairs.

Clay's ideas run something along this line. In the first place we should make up our minds whether or not we are prepared to make any interference with our access to Berlin, including civilian traffic as well as our military, a casus belli. Not only must we make this determination, but we have to state it clearly and at the outset so that the Russians and the world understand it. This is a sine qua non of any attempt to negotiate a satisfactory solution to the Berlin problem. Clay feels very strongly that the Russians will not go to war over Berlin but unless it is made clear that we would, there is no base from which we can negotiate. If this is not our position, he could see no satisfactory intermediate ground we could hold. . . .

At a certain point, Clay feels that it is more a matter of semantics than reality for the West Germans to refuse to deal with the East Germans, although no indication at this time should be given that we would countenance this. West Germany is already dealing with the East Germans on a low level de facto basis and he is inclined to feel that in dealing with East German Communists there may be advantages to be gained through them rather than the Russians.

As for my own views, I am clear that we should give a resounding "no" to Khrushchev's proposals. We should make clear the history which led up to our arrangements in respect to West Germany and Berlin, pointing out the gross distortions of Khrushchev's account, bearing down again on the fact of the German-Russian alliance which Khrushchev ignores in his survey of past history. I would also emphasize that we exchanged a very large part of East Germany for the part we occupy in Berlin. This last point is very strong, I think. We have a right to ask them to withdraw from that part of East Germany which we occupied if they are asking us to withdraw from Berlin.

Source: Letter from John McCloy to Assistant Secretary Merchant, in *FRUS, 1958–60, Berlin*, 164–68.

DOCUMENT 127: Ambassador Bruce's Diary on Use of Threats (10 December 1958)

Fought as usual today for firmness in Berlin. I see no way for the U.S. Government to avoid a decision, to be made known privately to the Soviets, that we are ready to preserve our rights in Berlin by force. This means an ultimate recourse to war, not waged in Berlin but between the US and the USSR. It would be difficult to persuade our allies to adopt such a course, but unless we have the firm intention, if driven to it, to employ force no matter what the risks, we will never in my opinion reach a satisfactory arrangement with the Soviet Government. However we should decide, there should be no publicity or use of threats, but our stand should be conveyed privately to Khrushchev so that at least he would make no miscalculations.

Source: FRUS, 1958–60, Berlin, 171.

DOCUMENT 128: President Eisenhower's National Security Meeting (11 December 1958)

The President called this meeting as the result of learning that the contingency plans currently in effect covering a possible closing of the corridors to Berlin are not adequate. He began the meeting by announcing that we are here to consider the attitude that we will take in the face of the current Berlin situation. . . .

The President agreed that this [State Department contingency plan] message would be all right for discussion purposes with our allies. He then went on to explain some of the difficulties which he visualizes. First of all, the U.S. now finds itself in a different situation from that in which the present agreements were formulated. These agreements came about at a time when all four powers were occupiers, which we no longer are. In the President's view, the U.S. made an error in attempting to control Germany from Berlin, so far behind the Russian lines. But he also recognizes that we now have pledges in the form of two million Germans in West Berlin, and we must stay there for their protection if nothing else. Since the present agreements were formulated, we have recognized West Germany and the Soviets have recognized East Germany. Since we refuse to recognize East Germany, our position with respect to Berlin can best be described as a "can of worms." . . .

General [Maxwell] Taylor proceeded to outline the position of the Joint Chiefs of Staff, to wit, that it is difficult to tell how far we will go ultimately in our use of force. The important thing, in the view of the JCS, is to verify that we have been stopped, not by our own backing down, but by actual use of force on the part of the Soviets. From there we may have to proceed to an airlift as the next step; but this is the least desirable course of action and is regarded as a form of defeat. In short, an attempt on the part of an armed convoy may be regarded as a "reconnaissance in force." Its failure would leave us facing two choices: the use of more force, or the use of an airlift.

The Vice President then posed the question of what Khrushchev is after. Mr. Nixon considers it improbable that Khrushchev is seeking a fight but believes that Khrushchev may be seeking a conference.

On this, Mr. Dulles ventured that Khrushchev is probably looking for a way out at this time. His first motive had been to point up Europe since things in the world had been going rather well for the U.S. (Lebanon and Quemoy).

Mr. Nixon pointed out the parallel between this situation and the Quemoy situation in that the Soviets had stirred up trouble as a device to lure us into a conference. He then asked if the U.S. is willing at this time to have a conference.

Mr. Herter, still referring to the question of Khrushchev's motives, stated the view that Khrushchev had felt a need to bolster East Germany. Many people were making their escape from East Germany through Berlin. A high percentage of these people comprised intellectuals. Mr. Dulles agreed with Mr. Herter, stating that if a free election were held in East Germany, only 10% would vote Communist. . . .

Mr. [Donald] Quarles now brought up the subject of a tack to be used in our approach to the Soviets. He feels that we should emphasize the rights of the two million people of West Berlin rather than the military rights of the occupying powers.

Source: FRUS, 1958–60, Berlin, 172–77.

DOCUMENT 129: Foreign Ministers' Communiqué Reaffirms Quadripartite Responsibilities in Berlin (Paris, 14 December 1958)

The Foreign Ministers of France, the United Kingdom and the United States once more reaffirmed the determination of their governments to maintain their position and their rights with respect to Berlin including the right of free access.

They found unacceptable a unilateral repudiation by the Soviet Government of its obligations to the Governments of France, the United Kingdom and the United States in relation to their presence in Berlin and the freedom of access to that city or the substitution of the German authorities of the Soviet Zone for the Soviet Government insofar as those rights are concerned.

After further discussion of the Soviet notes of November 27, 1958 the four Foreign Ministers found themselves in agreement on the basic issues to be dealt with in the replies to those notes. They will consult with their allies in the NATO Council, following which the four governments will formulate their replies.

Source: U.S. Department of State, *Documents on Germany, 1944–1985,* 559.

DOCUMENT 130: North Atlantic Council Denies the USSR's Right to Unilaterally Renounce Responsibility for Free Access to Berlin (Paris, 16 December 1958)

1. The North Atlantic Council examined the question of Berlin.

2. The Council declares that no state has the right to withdraw unilaterally from its international engagements. It considers that the denunciation by the Soviet Union of the interallied agreements on Berlin can in no way deprive the other parties of their rights or relieve the Soviet Union of its obligations. Such methods destroy the mutual confidence between nations which is one of the foundations of peace.

3. The Council fully associates itself with the views expressed on the subject by the Governments of the United States, the United Kingdom, France and the Federal Republic of Germany in their statement of 14th December.

4. The demands expressed by the Soviet Government have created a serious situation which must be faced with determination. . . .

6. The Council considers that the Berlin question can only be settled in the framework of an agreement with the U.S.S.R. on Germany as a whole. It recalls that the western powers have repeatedly declared themselves ready to examine this problem, as well as those of European security and disarmament. They are still ready to discuss all these problems.

Source: U.S. Department of State, *Documents on Germany, 1944–1985,* 560.

DOCUMENT 131: President Eisenhower Recalls Drafting the American Response to Soviets' 27 November Note (11–31 December 1958)

On December 11, immediately following the regularly scheduled meeting of the National Security Council, I asked the Vice President and a dozen others to come into my office. Before the meeting I had been informed by Foster Dulles that certain assumptions or attitudes about Berlin on which our previous planning had been based had turned out to be obsolete or invalid. For example, the State Department had thought it possible that when Khrushchev announced his intention of turning over controls of access routes to the East Germans the West should simply announce its intention to treat the East Germans as the "agents" of the Soviets. There were precedents for dealing with unrecognized Communist governments on specific problems. In Korea we had negotiated with the North Koreans and the Chinese Communists; in Indochina we had sat at the table with the North Vietnamese; indeed, in Germany, East Germans had administered transportation, utility, and other systems with our tacit approval on the assumption that they were responsible to the Soviets. Now, however, Khrushchev's belligerent message of November 27 left no doubt in anyone's mind that the East Germans would act in their own right, officially at least, once control of facilities should be turned over to them.

This position surprised me. Until that meeting, I said, I had not been aware that our petty dealings with the East Germans had become, by any distorted interpretation, a basis for virtual recognition of East Germany. I had no difficulty in rejecting the State Department's proposed "agent" expedient. An individual could be treated as an agent; a nation could not. However, I was troubled that up to this time we had always justified our position in Berlin solely on our rights as "conquerors." After all, we had recognized the Federal Republic of Germany (West Germany) as a sovereign nation four years before, and she had joined the North Atlantic Treaty Organization. The soundest basis for our remaining in Berlin, I felt, was our solemn obligation expressed to the two million Germans of West Berlin and to the entire world to stand by a city that had freely chosen to stay with the West and the cause of freedom. If our word to them would be broken, then no one in the world could have confidence in any pledge we made.

Source: Eisenhower, *Waging Peace*, 336–38.

DOCUMENT 132: U.S. Diplomatic Note to USSR on Status of Berlin (31 December 1958)

The agreements made by the Four Powers cannot be considered obsolete because the Soviet Union has already obtained the full advantage therefrom and now wishes to deprive the other parties of their compensating advantages. These agreements are binding upon all of the signatories so long as they have not been replaced by others following free negotiations.

Insofar as the Potsdam Agreement is concerned, the status of Berlin does not depend upon that agreement. Moreover, it is the Soviet Union that bears responsibility for the fact that the Potsdam Agreement could not be implemented. . . .

The United States Government cannot prevent the Soviet Government from announcing the termination of its own authority in the quadripartite regime in the sector which it occupies in the city of Berlin. On the other hand, the Government of the United States will not and does not, in any way, accept a unilateral denunciation of the accords of 1944 and 1945; nor is it prepared to relieve the Soviet Union from the obligations which it assumed in June 1949. Such action on the part of the Soviet Government would have no legal basis, since the agreements can only be terminated by mutual consent. The Government of the United States will continue to hold the Soviet Government directly responsible for the discharge of its obligations undertaken with respect to Berlin under existing agreements. . . .

The continued protection of the freedom of more than two million people of West Berlin is a right and responsibility solemnly accepted by the Three Western Powers. . . . The rights of the Three Powers to remain in Berlin with unhindered communications by surface and air between that city and the Federal Republic of Germany are under existing conditions essential to the discharge of that right and responsibility. Hence the proposal for a so-called 'free city' for West Berlin as put forward by the Soviet Union, is unacceptable.

Source: U.S. Department of State, *Documents on Germany, 1944–1985,* 573–76.

DOCUMENT 133: Excerpt from President Eisenhower's State of the Union Address (9 January 1959)

We cannot build peace through desire alone. Moreover, we have learned the bitter lesson that international agreements, historically considered by us as sacred, are regarded in Communist doctrine and in practice to be mere scraps of paper. The most recent proof of their disdain of international obligations, solemnly undertaken, is their announced intention to abandon their responsibilities respecting Berlin.

As a consequence, we can have no confidence in any treaty to which Communists are a party except where such a treaty provides within itself for self-enforcing mechanisms. Indeed, the demonstrated disregard of the Communists of their own pledges is one of the greatest obstacles to success in substituting the Rule of Law for rule by force.

Source: Public Papers of the Presidents, Dwight D. Eisenhower, 1959 (Washington: GPO, 1965), 327.

DOCUMENT 134: President Eisenhower's Conference with His Advisers (29 January 1959)

In late January President Eisenhower called a meeting of Defense and State Department officials to discuss developments in Berlin. On the question of the Soviet desire to turn control of Berlin access over to the East Germans, he reaffirmed the U.S. demand that the USSR observe its obligations.

The central point was that all rights the allies had in Berlin were brought about by agreement with the Soviet government, not with the puppets they had installed in a fragmented part of Germany. There would be no way in which we could hold the East Germans responsible for carrying out Soviet promises made years before. Chris Herter supplied what I thought was an apt phrase: Acquiescence in the substitution of East German officials for Soviets at a checkpoint would "simply start us down a slippery slope toward East German control of everything."

To show the Soviets that we meant business, the Chiefs of Staff were instructed to send sufficient replacements to Europe to fill out the rosters of all our military units, both combat and support. This routine movement of replacements would be done quietly but quickly; it was certain that the Soviets would detect the movements and probably interpret them correctly as evidence of our determination.

One disagreement at this meeting was between Foster Dulles and the Joint Chiefs of Staff. The Joint Chiefs believed that the United States should be prepared to go into action with a fairly substantial force—one division—on the day the first truck convoy should be stopped. Foster objected: world opinion, he argued, would not be sufficiently mobilized on May 27 to permit the immediate use of a force this size.

I tended to side with Foster, but for different reasons. One division was far too weak to fight its way through to Berlin and far more than necessary to be a mere "show of force" or evidence of determination. The deployment of an entire division would be played up in the press and would put the pressure on the Soviets to "Put up or shut up." Such a move could be regarded, elsewhere, as aggression. . . .

Once action was called for, the move would obviously have to be swift; delay could only confirm to the Soviets and to the world that we had accepted the new status quo.

The plan, as I approved it at the meeting, included these steps: (a) A refusal to acquiesce in any substitution of East Germans for Soviet officials in checking the Western occupying powers' movement to and from Berlin. (While it would be permissible to show an East German official a pass for identification purposes, such official would not be permitted to stamp a pass); (b) A decision to begin quiet military preparations in West Germany and Berlin prior to May 27, sufficient to be detected by Soviet intelligence but not sufficient to create public alarm; (c) Should there be any substitution of East German officials for Soviets, a small convoy with armed protection would attempt to go through, and if this convoy were stopped, the effect would be discontinued and the probe would fire only if fired upon; (d) Transit would then be suspended and pressure would be brought to bear on the Soviets by publicizing the blockade and taking the matter to the United Nations Security Council and, if necessary, to the General Assembly. In these circumstances our further military preparations would be intensified by observable means such as the evacuation of dependents from West Berlin and possibly from all Germany; (e) in the event that this moral and other pressure was not sufficient, use of additional force would be subject to governmental decision; (f) We would at once attempt to bring about a foreign ministers' meeting with the Soviet Union to be held about the middle of April.

Source: Eisenhower, *Waging Peace*, 340–41.

DOCUMENT 135: American Note Accepting Soviet Proposal for a Foreign Ministers Meeting on Germany-Berlin (16 February 1959)

The position of the Western Powers . . . has been made clear in their note of December 31. They have no choice but to declare again that they reserve the right to uphold by appropriate means their communications with their sectors of Berlin. . . .

The United States Government is prepared to participate in a conference of the Ministers of Foreign Affairs of the USSR, France, the United Kingdom, and the United States, and is ready to consider any suggestions as to a date and place, which would be fixed by mutual agreement. The place and date should be settled th[rough] diplomatic channels.

The conference should deal with the problem of Germany in all its aspects and implications as raised in the recent exchange of notes. . . .

It is suggested that German advisers should be invited to the conference and should be consulted.

Source: U.S. Note to the USSR Proposing a Foreign Ministers Meeting on Germany, February 16, 1959, in U.S. Department of State, *Documents on Germany, 1944–1985*, 607–8.

DOCUMENT 136: British Prime Minister Harold Macmillan's "Voyage of Discovery" to Moscow for Talks with Khrushchev Concerning Tension over Berlin (25 February 1959)

[Khrushchev] pretended not to be able to understand what the West wanted of the Soviet Government. He had advanced certain proposals about Germany. We had advanced none. Our last note of 16 February was not a reply to his note—it had no connection except a reference to the date. . . .

After saying this in a solemn way, he added that the Soviet Government were prepared for negotiation at any time. This repeated accusation of the allied desire to 'preserve the state of war' was, as he well knew, the common jargon which it suited the Russians to use in the complicated situation which followed the occupation and division of Berlin. By a curious paradox the freedom of West Berlin was and is still maintained by a nominal state of war, or at any rate the absence of a peace treaty with the whole of Germany. The Russian plan would involve the surrender of the people of West Berlin and their ultimate absorption into a Communist society.

In the course of a long discussion in which Selwyn Lloyd and Gromyko now took a leading part, one or two interesting points emerged. The Foreign Secretary pointed out that it was of no military advantage to us to maintain our garrisons in West Berlin. On the contrary they were somewhat of a liability. He had asked Mr. Gromyko why the Berlin situation worried the Soviet Government so much, and Mr. Gromyko had referred to our espionage organisations in West Berlin which he said numbered more than one hundred. Khrushchev intervened in an excited way and said that West Berlin was a Western base on the territory of a Soviet ally.

Source: Harold Macmillan, *Riding the Storm, 1956–1959* (New York: Harper and Row, 1971), 607–14.

DOCUMENT 137: President Eisenhower Meets with Congressional Leaders (6 March 1959)

With the country so concerned, I thought it was advisable to hold a conference with the legislative leaders of both parties. On the morning of March 6, 1959, I met with a few of them, along with some of my closest advisers. The value of this meeting was so obvious to all of us that I held another later that evening with broader congressional representation. These meetings, held in ordinary times as well as when the nation approached an emergency, often brought out the best in men. Their concerns reflected the concerns of our people; their sense of national interest could transcend party. This did not mean that such sessions were easy-going, rubber-stamp get-togethers. On the contrary, the quality of brisk give and take was among their finest features.

These encounters also revealed something about the character and interests of the legislators. Sam Rayburn, for example, was always anxious to make certain that the United States would do everything possible to negotiate. Senator Lyndon Johnson, on the other hand, appeared to be anxious to be able to take some action, visible to the world, to indicate we had—or the Senate had—strengthened our Armed Forces.

I assured Speaker Rayburn that we would not go to war because of rigidity in attitude and emphasized the recent exchange of notes in which

we kept the chances for negotiation open. To Lyndon Johnson, I reiterated my confidence in the nation's military power. In fact, I said, "If we were to release our nuclear stockpile on the Soviet Union, the main danger would arise not from retaliation but from fallout in the earth's atmosphere." . . .

The recurring question was the seeming contradiction between our plans, made much earlier, for reductions in the size of our Armed Forces and our need to be prepared to defend West Berlin. "The Soviets are engaged in confronting the United States with a series of crises," I said. "The United States has the need for an efficient military system. But it has to be realized that if we program for the sum total of all recommendations for increasing military strength, the mounting burden would call for full mobilization," putting our country on a wartime footing. I said that we could not have ground forces to match those that the Soviets could mobilize in middle Europe.

Source: Eisenhower, *Waging Peace*, 347–48.

DOCUMENT 138: President Eisenhower's Radio-TV Address on Berlin (16 March 1959)

My Fellow Americans, tonight I want to talk with you about two subjects:

One is about a city that lies four thousand miles away.

It is West Berlin. In a turbulent world it has been, for a decade, a symbol of freedom. But recently its name has come to symbolize, also, the efforts of Imperialistic Communism to divide the free world, to throw us off balance and to weaken our will for making certain of our collective security.

Next, I shall talk to you about the state of our nation's posture of defense and the free world's capacity to meet the challenges that the Soviets incessantly pose to peace and to our own security.

First, West Berlin. . . . Last November, the Soviets announced that they intended to repudiate these solemn obligations. They once more appear to be living by the Communist formula that "Promises are like pie crusts, made to be broken." . . .

Now a matter of principle—the United States cannot accept the asserted right of any government to break, by itself, solemn agreements to which we, with others, are parties. But in the Berlin situation, both free people and principle are at stake. . . .

The risk of war is minimized if we stand firm. War would become more likely if we gave way and encouraged a rule of terrorism rather than a rule of law and order. Indeed, this is the core of the peace policy which we are striving to carry out around the world. . . .

Now our final choice is negotiation, even while we continue to provide for our security against every threat. We are seeking meaningful negotiation at this moment. The United States and its allies stand ready to talk with Soviet representatives at any time and under any circumstances which offer prospects of worth-while results. . . .

Our position, then, is this: We will not retreat one inch from our duty. We shall continue to exercise our right of peaceful passage to and from West Berlin. We will not be the first to breach the peace; it is the Soviets who threaten the use of force to interfere with such free passage. We are ready to participate fully in every sincere effort at negotiation that will respect the existing rights of all and their opportunity to live in peace.

Source: President Eisenhower's Report on Berlin and Security in the Free World, March 16, 1959, in U.S. Department of State, *Documents on Germany, 1944–1985,* 611–15.

DOCUMENT 139: President Eisenhower's Effort to Provide Khrushchev with "a Remarkable Diplomatic Retreat" (27 May 1959)

During the following sixteen weeks, Premier Khrushchev executed a remarkable diplomatic retreat. So skillful and subtle was each step backward that its significance was hardly noticed and for this reason the retreat, although absolute, caused scarcely any loss in Khrushchev's public standing. The Western governments deliberately encouraged this evolution. . . .

Khrushchev. . . . seemed to be showing signs of amenability. True, the Communists had held up a Western convoy for over two days, after it had proceeded from Berlin to the very door of Western Germany, and Khrushchev was still boasting of his missile strength. However, at the meeting of the 21st Congress of the Communist Party, he had expressed the desire for an early end to the cold war and, surprisingly, had invited me to make a visit to the Soviet Union, claiming that I would be received with "heartfelt hospitality." In addition we were getting high-level Soviet hints of a possible postponement of the May 27 Berlin deadline.

Source: Eisenhower, *Waging Peace,* 342–43.

DOCUMENT 140: Following Their "Kitchen Debate" in Moscow, Vice President Richard Nixon and Chairman Khrushchev Discuss East-West Tension (July 1959)

In July 1959 Vice President Richard Nixon visited Moscow with an American trade show and held informal discussions with the Soviet leadership. In a rare joint appearance before a live television audience, Vice President Nixon and Premier Khrushchev debated the underlying principles of their opposing economic systems. Vice President Nixon later recalled his private discussion with the Soviet leader.

For the last two hours of our discussion we [discussed] the German problem. I pointed out that it was the Soviet proposal to sign a separate peace treaty with East Germany that was creating the present crisis.... I emphasized repeatedly that the vital interests of both our countries were involved in the Berlin and German problems and that neither side should confront the other with an impossible situation.

Ambassador [Llewellyn] Thompson, upon my suggestion that he outline the details of the Western proposals for a Berlin solution, declared that if the Soviets pushed the situation to a crisis, it would be hard to reconcile this with their words about peace. For the first and only time that afternoon, Khrushchev seemed to have a burst of temper and raised his voice. The Ambassador should be careful when using the word peace, he warned; what he had said sounded like a threat. The Soviet Union would sign a peace treaty and the West could declare war if it wished.

Source: Richard M. Nixon, *Six Crises* (Garden City, N.Y.: Doubleday, 1962), 268–69.

DOCUMENT 141: Four Power (Britain, France, USSR, and U.S.) Communiqué Agreeing to a Negotiated Settlement of Situation in Germany and Berlin (5 August 1959)

The Conference of Foreign Ministers met in Geneva from May 11 to June 20 and from July 13 to August 5, 1959 [and] considered questions relating to Germany, including a peace treaty with Germany and the question of Berlin.

The positions of the participants in the Conference were set out on these questions.

A frank and comprehensive discussion took place on the Berlin question.

The positions of both sides on certain points became closer.

The discussions which have taken place will be useful for the further negotiations which are necessary in order to reach an agreement.

Furthermore the Conference provided the opportunity for useful exchanges of views on other questions of mutual interest.

The Foreign Ministers have agreed to report the results of the Conference to their respective governments.

The date and place for the resumption of the work of the Conference will be settled through diplomatic channels.

Source: Communiqué of Foreign Ministers Meeting, Geneva, August 5, 1959, in U.S. Department of State, *Documents on Germany, 1944–1985*, 683.

The Berlin Crisis of 1961

KENNEDY-KHRUSHCHEV

DOCUMENT 142: Presidential Adviser Charles Bohlen's Memoirs on the Vienna Summit Between Soviet Chairman Khrushchev and President Kennedy (3–4 June 1961)

On 3 June 1961 President Kennedy met Premier Khrushchev in Vienna at the residence of the American Ambassador to Austria. Charles Bohlen, one of the State Department's foremost Soviet specialists, was along as an adviser and later recalled the Kennedy-Khrushchev Vienna Summit meetings.

After the first session, Kennedy was a little depressed. He had not been able to get Khrushchev to understand that the new American government was seeking a détente based on a realistic balance of power in the world. I told the President there had been no hardening of Soviet policy. The Soviets always talk tough.

There were only two days of meetings in Vienna, involving not more than four or five hours of talks. Kennedy did most of the talking for our side, and Khrushchev for the Russians. Occasionally, Rusk or Gromyko would interject a thought. The rest of us listened. . . .

The results of the discussions were meager. There was an agreement to hold a conference on Laos, which gratified the President. . . . On Germany and Berlin, there was no progress at Vienna. Khrushchev emphasized his intention to sign, in December, a peace treaty with East Germany—an act he had been threatening since 1958—turning over to the satellite the responsibility of dealing with Allied access rights to Berlin. Kennedy argued, but got nowhere. . . .

Whatever the effect on Khrushchev, the Vienna talks had a lasting impact on the President. For weeks thereafter, he commented to his associates on Khrushchev's remarks. . . . He read and reread the [Summit's transcript] sections on Berlin. I believe that the Vienna talks conditioned the President for the crises on Berlin and Cuba that were soon to follow.

Source: Charles E. Bohlen, *Witness to History, 1929–1969* (New York: Norton, 1973), 480–83.

DOCUMENT 143: Secretary of State Dean Rusk Recalls President Kennedy's Prediction of "a Very Cold Winter" Following the Vienna Summit (3–4 June 1961)

At the summit Khrushchev began with a long ideological screed about communism and the inevitability of the world revolution. When he got through, Kennedy said to him, "Well, Mr. Chairman, you're not going to make a communist out of me and I'm not going to make a capitalist out of you, so let's get down to business."

But once the two did get down to business, they made some headway on Laos and set some guidelines that helped us establish the Laos accords of 1962. However, when the discussion turned to Berlin, the conversation became very rough. At one point Khrushchev said to Kennedy, "We are going to negotiate a new agreement with East Germany, and the access routes to Berlin will be under their control. If there is any effort by the West to interfere, there will be war."

Diplomats almost never use the word "war"; they always talk about "gravest possible consequences" or something like that. But Kennedy went right back at him, looked him in the eye, and said, "Then there will be war, Mr. Chairman. It's going to be a very cold winter."

Clearly at the Vienna summit, held only two months after the Bay of Pigs fiasco, Khrushchev set out to intimidate this new, young president of the United States. The experience sobered and shook Kennedy. He stood head to head with Khrushchev in their verbal duel, but for the first time he felt the full weight of Soviet pressure and ideology. It was a brutal moment, and Kennedy was clearly startled that Khrushchev would try to roll over an American president. What bothered Kennedy even more than the Berlin issue itself was that Khrushchev would even make such an attempt.

Khrushchev also presented us with a formal aide-mémoire setting December 1961 as the deadline for a peace treaty. If one were not signed by then, the Russians would go forward on their own. But how serious were the Russians? My own belief was that if the Soviets went public with their demands, they were deadly serious, and on June 10 my worst fears were confirmed: The Soviets published the aide-mémoire.

Source: Dean Rusk, *As I Saw It* (New York: Norton, 1990), 220–21.

DOCUMENT 144: Aide-Mémoire from Soviets to President Kennedy Proposing "Peace Treaty" with Germany and "Free City" of West Berlin (4 June 1961)

1. The years-long delay in arriving at a peace settlement with Germany has largely predetermined the dangerous course of events in Europe in the postwar period. . . .

2. The Soviet Government is earnestly striving towards removing the sources of tension between the United States and the USSR. . . . The conclusion of a German peace treaty would allow the two countries to come much closer to the attainment of this goal. . . .

3. Proceeding from a realistic evaluation of the situation, the Soviet Government stands for the immediate conclusion of a peace treaty with Germany. . . . The point is who will conclude it and when, and whether this will entail unnecessary costs. . . .

4. In the interests of achieving agreement on a peace treaty the Soviet Union does not insist on the immediate withdrawal of the FRG from NATO. Both German states could for a certain period, even after the conclusion of a peace treaty, remain in the military alliances to which they now belong. . . .

5. The conclusion of a German peace treaty would also solve the problem of normalizing the situation in West Berlin. Deprived of a stable international status, West Berlin at present is a place where the Bonn revanchist circles continually maintain extreme tension and organize all kinds of provocations very dangerous to the cause of peace. . . .

At present, the Soviet Government does not see a better way to solve the West Berlin problem than by transforming it into a demilitarized free city. The implementation of the proposal to turn West Berlin into a free city, with the interests of all parties duly taken into consideration, would normalize the situation in West Berlin. The occupation regime now being maintained has already outlived itself and has lost all connection with the purposes for which it was established, as well as with the Allied agreements concerning Germany that established the basis for its existence. The occupation rights will naturally be terminated upon the conclusion of a German peace treaty, whether it is signed with both German States or only with the German Democratic Republic, within whose territory West Berlin is located.

All this considered, the settlement of the West Berlin problem should naturally take into account the necessity of respecting and strictly observing the sovereign rights of the German Democratic Republic, which, as is well known, has declared its readiness to adhere to such an agreement and respect it.

6. The Soviet Government proposes that a peace conference be called immediately, without delay, that a German peace treaty be concluded, and that the problem of West Berlin as a free city be solved in this way....

To avoid delaying a peace settlement it is essential to fix a time limit within which the Germans should seek possible ways for agreement on problems within their internal competence. The Soviet Government considers that not more than six months are needed for such negotiations....

7. The Soviet Government is prepared to consider any constructive proposals of the United States Government on a German peace treaty and on normalizing the situation in West Berlin.... But if the United States does not show that it realizes the necessity of concluding a peace treaty, we shall deplore it because we shall be obliged to sign a peace treaty, which it would be impossible and dangerous to delay, not with all the States but only with those that wish to sign it.

Source: Chairman Khrushchev's Aide-Mémoire to President Kennedy at Vienna Summit, 4 June 1961, in U.S. Department of State, *Documents on Germany, 1944–1985,* 729–32.

DOCUMENT 145: Secretary Rusk Recalls Drafting the State Department's Reply to Soviets' Aide-Mémoire (Mid-June 1961)

We now had a real crisis on our hands, and we spent much of the rest of June preparing a detailed U.S. and Western position on Berlin. No one favored conceding anything to the Soviets, but we differed on how to approach the issue. Dean Acheson, whom we called for advice, advocated a building up of NATO and U.S. nuclear and conventional forces to demonstrate Western resolve. He also wanted an allied ground probe along the autobahns if the Soviets tried to cut off access. Adlai Stevenson wanted a buildup of NATO and U.S. nuclear and conventional forces to defend our rights in Berlin, but he also wanted progress on resolving other Berlin issues. My own position, supported by Bob McNamara and our outside consultant Henry Kissinger, was to talk the question to death. I saw nothing that we could negotiate. We already had a Berlin policy, and it had stood firm for fifteen years. It was the Russians who wanted a new policy, who wanted to change the status quo. The Berlin problem could not be solved in my view, but neither did I want it to deteriorate into war. I also advocated passing the problem on to the United Nations.

When we returned to Washington after the Vienna summit, we drafted a specific response to Khrushchev's aide-mémoire and within a week or ten days at most delivered it from the State Department to the White House.

Source: Rusk, *As I Saw It*, 221–22.

DOCUMENT 146: Presidential Adviser Arthur Schlesinger, Jr., Notes the Debate Stirred in the Kennedy Administration over the "Hawkish" Acheson Memorandum on Berlin (July 1961)

Three weeks after the Vienna Summit former Secretary of State Dean Acheson penned a memorandum for the Kennedy White House with the basic thesis that West Berlin was not a problem but a pretext. Khrushchev's démarche had nothing to do with Berlin, Germany, or Europe. Acheson's "hawkish memo" emphasized that Khrushchev was primarily interested in testing the new administration's will to resist; according to Acheson, Khrushchev hoped that by making Kennedy back down on a sacred commitment, he could shatter American power and prestige. To Acheson, Vienna was a simple conflict of wills, and until Khrushchev learned otherwise, any effort to negotiate the Berlin issue would be fruitless. Since there was nothing for the United States to negotiate, any American willingness to go to the conference table would be taken in Moscow as evidence of weakness and only make the crisis worse.

Khrushchev had only dared precipitate the crisis, Acheson continued, because his fear of nuclear war had declined. Our problem was to convince him that this complacency was misplaced and that we would, in fact, go to nuclear war rather than abandon the status quo. This called for the build-up—prompt, serious and quiet—of both our conventional and nuclear forces. If Khrushchev signed his treaty with East Germany, we should not quibble about this or about changes in access procedures. But, the moment there was interruption of access itself, we must act: first an airlift—and then, if that could not be sustained against Soviet counter-measures, a ground probe in force too large to be stopped by East German troops alone. Acheson cited a joint Chiefs of Staff estimate that two Allied divisions could hold out indefinitely inside East Germany against an enemy of three or four divisions. The point would be, not to defeat the communist forces in the field, but to persuade Moscow that we had the resolve to go on, if necessary, to nuclear war. There was a substantial chance, Acheson said, that the necessary military prepara-tions would by themselves cause Khrushchev to alter his purpose; but he added frankly that there was also a substantial possibility that nuclear war might result. . . .

The first phase of the Berlin debate was under way. . . .

On 5 July Schlesinger received a visit from Georgi Kornienko of the Soviet Embassy who expressed his puzzlement over the American at-titude toward Berlin. The Russian diplomat seemed to be searching for a chance to get off a collison course with the West over the Berlin situation. Concerned that the Acheson policy of "talk tough" was too restrictive and too similar to the arguments that got Kennedy involved in the April 1961 fiasco in Cuba's Bay of Pigs, in his own memo of 6 July Schlesinger suggested another course to President Kennedy that became the "soft" approach.

The Cuban fiasco, [my] memorandum suggested, had resulted in large part from the "excessive concentration [in our advance planning] on mil-itary and operational problems and the wholly inadequate consideration of political issues. This error seems likely to be repeated here." The Ach-eson paper was excellent in analyzing the issues of last resort; it told us what we could fall back on when other alternatives were used up. But, if it were permitted to define our Berlin choices, there could be no sys-tematic effort to bring these alternatives to the surface. . . .

[My] memorandum concluded by mentioning another Cuban resem-blance—the tendency to define the issue, "to put it crudely, as: Are you chicken or not? When someone proposes something which seems tough, hard, put-up-or-shut-up, it is difficult to oppose it without seeming soft, idealistic, mushy, etc. Yet, as Chip Bohlen has often said, nothing would clarify more the discussion of policy toward the Soviet Union than the elimination of the words 'hard' and 'soft' from the language. People who had doubts about Cuba suppressed those doubts lest they seem 'soft.' It is obviously important that such fears not constrain free discussion of Berlin.''

Source: Arthur M. Schlesinger, Jr., A Thousand Days: John F. Kennedy in the White House (Boston: Houghton Mifflin, 1965), 380–88.

DOCUMENT 147: Soviet Defector Colonel Oleg Penkovsky Provides Information to the West on Khrushchev's Plans and Soviet Nuclear Capabilities (July 1961)

The defection of Soviet General Staff Officer for Intelligence (GRU) Colonel Oleg Penkovsky was of paramount importance to Western leaders in the summer of 1961. With the dangers of nuclear war inherent in the Berlin crisis, the information he provided to British and American intelligence agencies checked out and gave senior American officials a unique insight into Khrushchev's plans and capabilities. On 18 July, Penkovsky underwent his eighteenth debriefing, but his first debriefing by a joint American-British team, at a safe apartment near London.

Berlin was the burning issue. The CIA debriefer, George Kisevalter, asked Penkovsky a series of questions on Soviet strategy. Penkovsky's answers were sent to President Kennedy by Director Allen Dulles.

Colonel Penkovsky here recalls a comment he had heard from fellow General Staff Officer General Sergei Sergeyevitch Varentsov. This view, Penkovsky asserted, was shared by many officers of the Soviet General Staff.

We are definitely embarking on a risky action. Khrushchev is prepared to support the original clash with considerable reinforcements by tank forces. But he does not want the war to spread further. He realizes that the NATO powers have strong nuclear capabilities, but he is relying on the assumption that they would not use nuclear weapons in the first phases of such a conflict. If Khrushchev had such capabilities, his concept would be to launch an all-out initial smashing blow, but he does not have this.... The people do not want to fight for anything in East Germany.

The CIA debriefer then inquired whether or not the Soviet Union was ready for nuclear war.

They are not ready. Khrushchev's statements about this are all bluff, but he is preparing as fast as possible. Our officers do not want an atomic war. Local atomic strikes are possible since they have enough nuclear weapons to spit with, but insofar as blanketing important military centers or concentration points, they do not have the capability. . . .

> Kisevalter then asked Penkovsky to describe any new developments in the Soviet position since his last report in June.

The Soviet situation is as follows: first of all if it were possible [for the NATO allies] to deploy a huge army on a wide front, using only conventional weapons and no rockets with atomic warheads, there would probably be mass Soviet troop defections to our side [the West]. . . .

We [the West] should react with firmness if he [Khrushchev] blocks the access roads to Berlin. Those [Soviet] blocking forces should be smashed. This should be done without striking with atomic bombs at industrial centers or rear areas. Should Khrushchev attempt to do this [blockade Berlin], he should be repaid in kind and the whole world told that the West is protecting its vital interests, which Khrushchev trampled upon in violation of the Potsdam Agreement. If he expands the conflict to some degree, then he should be answered with corresponding counterblows. Actually Khrushchev and the Soviet Army at this time are unprepared.

Source: Jerrold L. Schecter and Peter S. Deriabin, "CIA Debriefing #18 of Colonel Penkovsky, July 18–19, 1961," in *The Spy Who Saved the World: How a Soviet Colonel Changed the Course of the Cold War* (New York: Charles Scribner's Sons, 1992), 205–9.

DOCUMENT 148: "The Penkovskiy Papers" and Their Insight on Soviet Military Preparedness and Khrushchev's Rhetorical Bluff on Berlin (July 1961)

Khrushchev will not consider the fact that our Army is not ready for a major war. [General Sergei] Varentsov says that we have no confidence in our state of readiness, that we are taking a great risk. Certainly we are training our troops, keeping them in combat readiness every moment, but we are not certain that we are ready in all respects.

. . . During the Berlin crisis [1958–1959] the entire Central Committee visited factories and plants, especially those involved with defense production. The city of Moscow was empty. Everyone had gone out on Khrushchev's orders. . . . All these representatives of the Central Committee visited factories and plants, appealing to the workers to work better and produce more. This happens not only during a crisis, it goes on all the time. It was especially noticeable during the Berlin crisis.

Khrushchev does not want a world war because he knows he cannot win it; but he will keep on trying to instigate various local conflicts. But if he feels that he can win in a specific place, such as in Berlin, and thus in a way slap down the U.S., England, and to some extent France, he might order a general attack, hoping that the West and the NATO countries will get into a squabble and split. Recently even the General Staff has begun to agree with Khrushchev's concept of delivering a sudden lightning strike, as Hitler used to do. The General Staff believes that there are advantages in such an attack, particularly if a mass missile strike is used, and right now they are preparing strenuously for this. The General Staff considers that if it is impossible to strike at all the targets at once, it is at least possible to hit the United States and England first, cause a split in the NATO alliance, and then pick up the pieces without a general war.

The Western leaders should have a secret meeting, without Khrushchev, and quickly decide what to do. It is urgent that the leaders of all the Western states meet to work out a firm, common line. A summit meeting should not be called; Khrushchev would attend such a meeting with pleasure in order to increase his prestige and authority. He will again try to steer any summit conference in his direction, using his propaganda of peaceful coexistence and disarmament.

The West has already won a small victory in the Berlin matter. Khrushchev began to write notes and talk about new negotiations. But this is an old story. This shows that the Western leaders acted wisely. This is the only correct way. He should be treated the same way in the future. Of course, he will continue to make long speeches about peaceful coexistence and disarmament, he may even lower his voice at the conference in order to be believed. Actually he is holding a rock inside his fist and keeping his powder dry.

I always wonder: Why does the West trust Khrushchev? It is difficult to understand. We in the GRU [Directorate of Intelligence for Soviet General Staff] sit around, talk, and laugh: What fools, they believed us again! Of course, the West must talk with Khrushchev, but it must maintain a firm policy. Do not retreat a single step from a firm policy, let Khrushchev know that the time of listening to his military psychosis has come to an end. Under no circumstances give any concessions to Khrushchev. He only gains time and by this prolongs his existence. If the West again makes even the smallest concession to Khrushchev, he will scream loudly about his power and will proclaim to the entire world: "See how powerful I am." . . .

Khrushchev has now become confused on the Berlin matter, particularly because he has realized that the West is firm there. He would like to pursue a hard policy and rattle his saber, but our country suffers from a great many shortages and difficulties which must be eliminated before the West is to be frightened further. Khrushchev will not scream so loudly if he feels that the West is holding a hard line in all directions. . . .

In 1961 the Soviet government was very unpleasantly surprised by the publication of Mr. Kennedy's statement regarding the three-billion-dollar increase in the military budget. This made a very strong impression. Good for him! That kicked them in the teeth! The Soviet High Command, moreover, is certain that the Western powers have still other secret funds (the Soviet Army has always had such funds) so they were sure that the budget was actually increased not by three but by six or nine billion dollars.

Our General Staff also knows that our nuclear weapons and plants are poorly hidden and camouflaged. The General Staff does not want a large-scale nuclear war, but it sometimes supports Khrushchev simply to please him, to curry his favor.

Our leaders proclaim loudly that our equipment is better, that we have more weapons in our arsenals, and that everything in the West is inferior. If this is indeed so, why do not the Western governments take urgent measures to improve their defense and increase their military forces? That is the elementary dialectic of survival. After all, they are responsible for the lives of their people! Every medium must be put to use—newspapers, radio, television; it must be demonstrated to the world where is truth and where is falsehood. It is Khrushchev, the Central Committee CPSU, and the Soviet government, together with the General Staff, who are responsible for the continuation of the cold war. . . .

The essence of Khrushchev's policy is to frighten the whole world with his missiles. As soon as a problem arises, or a hot spot develops, Khrushchev immediately begins to talk about missiles.

Source: Oleg Penkovskiy, *The Penkovskiy Papers*, translated by Peter Deriabin (Garden City, N.Y.: Doubleday, 1965), 214–20.

THE BERLIN WALL

DOCUMENT 149: Nikita Khrushchev Remembers the Berlin Crisis of 1961 (1974)

Walter Ulbricht and our other comrades in the GDR were facing serious troubles directly stemming from the ambiguous status of West Berlin. Berlin was an open city, which posed two problems: First, there was the problem of people crossing from East Berlin into West Berlin. The GDR had to cope with an enemy who was economically very powerful and therefore very appealing to the GDR's own citizens. West Germany was all the more enticing to East Germans because they all spoke the same language. An East German with adequate professional qualifications had no difficulty finding a job if he moved to West Germany. The resulting drain of workers was creating a simply disastrous situation in the GDR, which was already suffering from a shortage of manual labor, not to mention specialized labor. If things had continued like this much longer, I don't know what would have happened. I spent a great deal of time trying to think of a way out. . . .

The second problem was the problem of the West Berliners' easy access to East Berlin. Residents of West Berlin could cross freely into East Berlin, where they took advantage of all sorts of communal services like barbershops and so on. Because prices were much lower in East Berlin, West Berliners were also buying up all sorts of products which were in wide demand—products like meat, animal oil, and other food items, and the GDR was losing millions of marks. . . .

The GDR's economic problems were considerably relieved by the establishment of border control between East and West Berlin. Comrade Ulbricht himself told me that the economy of the GDR immediately began to improve after the establishment of border control. The demand for food products in East Berlin went down because West Berliners were no longer able to shop there. This meant that the limited supply of consumer products was available exclusively to the citizens of East Berlin.

Furthermore, the establishment of border control in Berlin had a very positive effect on the consciousness of the people. It strengthened them and reminded them that the task of building Socialism was a challenge of solid and lasting importance, dwarfing the temporary phenomenon of West German propaganda which had been used to tempt East Germans over to the side of capitalism. The establishment of border control restored order and discipline in the East Germans' lives (and Germans have always appreciated discipline). Seeing that their government had reasserted control over its own frontiers, the East Germans were heartened by the solidification and fortification of their state.

Source: Khrushchev, *Khrushchev Remembers*, 454–56.

DOCUMENT 150: Secretary Rusk's Reaction and Response to the Wall (August 1961)

On 13 August the East Germans began to build a barricade and to string barbed wire between East and West Berlin, the first step in what eventually became the Berlin Wall. This move caught American poli-cymakers by surprise, but it was quickly learned that the East Germans built the Berlin Wall to keep their own people in and not to keep anyone out. It was a startling demonstration of the nature of a paranoid communist regime.

We quickly decided that the wall was not an issue of war and peace between East and West; there was no way we would destroy the human race over it. By and large, even though we often thought their actions despicable, what Eastern European regimes did to their own people was not an issue of war and peace between East and West. So we did not seriously consider knocking the wall down. Had we done so, either we would have had an immediate confrontation with Soviet forces or they simply would have moved the wall back fifty or one hundred yards and started again. How far into East Germany would we go to keep knocking down walls? Some of our critics wanted us to threaten general war over the wall, but if you take that first step by military means, then you must think of the second, third, and fourth steps.

Source: Rusk, *As I Saw It*, 223–24.

DOCUMENT 151: Secretary Rusk Remarks that Germans "Voted with Their Feet" to Flee Communism in East Germany (13 August 1961)

The authorities in East Berlin and East Germany have taken severe measures to deny to their own people access to West Berlin. These mea-sures have doubtless been prompted by the increased flow of refugees in recent weeks. The refugees are not responding to persuasion or prop-aganda from the West but to the failures of communism in East Ger-many. These failures have created great pressures upon communist leaders who, in turn, are trying to solve their own problems by the dan-gerous course of threats against the freedom and safety of West Berlin. The resulting tension has itself stimulated flights from the East.

Having denied the collective right of self determination to the peoples of East Germany, communist authorities are now denying the right of individuals to elect a world of free choice rather than a world of coercion. The pretense that communism desires only peaceful competition is ex-posed; the refugees, more than half of whom are less than 25 years of age, have "voted with their feet" on whether communism is the wave of the future.

Available information indicates that measures taken thus far are aimed at residents of East Berlin and East Germany and not at the allied position in West Berlin or access thereto. However, limitation on travel within Berlin is a violation of the four-power status of Berlin and a flagrant violation of the right of free circulation throughout the city.

Source: Statement by Secretary of State Dean Rusk, 13 August 1961, in U.S. Department of State, *Documents on Germany, 1944–1985*, 776.

DOCUMENT 152: President Kennedy's Memorandum on the American Response to the Berlin Wall (14 August 1961)

1. What steps will we take this week to exploit politically propaganda-wise the Soviet-East German cut-off of the border?
2. This seems to me to show how hollow is the phrase "free city" and how despised is the East German government, which the Soviet Union seeks to make respectable.
3. The question we must decide is how far we should push this. It offers us a very good propaganda stick which if the situation were reversed would be well used in beating us. It seems to me this requires decisions at the highest level.

Source: Memo from President Kennedy to Secretary of State Rusk, August 14, 1961, in U.S. Department of State, *Foreign Relations of the United States, 1961–1963*, Vol. 14, *Berlin Crisis, 1961–1962* (Washington: GPO, 1993), 332.

DOCUMENT 153: State Department's Berlin Steering Group Reacts to the Berlin Wall (15 August 1961)

Turning to the immediate situation in Berlin, the Secretary of State asked [Deputy Assistant Secretary of State Loy] Kohler to summarize recent developments. Mr. Kohler described the progress which had been made through the Secretary's statement, the delivery of the protest of the three Western Commandants in Berlin, and preparation of a protest for delivery in Moscow. The Secretary of State noted that while the border closing was a most serious matter, the probability was that in realistic terms it would make a Berlin settlement easier. Our immediate problem is the sense of outrage in Berlin and Germany which carries with it a feeling that we should do more than merely protest. It was not easy to know just what else we should do.

In the following discussion it was generally agreed that economic countermeasures would be inappropriate; either they would be much too trivial to count, like withholding Western participation in the Leipzig Fair, or they might set in train a chain of challenges and responses which might affect our own deepest interest, and that of economic and human access to West Berlin.

Similar objections applied not only to such a course as general interruption of travel by East Germans to the West, but suspension of Temporary Travel documents. Moreover, it looks as if the new fence between East and West Berlin is there to stay, and we do not want to reply with temporary and incommensurate reprisals.

The one step for which there was substantial support in the group was the possibility of reinforcements of the West Berlin Garrison. There was no general agreement; and the Secretary of Defense indicated a specific reservation on the ground that such steps, taken as a gesture, were not desirable. His own inclination was to consider some reduction in U.S. military dependents abroad.

The discussion then turned to psychological measures and propaganda. Since it was agreed that, in the words of the Secretary of State, "we must keep shooting issues and non-shooting issues separate", and since it was further agreed that the closing of the border was not a shooting issue, the problem was essentially one of propaganda. We should reap a large harvest on this front. The Attorney General particularly pressed for a new and stronger organization of our efforts in this area; and it was agreed that there would be a special meeting on this subject at 6 P.M.

Source: Minutes of the Berlin Steering Group, August 15, 1961, in *FRUS, 1961–1963*, Vol. 14, *Berlin Crisis, 1961–1962*, 333–34.

DOCUMENT 154: American Note to USSR Condemning the Berlin Wall (17 August 1961)

On August 13, East German authorities put into effect several measures regulating movement at the boundary of the western sectors and the Soviet sector of the city of Berlin. These measures have the effect of limiting, to a degree approaching complete prohibition, passage from the

Soviet sector to the western sectors of the city. These measures were accompanied by the closing of the sector boundary by a sizable deployment of police forces and by military detachments brought into Berlin for this purpose.

All this is a flagrant, and particularly serious, violation of the quadripartite status of Berlin. Freedom of movement with respect to Berlin was reaffirmed by the quadripartite agreement of New York of May 4, 1949, and by the decision taken at Paris on June 20, 1949, by the Council of the Ministers of Foreign Affairs of the Four Powers. The United States Government has never accepted that limitations can be imposed on freedom of movement within Berlin. The boundary between the Soviet sector and the western sectors of Berlin is not a state frontier. The United States Government considers that the measures which the East German authorities have taken are illegal. It reiterates that it does not accept the pretension that the Soviet sector of Berlin forms a part of the so-called "German Democratic Republic" and that Berlin is situated on its territory. Such a pretension is in itself a violation of the solemnly pledged word of the U.S.S.R. in the Agreement on the Zones of Occupation in Germany and the administration of Greater Berlin. Moreover, the United States Government cannot admit the right of the East German authorities to authorize their armed forces to enter the Soviet sector of Berlin. . . .

The United States Government solemnly protests against the measures referred to above, for which it holds the Soviet Government responsible. The United States Government expects the Soviet Government to put an end to these illegal measures. This unilateral infringement of the quadripartite status of Berlin can only increase existing tension and dangers.

Source: U.S. Note to USSR Protesting Violation of the Quadripartite Status of Berlin, 17 August 1961, in U.S. Department of State, *Documents on Germany, 1944–1985*, 777–78.

DOCUMENT 155: Presidential Adviser Reports on Vice President Lyndon Johnson's Trip to Berlin and Reinforcement of the Berlin Garrison (17–19 August 1961)

President Kennedy immediately condemned the erection of the wall as a Soviet violation of agreements over the status of Berlin. He also decided to send Vice President Lyndon Johnson to Berlin for a brief visit to lift the morale of the Germans. President Kennedy also sent General Lucius Clay and diplomat Charles Bohlen to accompany the vice president. Clay, who had been the commander of the armed forces and the American High Commissioner for Germany at the time of the Berlin blockade, was a hero to the people of Berlin and thus a good choice for the trip. They arrived in Bonn on 18 August.

During our flight, General Clay said that if he had still been in command of American forces in Berlin, he would have ordered his troops to tear down the barricades and barbed wire that the East Germans had put up. . . . Johnson did not reply to Clay's statement. The Vice-President was much more of a listener than an asserter of policy on the trip, even though he was the senior American figure present. He asked my advice so often I felt flattered, and he was careful to make no mistakes.

Our Air Force Constellation [plane] arrived in Berlin at 5 P.M. The ride from Tempelhof Airport to City Hall was a triumphant procession. A half million people lined the streets to greet Johnson, and 250,000 cheered him at a rally at the City Hall. . . . While the Vice-President visited a refugee center, General Clay and Alan Lightner, the American political representative in Berlin . . . and I took an auto tour of East Berlin. Our military car was not stopped once. We saw East German soldiers on almost every corner and a dozen Soviet T-34 tanks, their engines running, at a square.

I wrote in my report to Secretary Rusk [that] the Vice President's visit and the arrival of the reinforcements "dramatized to the people of Berlin, American determination and will" to stay in the beleaguered city. The two events were a "complete and unqualified success." But, I added, "what is not so certain is the lasting effects." I asserted that Washington had underestimated the "profound" reaction of West Germans to the erection of the wall. I listed these factors in reaching that conclusion:

1. The fact that the East German regime, generally held in contempt by the West Berliners, had been permitted to carry out the action. If the sealing off had been done by Soviet troops, there would, of course, have been resentment, but it would have been accepted by the West Berliners as an illegal, but nonetheless more tolerable, action undertaken by one of the occupying powers.

2. There seemed to be a rather widespread feeling among West Berlin officials, shared in large measure by our representatives there, that our failure to react immediately and definitely in some manner, generally undefined, in the face of the East German action had increased Communist confidence to a point where further piecemeal restrictions and harassments were to be expected. There was a tendency to mix up the fact that the measure was taken because of the refugee flow with some idea that it was part of a calculated series of moves by the Communists.

3. Initially, there had been a great questioning of the willingness and

determination of the Allies to protect West Berlin and Allied rights in the future. The visit and the reinforcements went far to offset this feeling. We should recognize that the visit itself and the reaffirmation by the Vice-President in such circumstances increased, in the popular mind, American commitment to Berlin and might possibly be the subject of some overt interpretation.

I made only one specific recommendation:

> ... that we be prepared to react swiftly and decisively and, indeed, to overreact, if necessary, to any clear signs of harassment or any attempts by the Communists to erode our rights, and especially in regard to access (which includes the communications between West Berlin and the Federal Republic). Any hesitancy or delay in our reaction to any such attempts would rapidly cast the morale of the West Berliners back to the depths where it was immediately after August 13, and prior to the Vice President's visit.

Source: Bohlen, *Witness to History*, 483–86.

DOCUMENT 156: President Kennedy's Memo to Secretary of State Rusk (28 August 1961)

I should like to have a meeting of the Berlin Steering Group this week to go over the status of our Berlin contingency planning, in order to see what has been quadripartitely agreed and what is still under discussion. Are there any gaps in our planning which need to be covered? I am particularly interested in knowing what we are doing with regard to the following situations:

a. Interference with the civil air traffic into Berlin. This is very much in my mind.

b. Contingencies arising from the partitioning of Berlin (for example, conflicts between the West Berlin population and the East German police).

c. The extension of Live Oak planning [nuclear weapons] to take into account a greater reliance on conventional forces.

d. Actions to be taken in the case of an East German revolt.

Source: President Kennedy's Memo to Secretary of State Rusk, August 28, 1961, in *FRUS, 1961–1963*, Vol. 14, *Berlin Crisis, 1961–1962*, 379.

DOCUMENT 157: Secretary Rusk's Negotiations with British Foreign Minister Douglas-Home and Soviet Foreign Minister Gromyko (September–October 1961)

Despite [the] French and German hesitancy to talk, we and the British felt that we ought at least to meet with the Soviets. After all, Khrushchev had issued an ultimatum. We were operating against a deadline. Although we could not see any basis whatsoever for a fresh agreement on Berlin in the face of Russian demands, British Foreign Minister Alec Douglas-Home and I decided that we could talk just as long and just as repetitively as Gromyko. We may have surprised Gromyko—he wasn't used to Western long-windedness—but we just talked and talked. We repeated ourselves and made the same arguments over and over again. We even began to refer to our different positions by numbers; we'd say to Gromyko, "That is argument number four. Should we go over it or should we just pass on to another subject?" Even in this stale exercise we were taking some of the steam out of the crisis.

Source: Rusk, *As I Saw It*, 225–26.

DOCUMENT 158: Secretary Rusk Remembers His Discussions with Foreign Minister Gromyko and Ambassador Anatoly Dobrynin and Khrushchev's "Squeeze" Metaphor (1962–1963)

Soviet harassment of Western access to Berlin, particularly air traffic, began again in February 1962, but the Soviets still evidenced a desire to talk. From March 11 to 27 I talked almost daily with Andrei Gromyko at the Eighteen-Nation Disarmament Conference in Geneva. We accomplished nothing, but neither did the situation worsen; again, our long talks may have helped defuse the crisis. Shortly before I left Geneva, Gromyko suggested that the new Soviet ambassador to the United States, Anatoly Dobrynin, continue the discussions. Dobrynin and I discussed Berlin from mid-April to late May, and I must say I became rather good at saying the same thing over and over in different ways.

Berlin continued percolating and may have been a precipitating factor behind the Soviet decision to install missiles in Cuba later in 1962. And on occasion a sense of crisis returned. As late as September 1963 Soviet forces harassed the American military's access to Berlin on the autobahn, over the issue of tailgate inspections. To me, issues involving Berlin have always reminded me of the dance of the gooney birds on Wake Island— much posturing on both sides. Each event is loaded with symbolism, and issues such as the height of the tailgates on trucks and whether or not we would lower them for Soviet guards took on absurd political significance. We were as much concerned that the Soviets might try to nibble us to death with minor incidents—known as slicing the salami— as we were with more dramatic actions. After all, it was Khrushchev who said, "Berlin is the testicles of the West. Every time I want to make the West scream, I squeeze on Berlin." That was far too apt a metaphor.

Source: Rusk, *As I Saw It*, 225–27.

DOCUMENT 159: Circular Telegram from Secretary Rusk to All U.S. Embassies on Possible Link of Cuban Missile Crisis to Tension over Berlin (24 October 1962)

Policy. Unless you perceive objection, you should seek early occasion to complain to Foreign Minister or other appropriate official how this Government has viewed Soviet policy with respect to Cuban crisis.

Beginning in middle of summer, there were a number of indications that Khrushchev and Soviet Government had concluded there was no possibility Soviet Union could obtain its objectives with respect to Berlin through negotiation. There were also indications that Khrushchev felt too personally committed to achievement of his objectives in Berlin to retreat, as well as indications that factors which were pushing Soviet Government to a resolution of this problem were increasing (situation in East Germany, Communist Chinese pressure, etc.) and that Soviet Union had decided showdown on Berlin problem was inevitable within some months. There were also indications that Soviet Government and Khrushchev personally had developed doubts as to whether they could win in a showdown and that alternatives might be either an ignominious retreat or nuclear war.

Soviet Government privately and later publicly stated that while it would insist upon conclusive discussion of Berlin problem in relatively short period, it would not do so until after American Congressional elections. It maintained this position even though it was made clear to them that so far as US Government concerned, elections had no bearing on the problem.

A number of assurances were given by Soviet Government both privately and publicly that it would not arm Cuba with offensive weapons. This was not merely dialectical discussion but specific assurance against weapons that could reach the US. TASS statement of September 11 said that Soviet Union had no need to take such action. This statement, which was largely concerned with Cuban situation, related it to question of German peace treaty and other international problems.

When Gromyko saw President October 18, he made standard but strong statement about Berlin and German peace treaty issues and then made following statements about Cuba: Soviet assistance to Cuba "pursued solely the purpose of contributing to the defense capabilities of Cuba"; that "training by Soviet specialists of Cuban nationals in handling defensive armaments was by no means offensive" and that "if it were otherwise, the Soviet Government would have never become involved in rendering such assistance."

Khrushchev indicated to Ambassador [to the UN] Kohleri that he had virtually decided to come to UN meeting in New York latter part of November and Gromyko in his conversation with President confirmed this, although no specific date was set.

When Soviet action in arming Cuba with offensive nuclear missiles became evident, it was because of developments set forth above that this Government tended believe Soviet action was probably primarily geared to showdown on Berlin, intended to be timed with Khrushchev's arrival in US and completion of installation of these missiles in Cuba.

Addressees may discreetly use general line foregoing and particularly substance Gromyko's statement to President on Berlin on October 18, in background talks with foreign correspondents.

FYI. Purpose of this message is to improve understanding that any Berlin crisis will be due to Soviet action. In point of fact, Cuban crisis may well have effect of improving overall position of West in Berlin through clear-cut evidence of our resolution.

Source: State Department Circular Telegram to Certain Diplomatic Missions. October 24, 1962, in *FRUS, 1961–1963*, Vol. 15, *Berlin Crisis, 1962–1963* (Washington: GPO, 1994), 397–99.

DOCUMENT 160: Presidential Adviser Clark Clifford Makes a Connection Between the Superpower Tension over Berlin and the Cuban Missile Crisis (1961–1962)

[T]here was a particularly tragic aspect of the [Berlin Wall] affair: the CIA's best agent in the Soviet Union, Colonel Oleg Penkovsky, learned of the decision on August 9, but either failed or was unable to notify his handlers in the West. He was later caught and executed by the KGB after sending information concerning the next, and greatest, crisis in East-West relations . . . the Cuban Missile Crisis.

Source: Clark Clifford with Richard Holbrooke, *Counsel to the President: A Memoir* (New York: Random House, 1991), 356.

DOCUMENT 161: Nikita Khrushchev Recalls "Unpleasant Incidents" at the Berlin Wall (1974)

There were illegal attempts to cross over to the West, resulting in some incidents along the border, some of them with unpleasant outcome. Such unpleasantness had to be expected. Border guards were forced to use the means which had been put at their disposal to prevent violation of the border. The incidents were exploited by the West and blown completely out of proportion. . . .

We would introduce as much freedom as the material conditions would permit, but naturally under the dictatorship of the working class there can be no such thing as absolute freedom. As for other countries which brag about all their freedoms, if we analyze their societies carefully, we'll find that they have no such thing as absolute freedom either. In order to feel moral constraint, moral oppression, or moral bondage, a man must have a highly developed and highly refined conception of what human freedom is all about. Most people still measure their own freedom or lack of freedom in terms of how much meat, how many potatoes, or what kind of boots they can get for one ruble.

Source: Khrushchev, *Khrushchev Remembers*, 457–58.

DOCUMENT 162: President Kennedy's "ich bin ein Berliner" ["I Am a Berliner"] Speech at the Rudolph Wilde Platz in Berlin (26 June 1963)

On 26 June 1963, President Kennedy arrived in Berlin with retired General Lucius Clay to commemorate the fifteenth anniversary of the Berlin airlift. Before departing for Berlin, Robert Kennedy had suggested to the president that he say something to the West Berliners in German.

As *Air Force One* was flying into Berlin, McGeorge Bundy scribbled some phrases in German for the president. President Kennedy delivered a short speech that sunny afternoon on a raised platform in front of West Berlin's City Hall. A million roaring West Berliners had jammed onto Rudolph Wilde Platz that day and became energized by the "handsome and virile" American president and his words of encouragement. The speech was the first time President Kennedy had publicly denounced the Berlin Wall and would be remembered as one of his personal favorites. With the end of the Cold War and reunification of Germany some twenty-five years later, the speech also became one of his most visionary.

Two thousand years ago the proudest boast was *"civis Romanus sum."* Today, in the world of freedom, the proudest boast is *"ich bin ein Berliner!"*

There are many people in the world who really don't understand, or say they don't, what is the great issue between the free world and the Communist world. Let them come to Berlin! There are some who say that communism is the wave of the future. Let them come to Berlin! And there are some who say in Europe and elsewhere we can work with the Communists. Let them come to Berlin! And there are even a few who say that it is true that communism is an evil system, but it permits us to make economic progress. *Lass' sie nach Berlin kommen!* Let them come to Berlin!

Freedom has many difficulties and democracy is not perfect, but we have never had to put a wall up to keep our people in, to prevent them from leaving us. . . . I know of no town, no city, that has been besieged for 18 years that still lives with the vitality and the force, and the hope and the determination of the city of West Berlin. While the wall is the most obvious and vivid demonstration of the failures of the Communist system, for all the world to see, we take no satisfaction in it, for it is, as your Mayor [Willy Brandt] has said, an offense not only against history but an offense against humanity, separating families, dividing husbands and wives and brothers and sisters, and dividing a people who wish to be joined together.

What is true of this city is true of Germany—real, lasting peace in Europe can never be assured as long as one German out of four is denied the elementary right of free men, and that is to make a free choice. In 18 years of peace and good faith, this generation of Germans has earned the right to be free, including the right to unite their families and their nation in lasting peace, with good will to all people. You live in a defended island of freedom, but your life is part of the main. So let me ask you, as I close, to lift your eyes beyond the dangers of today, to the hopes of tomorrow, beyond the freedom merely of this city of Berlin, or your country of Germany, to the advance of freedom everywhere, beyond the wall to the day of peace with justice, beyond yourselves and ourselves to all mankind.

Freedom is indivisible, and when one man is enslaved, all are not free. When all are free, then we can look forward to that day when this city will be joined as one and this country and this great Continent of Europe in a peaceful and hopeful globe. When that day finally comes, as it will, the people of West Berlin can take sober satisfaction in the fact that they were in the front lines for almost two decades.

All free men, wherever they may live, are citizens of Berlin, and, therefore, as a free man, I take pride in the words *"ich bin ein Berliner!"*

Source: Public Papers of the Presidents, John F. Kennedy, 1963 (Washington: GPO, 1964), 524–25.

FURTHER READING

Dobrynin, Anatoly. *In Confidence: Moscow's Ambassador to America's Six Cold War Presidents* (1995).

Hanrieder, Wolfram F. *Germany, America, Europe: Forty Years of German Foreign Policy* (1989).

Harper, John L. *American Visions of Europe: Roosevelt, Kennan, and Acheson* (1995).

Immerman, Richard H., ed. *John Foster Dulles and the Diplomacy of the Cold War* (1990).

Kaplan, Lawrence S., and R. W. Clawson, eds. *NATO after Thirty Years* (1985).

Mayers, David. *The Ambassadors and America's Soviet Policy* (1995).

Preussen, Ronald W. *John Foster Dulles* (1982).

Schwartz, Thomas. *America's Germany* (1991).

Shick, Jack M. *The Berlin Crisis, 1958–62* (1972).

Slusser, Robert M. *The Berlin Crisis of 1961* (1973).

Smith, Jean Edward. *The Defense of Berlin* (1963).

Zelikow, Philip, and Condoleezza Rice. *Germany Unified and Europe Transformed: A Study in Statecraft* (1995).

Part V

The Cuban Missile Crisis, October 1962

The Cuban missile crisis began in April 1962 when Soviet Premier Nikita Khrushchev decided to place nuclear medium- and intermediate-range ballistic missiles in Cuba. He probably made his decision for three primary reasons: to respond to the existence of American missiles in Turkey aimed at the Soviet Union, to redress the Soviets' enormous inferiority in intercontinental ballistic missiles (in 1961 the United States possessed about seventy of these missiles to roughly six for the Soviets), and to counter a possible American invasion of the Caribbean island—the latter suggested by the failed CIA-sponsored Bay of Pigs invasion of April 1961 and by U.S. contingency plans (for such a purpose) developed in the fall of 1961. After confirming the missiles' existence with aerial reconnaissance photographs taken on 14 October 1962, President John F. Kennedy acted promptly to confront this bold Soviet military initiative because he saw the missiles as a challenge to the national security of the United States, to its international credibility, and to his own political future at home.

Kennedy's initial move was to put together a team of advisers, the Executive Committee of the National Security Council (Ex Comm), to consider American options. Resisting strong pressure from the military members of this group for an air strike and invasion, the president ultimately accepted his advisers' proposal for a naval blockade of Cuba, and on October 22 went on national television to announce that American naval warships would prevent the delivery of any additional offensive weapons to Cuba. This brought an immediate showdown with the Soviet Union, whose ships were moving rapidly toward the blockade line. Both sides went to a high state of military alert, and international tension grew as nuclear war seemed a distinct possibility. "The smell of burning," Khrushchev said, "hung in the air." Civilization, in fact, hung in the balance.

Soviet ships did not run the blockade. The crisis ended on 28 October when President Kennedy agreed to accept a Soviet proposal to withdraw the missiles under United Nations supervision, in return for an American pledge not to invade Cuba. A corollary agreement provided for American removal of its outdated Jupiter missiles from Turkey (a step it planned to take anyway) after the crisis ended.

Recent disclosures indicate that the crisis was even more dangerous than policymakers and the public thought at the time. Revelations from former Soviet officials indicate that in the fall of 1962 the Soviets had 42,000 military personnel in Cuba rather than the 12,000–16,000 that American officials assessed to be there, that the twenty-four 1,020 nautical-mile missiles were loaded with nuclear warheads, and, most important, that the Soviets had given their forces in Cuba six tactical rocket launchers and nine tactical nuclear warheads to use in the event of an American invasion. These latter missiles, it has also been learned, could have been fired at the discretion of the Soviet commander in Cuba. What this suggests is that if President Kennedy had gone ahead with an air strike followed by an invasion, as urged by his hawkish advisers, American troops would have been killed in massive numbers by Soviet nuclear weapons, and the United States almost certainly would have responded with a nuclear attack on the Soviet Union.

CHRONOLOGY

1959

January 1. Castro overthrows Batista regime in Cuba

October. Turkey agrees to U.S. deployment of nuclear missiles

1960

February. Castro signs economic pact with Soviet Union

May 1. Soviets shoot down American U-2 and capture pilot

May 7. USSR and Cuba establish diplomatic relations

November. Kennedy elected president

1961

April 17. Bay of Pigs invasion with CIA assistance

June 3–4. Vienna Summit between Kennedy and Khrushchev

August 13. Berlin Wall erected

October 21. Sec. Gilpatric's speech on Soviet nuclear bluff

November. "Operation Mongoose" plans to overthrow Castro

1962

March. Soviets initiate Operation Anadyr

June. Penkovsky debriefings on Soviet nuclear preparedness

August. USSR-Cuba draft agreement of military cooperation

October 14. U-2 photos disclose Soviet MRBM/IRBMs in Cuba

October 16–28. Cuban missile crisis' "Thirteen Days"

October 16. First secret session of Ex Comm to advise Kennedy

October 22. Kennedy's radio-TV address to the nation

October 25. Ambassador Stevenson's speech at the UN

October 26–27. Khrushchev's two letters regarding "deal"

October 27. Robert Kennedy meets with Ambassador Dobrynin

October 28. Khrushchev agrees to remove missiles from Cuba

October 28. Kennedy pledges not to invade Cuba

October 26–31. Khrushchev-Castro correspondence

November 20. Kennedy lifts "quarantine" against Cuba

1963

June. Kennedy's détente address at American University

July. Limited Test Ban Treaty between U.S. and USSR

November 1. South Vietnam's President Diem assassinated

November 22. Kennedy assassinated; Johnson becomes president

1992

January. Oral History Conference in Havana on missile crisis

NUCLEAR BRINKSMANSHIP

The following documents address the issue of Khrushchev's motives and expectations in placing missiles in Cuba. One factor might have been a rational recognition by the Soviet leadership of their strategic inferiority to the United States in intercontinental ballistic missiles. Another motive was probable concern that the United States was preparing to destroy Fidel Castro's Cuban Revolution and deprive the Soviets of a valuable, strategically located client state.

DOCUMENT 163: National Security Adviser McGeorge Bundy Comments on Deputy Secretary of Defense Roswell Gilpatric's Speech Designed to Expose the Soviets' Pretension to Nuclear Superiority (October 1961)

McGEORGE BUNDY: In reality, there never was a missile gap, and by the fall of 1961 the new American administration had full confidence in its strategic strength. The decisive American exposure of Khrushchev's fraudulent pretension to superiority came on October 21, 1961, in a speech delivered to the Business Council by Deputy Secretary of Defense Roswell Gilpatric. Gilpatric's speech was his own, in the sense that he himself put the argument together, with staff help inside the Pentagon. But it was also an administration statement, encouraged by the president, and Gilpatric reviewed his text in advance in separate face-to-face meetings with Rusk, with McNamara, and with me. . . .

Here is an excerpt from Deputy Secretary Gilpatric's speech to which Bundy refers.

Our confidence in our ability to deter Communist action, or resist Communist blackmail, is based upon a sober appreciation of the relative military power of the two sides. We doubt that the Soviet leadership has in fact any less realistic views, although this may not be always apparent from their extravagant claims. While the Soviets use rigid security as a military weapon, their Iron Curtain is not so impenetrable as to force us to accept at face value the Kremlin's boasts.

The fact is that this nation has a nuclear retaliatory force of such lethal power that an enemy move which brought it into play would be an act of self-destruction on his part. The U.S. has today hundreds of manned intercontinental bombers capable of reaching the Soviet Union, including 600 heavy bombers and many more medium bombers equally capable of intercontinental operations because of our highly developed in-flight refueling techniques and world-wide base structure. The U.S. also has 6 *POLARIS* submarines at sea carrying a total of 96 missiles, and dozens of intercontinental ballistic missiles. Our carrier strike forces and land-based theater forces could deliver additional hundreds of megatons. The total number of our nuclear delivery vehicles, tactical as well as strategic, is in the tens of thousands; and of course, we have more than one warhead for each vehicle.

Our forces are so deployed and protected that a sneak attack could not effectively disarm us. The destructive power which the United States could bring to bear even after a Soviet surprise attack upon our forces would be as great as—perhaps greater than—the total undamaged force which the enemy can threaten to launch against the United States in a first strike. In short, we have a second strike capability which is at least as extensive as what the Soviets can deliver by striking first.

Source: McGeorge Bundy, *Danger and Survival: Choices about the Bomb in the First Fifty Years* (New York: Random House, 1988), 381; Gilpatric's speech in United States Arms Control and Disarmament Agency, *Documents on Disarmament, 1961* (Washington: GPO, 1962), 544–45.

DOCUMENT 164: Robert Kennedy's "The Cuba Project" with Plan for Operation Mongoose to Overthrow the Regime of Fidel Castro (20 February 1962)

The Goal. In keeping with the spirit of the Presidential memorandum of 30 November 1961, the United States will help the people of Cuba overthrow the Communist regime from within Cuba and institute a new government with which the United States can live in peace. . . .

Time is running against us. The Cuban people feel helpless and are losing hope fast. They need symbols of inside resistance and of outside interest soon. They need something they can join with the hope of starting to work surely towards overthrowing the regime. Since late November, we have been working hard to re-orient the operational concepts within the U.S. government and to develop the hard intelligence and operational assets required for success in our task.

The next National Intelligence Estimate on Cuba (NIE 85-62) promises to be a useful document dealing with our practical needs and with due recognition of the sparsity of hard facts. The needs of the Cuba project, as it goes into operation, plus the increasing U.S. capability for intelligence collection, should permit more frequent estimates for our guidance. These will be prepared on a periodic basis.

Premise of Action. Americans once ran a successful revolution. It was run from within, and succeeded because there was timely and strong political, economic, and military help by nations outside who supported our cause. Using this same concept of revolution from within, we must now help the Cuban people to stamp out tyranny and gain their liberty.

On 18 January, the Chief of Operations [Brig. General Edward Lansdale] assigned thirty-two tasks to Departments and Agencies of the U.S. government, in order to provide a realistic assessment and preparation of U.S. capabilities. The Attorney General [Robert Kennedy] and the Special Group were apprised of this action. The answers received on 15 February provided the basis for planning a realistic course of action. The answers also revealed that the course of action must contain continuing coordination and firm overall guidance.

The course of action set forth herein is realistic within present operational estimates and intelligence. Actually, it represents the maximum target timing which the operational people jointly considered feasible. It aims for a revolt which can take place in Cuba by October 1962. It is a series of target actions and dates, not a rigid time-table. The target dates are timed as follows:

Phase 1, *Action*, March 1962. Start moving in.

Phase 2, *Build-up*, April-July 1962. Activating the necessary operations inside Cuba for revolution and concurrently applying the vital political, economic, and military-type support from outside Cuba.

Phase 3, *Readiness*, 1 August 1962. Check for final policy decision.

Phase 4, *Resistance*, August–September 1962. Move into guerrilla operations.

Phase 5, *Revolt*, first two weeks of October 1962. Open revolt and overthrow of Communist regime.

Phase 6, *Final*, during month of October 1962. Establishment of new government.

Plan of Action. Attached is an operational plan for the overthrow of the Communist regime in Cuba, by Cubans from within Cuba, with outside help from the U.S. and elsewhere. Since this is an operation to prompt and support a revolt by the people in a Communist police state, flexibility is a must for success. Decisions on operational flexibility rest with the Chief of Operations, with consultation in the Special Group when policy matters are involved. . . .

Early Policy Decisions. The operational plan for clandestine U.S. support of a Cuban movement inside Cuba to overthrow the Communist regime is within policy limits already set by the President. A vital decision, still to be made, is on the use of open U.S. force to aid the Cuban people in their liberty. If conditions and assets permitting a revolt are achieved in Cuba, and if U.S. help is required to sustain this condition, will the U.S. respond promptly with military force to aid the Cuban revolt? The contingencies under which such military deployment would be needed, and recommended U.S. responses, are detailed in a memorandum being prepared by the Secretaries of State and of Defense. An early decision is required, prior to deep involvement of the Cubans in this program.

Source: Laurence Chang and Peter Kornbluh, eds., *The Cuban Missile Crisis, 1962: A National Security Archive Documents Reader* (New York: The New Press, 1992), 23–25.

DOCUMENT 165: Nikita Khrushchev's Objective to Defend Cuba from U.S. Invasion (Spring 1962)

The fate of Cuba and the maintenance of Soviet prestige in that part of the world preoccupied me even when I was busy conducting the affairs of state in Moscow and traveling to the other fraternal countries.

While I was on an official visit to Bulgaria, for instance, one thought kept hammering away at my brain: what will happen if we lose Cuba? I knew it would have been a terrible blow to Marxism-Leninism. It would gravely diminish our stature throughout the world, but especially in Latin America. If Cuba fell, other Latin American countries would reject us, claiming that for all our might the Soviet Union hadn't been able to do anything for Cuba except to make empty protests to the United Nations. We had to think up some way of confronting America with more than words. We had to establish a tangible and effective deterrent to American interference in the Caribbean. But what exactly? The logical answer was missiles. The United States had already surrounded the Soviet Union with its own bomber bases and missiles. We knew that American missiles were aimed against us in Turkey and Italy, to say nothing of West Germany. Our vital industrial centers were directly threatened by planes armed with atomic bombs and guided missiles tipped with nuclear warheads. As Chairman of the Council of Ministers, I found myself in the difficult position of having to decide on a course of action which would answer the American threat but which would also avoid war. Any fool can start a war, and once he's done so, even the wisest of men are helpless to stop it especially if it's a nuclear war.

It was during my visit to Bulgaria [14–20 May 1962] that I had the idea of installing missiles with nuclear warheads in Cuba without letting the United States find out they were there until it was too late to do anything about them. I knew that first we'd have to talk to Castro and explain our strategy to him in order to get the agreement of the Cuban government.

Source: Nikita S. Khrushchev, *Khrushchev Remembers: The Last Testament*, translated by Strobe Talbott (Boston: Little, Brown, 1974), 493–94.

DOCUMENT 166: Soviet Chief of Staff General Anatoly Gribkov Comments on Operation Anadyr, Summer–Fall 1962 (Havana Conference, 1992)

Beginning in March 1987, James G. Blight and David A. Welch conducted a series of group conversations with both American and Soviet participants who witnessed the crisis firsthand. While these oral histories have serious limitations due to their "reunion atmosphere" some thirty years after the event, they have proven an important supplement to the available documents on the decision-making process during those critical hours of October 1962. Three major conferences were held under the direction of Blight, Welch, and Bruce J. Allyn—in Moscow in January 1989, Antigua in 1991, and Havana in January 1992. In addition to key U.S. (Secretary of Defense Robert McNamara, CIA Director Ray Cline, and State Department Officer Raymond Garthoff) and Soviet policymakers (Soviet Chief of Staff General Anatoly Gribkov), these last three conferences included a Cuban delegation, with Fidel Castro joining the discussion at Havana. Here follows one of the most striking revelations of the Havana Conference: the presence of armed Soviet tactical nuclear missiles, the *Luna*, in Cuba at the time of the crisis.

In 1962, I was the head of a bureau of the Main Operations Directorate of the Soviet General Staff. . . . We presented our government with a proposed plan to deploy troops and equipment in Cuba, but we had to consider how we were going to represent the operation. Our cover was that we were going to carry out a strategic exercise through the deployment of Soviet troops in the north. The troops themselves were later told that they were going to go to Cuba to defend the island's independence. The name of the operation was "Anadyr." That is the name of a river in the northern region of our country, in a very cold region. . . .

What was the force that we would have to train in our country in a very short span of time and transport to the other side of the ocean? This was its composition:

• A medium-range missile division. We saw this unit as a means to prevent aggression; I repeat, as a means to deter aggression. This division was made up of five regiments. Three were R-12 [NATO designation SS-4] regiments, with missiles whose range was 2,500 km (24 launchers with a complement of 1 1/2 missiles for each launcher). Two were R-14 [SS-5] missile regiments (sixteen launchers, also 1 1/2 missiles per launcher). Forty launchers were foreseen in all, together with the appropriate number of missiles [sixty]. I would like to add that at the beginning of the crisis—that is, on October 22nd—three R-12 regiments were already in Cuba, and two regiment sites were already laid out in their deployment areas. The third regiment site was under construction. The two R-14 regiments were still en route at sea, and in accordance with the instructions of the Soviet government, returned to the Soviet Union.

• Two air defense missile divisions comprised of twenty-four missile sites: 144 S-75 [NATO designation SA-2] launchers. The Americans are probably familiar with these data, but I can repeat their range (65 km) and altitude (100 m to 30 km).

• Four motorized rifle regiments, reinforced by three tactical nuclear missile batteries—six launchers for *Luna* [NATO designation FROG (Free Rocket Over Ground)] missiles with a 60 km range. We initially considered calling these units brigades, but then we changed our minds and decided to call them regiments that we were going to deploy there to defend the shores and the missile sites, jointly with the Cuban troops.

• The Air Force had a regiment of forty MiG-21 aircraft in Cuba; thirty[-three] tactical aircraft (IL-28s); and a separate naval squadron of nine IL-28 aircraft. At the onset of the crisis, only six planes had been assembled, and only a few flights had been made.

• Two regiments of tactical cruise missiles were also provided. In each regiment there were ten launchers: one for training, and nine for combat. There were eighteen combat launchers in all. Range: 150 km. We brought over eighty conventional cruise missiles for these two regiments.

• We also had an Mi-8 transport helicopter regiment, and a transport air squadron with nine already-obsolete Li-2 planes.

• We planned to deploy two squadrons to Cuba: one squadron of surface ships, comprising two cruisers and two destroyers; and a squadron of submarines, comprising eleven submarines. These two squadrons never went to Cuba. . . .

• A missile regiment for coastal defense, with the *Sopka* missile, had eight launchers at four sites on the coast. Thirty-two cruise missiles were brought for these eight launchers. . . .

• Finally, there was a brigade of twelve missile-launching [Komar] patrol boats, with two P-15 missiles each, with a range of 40 km. . . .

Before the crisis, we had foreseen bringing in 45,000 men. By the time of the crisis, we had brought in 42,000. Never before in the history of the Soviet Armed Forces and in the history of Russia had we transported so many troops to the other side of the ocean. Consequently, when we were entrusted by the government with the planning of this operation, we said that there were many issues and unknowns to be taken into account. We devoted day and night to these preparations. We made all the necessary calculations, but these had to be done in absolute secrecy. To transport these troops, we had to use eighty-five ships from our merchant marine, and to assemble in secrecy ships of various kinds scattered all over the seas. They had to be equipped with special technology and with the necessary crew, a special crew. Consequently, the merchant marine had to make great efforts to accomplish this task.

The Navy got the necessary ships, and 185 trips were made with these ships transporting the forces. The ships were distributed among seven ports in the White Sea, the Barents Sea, the Baltic Sea, [and] the Black Sea. Aside from the plan for transporting the troops, we also prepared a plan to cover these operations, replete with the necessary diversionary tactics and disinformation, as is done by all armed forces. The steps that we took in this regard were generally successful. . . .

Simultaneously, we prepared the command structure. . . . General Issa Alexandrovich Pliyev was appointed overall commander. He had actively participated in the Second World War and was twice named a Hero of the Soviet Union. . . .

To identify the area for the deployment of troops in Cuba, in keeping with the agreement, we sent a group to Cuba headed by Pliyev. Each service was represented. We sent them by plane, and, jointly with Cubans, they selected the sites for the deployment of forces. . . .

I would like to quote [Minister of Defense Marshal Rodion] Malinovsky when he gave me the order to convey Khrushchev's and the defense minister's instructions to Pliyev: "The missile forces will fire only if authorized by Nikita Sergeievich Khrushchev"—it was repeated—"only if instructed by the Supreme Commander-in-Chief himself." . . . The tactical nuclear forces—the six *Luna* launchers I've mentioned—could be employed with nuclear weapons during a direct invasion by the aggressor. It was said that before arriving at a decision on employ[ing] the tactical missiles, the situation had to be very thoroughly and carefully assessed, and, in case of extreme need only, then could the decision be made. That was my mission when I was sent to Cuba.

Source: Havana Oral History Conference, 9–12 January 1992: see James G. Blight, Bruce J. Allyn, and David A. Welch, *Cuba on the Brink: Castro, the Missile Crisis and the Soviet Collapse* (New York: Pantheon, 1993), 56–63.

DOCUMENT 167: Draft Cuban-Soviet Agreement on Military Cooperation and Mutual Defense in the Event of Aggression (never signed) (August 1962)

The Government of the Republic of Cuba and the Government of the Union of Soviet Socialist Republics, . . .

Desiring to agree on all questions relating to the support which the Soviet Armed Forces will provide in the defense of the national territory of Cuba in the event of aggression, have agreed to subscribe to the present agreement.

Article 1

The Soviet Union will send to the Republic of Cuba armed forces to reinforce its defenses in the face of the danger of an external aggression and to contribute to the preservation of world peace. . . .

Article 2

In the event of aggression against the republic of Cuba or against the Soviet Armed Forces on the territory of the Republic of Cuba, the Government of the Union of Soviet Socialist Republics and the Government of the Republic of Cuba, making use of the right to individual or collective defense, provided for in Article 51 of the United Nations Organization Charter, will take all necessary measures to repel the aggression. . . .

Article 4

The Government of the Union of Soviet Socialist Republics will assume the upkeep costs of the Soviet Armed Forces based on the territory of the Republic of Cuba by virtue of this agreement. . . .

Article 10

Both parties agree that the military units of each state will be under the command of their respective governments who will, in coordination, determine the use of their respective forces to repel external aggression and restore the peace. . . .

Article 13

This agreement is valid for a five year term. Either party may annul the agreement, notifying the other party within one year before the expiration date of this agreement.

In the event that the five year term is concluded without either party requesting its annulment, this agreement will be in force for five more years. . . .

Article 14

After the conclusion of this agreement's validity, the Soviet Armed Forces will abandon the territory of the Republic of Cuba.

Source: Chang and Kornbluh, *Cuban Missile Crisis, 1962*, 54–56.

DOCUMENT 168: CIA Director John McCone's "Honeymoon Cables from Paris" Directing Extensive Search for Soviet Medium-Range Ballistic Missiles (MRBMs) in Cuba (7–20 September 1962)

On 7 September 1962, CIA Director John McCone wired Acting CIA Director Lt. Gen. Marshal S. Carter as follows:

[U]rge frequent repeat missions of recent reconnaissance operations which [Deputy Secretary of Defense Roswell] Gilpatric advises informative. Also I support use of R-101 [Low Altitude Reconnaissance Aircraft] if necessary. My hunch is we might face prospect of Soviet short-range surface-to-surface missiles of portable type in Cuba which could command important targets of southeast United States and possibly Latin American Caribbean areas. You might suggest to Rusk that we develop joint policies for action in Cuba with selected Caribbean, South American states as an alternative to seeking unanimous OAS action which most certainly will be an ineffective compromise solution if past history is any indicator.

On 10 September Director McCone wired Carter as follows:

Difficult for me to rationalize extensive costly defenses being established in Cuba as such extreme costly measures to accomplish security and secrecy not consistent with other policies such as refugees, legal travel, etc. Appears to me quite possible measures now being taken are for purpose of insuring secrecy of some offensive capability such as MRBMs to be installed by Soviets after present phase completed and country secured from overflights. Suggest BNE [Board of National Estimates] study motives behind these defensive measures which even seem to exceed those provided most satellites. . . .

On 16 September Director McCone cabled Carter as follows:

Also believe we must carefully study the prospect of secret importation and placement of several Soviet MRBMs which could not be detected by us if Cuban defenses deny overflight. In reflecting on my observations of Thor installation in Britain and Jupiters in Italy I can envisage a Soviet plan to package missile, control and operating equipment in such a way that a unit could be made operational a few hours after a site cleared and with a modest concrete pad poured. Do not wish to be overly alarming this matter but believe CIA and community must keep government informed of danger of a surprise and also that detection of preparatory steps possibly beyond our capability once Cuban defense system operative. Thrust of press reports reaching me is that there exists a clear demarcation between defensive and offensive preparations and I question if we can be sure of this. I recognize Cuban policy decisions most delicate and beyond Agency or my competence. However believe we must give those making decision our best estimate of possible developments and alternative situations which might evolve and unexpectedly confront us.

On 19 September Carter communicated the summary of the conclusions of Cuban SNIE (Special National Intelligence Estimate) of that date, stating that the establishment of MRBMs in Cuba would be incompatible with Soviet policy—and would indicate a greater willingness to increase risk in U.S./Soviet relations than the Soviet Union has displayed so far.

On 20 September McCone responded as follows:

Suggest most careful consideration to conclusion last sentence paragraph D. As an alternative I can see that an offensive Soviet Cuban base will provide Soviets with most important and effective trading position in connection with all other critical areas and hence they might take an unexpected risk in order to establish such a position.

Source: Central Intelligence Agency, *The Secret Cuban Missile Crisis Documents* (Washington: Brassey's, 1994), 13–17.

DOCUMENT 169: CIA Special National Intelligence Estimate (SNIE) 85-3-62, "The Military Buildup in Cuba" (19 September 1962)

CONCLUSIONS

We believe that the USSR values its position in Cuba primarily for the political advantages to be derived from it, and consequently that the main purpose of the present military buildup in Cuba is to strengthen the Communist regime there against what the Cubans and the Soviets conceive to be a danger that the US may attempt by one means or another to overthrow it. . . .

The USSR could derive considerable military advantage from the establishment of Soviet medium and intermediate range ballistic missiles in Cuba, or from the establishment of a Soviet submarine base there. As between these two, the establishment of a submarine base would be the more likely. Either development, however, would be incompatible with Soviet practice to date and with Soviet policy [as] we presently estimate it. It would indicate a far greater willingness to increase the level of risk in US-Soviet relations than the USSR has displayed thus far, and consequently would have important policy implications with respect to other areas and other problems in East-West relations.

Source: SNIE 85-3-62, in Central Intelligence Agency, *The Secret Cuban Missile Crisis Documents*, 91–93.

DOCUMENT 170: Soviet Defector Oleg Penkovsky, Code Name HERO, Provides Western Intelligence with Vital Information on Soviet Nuclear Capability (June 1962)

Khrushchev is blabbing that we are ready, we have everything. This is just so much idle talk. He himself probably does not see the whole picture. He talks about the Soviet Union's capability to send missiles to every corner of the world, but he has not done anything about it because he knows that we are actually not ready. Of course, we can send our missiles in different directions as far as the United States, or Cuba, etc. But as far as launching a planned missile attack to destroy definite targets is concerned, we are not yet capable of doing it. We simply do not have missiles that are accurate enough. . . .

[M]any of our big missiles are still on the drawing boards, in the prototype stage, or are still undergoing tests. There are altogether not more than a few dozen of these, instead of the "shower" of missiles with which Khrushchev has been threatening the West. The launching of the first sputnik required the combined efforts of all Soviet scientists and technical personnel with the entire technological capacity of the country at their disposal.

Several sputniks were launched into the stratosphere and never heard from again. They took the lives of several specially trained astronauts.

Khrushchev's boasting is also meant to impress the Soviet people and to show them that we are strong. Of course, there have been some fine achievements in the development and improvement of tactical and operational short-range missiles. It is still too early, however, to speak of strategic missiles as perfected. Accidents and all sorts of troubles are daily occurrences. In this connection, there is much talk about shortcomings in the field of electronics.

There have been many cases during the test launchings of missiles . . . deviating several hundred kilometers from their prescribed course. The vigilance of the Western powers, however, must not be weakened by these shortcomings. If at the present time the Soviet ballistic missiles are still far from being perfect, in two or three years—perhaps even sooner— Khrushchev will have achieved his goal; this is something for everyone to keep in mind. Right now we have a certain number of missiles with nuclear warheads capable of reaching the United States or South America; but these are single missiles, not in mass production, and they are far from perfect. Every possible measure is taken to improve the missiles and their production. Money is saved everywhere and allocated to the building of "kindergartens," the slang expression we use for missile production. Scientific and technical personnel are being mobilized.

Source: Oleg Penkovskiy, *The Penkovskiy Papers,* translated by Peter Deriabin (Garden City, N.Y.: Doubleday, 1965), 339–40.

DOCUMENT 171: Soviet Historian Sergei Khrushchev Asks What Impact Western Intelligence Sources Had on U.S. Policymakers' Attitudes about Soviet Nuclear Capability in 1962 (Havana Conference, 1992)

SERGEI KHRUSHCHEV (Nikita Khrushchev's son): I've posed [this question] many times, but finally I'm going to address it to Mr. Cline. He said that with the aid of satellites it was discovered that the Soviet Union had many fewer missiles than the United States supposed. This is a very important point, in my view, since we know that as of the beginning of the Cold War, the Soviet Union lived under the threat of a U.S. nuclear strike, and the Soviet Union was always looking for a chance to respond to this strike. And this led to the development of missiles in our country, although, in view of the events of the October crisis, we overestimated our potential.

The United States learned that we did not have as many missiles as they thought. At one point, Khrushchev said that we built missiles like sausages. I said then, "How can you say that, since we only have two or three?" He said, "The important thing is to make the Americans believe that. And that way we prevent an attack." And on these grounds our entire policy was based. We threatened with missiles we didn't have. That happened in the case of the Suez crisis, and the Iraqi crisis. But it happened that in 1962 the United States discovered the real balance of forces in terms of missiles.

I think that this can be traced to Penkovsky. Penkovsky was the one who obtained this intelligence. After this, the Americans started their reconnaissance flights in outer space. And I've always thought that it was impossible in 1962 to take pictures of the whole territory of the Soviet Union and determine the exact number of missiles that we had. That is, the system was not fully operational. We found film capsules from these reconnaissance satellites which would crash in Kazakhstan. So my question is: how did your intelligence activity correlate to Penkovsky's activity, and what was the role of surveillance from outer space? . . .

RAY CLINE: I believe that Penkovsky was a very important source of information for the intelligence services in Washington. He gave us hundreds and hundreds of documents. He was not a current operations officer, but he did manage to provide the CIA with literally thousands of pages of documents about the structure of the military system. However, while we were getting those documents, we didn't know at that time—and I'm talking about 1960 and 1961—what the actual current data were. And the Pentagon in particular—it was the Air Force primarily—were absolutely convinced that the Soviet Union had hundreds of missiles.

Well, in August 1961, as I recall, we did fly the first effective reconnaissance satellite mission. And I remind you that this is an extraordinary achievement. The satellite flew ninety miles above the Earth, and still took useful photographs. And it also, as I recall, circled the Earth every ninety minutes. Of course, as the world turns, you could move across the Soviet Union, and cover an enormous area of the country. Actually, that's why we put the satellites up—because there were eleven time zones in the Soviet Union, and we were able to cut across them. So, what I want to say is that the actual photography from satellites was the key, and what made the United States feel that it had confidence in protecting ourselves. . . .

RAYMOND GARTHOFF: I want briefly to add a little to what Ray Cline has said. First, I went to the Department of State in September 1961, and I was there during the Cuban missile crisis. But in preceding years, I had been working on Soviet affairs for Ray Cline's predecessor at the [Central Intelligence Agency]. So I was there, for example, during the Penkovsky period, and for most of it—the earlier part—I was probably one of the few people who read all those hundreds of pages, the hundreds of documents he provided. It was very valuable information. But some of the material he provided was things he had picked up, gossip picked up around Ministry of Defense and elsewhere. Some of it was very interesting and probably true. Some of it was interesting and probably not true, and it was sometimes very difficult to tell. So much depended on the kind of information, and the source. But he did, for example, provide us with the full characteristics of, and other data with respect to, the R-12 and R-14 systems [Russian designations for SS-4 and SS-5 nuclear missiles deployed in Cuba]. We even learned those designations from him for the first time.

But to go back to the point, Colonel Penkovsky did not tell us—he did not learn, at least in time to tell us anything—about the missiles going to Cuba. He did give us information, some of which was helpful and some of which was not, with respect to intentions during the Berlin crisis in 1961. He had begun reporting in April 1961, and this lasted until shortly before he was arrested on the 22nd of October 1962. But if I may slightly amend what Ray Cline said, the first successful space reconnaissance mission was in August 1960, not August 1961, and we began to get useful information in early 1961 which permitted Secretary McNamara, when he first came in office in February, to make a statement— perhaps politically prematurely—to the effect that there wasn't any missile gap, right after President Kennedy had just won an election running on the theme that there was one. . . .

At that same time, in October 1962, we rushed some of our missiles along which were being deployed, and by October 31st we had 172 operational ICBMs on alert—on station—and 144 Polaris missiles at sea on station. I say nothing, of course, of the discrepancy in bombers, where we had 1,450 strategic bombers on alert status, with a total initial salvo of 2,952 weapons on the strategic bombers and intercontinental missiles. So the discrepancy between actual operational American and Soviet intercontinental strategic forces was very great, and in that sense, an addition of (let's say) twenty-four R-12s in Cuba doubled, perhaps, the Soviet force if they were fired first, and could have taken under fire additional soft targets—lucrative targets in the United States, such as SAC bases, for which there were not enough ICBMs in the Soviet Union at that time. So in that sense, the Soviet deployment added a lot. It changed the strategic balance.

Source: Blight, Allyn, and Welch, *Cuba on the Brink*, 130–35.

DOCUMENT 172: The View that Cuba Had Reason to Prepare for U.S. Invasion and that Policymakers Must "Stand in the Other Guy's Shoes," Summer 1962 (Moscow Conference, 1989)

ROBERT McNAMARA: . . . [O]ne of the most important lessons of this event is that we must look at ourselves from the point of view of others. I want to state quite frankly that with hindsight, if I had been a Cuban leader, I think I might have expected a U.S. invasion. Why? Because the U.S. had carried out what I have referred to publicly as a debacle—the Bay of Pigs invasion—we'd carried it out in the sense that we had supported it. We did not support it militarily and I think this should be recognized and emphasized, as it was specifically the decision of President Kennedy *not* to support it with the use of U.S. military force—but in any event, we'd carried it out, and after the debacle, there were many voices in the United States that said the error was not in approving the Bay of Pigs operation; the error was in the failure to support it with military force, the implication being that at some point in the future, force would be applied.

Secondly, there were covert operations. The Cubans knew that. There were covert operations extending over a long period of time. . . . [My] recollection is that they extended from the late 1950s into the period we're discussing, the summer and fall of 1962 [Operation Mongoose].

And thirdly, there were important voices in the United States—important leaders of our Senate, important leaders of our House—who were calling for the invasion of Cuba. . . . So I state quite frankly again that if I had been a Cuban leader at that time, I might well have concluded that there was a great risk of U.S. invasion. And I should say, as well, if I had been a Soviet leader at the time, I might have come to the same conclusion.

Source: Bruce J. Allyn, James G. Blight, and David A. Welch, eds., *Back to the Brink: Proceedings of the Moscow Conference on the Cuban Missile Crisis, January 27–28, 1989* (Lanham, Md.: University Press of America, 1992), 160.

DOCUMENT 173: The View that Placing Nuclear Missiles in Cuba Was Khrushchev's Gambit to Alter the East-West "Correlation of Forces," Summer 1962 (Havana Conference, 1992)

RAY CLINE: . . . I talked to President Kennedy most of that summer about the evidence we found—that he did not anticipate that Khrushchev would put the missiles in Cuba. He didn't think it was true. They had some rather preliminary exchanges of letters. President Kennedy anticipated that any conflict with the Soviet Union over Cuba would be conducted on the diplomatic level, and that he would not be forced to deal with the presence of a nuclear missile system in the Western Hemisphere.

. . . My boss, [CIA Director] John McCone, had a strong feeling that Soviet missiles would be put in Cuba. He said it was just a hunch; he didn't have any evidence any more than we did. But he said he wanted to make sure that we searched as thoroughly as necessary to find evidence of missile installations. Well, John McCone went to France on a honeymoon—he married a second wife, and he went to the Riviera [23 August–23 September 1962]. He was so frustrated that he kept firing me messages from the Riviera on his honeymoon all the time saying, "You've got to do something more about this. Get this evidence out and tell President Kennedy what to say." . . .

Another point that I wanted to mention was that I briefed Kennedy on the CIA satellite reconnaissance system. At that time it was totally secret; nobody knew about orbiting satellite systems. They went around the Earth every ninety minutes, and you could map huge areas of the Soviet Union or any other part of the world. I revealed that the Soviet Union was boasting about enormous missile superiority—we called it the missile gap at that time. But when we managed to get all the photographs from the National Photo Interpretation Center, I found that they had many fewer missiles than the United States had; it was about four to one. And that was very hard for us to believe, because many of the military people were confident that Khrushchev had created a superior missile system. In fact, it turned out that, since we started up our missile production very efficiently and very promptly, we ended up with four times the number of Soviet missiles.

. . . I talked to Kennedy about that. I said, "Look, we have real intercontinental strategic superiority, and they will not use it against us. They would be crazy to use it against us. We don't want a war; we don't want a military conflict. But if the missiles are in Cuba, then we have to respond in a firm and strategic way." And we did. We forced Khrushchev to retreat, and I think that was wise. . . . After all, we had a cold war with the Soviet Union beginning in the Stalin days that had nothing to do with Cuba. President Fidel Castro came along in 1959, and he was not the primary actor in this situation. It was a very direct conflict between Moscow and Washington. So I felt that the priority for the Soviet Union was to change the balance of strategic military power—what Russians always called the "correlation of forces"—and I believe that was their major goal. . . .

I thought the Soviets' second priority was to force the United States military out of Berlin. This was an issue for many years, and Khrushchev was very anxious to somehow force—particularly Kennedy to retreat from Berlin. And while we would have tried to solve the Cuban crisis by diplomatic and political measures, President Kennedy insisted that we couldn't get out of Berlin.

In my view—contrary to what I think many people here believe—the defense of Cuba was only the third Soviet priority. . . .

I am sure there was an interest in saving the Cuban commonwealth, the Cuban system. But I felt that the primary objective was to develop the new balance of power, because the Russians were falling behind in intercontinental missiles. So I felt—and this was my judgment, but I think the CIA people generally agreed with it—that if he put missiles in Cuba, it would indeed change the balance of power, because we thought there would probably end up being about eighty-four missiles. Of course, originally it was only forty-two, but we thought that if the missiles got established in Cuba, they would build them up, and it would be a real hazard for the United States. Now, one of the reasons was that we had set up a defense system which was all oriented toward the Soviet Union, the northern Atlantic, and the northern Pacific. We had very little in the way of defenses in the southern part of the United States. I think that's why those missiles were significant.

Source: Blight, Allyn, and Welch, *Cuba on the Brink*, 125–30.

MISSILES OF OCTOBER

DOCUMENT 174: Imagery Confirmation of Offensive Missiles in Cuba (14–15 October 1962)

Delayed by bad weather until October 14, the U-2 flew in the early morning hours of that cloudless Sunday high over western Cuba, moving from south to north. Processed that night, the long rolls of film were scrutinized, analyzed, compared with earlier photos, and reanalyzed throughout Monday by the extraordinarily talented photo interpreters of the U.S. Government's intelligence network; and late that afternoon they spotted in the San Cristóbal area the first rude beginnings of a Soviet medium-range missile base.

By Monday evening, October 15, the analysts were fairly certain of their findings. Between 8 and 10 P.M. the top CIA officials were notified and they notified in turn the Defense and State intelligence chiefs and, at his home, McGeorge Bundy. Bundy immediately recognized that this was no unconfirmed refugee report or minor incident. He decided, however, and quite rightly, I believe—not to call the President but to brief him in person and in detail the next morning. . . .

Around 9 A.M. Tuesday morning, October 16, having first received a detailed briefing from top CIA officials, Bundy broke the news to the President as he scanned the morning papers in his bedroom.

Source: Theodore C. Sorensen, *Kennedy* (New York: Harper and Row, 1965), 672–73.

DOCUMENT 175: CIA's National Photographic Interpretation Center Memo on "Mission 3101" (16 October 1962)

1. An examination of photography from Mission 3101 dated 14 October 1962 has revealed an MRBM Launch Site and two new military

encampments located along the southern edge of the Sierra Del Rosario in west central Cuba.

2. The Launch Site and one of the encampments contains a total of at least 14 canvas-covered missile trailers measuring approximately 67 feet in length and 9 feet in width. The overall length of the trailers including the tow bar is approximately 80 feet. . . .

4. Detail and equipment for each area is as follows:

a. Area 1—MRBM Launch Site located in a wooded area at 22-40-05N 83-17-55W, 4.0 NM ENE of San Diego de los Banos. Site contains at least 8 canvas-covered missile trailers and 4 deployed probable missile erector/launchers (unrevetted). . . .

b. Area 2—Military Encampment (missile) located in a wooded area at 22-40-50N 83-15-OOW, 5.8 NM north of Los Palacios. . . .

c. Area 3—Military Encampment located in a wooded area at 22-42-40N 83-08-15W, 4.2 NM West of San Cristobal.

Source: Central Intelligence Agency, *Secret Cuban Missile Crisis Documents*, 155–56.

DOCUMENT 176: CIA Operations Officer Richard Helms' Memorandum on Operation Mongoose as the Covert Effort to Overthrow or Remove Castro from Power in Cuba (16 October 1962)

The Attorney General [Robert Kennedy] opened the meeting [afternoon of 16 October] by expressing the "general dissatisfaction of the President" with Operation MONGOOSE. He pointed out that the Operation had been under way for a year, that the results were discouraging, that there had been no acts of sabotage, and that even the one which had been attempted had failed twice. He indicated that there had been noticeable improvement during the year in the collection of intelligence but that other actions had failed to influence significantly the course of events in Cuba. He spoke of the weekly meetings of top officials on this problem and again noted the small accomplishments despite the fact that Secretaries Rusk and McNamara, General [Maxwell] Taylor, McGeorge Bundy, and he personally had all been charged by the president with finding a solution. He traced the history of General Lansdale's personal appointment by the president a year ago. The Attorney General then stated that in view of this lack of progress, he was going to give Operation MONGOOSE more personal attention. In order to do this, he will hold a meeting every morning at 0930 with the MONGOOSE operational representatives from the various agencies.

Source: Central Intelligence Agency, *Secret Cuban Missile Crisis Documents*, 153–54.

DOCUMENT 177: Attorney General Robert Kennedy's Account of the NSC's "Executive Committee" (Ex Comm) and Its Initial Decisions (17–20 October 1962)

[T]he "Ex Comm" (the Executive Committee of the National Security Council) included Secretary of State Dean Rusk; Secretary of Defense Robert McNamara; Director of the Central Intelligence Agency John McCone; Secretary of the Treasury Douglas Dillon; President Kennedy's adviser on national-security affairs, McGeorge Bundy; Presidential Counsel Ted Sorensen; Under Secretary of State George Ball; Deputy Under Secretary of State U. Alexis Johnson; General Maxwell Taylor, Chairman of the Joint Chiefs of Staff; Edward Martin, Assistant Secretary of State for Latin America; originally, Chip Bohlen, who, after the first day, left to become Ambassador to France and was succeeded by Llewellyn Thompson as the adviser on Russian affairs; Roswell Gilpatric, Deputy Secretary of Defense; Paul Nitze, Assistant Secretary of Defense; and, intermittently at various meetings, Vice-President Lyndon B. Johnson; Adlai Stevenson, Ambassador to the United Nations; Ken O'Donnell, Special Assistant to the President; and Don Wilson, who was Deputy Director of the United States Information Agency. This was the group that met, talked, argued, and fought together during that crucial period of time. From this group came the recommendations from which President Kennedy was ultimately to select his course of action. . . .

It was during the afternoon and evening of that first day, Tuesday, that we began to discuss the idea of a quarantine or blockade. Secretary McNamara, by Wednesday, became the blockade's strongest advocate. He argued that it was limited pressure, which could be increased as the circumstances warranted. Further, it was dramatic and forceful pressure, which would be understood yet, most importantly, still leave us in control of events. Later he reinforced his position by reporting that a surprise air strike against the missile bases alone—a surgical air strike, as it came to be called—was militarily impractical in the view of the Joint Chiefs of Staff, that any such military action would have to include all military installations in Cuba, eventually leading to an invasion. Perhaps we would come to that, he argued. Perhaps that course of action would turn out to be inevitable. "But let's not start with that course," if by chance that kind of confrontation with Cuba, and of necessity with the Soviet Union, could be avoided.

Those who argued for the military strike instead of a blockade pointed out that a blockade would not in fact remove the missiles and would not even stop the work from going ahead on the missile sites themselves. The missiles were already in Cuba, and all we would be doing with a blockade would be "closing the door after the horse had left the barn." Further, they argued, we would be bringing about a confrontation with the Soviet Union by stopping their ships, when we should be concentrating on Cuba and Castro.

Their most forceful argument was that our installation of a blockade around Cuba invited the Russians to do the same to Berlin. If we demanded the removal of missiles from Cuba as the price for lifting our blockade, they would demand the removal of missiles surrounding the Soviet Union as the reciprocal act. . . .

The members of the Joint Chiefs of Staff were unanimous in calling for immediate military action. They forcefully presented their view that the blockade would not be effective. General Curtis LeMay, Air Force Chief of Staff, argued strongly with the President that a military attack was essential. When the President questioned what the response of the Russians might be, General LeMay assured him there would be no reaction. President Kennedy was skeptical. "They, no more than we, can let these things go by without doing something. They can't, after all their statements, permit us to take out their missiles, kill a lot of Russians, and then do nothing. If they don't take action in Cuba, they certainly will in Berlin." . . .

Later, Secretary McNamara, although he told the President he disagreed with the Joint Chiefs and favored a blockade rather than an attack, informed him that the necessary planes, men, and ammunition were being deployed and that we could be ready to move with the necessary air bombardments on Tuesday, October 23, if that was to be the decision. The plans called for an initial attack, consisting of five hundred sorties, striking all military targets, including the missile sites, airfields, ports, and gun emplacements.

I supported McNamara's position in favor of a blockade. This was not from a deep conviction that it would be a successful course of action, but a feeling that it had more flexibility and fewer liabilities than a military attack.

Source: Robert F. Kennedy, *Thirteen Days: A Memoir of the Cuban Missile Crisis,* 3rd ed. (New York: Norton, 1971), 8–15.

DOCUMENT 178: Memorandum by Ambassador Charles Bohlen, a Soviet-Specialist State Department Officer and Presidential Adviser, to President Kennedy (18 October 1962)

That evening [October 18] . . . I wrote in longhand on a yellow legal pad my suggestions of what the President ought to do about the Soviet missiles in Cuba. . . .

They are as follows: . . .

3. No one can guarantee that this [the elimination of Soviet missiles from Cuba] can be achieved by diplomatic action—but it seems to me essential that this channel should be tested out before military action is employed. If our decision is firm (and it must be) I can see no danger in communicating with Khrushchev privately, worded in such a way that he realizes that we mean business. . . .

8. In general I feel that a declaration of war [against Cuba] would be valuable since it would open up every avenue of military action—air strike, invasion, or blockade. But we would have to make a case before our allies to justify such a declaration of war. But if we acted first and sought to justify it later we would be in a spot of great consequence.

9. Finally, I feel very strongly that any belief in a limited quick action is an illusion and would lead us into a full war with Cuba on a step by step basis which would greatly increase the possibility of general war.

The best course in my view would be a carefully worded and serious letter to Khrushchev, and when the reply is received (if it is unsatisfactory) communicate with our principal allies to inform them of our intention and then ask Congress for a declaration of war with a suitable statement of the reason and all adequate preparations.

Source: Charles E. Bohlen, *Witness to History, 1929–1969* (New York: Norton, 1973), 489–92.

DOCUMENT 179: The LET [Presidential Adviser Llewellyn E. Thompson?] Memo on Behalf of Air Strike Option (19 October 1962)

Steps which would make air strike more acceptable to blockade group.
1. Prior notice to Khrushchev by message from the President giving

Soviets possibility of backing down and strengthening our case with our Allies and world opinion in the event that Khrushchev takes such action as blockading Berlin.

2. Some effort to try to minimize numbers of Soviets killed, or at least show we wanted to avoid this. Message to Khrushchev might urge him to remove Soviet technicians immediately.

3. Prior notice to our principal Allies, and particularly Turkey and Italy (because of our missiles there).

4. Prior ultimatum to Castro giving him chance to fold.

5. Prior notification to certain Latin American Governments to allow them to take steps to prevent being overthrown.

(All these notifications could be short but should be minimum military considerations would allow. None of them need spell out our proposed actions, but should indicate it will be extremely serious.)

6. Some improvement in our position before world opinion. Example—President might make reference to Soviet construction of "Fishing Port" in Cuba, saying that in view other Soviet actions we are convinced Soviets were constructing naval base.

7. No attack on Havana to avoid killing foreign diplomats and thus arousing public opinion against us in those countries.

Source: Central Intelligence Agency, *Secret Cuban Missile Crisis Documents*, 195.

DOCUMENT 180: Conclusions of CIA Estimate "Soviet Missile Threat in Cuba" Which Incorporate Sensitive Penkovsky "IRONBARK" Debriefings (18–19 October 1962)

Offensive Missiles

1. At least one Soviet regiment consisting of eight launchers and sixteen 1020-nm [nautical mile] (SS-4) medium range ballistic missiles is now deployed in western Cuba at two launch sites. These sites presently contain unrevetted, field-type launchers which rely on mobile erection, checkout, and support equipment. These missiles are probably those reported moving into this area during September. Although there is continuing improvement of these sites, these mobile missiles must be considered operational now and could be launched within 18 hours after the decision to launch. A refire from each launcher could be accomplished within 5 hours after the initial firing.

2. Fixed, soft sites which could achieve initial operational capability during December 1962 are now being developed near Havana. We be-

lieve that the 2200-nm (SS-5) intermediate range ballistic missile is probably intended for these sites. Photography of these sites show[s] eight, fixed launch pads under construction which probably equate to an additional missile regiment with eight ready missiles and eight for refire.

3. All of these offensive missile systems are Soviet manned and controlled. We believe that offensive action by these systems would be commanded from the Soviet Union but have not yet found the command and control communication links. . . .

Coastal Defense Missiles

6. Three coastal defense missile sites have now been identified in Cuba, two of which must now be considered operational (Banes and Santa Cruz del Norte). In an alert status, these cruise missiles can be fired in about 10 minutes, with subsequent firings from each launcher at 5 minute intervals.

Air Defense Missiles

7. There are now 22 surface-to-air missile (SA-2) sites located in Cuba, nine of which are believed to be individually operational at the present time. The remaining SA-2 sites could be operational in two to three weeks. Each site contains six missiles with six additional missiles in an adjacent hold area. The initial firing can take place anytime after an alert, providing the site has reached readiness. Refire from a single launcher will take approximately 3 to 5 minutes. . . .

Significance

11. The magnitude of the total Soviet missile force being deployed indicates that the USSR intends to develop Cuba into a prime strategic base, rather than as a token show of strength.

12. A mixed force of 1020- and 2200-nm missiles would give the USSR a significant strategic strike capability against almost all targets in the U.S. By deploying stockpiled shorter range ballistic missiles at overseas bases against which we have no BMEWS [Ballistic Missile Early Warning System] warning capability, the Soviet Union will supplement its ICBM home force in a significant way. This overseas strategic force is protected by an extensive SA-2 deployment in Cuba.

Source: Central Intelligence Agency, *Secret Cuban Missile Crisis Documents*, 187–91.

DOCUMENT 181: Special National Intelligence Estimate 11-18-62: Possible Soviet Reactions to U.S. Action (19 October 1962)

---

1. A major Soviet objective in their military buildup in Cuba is to demonstrate that the world balance of forces has shifted so far in their

favor that the US can no longer prevent the advance of Soviet offensive power even into its own hemisphere. In this connection they assume, of course, that these deployments sooner or later will become publicly known.

2. It is possible that the USSR is installing these missiles primarily in order to use them in bargaining for US concessions elsewhere. We think this unlikely, however. The public withdrawal of Soviet missiles from Cuba would create serious problems in the USSR's relations with Castro; it would cast doubt on the firmness of the Soviet intention to protect the Castro regime and perhaps on their commitments elsewhere.

3. If the US accepts the strategic missile buildup in Cuba, the Soviets would continue the buildup of strategic weapons in Cuba. We have no basis for estimating the force level which they would wish to reach, but it seems clear already that they intend to go beyond a token capability. They would probably expect their missile forces in Cuba to make some contribution to their total strategic capability vis-à-vis the US. . . .

SOVIET REACTION TO USE OF MILITARY FORCE

9. If the US takes direct military action against Cuba, the Soviets would be placed automatically under great pressure to respond in ways which, if they could not save Cuba, would inflict an offsetting injury to US interests. This would be true whether the action was limited to an effort to neutralize the strategic missiles, or these missiles plus airfields, surface-to-air missile sites, or cruise missile sites, or in fact an outright invasion designed to destroy the Castro regime. . . .

13. We believe that whatever course of retaliation the USSR elected, the Soviet leaders would not deliberately initiate general war or take military measures, which in their calculation, would run the gravest risks of general war.

Source: Central Intelligence Agency, *Secret Cuban Missile Crisis Documents*, 197–202.

DOCUMENT 182: Secretary of State Dean Rusk Recalls the Opposing Opinions of Ex Comm Members, and Meeting with Congressional Leaders (17–22 October 1962)

Although I realized the missiles would have to be removed, I didn't commit myself to any policy line or join any task force at first, although I consulted with all. Others were more vocal—notably Paul Nitze and Maxwell Taylor, who argued for an air strike to destroy the missiles. Bob McNamara and George Ball opposed an air strike, and McNamara even argued that Soviet missiles in Cuba did little to change the strategic equation. . . .

The atmosphere at our Ex Comm meetings was extremely serious, but I would not call it emotional. Although this was the worst crisis we ever faced, most of us had been there before. The emotion that Bobby Kennedy portrayed in his book *The Thirteen Days* and that was reflected in the television program "The Missiles of October" was unique to Bobby; this was his first major crisis. His brother set the tone for us all, however. Throughout, John Kennedy was cool as a cucumber. That alone—keeping his cool—was JFK's greatest contribution in the crisis. . . .

Legal issues also led us toward a naval "quarantine" instead of a "blockade." In international law a blockade can mean a number of things, but over the years the blockade concept had become rigid and developed all sorts of barnacles. A blockade was hard to apply in strict accordance with international law. To shed the barnacles and allow for maximum flexibility, we hit upon a new term, "quarantine," partly because no one knew exactly what a quarantine meant. Ironically, this created problems since our Navy insisted the quarantine was a blockade. Bob McNamara had to ride herd on the Navy in implementing the quarantine. . . .

Two hours before Kennedy went on television [22 October], he called about thirty congressional leaders to the White House for their first briefing about the missiles. They were as shocked as we were. The facts spoke for themselves. Kennedy told the group we would respond with a naval quarantine. One elderly senator just groaned and fell over on the table with his head in his hands and stayed there for a while.

When it came their turn to talk, some senators, William Fulbright and Richard Russell in particular, pressed hard for an immediate strike on Cuba. Nevertheless, at meeting's end the group supported Kennedy, and despite their misgivings, neither Fulbright nor Russell publicly questioned the president's decision. Equally important, no one present questioned whether Kennedy had constitutional authority to initiate a quarantine. No one suggested that Kennedy come to Congress for authorization. In fact, one senator told me upon leaving, "Thank God I am not the president of the United States!"

Source: Dean Rusk as Told to Richard Rusk. Edited by Daniel S. Papp, *As I Saw It* (New York: Norton, 1990), 229–35.

DOCUMENT 183: National Security Adviser McGeorge Bundy Describes the Dilemma over the Air Strike or the Blockade Response (16–20 October 1962)

Robert Kennedy and Robert McNamara had become settled advocates of a naval blockade, and they had the strong support of [Theodore] Sorensen. . . . A blockade might produce a deeply embarrassing counterblockade, most obviously in Berlin, and it might require deadly force in its application. But it did not begin with sudden death, and it was a first step, not a last. . . .

A particularly impressive and influential advocate of the blockade was [former Secretary of Defense] Robert Lovett, whose role is often neglected because his advice was given in a very small group. . . . When he came to Washington [18 October] at the president's request, he talked first with me and then with briefing officers . . . and his quick conclusion was that a good strong blockade was the right first step. . . .

The advocates of an air strike . . . never managed to concert their varied approaches into anything Kennedy found acceptable. . . . The most formidable of them was Dean Acheson, whose argument was characteristically brisk. . . . But where Acheson intended the air attack as a sharply limited blow against the missile sites alone, the Joint Chiefs . . . saw it as a blow that should be struck with all the additional military measures appropriate to traditional air warfare.

Source: Bundy, *Danger and Survival*, 398–400.

DOCUMENT 184: Press Secretary Pierre Salinger's "White Lie" that President Kennedy Has "a Cold" (20 October 1962)

The next morning, a Saturday [20 October], I met with the press . . . to outline the President's schedule for the day [in Chicago, St. Louis and Albuquerque]. . . . Midway through the briefing, [I was told] that I was to go to the President's suite immediately.

I found JFK . . . with [Ken] O'Donnell, Dave Powers, and Rear Admiral George G. Burkley, the White House physician. President was playing it straight.

"I have a temperature and a cold," he told me. "You have better go back downstairs and tell the press I'm returning to Washington on the advice of Dr. Burkley." Then, as I was halfway to the door, "Wait a minute. Let's be sure we're all saying the same thing."

He then took out a piece of Sheraton-Blackstone stationery and wrote: "*99.2 degrees temperature. Upper respiratory infection. Doctor says he should return to Washington.*"

He gave it to me. "There, tell them that."

Source: Pierre Salinger, *With Kennedy* (Garden City, N.Y.: Doubleday, 1966), 252.

DOCUMENT 185: Press Secretary Salinger Recalls Plan to Convert National Government to Wartime Posture (21 October 1962)

Shortly before noon that Sunday [21 October], I met in my office with Colonel Justice Chambers, deputy director of the Office of Emergency Planning. The colonel, a Congressional Medal of Honor winner in World War II, had conferred with me frequently over the past twenty-two months to update our emergency information procedures. All we had to do that morning was set the plan in motion.

The colonel's first action was to place on standby alert a nation-wide communications system, most of it underground. This system would be available if war came only to top government officials and the news services and networks. Our next concern was the pool of White House correspondents and photographers who would accompany the President if he had to evacuate Washington and who would remain with him for the duration. Colonel Chambers and I reviewed pre-evacuation instructions for the reporters we had previously worked out and that I was to relay them at the appropriate time.

Source: Salinger, *With Kennedy*, 257.

DOCUMENT 186: CIA Memo Suggests Vice President Lyndon Johnson Favored Surprise Air Strike Against Soviet Missile Sites in Cuba (21 October 1962)

On Sunday night, October 21 at 8:30 I [CIA Director John McCone] briefed Vice President Lyndon Johnson at the request of the President.

The briefing involved a review of photography by Lundahl [National Photographic Interpretation Center (NPIC) Director] paralleling briefings given to General Eisenhower and others. . . .

The thrust of the Vice President's thinking was that he favored an unannounced strike rather than the agreed plan which involved blockade and strike and invasion later if conditions warranted. He expressed displeasure at "telegraphing our punch" and also commented the blockade would be ineffective because we in effect are "locking the barn after the horse was gone."

. . . The Vice President finally agreed reluctantly but only after learning among other things the support indicated by General Eisenhower [afternoon of 21 October].

Source: Central Intelligence Agency, *Secret Cuban Missile Crisis Documents*, 245.

DOCUMENT 187: President Kennedy Speaks to the American People (22 October 1962)

This Government, as promised, has maintained the closest surveillance of the Soviet military buildup on the island of Cuba. Within the past week, unmistakable evidence has established the fact that a series of offensive missile sites is now in preparation on that imprisoned island. The purpose of these bases can be none other than to provide a nuclear strike capability against the Western Hemisphere. . . .

The characteristics of these new missile sites indicate two distinct types of installations. Several of them include medium range ballistic missiles, capable of carrying a nuclear warhead for a distance of more than 1,000 nautical miles. Each of these missiles, in short, is capable of striking Washington, D.C., the Panama Canal, Cape Canaveral, Mexico City, or any other city in the southeastern part of the United States, in Central America, or in the Caribbean area.

Additional sites not yet completed appear to be designed for intermediate range ballistic missiles—capable of traveling more than twice as far—and thus capable of striking most of the major cities in the Western Hemisphere, ranging as far north as Hudson Bay, Canada, and as far south as Lima, Peru. In addition, jet bombers, capable of carrying nuclear weapons, are now being uncrated and assembled in Cuba, while the necessary air bases are being prepared.

This urgent transformation of Cuba into an important strategic base— by the presence of these large, long-range, and clearly offensive weapons of sudden mass destruction—constitutes an explicit threat to the peace and security of all the Americas, in flagrant and deliberate defiance of the Rio Pact of 1947, the traditions of this Nation and hemisphere, the joint resolution of the 87th Congress, the Charter of the United Nations, and my own public warnings to the Soviets on September 4 and 13. This action also contradicts the repeated assurances of Soviet spokesmen, both publicly and privately delivered, that the arms buildup in Cuba would retain its original defensive character, and that the Soviet Union had no need or desire to station strategic missiles on the territory of any other nation. . . .

The 1930s taught us a clear lesson: aggressive conduct, if allowed to go unchecked and unchallenged, ultimately leads to war. This nation is opposed to war. We are also true to our word. Our unswerving objective, therefore, must be to prevent the use of these missiles against this or any other country, and to secure their withdrawal or elimination from the Western Hemisphere. . . .

Acting, therefore, in the defense of our own security and of the entire Western Hemisphere, and under the authority entrusted to me by the Constitution as endorsed by the resolution of the Congress, I have directed that the following initial steps be taken immediately:

First: To halt this offensive buildup, a strict quarantine on all offensive military equipment under shipment to Cuba is being initiated. All ships of any kind bound for Cuba from whatever nation or port will, if found to contain cargoes of offensive weapons, be turned back. This quarantine will be extended, if needed, to other types of cargo and carriers. . . .

Second: I have directed the continued and increased close surveillance of Cuba and its military buildup. The foreign ministers of the OAS, in their communiqué of October 6, rejected secrecy on such matters in this hemisphere. Should these offensive military preparations continue, thus increasing the threat to the hemisphere, further action will be justified. I have directed the Armed Forces to prepare for any eventualities; and I trust that in the interest of both the Cuban people and the Soviet technicians at the sites, the hazards to all concerned of continuing this threat will be recognized.

Third: It shall be the policy of this Nation to regard any nuclear missile launched from Cuba against any nation in the Western Hemisphere as an attack by the Soviet Union on the United States, requiring a full retaliatory response upon the Soviet Union.

Fourth: As a necessary military precaution, I have reinforced our base at Guantanamo, evacuated today the dependents of our personnel there, and ordered additional military units to be on a standby alert basis.

Fifth: We are calling tonight for an immediate meeting of the Organ of Consultation under the Organization of American States, to consider this threat to hemispheric security and to invoke articles 6 and 8 of the Rio Treaty in support of all necessary action. . . .

Sixth: Under the Charter of the United Nations, we are asking tonight that an emergency meeting of the Security Council be convoked without delay to take action against this latest Soviet threat to world peace. Our resolution will call for the prompt dismantling and withdrawal of all offensive weapons in Cuba, under the supervision of U.N. observers, before the quarantine can be lifted.

Seventh: I call upon Chairman Khrushchev to halt and eliminate this clandestine, reckless, and provocative threat to world peace and to stable relations between our two nations.

Source: Radio and television report to the nation, October 22, 1962, *Public Papers of the Presidents: John F. Kennedy, 1962* (Washington: GPO, 1963), 806–9.

DOCUMENT 188: President Castro's Speech to the Cuban People (22 October 1962)

. . . If they blockade our country they will exalt our nation, because we will resist. . . . We are part of humanity and we run the necessary risks, yet, we are not afraid. We must learn how to live in our allotted times and with the dignity with which we know how to live. Everybody, men and women, young and old, we are all one in this moment of danger.

Source: Blight, Allyn, and Welch, *Cuba on the Brink*, xv.

DOCUMENT 189: Soviet General Gribkov Comments on Readiness of Soviet Forces in Cuba, 22 October 1962 (Havana Conference, 1992)

On October 22nd, the day when Kennedy spoke on the radio and on television, we already had 42,000 troops in Cuba and three missile regiments (one division). The sites were ready for two regiments (not yet for the third). None of the missiles was placed in combat readiness. They had not yet been fueled, nor supplied with oxidating agents. The warheads were some 250 or 300 kilometers from the launch sites, and had not yet been released for use. . . .

The fighter planes were ready for combat. All the planes—forty MiG-21s—had been assembled and were ready for combat. But despite this, no one fired on the American planes that were flying over Cuba. These included high-altitude U-2s, and other low-level reconnaissance planes that flew so low that, in some cases, we could even see the pilots. We later learned that negotiations were taking place between Khrushchev and Kennedy. But, while they were in Cuba, the commanders of our troops were not informed of these secret negotiations. . . .

I must say that the fighting spirit of the Cuban Revolutionary Armed Forces and of the Cuban people, and the fighting spirit of the Soviet troops in Cuba, was high. We were all ready and willing to fight to the very last man. We didn't just plan an initial resistance. We even decided that if it proved necessary—if large tracts of the island were occupied— we would form guerrilla units in order to continue defending the inter- ests of revolutionary Cuba. . . . Allow me to say that, considering all the possible options in the event of an attack against Cuba, the aggressor would have suffered great losses, either in the event of an air attack with a subsequent landing, or in a direct assault. An air attack would not have destroyed all the missiles. Even if the three intermediate-range mis- sile regiments had been destroyed, leaving only the six *Luna* launchers (which were very hard to destroy), they would have been made ready with nuclear weapons, and we are all perfectly aware of the fact that losses would have been tremendous.

Source: Blight, Allyn, and Welch, *Cuba on the Brink*, 56–62.

DOCUMENT 190: Dean Rusk Recalls the American Diplomatic Effort to Resolve the Crisis (23–25 October 1962)

Although we took the missile crisis to the UN, we knew this alone would not get the job done. With their veto, the Russians could postpone discussion and action in the Security Council until the missile sites be- came fully operational. Nevertheless, although the Cuban missile crisis was directly resolved between Washington and Moscow, it was very important that the Security Council take it up. Prolonged discussion less- ened the chance that one side would lash out in a spasm and do some- thing foolish. The UN earned its pay for a long time to come just by being there for the missile crisis.

In another prong of our diplomatic effort, seeking support from our Latin American neighbors, on Tuesday, October 23, we met in an all-day meeting with the OAS [Organization of American States]. I worked closely with Edwin Martin, assistant secretary for Latin American affairs. All twenty OAS members voted in favor of a resolution demanding that the Soviets withdraw all offensive missiles from Cuba. They also authorized the use of force individually or collectively in a limited blockade. We were delighted with the vote. I am convinced the overwhelming support we received from the international community—and Castro's neighbors in particular—helped persuade Khrushchev to withdraw the missiles. Support came willingly at that Tuesday morning OAS meeting in Washington; I didn't have to twist arms or bludgeon anyone. OAS members believed Soviet missiles in Cuba were dangerous for the hemisphere and something had to be done about it.

The Soviets' initial reactions to Kennedy's speech worried us. They denied the missiles were offensive and condemned American "aggression." They continued to build their missile sites as twenty-five Soviet ships moved toward the quarantine line. The Soviets officially rejected our quarantine on Wednesday, October 24, and sent submarines to join their cargo vessels.

We imposed the quarantine very carefully, looking for maximum flexibility. Since it affected only offensive weapons, we allowed ships carrying weapons to go on to Cuba. We let a Soviet tanker through the blockade because it appeared to hold nothing but oil, and for our first boarding and inspection, we stopped a ship from another country rather than begin with a Soviet ship. At one point we moved our naval forces closer toward Cuba, reducing the radius of our blockade line from five hundred miles out to something less, to give Soviet ships steaming toward Cuba—and the Kremlin—more time. The crisis was building, and how it would end was unclear.

Source: Rusk, *As I Saw It*, 236–37.

DOCUMENT 191: Robert Kennedy Recalls a Stressful Ex Comm Meeting (24 October 1962)

The next morning, Wednesday [24 October], the quarantine went into effect, and the reports during the early hours told of the Russian ships coming steadily on toward Cuba. I talked with the President for a few moments before we went in to our regular meeting. He said, "It looks really mean, doesn't it? But then, really there was no other choice. If they get this mean on this one in our part of the world, what will they do on the next?" "I just don't think there was any choice," I said, "and not only that, if you hadn't acted, you would have been impeached." The President thought for a moment and said, "That's what I think—I would have been impeached." . . .

Then it was 10:25—a messenger brought in a note to John McCone. "Mr. President, we have a preliminary report which seems to indicate that some of the Russian ships have stopped dead in the water."

Stopped dead in the water? Which ships? Are they checking the accuracy of the report? Is it true? I looked at the clock. 10:32. "The report is accurate, Mr. President. Six ships previously on their way to Cuba at the edge of the quarantine line have stopped or have turned back toward the Soviet Union. A representative from the Office of Naval Intelligence is on his way over with the full report." A short time later, the report came that the twenty Russian ships closest to the barrier had stopped and were dead in the water or had turned around.

"So no ships will be stopped or intercepted," said the President. I said we should make sure the Navy knew nothing was to be done, that no ships were to be interfered with. Orders would go out to the Navy immediately.

Source: Kennedy, *Thirteen Days,* 46–50.

DOCUMENT 192: Secretary of State Rusk's "Eyeball to Eyeball" Remark (25 October 1962)

The moment of truth would not come until we stopped Soviet ships that carried missiles. Fortunately we never got that far since on Thursday several ships we suspected of carrying missiles stopped dead in the water, then turned around and headed back to the Black Sea. When we heard the news, I said to my colleagues, "We are eyeball to eyeball, and the other fellow just blinked."

Source: Rusk, *As I Saw It,* 237.

DOCUMENT 193: UN Ambassador Adlai Stevenson's Speech to "the Courtroom of World Opinion" (25 October 1962)

On Thursday evening [25 October] at the UN Stevenson [flanked by photo interpreters and intelligence analysts] returned to the debate in the Security Council. He crisply dismissed the communist argument that the United States had created the threat to the peace [by claiming the CIA had manufactured the evidence]: "This is the first time that I have ever heard it said that the crime is not the burglary, but the discovery of the burglar." As for those who thought the quarantine too extreme a remedy: "Were we to do nothing until the knife was sharpened? Were we to stand idly by until it was at our throats? . . . The course we have chosen seems to me perfectly graduated to meet the character of the threat."

[Soviet UN Ambassador V. A.] Zorin made a cocky but evasive reply. Now Stevenson took the floor again. Ironically regretting that he lacked his opponent's "talent for obfuscation, for distortion, for confusing language and for double-talk," saying sternly "those weapons must be taken out of Cuba," he turned on the Russian with magnificent scorn:

Do you, Ambassador Zorin, deny that the USSR has placed and is placing medium and intermediate-range missiles and sites in Cuba? Yes or no? Don't wait for the translation. Yes or no?

Zorin muttered something about not being in an American courtroom. Stevenson, cold and controlled:

You are in the courtroom of world opinion. You have denied they exist, and I want to know if I understood you correctly. I am prepared to wait for my answer until hell freezes over. And I am also prepared to present the evidence in this room—now!

Source: Arthur M. Schlesinger, Jr., *A Thousand Days: John F. Kennedy in the White House* (Boston: Houghton Mifflin, 1965), 820–24.

DOCUMENT 194: Dean Rusk Recalls the Confusing Signals from Soviet Sources and American Perception that Khrushchev Was Losing Control (26 October 1962)

On Friday, the twenty-sixth, came encouraging news; Alexander Fomin, the top Soviet intelligence officer in the United States, asked ABC's State Department correspondent John Scali to see if we would issue a public promise not to invade Cuba if the Soviets removed their missiles, pledged never to reintroduce them, and allowed UN inspectors to verify their removal. I gave Scali a note stating that we thought this could be worked out but that time was short. I told Scali to tell Fomin that our reply came from "the highest levels."

Kennedy also received a long message from Khrushchev, which we all believed bore Khrushchev's personal stamp. The letter encouraged us since Khrushchev obviously realized how grave the crisis was and indicated he wanted to avoid war, even implying that he might withdraw the missiles if we pledged not to invade Cuba. But its distraught and emotional tone bothered us, because it seemed the old fellow might be losing his cool in the Kremlin.

Source: Rusk, *As I Saw It*, 238–39.

DOCUMENT 195: General Gribkov Emphasizes that a Soviet Officer Ordered, and a Soviet Missile Crew Executed, the Shootdown of the American U-2 on 27 October 1962 (Havana Conference, 1992)

BRUCE ALLYN: This is just a follow-up question to General Gribkov about the U-2 shoot-down on the 27th of October. . . . There was a rumor that it was shot down by the Cubans, and this was certainly not possible because the Soviets were in control of the SAM sites. As President Castro said yesterday, he would quite happily have shot down the U-2s had Cubans had control of the SAMS. . . . We know that Marshal Malinovsky apparently sent a strong letter of rebuke to the Soviet commander in Cuba, complaining that the U-2 had been shot down without authorization from Moscow. This whole question of whether it could have been shot down without authorization from Moscow became even more interesting yesterday, when we learned that the authority to use the tactical nuclear weapons may have been vested in the local commander in Cuba. . . . When we learned the story of how the U-2 was shot down as the result of the decision of two Soviet generals in Cuba, that did clarify the basic question. But I wonder if you could help us understand how the rumor persisted that the plane had been shot down by the Cubans.

ANATOLY GRIBKOV: The U-2 manned by Major [Rudolf] Anderson was shot down with a Soviet missile under Soviet command. The order was issued by General Pliyev's deputy, General [Stepan Naumovich] Grechko. The order reached those under their command, and at 10:21 the plane was shot down. There were no orders from Moscow. It is also totally incorrect that the commander-in-chief of the Cuban Revolutionary Armed Forces, our dear Comrade Fidel Castro, pressed the button to shoot down the U-2. From the very beginning we said that the Soviet troops were commanded by Soviets, and there was no order issued by Commander Fidel Castro. He can corroborate here.

Source: Blight, Allyn, and Welch, *Cuba on the Brink*, 104–6.

DOCUMENT 196: Fidel Castro Presents the Cuban Perspective for Downing the American U-2 on 27 October 1962 (Havana Conference, 1992)

FIDEL CASTRO: The situation grew increasingly tense [afternoon 26 October], and low-level overflights more frequent, and we became convinced that it was extremely dangerous to allow low-level overflights. That was our conviction. It was our territory. We considered that we had the right to take whatever steps we deemed pertinent using our weapons in our territory, and we contacted the Soviet command, that is, the head of all the Soviet troops, General Pliyev. He had his command post here, southwest of the capital. We had a long meeting with him and his staff, and I told them that we had decided to fire against the low-level flights—those were the only ones we could reach. Yesterday I said that we were not so worried about the high-altitude aircraft flying at 20,000 meters, because those were not war planes. The danger was posed by the planes which overflew us every day at a low level. Those were flying not just for observation, but also to demoralize our troops. These planes were, in effect, training daily on how they could destroy our weapons. I told them that we had decided to shoot down low-flying planes, that we felt it was our duty, I told them we had reached this decision: we cannot tolerate these low-level overflights under these conditions, because any day at dawn they're going to destroy all these units. . . .

So, the next day, in the morning, when the planes started to come all over the place—they flew over San Cristóbal—our batteries opened fire. All our batteries fired on all low-level flights on the morning of the 27th when the planes appeared at their usual time. So the order was fulfilled. Now, we didn't have ground-to-air missiles. I explained to the Soviet commander the seriousness of these overflights, and I explained our point of view, to persuade them that our order had been correct. We could say that the war started in Cuba on October the 27th in the morning. Of course, those fast-flying jet planes, as soon as they heard the first shots, went higher to evade our artillery. Our artillerymen were not experts; the planes were flying at an altitude of 100 or 150 meters. I saw them more than once. I saw them flying over; the planes seemed quite vulnerable, but we couldn't shoot down any of the low-flying planes. But we demonstrated our resistance.

The U-2 planes overflew us almost every day. It's still a mystery what led the Soviet commander and the commander of that battery to issue the order to open fire. Obviously, we couldn't give them any orders, but we cannot say that they were solely responsible. And we were in total agreement with their firing against the U-2, because even though they did not pose the same danger from the military standpoint, the principle was the same. I said yesterday that we should not have tolerated the flight of the U-2s. . . .

These soldiers were all together. They had a common enemy. The firing started and, in a basic spirit of solidarity, the Soviets decided to fire as well. That is my interpretation. Our batteries opened fire that morning. When the planes started overflying from the west, sometime later a plane was shot down overflying Oriente. Prior to that, the radars usually were not operating; one of the issues that we had discussed with the Soviets on the evening of the 26th was that we had to activate the radars. We couldn't leave them off. We had to have time to be warned of the planes' approach. . . .

I can add that Khrushchev for some time believed that we had shot down the plane. He said, "You shot down a plane. You shot down a plane and you didn't do that before." That is really what he said; he was pointing the finger at us.

Source: Blight, Allyn, and Welch, *Cuba on the Brink,* 106–13, 120–21.

DOCUMENT 197: Two Soviet Generals Describe the Russian Perspective Behind the Downing of the American U-2 by a Soviet Missile Crew on 27 October 1962 (Havana Conference, 1992)

GENERAL GRIBKOV: When Anderson's airplane was shot down, we wrote a report to the minister of defense, Marshal of the Soviet Union Malinovsky. We explained how the airplane was shot down by our anti-aircraft batteries. [Gen. Georgy] Titov and I wrote the report. Titov was head of the operational department of the troops in Cuba. When our report was received in Moscow—signed by Comrade Pliyev—we received a brief and severe reply signed by Malinovsky. It said, more less, "You were hasty in shooting down the American U-2 while the talks were under way successfully with the American side." We were expecting to be punished for having shot down the plane, so the reply was actually light. But even before that, we had requested authorization to open fire from the minister of defense—and, of course, through him, from the political leadership. We had warned them that American planes were making low-level and high-level overflights, and we requested authorization to open fire. They, however, refused that authorization. However, when Commander-in-Chief Fidel Castro ordered his troops—his anti-aircraft batteries—to fire, our commander also issued the order to be in a state of maximum alert. He ordered that our batteries be ready, that our radars be operational. The order to shoot down the plane was given by General Stepan Naumovich Grechko at the regiment commander's headquarters. From there it was transferred to the regiments, and then to the battery commander. Immediately after the information arrived, the aircraft was shot down.

GENERAL GEORGY TITOV: I would like to shed a little light on the question of the shooting down of the aircraft. One has to understand the situation at the time. I recall that on the 25th, 26th, and 27th, we were expecting a strike by the U.S. armed forces. We were at the command posts, and we felt that we were about to launch into military operations, because U.S. aircraft were flying over Cuban territory and inspecting it indiscriminately. Our troops were in defensive positions then, and we could not allow a total discovery of our defensive dispositions. This was a definite possibility because we were being watched by these aircraft that were flying over Cuba constantly. On a number of occasions we requested authorization to fire on these aircraft, because they had in fact already begun what we considered to be military operations. While we were awaiting a decision from Moscow, our commander, Pliyev, made the decision to shoot down the U-2. The order was given by Grechko, as Grechko said he was the general commanding troops in Cuba.

Source: Blight, Allyn, and Welch, *Cuba on the Brink*, 113–14, 119–20.

DOCUMENT 198: Khrushchev's "Hard" Cable to Kennedy Proposing Swap of Soviet Missiles in Cuba for U.S. "Analogous Weapons" in Turkey (27 October 1962)

Dear Mr. President,

I have studied with great satisfaction your reply to Mr. Thant concerning measures that should be taken to avoid contact between our vessels and thereby avoid irreparable and fatal consequences. This reasonable step on your part strengthens my belief that you are showing concern for the preservation of peace, which I note with satisfaction. . . .

You wish to ensure the security of your country, and this is understandable. But Cuba, too, wants the same thing; all countries want to maintain their security. But how are we, the Soviet Union, our Government, to assess your actions which are expressed in the fact that you have surrounded the Soviet Union with military bases; surrounded our allies with military bases; placed military bases literally around our country; and stationed your missile armaments there? This is no secret. Responsible American personages openly declare that it is so. Your missiles are located in Britain, are located in Italy, and are aimed against us. Your missiles are located in Turkey.

You are disturbed over Cuba. You say that this disturbs you because it is 90 miles by sea from the coast of the United States of America. But Turkey adjoins us; our sentries patrol back and forth and see each other. Do you consider, then, that you have the right to demand security for your own country and the removal of the weapons you call offensive, but do not accord the same right to us? You have placed destructive missile weapons, which you call offensive, in Turkey, literally next to us. How then can recognition of our equal military capacities be reconciled with such unequal relations between our great states? This is irreconcilable. . . .

I therefore make this proposal: We are willing to remove from Cuba the means which you regard as offensive. We are willing to carry this out and to make this pledge in the United Nations. Your representatives will make a declaration to the effect that the United States, for its part, considering the uneasiness and anxiety of the Soviet State, will remove its analogous means from Turkey. Let us reach agreement as to the period of time needed by you and by us to bring this about. And, after that, persons entrusted by the United Nations Security Council could inspect on the spot the fulfillment of the pledges made. . . .

The United States Government will . . . declare that the United States will respect the inviolability of Cuba's borders and its sovereignty, will pledge not to interfere in its internal affairs, not to invade Cuba itself or make its territory available as a bridgehead for such an invasion.

Source: Chang and Kornbluh, *Cuban Missile Crisis, 1962,* 197–99.

DOCUMENT 199: U.S. Ambassador to Turkey Cables Turkish Objections to American-Soviet Missile Swap (27 October 1962)

As recognized . . . removal Jupiters from Turkey in context Cuban situation would present major problem not only in terms of bilateral Turkish-American relationship but also NATO association. Problem would be partly psycho-political, partly substantive; psycho-political, in sense that Turks are proud courageous people who do not understand concept or process of compromise. It is this quality of steadfast, even stolid, courage in both spirit and policy, together with traditional Turkish military skill which is actually their greatest asset to US and to West generally and by same token it is here that we would have most to lose if in process of Jupiter removal Turks should get the impression that their interests as an ally were being sacrificed in order to appease an enemy. Furthermore, as brought out in conversation with Foreign Minister Erkin yesterday, Turks deeply resent any coupling of Turkey and Cuba on ground that situations completely different and that suggestions to that effect, especially when coming from Western sources, are both inexcusable and seriously damaging; and all the more so when associated with idea that Turkish relationship with US can be equated with stooge status of Cuba with USSR.

The Turks, as we well know, set great store on arms which they feel necessary [*sic*] meet their needs and were adamant in refusing our suggestion last year that Jupiter project not be implemented. No indication in meantime that their position has changed and can therefore be assumed that . . . demand for arms to fill vacuum would be specific and sizeable.

Source: "U.S. Ambassador to Turkey Raymond Hare to State Department," in Chang and Kornbluh, *Cuban Missile Crisis, 1962,* 221–22.

DOCUMENT 200: Secretary of State Rusk Recalls Decision to Swap U.S. Missiles in Turkey for Soviet Missiles in Cuba (27 October 1962)

The next day, Saturday [27th], we got another long message from Khrushchev, but this one was clearly a collective effort, a foreign ministry type of letter. It raised the red herring of U.S. Jupiter missiles in Turkey and offered to withdraw Soviet missiles in Cuba for our Jupiters in Turkey.

Those Jupiters had long been a problem for us. When Kennedy took office, he had on his desk a very negative report from the congressional Joint Atomic Energy Committee criticizing deployment of Jupiters in Turkey and Italy. The Eisenhower administration had built these medium-range missiles without knowing what to do with them. They could not be based in the United States since they couldn't reach the Soviet Union. So Eisenhower, casting about, managed to persuade both the Turks and the Italians to accept some missiles, and there they sat. . . .

Soon after taking office, Kennedy and I discussed the matter and decided we should withdraw the missiles. But during a Central Treaty Organization (CENTO) meeting in Ankara, Turkey, in spring of 1961, I had a walk in the garden with Selim Sarper, Turkey's foreign minister. I raised the question with him, and he expressed great concern. His government had just convinced the Turkish Parliament to appropriate money for the Turkish costs of putting those missiles in, and it would be very embarrassing to go back so soon to Parliament to say the missiles were being dismantled.

Second, he said that Turkish morale would be seriously affected if the Jupiters were withdrawn without substituting another weapons system such as Polaris submarines in the Mediterranean. But these submarines were not going to be available until spring of 1963.

I came home and discussed this fully with President Kennedy. He disliked further delay but understood the Turkish point of view. Also, we couldn't withdraw the missiles without consulting NATO. But reports that Kennedy blew his top during the Cuban missile crisis because the Jupiters were still in place were simply untrue. We regretted the Jupiters were still there because if we had destroyed the missile sites in Cuba, the Jupiters were likely targets. Early in the crisis, to discourage this kind of swap and lessen the threat the Soviets felt from the Jupiters, Kennedy ordered American personnel to remove their warheads and to do so conspicuously so the Soviets would see this.

All this occurred before Khrushchev's second letter of Saturday, October 27. In framing a response, the president, Bundy, McNamara, Bobby Kennedy, and I met in the Oval Office, where after some discussion I suggested that since the Jupiters in Turkey were coming out in any event, we should inform the Russians of this so that this irrelevant question would not complicate the solution of the missile sites in Cuba. We agreed that Bobby should inform Ambassador Dobrynin orally. Shortly after we returned to our offices, I telephoned Bobby to underline that he should pass this along to Dobrynin only as information, not a public pledge. Bobby told me that he was then sitting with Dobrynin and had already talked with him. Bobby later told me that Dobrynin called this message "very important information."

Later Dobrynin brought back to Bobby Kennedy a memo of conversation recording their exchange on the Turkish Jupiters, implying that we had made an official agreement. That memo was returned to Dobrynin as inappropriate in the circumstances.

Although most people credit Bobby Kennedy, actually Llewellyn Thompson came up with the idea of how to respond to Khrushchev's linking American Jupiters in Turkey to Soviet missiles in Cuba; Tommy suggested we simply ignore the second letter and respond to the first.

Bobby got the credit because he proposed it at the Ex Comm meeting, but it was Thompson's idea.

It worked. We ignored the second letter entirely, picked up on Khrushchev's feeler in his first letter about an American pledge not to invade Cuba if the Soviets withdrew their missiles, and attributed the idea to Khrushchev. That was the key that defused the crisis.

Source: Rusk, *As I Saw It*, 239–40.

DOCUMENT 201: Robert Kennedy's Meeting with Soviet Ambassador Anatoly Dobrynin over Status of U.S. Missiles in Turkey (27 October 1962)

I telephoned Ambassador Dobrynin [on Saturday, 27 October] about 7:15 P.M. and asked him to come to the Department of Justice. We met in my office at 7:45. I told him first that we knew that work was continuing on the missile bases in Cuba and that in the last few days it had been expedited. I said that in the last few hours we had learned that our reconnaissance planes flying over Cuba had been fired upon and that one of our U-2s had been shot down and the pilot killed. That for us was a most serious turn of events. . . .

He said the Cubans resented the fact that we were violating Cuban air space. I replied that if we had not violated Cuban air space, we would still be believing what Khrushchev had said—that there would be no missiles placed in Cuba. In any case, I said, this matter was far more serious than the air space of Cuba—it involved the peoples of both of our countries and, in fact, people all over the globe. . . .

He asked me what offer the United States was making, and I told him of the letter that President Kennedy had just transmitted to Khrushchev. He raised the question of our removing the missiles from Turkey. I said that there could be no quid pro quo or any arrangement made under this kind of threat or pressure, and that in the last analysis this was a decision that would have to be made by NATO. However, I said, President Kennedy had been anxious to remove those missiles from Turkey and Italy for a long period of time. He had ordered their removal some time ago, and it was our judgment that, within a short time after this crisis was over, those missiles would be gone.

Source: Kennedy, *Thirteen Days*, 79–87.

DOCUMENT 202: Secretary of State Rusk Remembers the "Cordier Ploy" to Swap Missiles Through UN Auspices (27 October 1962)

There is a postscript to the saga of the Jupiter missiles. Neither Kennedy nor I, nor anyone on the Ex Comm with the exception of Adlai Stevenson and John J. McCloy, thought a missile trade with the Soviets wise because it smacked of blackmail and could set a dangerous precedent. Nevertheless, Kennedy clearly didn't want the Jupiters to impede the removal of the missile sites in Cuba and perhaps lead to war with the Soviet Union, since the Jupiters were coming out in any event. That Saturday night—October 27—the president remained troubled, and so did I; what would we do if Khrushchev refused to accept what Robert Kennedy had discussed with Dobrynin? We needed a final option, and instinctively I thought of the United Nations.

I suggested to Kennedy that he let me telephone Andrew Cordier, then at Columbia University, and dictate to him a statement which would be made by Secretary-General U Thant at the United Nations, proposing the removal of both the Jupiters and Soviet missiles in Cuba. I had known Andrew Cordier for many years in New York, and I trusted him. During his years at the UN he was known as an expert parliamentarian. He sat next to the president of the Security Council during all the debates. He also had ready access to U Thant.

Kennedy readily agreed. U Thant was in a better position to make this proposal than we, because the Soviets could more easily respond to a United Nations plea. From the U.S. point of view, the Jupiters were a red herring—they were coming out—and responding to U Thant wouldn't have been a serious concession on our part. The swap might have created strain within NATO, but a temporary disruption of the alliance or our relations with Turkey was preferable to war.

Kennedy never decided in advance to go to the UN; it simply gave him an additional option if the Soviets didn't withdraw their missiles. I called Cordier, and he quietly took the message. Cordier was to put the statement in the hands of U Thant only after a further signal from us. Fortunately we never had to send that signal.

Source: Rusk, *As I Saw It*, 240–41.

DOCUMENT 203: President Kennedy Decides to Respond to Khrushchev's "Soft" Cable (27 October 1962)

I have read your letter of October 26th with great care and welcomed the statement of your desire to seek a prompt solution to the problem. The first thing that needs to be done, however, is for work to cease on offensive missile bases in Cuba and for all weapons systems in Cuba capable of offensive use to be rendered inoperable, under effective United Nations arrangements.

Assuming this is done promptly, I have given my representatives in New York instructions that will permit them to work out this weekend—in cooperation with the Acting Secretary General and your representative—an arrangement for a permanent solution to the Cuban problem along the lines suggested in your letter of October 26th. As I read your letter, the key elements of your proposals—which seem generally acceptable as I understand them—are as follows:

1) You would agree to remove these weapons systems from Cuba under appropriate United Nations observation and supervision; and undertake, with suitable safeguards, to halt the further introduction of such weapons systems into Cuba.

2) We, on our part, would agree—upon the establishment of adequate arrangements through the United Nations to ensure the carrying out and continuation of these commitments—(a) to remove promptly the quarantine measures now in effect and (b) to give assurances against an invasion of Cuba. I am confident that other nations of the Western Hemisphere would be prepared to do likewise.

If you will give your representative similar instructions, there is no reason why we should not be able to complete these arrangements and announce them to the world within a couple of days. The effect of such a settlement on easing world tensions would enable us to work toward a more general arrangement regarding "other armaments," as proposed in your second letter which you made public. . . .

But the first ingredient, let me emphasize, is the cessation of work on missile sites in Cuba and measures to render such weapons inoperable, under effective international guarantees. The continuation of this threat, or a prolonging of this discussion concerning Cuba by linking these problems to the broader questions of European and world security, would surely lead to an intensification of the Cuban crisis and a grave risk to the peace of the world.

Source: John Kennedy's letter to Khrushchev, 27 October 1962, in *Public Papers of the Presidents: John F. Kennedy, 1962,* 813–14.

DOCUMENT 204: Khrushchev's Cable to Remove Missiles from Cuba (28 October 1962)

In order to eliminate as rapidly as possible the conflict which endangers the cause of peace, to give an assurance to all people who crave peace, and to reassure the American people, who, I am certain, also want peace, as do the people of the Soviet Union, the Soviet Government, in addition to earlier instructions on the discontinuation of further work on weapons construction sites, has given a new order to dismantle the arms which you described as offensive, and to crate and return them to the Soviet Union. . . .

I regard with respect and trust the statement you made in your message of 27 October 1962 that there would be no attack, no invasion of Cuba, and not only on the part of the United States, but also on the part of other nations of the Western Hemisphere, as you said in your same message. Then the motives which induced us to render assistance of such a kind to Cuba disappear.

It is for this reason that we instructed our officers—these means as I had already informed you earlier are in the hands of the Soviet officers—to take appropriate measures to discontinue construction of the aforementioned facilities, to dismantle them, and to return them to the Soviet Union. As I had informed you in the letter of 27 October, we are prepared to reach agreement to enable U.N. representatives to verify the dismantling of these means. Thus in view of the assurances you have given and our instructions on dismantling, there is every condition for eliminating the present conflict.

Source: Chang and Kornbluh, *Cuban Missile Crisis, 1962,* 226–29.

DOCUMENT 205: President Kennedy's Reply to Chairman Khrushchev (28 October 1962)

I am replying at once to your broadcast message of October twenty-eight, even though the official text has not yet reached me, because of the great importance I attach to moving forward promptly to the settlement of the Cuban crisis. I think that you and I, with our heavy responsibilities for the maintenance of peace, were aware that developments were approaching a point where events could have become unmanageable. So I welcome this message and consider it an important contribution to peace. . . .

You referred in your letter to a violation of your frontier by an American aircraft in the area of the Chukotsk Peninsula. I have learned that this plane, without arms or photographic equipment, was engaged in an air-sampling mission in connection with your nuclear tests. . . . The pilot made a serious navigational error which carried him over Soviet territory. . . . I regret this incident and will see to it that every precaution is taken to prevent recurrence.

Source: John Kennedy's letter to Khrushchev, 28 October 1962, in *Public Papers of the Presidents: John F. Kennedy, 1962,* 814–15.

DOCUMENT 206: Fidel Castro–Nikita Khrushchev Correspondence (26–31 October 1962)

Havana, October 26, 1962

Dear Comrade Khrushchev:

From an analysis of the situation and the reports in our possession, I consider that the aggression is almost imminent within the next 24 or 72 hours.

There are two possible variants: the first and likeliest one is an air attack against certain targets with the limited objective of destroying them; the second, less probable although possible, is invasion. I understand that this variant would call for a large number of forces and it is, in addition, the most repulsive form of aggression, which might inhibit them.

You can rest assured that we will firmly and resolutely resist attack, whatever it may be.

The morale of the Cuban people is extremely high and the aggressor will be confronted heroically.

At this time I want to convey to you briefly my personal opinion.

If the second variant is implemented and the imperialists invade Cuba with the goal of occupying it, the danger that that aggressive policy poses for humanity is so great that following that event the Soviet Union must never allow the circumstances in which the imperialists could launch the first nuclear strike against it.

I tell you this because I believe that the imperialists' aggressiveness is extremely dangerous and if they actually carry out the brutal act of invading Cuba in violation of international law and morality, that would be the moment to eliminate such danger forever through an act of clear legitimate defense, however harsh and terrible the solution would be, for there is no other. . . .

Fraternally, Fidel Castro

* * * * *

Moscow, 30 October 1962

Dear Comrade Fidel Castro:

. . . As we learned from our ambassador, some Cubans have the opinion that the Cuban people want a declaration of another nature rather than the declaration of the withdrawal of the missiles. It's possible that this kind of feeling exists among the people. But we, political and government figures, are leaders of a people who doesn't know everything and can't readily comprehend all that we leaders must deal with. Therefore, we should march at the head of the people and then the people will follow us and respect us.

Had we, yielding to the sentiments prevailing among the people, allowed ourselves to be carried away by certain passionate sectors of the population and refused to come to a reasonable agreement with the U.S. government, then a war could have broken out, in the course of which millions of people would have died and the survivors would have pinned the blame on the leaders for not having taken all the necessary measures to prevent that war of annihilation.

Preventing the war and an attack on Cuba depended not just on the measures adopted by our governments but also on an estimate of the actions of the enemy forces deployed near you. Accordingly, the overall situation had to be considered. . . .

We came to the conclusion that our strategic missiles in Cuba became an ominous force for the imperialists: they were frightened and because of their fear that our rockets could be launched, they could have dared to liquidate them by bombing them or launching an invasion of Cuba. And it must be said that they could have knocked them all out. Therefore, I repeat, your alarm was absolutely well-founded.

In your cable of October 27 [26 October] you proposed that we be the first to launch a nuclear strike against the territory of the enemy. You, of course, realize where that would have led. Rather than a simple strike, it would have been the start of a thermonuclear world war.

. . . I consider this proposal of yours incorrect, although I understand your motivation. . . . Cuba would have been burned in the fire of war. There's no doubt that the Cuban people would have fought courageously or that they would have died heroically. But we are not struggling against imperialism in order to die, but to take advantage of all our possibilities, to lose less in the struggle and win more to overcome and achieve the victory of communism.

Now, as a result of the measures taken, we reached the goal sought when we agreed with you to send the missiles to Cuba. We have wrested from the United States the commitment not to invade Cuba and not to permit their Latin American allies to do so. We have wrested all this from them without a nuclear strike.

We consider that we must take advantage of all the possibilities to defend Cuba, strengthen its independence and sovereignty, defeat military aggression and prevent a nuclear world war in our time.

And we have accomplished that. . . .

N. Khrushchev

* * * * *

Havana . . . 31 October 1962

Dear Comrade Khrushchev:

. . . Few times in history, and it could even be said that never before, because no people had ever faced such a tremendous danger, was a people so willing to fight and die with such a universal sense of duty.

We knew, and do not presume that we ignored it, that we would have been annihilated, as you insinuate in your letter, in the event of nuclear war. However, that didn't prompt us to ask you to withdraw the missiles, that didn't prompt us to ask you to yield. Do you believe that we wanted that war? But how could we prevent it if the invasion finally took place? The fact is that this event was possible, that imperialism was obstructing every solution and that its demands were, from our point of view, impossible for the USSR and Cuba to accept. . . .

. . . I did not suggest, Comrade Khrushchev, that in the midst of this crisis the Soviet Union should attack, which is what your letter seems to say; rather, that following an imperialist attack, the USSR should act without vacillation and should never make the mistake of allowing circumstances to develop in which the enemy makes the first nuclear strike against the USSR. And in this sense, Comrade Khrushchev, I maintain my point of view, because I understand it to be a true and just evaluation of a specific situation. You may be able to convince me that I am wrong, but you can't tell me that I am wrong without convincing me. . . .

I do not see how you can state that we were consulted in the decision you took. I would like nothing more than to be proved wrong at this moment. I only wish that you were right.

There are not just a few Cubans, as has been reported to you, but in fact many Cubans who are experiencing at this moment unspeakable bitterness and sadness. . . .

Fraternally, Fidel Castro

Source: Blight, Allyn, and Welch, *Cuba on the Brink*, 481–91.

CLOSE CALL

The Cuban missile crisis was the most dangerous event of the Cold War. One false step by either side could have brought nuclear catastrophe. This fact, and the difficulty in communicating directly and immediately with the Soviet government in Moscow, made the task of deciding on an appropriate response difficult for American policymakers. Students studying these documents may want to speculate as to who "won" and who "lost" in the end.

DOCUMENT 207: General Gribkov's Most Humiliating Experience, November 1962 (Havana Conference, 1992)

I am a military man who fought hard in 1939 and 1940. I was in a tank during the Second World War. I was a lieutenant. I had to fight. I know the bitterness of retreat, and we had victories. But during my long military career—in the fifty-four years that I have served as a military man—my most humiliating experience was the inspection of our ships at sea. You know what I am talking about. I believe that Fidel Castro did right when he refused to allow Cuban territory to be inspected, the ports and the territorial waters of Cuba; but our ships were inspected on the high seas. At that time, we had to tell the Americans the number of missiles that the ships were to carry, and then the American ships and helicopters came, inspected the ships, and said okay.

Source: Blight, Allyn, and Welch, *Cuba on the Brink*, 62–63.

DOCUMENT 208: President Kennedy's News Conference Lifting the "Quarantine" of Cuba (20 November 1962)

I have today been informed by Chairman Khrushchev that all of the IL-28 bombers now in Cuba will be withdrawn in 30 days. He also agrees that these planes can be observed and counted as they leave. Inasmuch as this goes a long way towards reducing the danger which faced this hemisphere 4 weeks ago, I have this afternoon instructed the Secretary of Defense to lift our naval quarantine.

In view of this action, I want to take this opportunity to bring the American people up to date on the Cuban crisis and to review the progress made thus far in fulfilling the understandings between Soviet Chairman Khrushchev and myself as set forth in our letters of October 27 and 28. Chairman Khrushchev, it will be recalled, agreed to remove from Cuba all weapons systems capable of offensive use, to halt the further introduction of such weapons into Cuba, and to permit appropriate United Nations observation and supervision to insure the carrying out and continuation of these commitments. We on our part agreed that once these adequate arrangements for verification had been established we would remove our naval quarantine and give assurance against an invasion of Cuba.

The evidence to date indicates that all known offensive missile sites in Cuba have been dismantled. The missiles and their associated equipment have been loaded on Soviet ships. And our inspection at sea of these departing ships has confirmed that the number of missiles reported by the Soviet Union as having been brought into Cuba, which closely corresponded to our own information, has now been removed. In addition, the Soviet Government has stated that all nuclear weapons have been withdrawn from Cuba and no offensive weapons will be reintroduced.

Source: John Kennedy's News Conference Statement, 20 November 1962, in *Public Papers of the Presidents: John F. Kennedy, 1962*, 830–31.

DOCUMENT 209: Ambassador Charles Bohlen's Assessment of the Crisis (1969)

There are those who still believe that the United States should have bombed out the missile sites and with them the Castro government. The simplicity of such a course is attractive, but the results would have been questionable. The missiles would have been removed from Cuba all right. But thousands of Soviet technicians might have been killed. Because it sometimes reacts instinctively, the Kremlin might have responded, without thought of the consequences, with a direct military counterblow. The United States would have won the nuclear war that followed. We still maintained an advantage over the Soviets in missiles and atomic weapons. But millions of lives would have been lost, and the onus for starting the war would have been on us. Kennedy succeeded in getting the missiles removed without a war. The Cuban missile crisis showed that Kennedy would have been a strong President if he had lived.

Source: Bohlen, *Witness to History, 1929–1969*, 495–96.

DOCUMENT 210: Fidel Castro Asks Robert McNamara When Nuclear Balance Was Achieved Between the United States and the Soviet Union (Havana Conference, 1992)

FIDEL CASTRO: Mr. McNamara, when was the nuclear balance achieved—the nuclear balance that has been so much discussed in recent years in the negotiations between the United States and the USSR?

ROBERT McNAMARA: Mr. President, . . . we [are] defining parity, deterrence, sufficiency and so on; . . . I can't tell you when nuclear balance was achieved, if by "balance" you mean the term "parity." But I can tell you when it existed. . . . I believed parity existed in October 1962, in the following sense—and this is why I have never felt that the movement of the missiles into Cuba changed the strategic balance, because parity existed before the missiles were put into Cuba. There was a gross imbalance in numbers. We estimated—I think probably we overestimated the total number of Soviet strategic nuclear warheads—but we estimated that we had roughly 5,000 to the Soviets' 300. How can I possibly say parity existed? Because we in the U.S., contrary to what the Soviets believed—and they had reason for their belief, but they were in error—contrary to what they believed, we did not believe we had a first strike capability. We did not believe prior to the missile crisis or during the missile crisis, when it was a question that had to be considered—Kennedy and I did not believe—that we could launch our 5,000 warheads against the Soviet Union and destroy a sufficient number of what we thought were 300 (perhaps less) so that the number remaining could not inflict unacceptable damage on us. And, therefore, neither Kennedy nor I believed before the missiles were emplaced in Cuba that we had a first strike capability. Now, the Soviets might have thought we did, and if they thought that, they might have acted to try to change our thinking. But we did not have a first strike capability before the missiles were placed in Cuba.

We did not have a first strike capability, but we had confidence in our deterrent. We believed that our 5,000 warheads would deter the Soviets from ever initiating the use of their 300 in a first strike. So we believed we were deterring them. . . . I know how absurd this sounds, in a sense. It sounds absurd to say that we had a "balance" in October '62 when we had 5,000 and they had 300. But in terms of strategic theory, in terms of strategic deterrence, a balance did exist.

Source: Blight, Allyn, and Welch, *Cuba on the Brink*, 136–37.

DOCUMENT 211: CIA Report on U.S. Intelligence Agencies' Effectiveness During the Crisis (28 February 1963)

1. Although the intelligence community's inquiry into its actions during the Cuban crisis revealed certain areas where shortcomings existed and where improvements should be made in various areas of intelligence collection and processing, the intelligence community operated extensively and well in connection with Cuba. Every major weapon system introduced into Cuba by the Soviets was detected, identified, and reported (with respect to numbers, location and operational characteristics) before any one of these systems attained an operational capability.

2. A relatively short period of time ensued between the introduction of strategic weapons into Cuba, particularly strategic missiles, and the commencement of the flow, although meager, of tangible reports of their presence; detection of their possible presence and targeting of the suspect areas of their location was accomplished in a compressed time frame; and the intelligence cycle did move with extraordinary rapidity through the stages of collection, analysis, targeting for verification, and positive identification.

3. The very substantial effort directed toward Cuba was originated by an earlier concern with the situation in Cuba and the effort, already well under way, contributed to the detection and analysis of the Soviet build-up.

4. Information was disseminated and used.

5. Aerial photography was . . . our best means of establishing hard intelligence.

6. The procedures adapted in September delayed photographic intelligence, but this delay was not critical, because photography obtained prior to about 17 October would not have been sufficient to warrant action of a type which would require support from Western Hemisphere NATO allies.

7. Agent reports helped materially; however, none giving significant information on offensive missiles reached the intelligence community or

policy-makers until after mid-September. When received, they were used in directing aerial photography.

8. Some restrictions were placed on dissemination of information, but there is no indication that these restrictions necessarily affected analytical work or actions by policy-makers.

9. The 19 September estimate, while indicating the improbability that the Soviet Union would place MRBMs and IRBMs in Cuba, did state that "this contingency must be examined carefully, even though it would run counter to current Soviet policy"; the estimators in preparing the 19 September estimate gave great weight to the philosophical argument concerning Soviet intentions and thus did not fully weigh the many indicators.

10. The estimate of 19 October on probable Soviet reactions [to U.S. options] was correct.

Source: Central Intelligence Agency, *Secret Cuban Missile Crisis Documents*, 373–76.

DOCUMENT 212: Robert McNamara and Fidel Castro Discuss the Role of the Soviet *Lunas* in the Defense of Cuba and Their Relevance to the Crisis (Havana Conference, 1992)

ROBERT McNAMARA: I think the most extraordinary statement I have heard here—at least with respect to the military aspects of the crisis—was that of General Gribkov, who, if I understood him correctly, stated that the Soviet Union anticipated the possibility of a large-scale U.S. invasion of the type that we were equipped for by October 27. I think Ray Garthoff summarized it. . . . Let me just repeat it very quickly: something on the order of 1,190 air sorties the first day, five army divisions, three marine divisions, 140,000 U.S. ground troops. The Soviet Union, as I understand it, to some degree anticipated that, and equipped their forces here—the 42,000 Soviet troops—with six what they call *Luna* launchers—we call them FROGs—and nine tactical nuclear warheads. Later, perhaps, we should extend the discussion of the implications of that for the future of a nuclear world. It strikes me in one sense as the most dangerous element of the entire episode. But, my question to you, sir, is this: Were you aware that the Soviet forces (a) were equipped with six *Luna* launchers and nine nuclear warheads; and (b)—something I never could have conceived of—that because the Soviets were concerned about the ability of the Soviet troops and the Cuban troops to repel the possible U.S. invasion using conventional arms, the Soviets authorized the field commanders in Cuba, without further consultation with the Soviet Union—which of course would have been very difficult because of communication problems—to utilize those nuclear launchers and nuclear warheads?;

(a) Were you aware of it? (b) What was your interpretation or expectation of the possible effect on Cuba? How did you think the U.S. would respond, and what might the implications have been for your nation and the world?

FIDEL CASTRO: Well, I actually thought that there were *more* tactical nuclear weapons. There was mention of tactical nuclear weapons in the report of the Soviet Command. There was mention of the *Luna* missiles. I don't know whether the naval forces had them, too. There was mention of the tactical nuclear weapons, and the motorized, or mechanized, regiments. . . .

. . . We've always thought that in a nuclear war, the whole world would be included in it, and it would affect everyone. . . . I also think that if it was a matter of defending Cuba without creating an international problem, the presence of tactical weapons would not have created the same problem that the strategic weapons did. It couldn't have been said that tactical nuclear weapons in Cuba represented a threat to the United States. It might even have been considered an appropriate formula. If the intent was simply to defend Cuba, a number of tactical weapons for the mechanized units would have been more practical.

Now, we started from the assumption that if there was an invasion of Cuba, nuclear war would erupt. We were certain of that. If the invasion took place in the situation that had been created, nuclear war would have been the result. Everybody here was simply resigned to the fate that we would be forced to pay the price, that we would disappear. We saw that danger . . . and the conclusion that we might derive is that if we were going to rely on fear, we would never be able to prevent a nuclear war. The danger of nuclear war has to be eliminated by other means; it cannot be prevented on the basis of fear of nuclear weapons, or that human beings are going to be deterred by the fear. . . .

You want me to give you my opinion in the event of an invasion with all the troops, with 1,190 sorties? Would I have been ready to use nuclear weapons? Yes, I would have agreed to the use of nuclear weapons. Because, in any case, we took it for granted that it would become a nuclear war anyway, and that we were going to disappear. Before having the country occupied—totally occupied—we were ready to die in the defense of our country. I would have agreed, in the event of the invasion that you are talking about, with the use of tactical nuclear weapons. You've asked me to speak frankly and, in all frankness, I must say that I would have had that opinion. If Mr. McNamara or Mr. Kennedy had been in our place, and had their country been invaded, or if their country was going to be occupied—given an enormous concentration of conventional forces—they would have used tactical nuclear weapons. And after the experience of what happened, do you want me to tell you something? I am glad that the military here had the authority, and that they did not have to consult.

. . . If I'd known this information [about the nuclear balance favoring the United States], and [Khrushchev and I] had discussed the deployment on the basis of the strategic issues—I continue to believe that this was what was at the bottom of the issue—I would have counseled prudence, since for us there was no anxiety, no fear, in the thought that we were going to be invaded, and that they were going to crush us. After all, we had developed the mentality of fighters, of patriots ready to fight. We were not afraid of fighting. [W]e are calm. I'm not boasting. It is a philosophy. It is a way of thinking. If we had known that this was the correlation of forces, we would have advised prudence. "Don't bring that kind of missile," I would have said, "because under these conditions you can't do that. You shouldn't do that."

Source: Blight, Allyn, and Welch, *Cuba on the Brink*, 250–55.

FURTHER READING

Allison, Graham T. *Essence of Decision* (1971).

Beschloss, Michael. *The Crisis Years* (1991).

Blight, James G., and David A. Welch. *On the Brink* (1990).

Brugioni, Dino A. *Eyeball to Eyeball: The Inside Story of the Cuban Missile Crisis* (1991).

Chang, Laurence, and Peter Kornbluh, eds. *The Cuban Missile Crisis, 1962: A National Security Archive Documents Reader* (1992).

Cohen, Warren I. *Dean Rusk* (1980).

Garthoff, Raymond. *Reflections on the Cuban Missile Crisis* (1989).

Higgins, Trumbull. *The Perfect Failure* (1987).

Kern, Montague. *The Kennedy Crises: The Press, the Presidency, and Foreign Policy* (1983).

McAuliffe, Mary S., ed. *CIA Documents on the Cuban Missile Crisis, 1962* (1992).

Nathan, James A., ed. *The Cuban Missile Crisis Revisited* (1992).

Paterson, Thomas G., ed. *Kennedy's Quest for Victory* (1989).

Thompson, Robert S. *The Missiles of October: The Declassified Story of John F. Kennedy and the Cuban Missile Crisis* (1992).

Part VI

The War in Vietnam, 1954–1975

Vietnam was not only America's longest war, but in many respects its most tragic. A colony of the French in the nineteenth and early twentieth centuries, and under Japanese control during World War II, Vietnam drew the attention of the United States during the early years of the Cold War. American support for France in Europe all too early became translated into U.S. underwriting of a French effort to defeat a communist-led nationalist struggle for an independent Vietnam. The United States found itself, at first inadvertently, and then later deliberately, supporting French efforts to reassert colonial control.

After the Geneva Agreement of 1954, which evicted the French and divided the country at the 17th parallel, the Eisenhower Administration took up the task of providing aid to a noncommunist regime headquartered in the southern city of Saigon (now Ho Chi Minh City). This American involvement effectively obstructed any hope for a peaceful unification of the country under a communist government centered in the northern industrial city of Hanoi. In the late 1950s and early 1960s the United States increased its aid to the government of South Vietnam to thwart the attempts of the communists to unite the country by force. In 1965 President Lyndon Johnson increased American commitment exponentially, so that by 1969 some 500,000 U.S. troops were involved in military operations in Southeast Asia.

What informed the increased American involvement under both Presidents Kennedy and Johnson was concern about the aggressive behavior of the People's Republic of China, a belief in particular of a "domino effect" in which China would eventually revolutionize and control the entire region. After all, American officials reasoned, the United States had become engaged in World War II largely because of threatened Japanese domination of Southeast Asia. Other factors influencing U.S. policy were the perceived need to combat wars of national liberation and prove American credibility as a guarantor.

Richard Nixon came to the presidency determined to extricate the United States from this Asian conflict, because he saw it as frittering away American power and because, over a four-year period, the war had done serious damage to the fabric of American society. It tore at the heart of the nation's institutions, including its families, as few developments before it had done; and it led to massive protests within the United States. Unfortunately, Nixon's plan to end the conflict with American honor intact led to the deaths of 20,000 more American troops and over 600,000 Vietnamese, took roughly four more years to accomplish, and resulted in an agreement of January 1973 that could not, given the climate of the time, ensure the peace. Fortunately, Nixon's simultaneous efforts to build new relationships with China and the Soviet Union did much to mitigate his failure in Vietnam, helping in the end—even though his own resignation occurred in August 1974 following the Watergate scandal—to offset the total collapse of the Saigon regime in April 1975 to units of the North Vietnamese Army.

CHRONOLOGY

1954

March–May. Battle of Dienbienphu in Vietnam

May–July. Geneva Conference and Agreement of Vietnam

September. Southeast Asia Treaty Organization (SEATO) created

November. Quemoy-Matsu/Taiwan Straits crisis with China

1963

November 1. South Vietnam's President Diem assassinated

November 22. Kennedy assassinated; Johnson becomes president

1964

August 4–5. U.S. destroyers allegedly attacked in Gulf of Tonkin

August 7. Gulf of Tonkin Resolution

November. Johnson elected president

1965

February 7. U.S. air strikes over North Vietnam begin

March 8. American Marines arrive at Da Nang in South Vietnam

March–June. Antiwar "teach-ins" begin on many U.S. campuses

April–May. U.S. Marines land in Dominican Republic

1966

Gen. Westmoreland commands some 362,000 U.S. troops in Southeast Asia

1967

March. Antiwar march on Washington

April 4. Martin Luther King, Jr., denounces the war

1968

January 30–February 24. Tet offensive by North Vietnam

March 16. My Lai massacre

March 22. Westmoreland relieved of command

March 31. Johnson withdraws from presidential race

April 4. Martin Luther King, Jr., assassinated

April 4–11. Urban riots in 168 cities

June 4. Robert Kennedy assassinated

August 29. Antiwar rioting in Chicago at Democratic Convention

November. Nixon elected president

1969

May 14. Nixon televised speech on 8-point negotiating position

September 2. Ho Chi Minh dies

October 15. Antiwar moratorium includes many U.S. servicemen

1970

February. Kissinger–Le Duc Tho secret peace talks in Paris

April 29. U.S. and ARVN troops invade Cambodia

May. Protest demonstrations; killings at Kent and Jackson State

June 24. Senate repeals Gulf of Tonkin Resolution

December. Congress bans combat troops in Laos and Cambodia

1971

April. Massive antiwar demonstration in Washington

June. The *New York Times* publishes *The Pentagon Papers*

October. Thieu elected president of South Vietnam

1972

February. Nixon visits China

May. Nixon orders mining of Haiphong Harbor

June. Watergate break-in

October. Secretary Kissinger's "Peace is at hand" speech

November. Nixon reelected

December 18–31. Bombing of North Vietnam resumes

1973

January 27. Vietnam peace agreement

February. Nixon pledges $4 billion in U.S. aid to North Vietnam

March. U.S. combat troops are withdrawn from Vietnam

March. U.S. POWs released by North Vietnam: Operation Homecoming

March. U.S. draft ended

July 1. Congress forbids further funding for combat in Vietnam

November. War Powers Act

1974

January–May. Cease-fire breaks down; Saigon launches offensive

May. House Judiciary Committee begins impeachment hearings

August 9. Nixon resigns; Ford becomes president

1975

January–April. Fall of South Vietnam; Thieu resigns

April 30. Saigon surrenders; helicopter airlift of U.S. personnel

May 16. U.S. imposes trade embargo on Vietnam

1976

Vietnam unified with Hanoi as capital; Saigon renamed Ho Chi Minh City

November. Jimmy Carter elected president

1982

November. Vietnam Veterans Memorial unveiled in Washington

1994

February. U.S. lifts trade embargo against Vietnam

1996

January. U.S. opens diplomatic relations with Vietnam

THE GENEVA CONFERENCE AND THE EISENHOWER-KENNEDY COURSE, 1954–1963

The French defeat at the battle of Dienbienphu in the spring of 1954 proved the coup de grâce for that nation's Southeast Asian colonial pretensions and led to a "settlement" on Indochina at Geneva—an agreement that divided the country at the 17th parallel while calling for a national election in 1956 to unify the country. The United States then began supporting the noncommunist government of Ngo Dinh Diem in the south and forced the cancellation of the election. Frustrated at its failure to unify the country through peaceful means, the

North Vietnamese government of Ho Chi Minh in Hanoi soon under-took to do so by force. This prompted a tentative buildup of American forces in the south under Presidents Eisenhower and Kennedy.

DOCUMENT 213: Geneva Conference's Indochina Cease-Fire Armistice (20 July 1954)

Article 1

A provisional military demarcation line shall be fixed, on either side of which the forces of the two parties shall be regrouped after their with-drawal, the forces of the People's Army of Viet-Nam to the north of the line and the forces of the French Union to the south.

The provisional military demarcation line is fixed [roughly along the 17th parallel].

It is also agreed that a demilitarized zone shall be established on either side of the demarcation line, to a width of not more than 5 kilometers from it, to act as a buffer zone and avoid any incidents which might result in the resumption of hostilities. . . .

Article 30

In order to facilitate, under the conditions shown below, the execution of provisions concerning joint actions by the two parties a Joint Com-mission shall be set up in Viet-Nam. . . .

Article 33

The Joint Commission shall ensure the execution of the following pro-visions of the Agreement on the cessation of hostilities:

(a) A simultaneous and general cease-fire in Viet-Nam for all reg-ular and irregular armed forces of the two parties.

(b) A re-groupment of the armed forces of the two parties.

(c) Observance of the demarcation lines between the re-grouping zones and of the demilitarized sectors. . . .

Article 43

If one of the parties refuses to put into effect a recommendation of the International Commission, the parties concerned or the Commission it-self shall inform the members of the Geneva Conference.

Source: U.S. Department of State, *Foreign Relations of the United States, 1952–1954,* Vol. 16, *The Geneva Conference* (Washington: GPO, 1981), 1474–81.

DOCUMENT 214: Report Detailing Efforts by CIA Operative Colonel Edward Lansdale and the Saigon Military Mission to Shore Up Diem Government in South (1954–1955)

This is the condensed account of one year in the operations of a "cold war" combat team, written by the team itself in the field. . . . The team is known as the Saigon Military Mission (SMM). The field is Vietnam. . . .

The Saigon Military Mission entered Vietnam on 1 June 1954 when its Chief [Colonel Edward G. Lansdale, USAF] arrived in Saigon [as the nominal Assistant Air Attaché]. However, this is the story of a team, and it wasn't until August 1954 that sufficient members arrived to constitute a team. . . .

The Saigon Military Mission received some blows from allies and the enemy in this atmosphere, as we worked to help stabilize the government and to beat the Geneva time-table of Communist takeover in the north. However, we did beat the time-table. The government did become stabilized. The Free Vietnamese are now becoming unified and learning how to cope with the Communist enemy. We are thankful that we had a chance to help in this work in a critical area of the world, to be positive and constructive in a year of doubt.

The Saigon Military Mission was born in a Washington policy meeting early in 1954, when Dien Bien Phu was still holding out against the encircling Vietminh. The SMM was to enter into Vietnam quietly and assist the Vietnamese, rather than the French, in unconventional warfare. The French were to be kept as friendly allies in the process, as far as possible.

The broad mission for the team was to undertake paramilitary operations against the enemy and to wage political-psychological warfare. Later, after Geneva, the mission was modified to prepare the means for undertaking paramilitary operations in Communist areas rather than to wage unconventional warfare.

Source: The Pentagon Papers: The Defense Department History of United States Decisionmaking on Vietnam, Gravel Edition, 5 vols. (Boston: Beacon Press, 1971), 1: 573–76.

DOCUMENT 215: Ngo Dinh Diem Statement Concerning Consultative Preparations for the 1956 Election of National Reunification (16 July 1955)

The National Government has emphasized the price it has paid for the defense of the unity of the country and of true democracy. We did not sign the Geneva Agreements. We are not bound in any way by these Agreements, signed against the will of the Vietnamese people. Our policy is a policy of peace, but nothing will lead us astray from our goal: the unity of our country—a unity in freedom and not in slavery.

Serving the cause of our nation more than ever, we will struggle for the reunification of our homeland. We do not reject the principle of free elections as peaceful and democratic means to achieve that unity. Although elections constitute one of the bases of true democracy, they will be meaningful only on the condition that they are absolutely free.

Faced now with a regime of oppression as practiced by the Vietminh, we remain skeptical concerning the possibility of fulfilling the conditions of free elections in the North. We shall not miss any opportunity which would permit the unification of our homeland in freedom, but it is out of the question for us to consider any proposal from the Vietminh if proof is not given that they put the superior interests of the national community above those of Communism, if they do not cease violating their obligations as they have done by preventing our countrymen of the North from going South or by recently attacking, together with the Communist Pathet Lao, the friendly state of Laos.

Source: Marvin E. Gettleman, Jane Franklin, Marilyn B. Young, and H. Bruce Franklin, *Vietnam and America: A Documented History* (New York: Grove Press, 1985), 107–9.

DOCUMENT 216: National Security Council Directive 5612 on U.S. Policy Toward North Vietnam (5 September 1956)

—Treat the Viet Minh as not constituting a legitimate government, and discourage other non-Communist states from developing or maintaining relations with the Viet Minh regime.

—Prevent the Viet Minh from expanding their political influence and territorial control in Free Viet Nam and Southeast Asia.

—Deter the Viet Minh from attacking or subverting Free Viet Nam or Laos.

—Probe weaknesses of the Viet Minh and exploit them internally and internationally whenever possible.

—Exploit nationalist sentiment within North Viet Nam as a means of weakening and disrupting Sino-Soviet domination.

—Assist the Government of Viet Nam to undertake programs of political, economic and psychological warfare against Viet Minh Communists.

—Apply, as necessary to achieve U.S. objectives, restrictions on U.S. exports and shipping and on foreign assets similar to those already in effect for Communist China and North Korea.

Source: U.S. Department of State, *United States–Vietnam Relations, 1945–1967*, Vol. 10 (Washington: GPO, 1975), 1082–95.

DOCUMENT 217: North Vietnam's Communist Party General Secretary, Le Duan, Provides Guidelines to North Vietnam's Lao Dong Party for "The Path of Revolution in the South" (November 1956)

During two years of struggle for peace, unification, independence and democracy, the people of the South have shown clearly their earnest feelings of patriotism and the firm will of Vietnamese.

Meanwhile, the past two years have also made the people of South Vietnam see clearly the poisonous scheme of the Aggressive American imperialists, and the traitorous, country-selling crimes of Ngo Dinh Diem.

On July 20, 1956, was the day the ceasefire agreement was signed at the Geneva Conference, requiring a free national general election to unify Vietnam, but has not been carried out. The reason is the Aggressive American imperialists and dictatorial feudalist Ngo Dinh Diem have sought by every means to sabotage and not carry out the agreement with hope of maintaining long-term division of our country, and turning the South into a colony and military base of the imperialists in order to provoke war and hoping to rob us of our rivers and mountains....

Three Main Tasks of the Whole Nation at Present

In order to cope with that situation created by the U.S.-Diem, and in order to complete the work of national liberation, to liberate the Southern people from the imperialist-feudalist yoke, the Party Central has put forward three main tasks to make a general line for the whole revolution work at present for the entire country.

Those tasks are: 1) Firmly consolidate the North. 2) Strongly push the Southern revolutionary movement. 3) Win the sympathy and support of the people who love peace, democracy and national independence in the world.

Source: Gareth Porter, ed., *Vietnam: The Definitive Documentation of Human Decisions*, 2 vols. (Stanfordville, N.Y.: Coleman Enterprises, 1979), 2:24–25. Document obtained in South Vietnam in 1957.

DOCUMENT 218: U.S. Ambassador to Vietnam Eldridge Durbrow Reports on the Diem Government in Saigon and Viet Cong Intentions and Potential in South Vietnam (7 March 1960)

Indications are growing that the VC [the organized and militant communists of South Vietnam were called Viet Cong] are mounting a special campaign aimed at undermining the Diem Government. According to CAS [CIA] sources, VC armed cadre strength has increased to about 3,000 in the southwest, double the number in September. VC groups now operate in larger strength, and their tactics have changed from attacks on individuals to rather frequent and daring attacks on GVN [Government of Vietnam] security forces. A recent CAS report has indicated a VC intention to press general guerrilla warfare in South Viet-Nam in 1960, and indicates the VC are convinced they can mount a coup d'état this year. President Diem also told me in late February about the capture of a VC document indicating their intention to step up aggressive attacks all over the country, including Saigon, beginning in the second quarter.

These signs indicate that aggressively worded statements emanating from the DRV [Democratic Republic of (North) Vietnam] in 1959 may accurately reflect DRV intentions. In May 1959 the central committee of the Lao Dong Party passed a resolution stating that the struggle for reunification of Viet-Nam should be carried out by all "appropriate means". Subsequently in conversations with Western officials, Prime Minister Pham Van Dong made statements to the effect that "We will be in Saigon tomorrow" and "We will drive the Americans into the sea." . . .

At the same time that the DRV guerrilla potential has increased in the South, weaknesses have become more apparent in the GVN security forces. GVN leaders have in recent weeks stressed the need for more anti-guerrilla training of ARVN [Army of the Republic of (South) Vietnam]. The desirability of centralized command in insecure areas and a centralized intelligence service has also become more evident. The need for a capable, well-equipped, well-trained, centrally-controlled Civil Guard is even more keenly felt than previously.

Likewise, at the same time, signs of general apathy and considerable dissatisfaction which the VC can play upon have become more evident among the people in rural areas. Fear among the peasants engendered by sustained VC terrorist activities against which the GVN has not succeeded in protecting them is combined with resentment of the GVN because of the methods which are all too often employed by local officials. Coercion rather than persuasion are often used by these officials in carrying out the programs decided upon in Saigon. There is a tendency to disregard the desires and feelings of the peasantry by, for instance, taking them away from their harvests to perform community work.

Source: U.S. Department of State, *Foreign Relations of the United States, 1958–1960,* Vol. 1 (Washington: GPO, 1986), 300–303.

DOCUMENT 219: National Security Council's Policy Planning for Counterinsurgency in Vietnam (19 June 1962)

The President has approved the following statement and proposed assignments of responsibilities to various agencies as recommended by the Special Group Counterinsurgency:

The study of U.S. and indigenous paramilitary resources . . . reflects gratifying progress in the development of an adequate U.S. capability to support both the training and active operations of indigenous paramilitary forces. Certain deficiencies, however, were clearly revealed. The deficiencies, to which all efforts and shortcomings to date are related, should be the basis upon which internal defense requirements are established for each country to be assisted. . . .

6. *Increased Use of Third Country Personnel*

The Department of Defense, in collaboration with the Department of State and the Central Intelligence Agency, will undertake a study to determine on a selective basis the feasibility of the concept of the increased use of third-country personnel in paramilitary operations. Particular attention will be given to the following:

(a) The whole range of this concept from the current limited use of Thai and Filipino technicians in Laos to the creation of simply equipped regional forces for use in remote jungle, hill and desert country. Such forces would be composed of foreign volunteers supported and controlled by the U.S.

(b) The feasibility of using third-country military or paramilitary forces to operate under their own or other national auspices in crisis areas.

7. *Exploitation of Minorities*

In view of the success which has resulted from CIA/US Army Special Forces efforts with tribal groups in Southeast Asia, continuing efforts will be made to determine the most feasible method of achieving similar results in other critical areas. On a selective basis, CIA and the Department of Defense will make studies of specific groups where there is reason to believe there exists an exploitable minority paramilitary capability. . . .

9. *Research and Development for Counterinsurgency*

The Department of Defense and the Central Intelligence Agency will carry in their research and development programs a special section devoted to the requirements of counterinsurgency. The Special Group (Counterinsurgency) will follow up on this action and receive reports from time to time with regard to progress in developing modern equipment suitable to meet the requirements of counterinsurgency.

Source: Pentagon Papers, Gravel Edition, 2:681–84.

THE GULF OF TONKIN AND THE AMERICANIZATION OF VIETNAM'S WAR, 1964–1967

Having determined that only a major injection of American power could prevent the fall of South Vietnam, President Johnson used an attack by North Vietnamese torpedo patrol boats on a U.S. destroyer in early August 1964 to get the U.S. Congress to support his plan to "Americanize" the Vietnamese civil war. The resulting Tonkin Gulf Resolution thereby became Johnson's congressional authorization to conduct military operations against North Vietnam, and he soon initiated a major bombing campaign against North Vietnam and sent hundreds of thousands of U.S. troops to South Vietnam.

DOCUMENT 220: Joint Chiefs of Staff Memorandum (JCSM) 471-64, "Objectives and Courses of Action—Southeast Asia" with Chairman Maxwell Taylor's Addendum (2–5 June 1964)

The Joint Chiefs of Staff conclude that:

a. There is no basis to be hopeful about the situation in Southeast Asia until and unless North Vietnam is forced to stop supporting the insurgent activities in Laos and South Vietnam.

b The best way to achieve this objective is through destruction of the North Vietnamese will and capabilities as necessary to compel the DRV to cease providing such support.

c. If there should be a national decision that the United States will resort to lesser measures to cause the North Vietnamese to make a decision to terminate their subversive activities, then we should not waste critical time and more resources in another protracted series of "messages," but rather we should take positive, prompt, and meaningful military action to underscore our meaning that after more than two years of tolerating this North Vietnamese support we are now determined that it will stop.

d. Just as it is essential to convey a meaningful "message" to the North Vietnamese, it is obviously also important that we convey to our Allies [in the region] the will and determination of the United States in this matter.

6. In summary, the Joint Chiefs of Staff recommend that:

a. In any national level discussions of action against North Vietnam, you seek precise delineations of both objectives and their supporting courses of action.

b. In defining objectives, it be recognized that the Joint Chiefs of Staff consider that termination of North Vietnamese support efforts in both South Vietnam and Laos can be assured only through destruction of North Vietnamese will and capabilities as necessary to compel the DRV to cease providing such support; based on military considerations, the Joint Chiefs of Staff advocate acceptance of this objective and the initiation now of measures designed to increase readiness for its achievement.

[Chairman JCS Addendum]

. . . It appears to me [General Taylor] that there are three patterns from among which we may choose to initiate the attack on North Vietnam. In descending order of weight, they are the following:

a. A massive air attack on all significant military targets in North Vietnam for the purpose of destroying them and thereby making the enemy incapable of continuing to assist the Viet Cong and the Pathet Lao.

b. A lesser attack on some significant part of the military target system in North Vietnam for the dual purpose of convincing the enemy that it is to his interest to desist from aiding the Viet Cong and the Pathet Lao, and, if possible, of obtaining his cooperation in calling off the insurgents in South Vietnam and Laos.

c. Demonstrative strikes against limited military targets to show US readiness and intent to pass to alternatives 3b or 3a above. These demonstrative strikes would have the same dual purpose as in alternative 3b.

Source: U.S. Department of State, *Foreign Relations of the United States, 1964–1968*, Vol. 1, *Vietnam, 1964* (hereafter *FRUS, VN-1964*) (Washington: GPO, 1992), 436–40, 457–58.

DOCUMENT 221: U.S. Undersecretary of State George Ball's Discussion with French President Charles de Gaulle (5 June 1964)

We agree with what we understand to be General de Gaulle's idea— that stabilization in the area requires the agreement and acquiescence of Peking. But we do not see the present situation presenting the balance of force which would make this possible.

There are certain elements of the problem that seem to be a matter of disagreement between the US and France. One results from a different appreciation of the phasing of the Communist revolution in China. We see that the Chinese revolution is in a phase reminiscent of the primitive Soviet Communism of 1917 which was both bellicose and expansionist. We do not think that Peking would accept any arrangement that would limit or prevent the spread of Communism in Southeast Asia or that it would abide by any such arrangement if made.

In our experience agreements with the Communists only succeed when there were countervailing powers that produced a kind of equilibrium. Examples were Austria and Finland. But if there is no countervailing force in the area the Communists will continue their subversive efforts. They will profit by the advantage that accrues to those who engage in covert and dishonest operations as compared with the open and aboveboard operations of their adversaries. He said we would have to insist on some countervailing force in the area. . . .

War was, of course, a possibility which the US could envisage. General

MacArthur had thought it was a good idea. However, he said, the French would never resume war in Asia. He had told this to President Kennedy. The French consider that Southeast Asia is a "rotten" territory in which to fight. Even if the US were involved France would not get into a war in Asia, as an ally or otherwise.

Source: FRUS, VN-1964, 464–70.

DOCUMENT 222: CIA Estimate on the "Domino Effect" in the Far East (9 June 1964)

1. The "domino effect" appears to mean that when one nation falls to communism the impact is such as to weaken the resistance of other countries and facilitate, if not cause, their fall to communism. Most literally taken, it would imply the successive and speedy collapse of neighboring countries, as a row of dominoes falls when the first is toppled—we presume that this degree of literalness is not essential to the concept. Most specifically it means that the loss of South Vietnam and Laos would lead almost inevitably to the communization of other states in the area, and perhaps beyond the area.

2. We do not believe that the loss of South Vietnam and Laos would be followed by the rapid, successive communization of the other states of the Far East. Instead of a shock wave passing from one nation to the next, there would be a simultaneous, direct effect on all Far Eastern countries. With the possible exception of Cambodia, it is likely that no nation in the area would quickly succumb to communism as a result of the fall of Laos and South Vietnam. Furthermore, a continuation of the spread of communism in the area would not be inexorable, and any spread which did occur would take time—time in which the total situation might change in any of a number of ways unfavorable to the Communist cause.

3. The loss of South Vietnam and Laos to the Communists would be profoundly damaging to the US position in the Far East, most especially because the US has committed itself persistently, emphatically, and publicly to preventing Communist takeover of the two countries. Failure here would be damaging to US prestige, and would seriously debase the credibility of US will and capability to contain the spread of communism elsewhere in the area. Our enemies would be encouraged and there would be an increased tendency among other states to move toward a greater degree of accommodation with the Communists. However, the extent to which individual countries would move away from the US

towards the Communists would be significantly affected by the substance and manner of US policy in the period following the loss of Laos and South Vietnam. . . .

9. *Communist Asia*. Aside from the immediate joy in the DRV over achievement of its national goals, the chief effect would be upon Communist China, both in boosting its already remarkable self-confidence and in raising its prestige as a leader of World Communism. Peiping has already begun to advertise South Vietnam as proof of its thesis that the underdeveloped world is ripe for revolution, that the US is a paper tiger, and that local insurgency can be carried through to victory without undue risk of precipitating a major international war. The outcome in South Vietnam and Laos would conspicuously support the aggressive tactical contentions of Peiping as contrasted with the more cautious position of the USSR. To some degree this will tend to encourage and strengthen the more activist revolutionary movements in various parts of the underdeveloped world.

Source: FRUS, VN-1964, 484–87.

DOCUMENT 223: President Johnson's Tonkin Gulf Message to Congress (5 August 1964)

Last night I announced to the American people that the North Vietnamese regime had conducted further deliberate attacks against U.S. naval vessels operating in international waters, and that I had therefore directed air action against gunboats and supporting facilities used in these hostile operations. This air action has now been carried out with substantial damage to the boats and facilities. Two U.S. aircraft were lost in the action.

After consultation with the leaders of both parties in the Congress, I further announced a decision to ask the Congress for a resolution expressing the unity and determination of the United States in supporting freedom and in protecting peace in southeast Asia.

These latest actions of the North Vietnamese regime have given a new and grave turn to the already serious situation in southeast Asia. Our commitments in that area are well known to the Congress. They were first made in 1954 by President Eisenhower. They were further defined in the Southeast Asia Collective Defense Treaty approved by the Senate in February 1955. . . .

I recommend a resolution expressing the support of the Congress for all necessary action to protect our Armed Forces and to assist nations covered by the SEATO Treaty. At the same time, I assure the Congress that we shall continue readily to explore any avenues of political solution that will effectively guarantee the removal of Communist subversion and the preservation of the independence of the nations of the area.

The resolution could well be based upon similar resolutions enacted by the Congress in the past to meet the threat to Formosa in 1955, to meet the threat to the Middle East in 1957, and to meet the threat in Cuba in 1962. It could state in the simplest terms the resolve and support of the Congress for action to deal appropriately with attacks against our Armed Forces and to defend freedom and preserve peace in southeast Asia in accordance with the obligations of the United States under the Southeast Asia Treaty. I urge the Congress to enact such a resolution promptly.

Source: Papers of the Presidents: Lyndon B. Johnson, 1963–1964, Book 2 (Washington: GPO, 1965), 926–28.

DOCUMENT 224: Senator Wayne Morse Questions Secretaries Rusk and McNamara and Explains His Opposition to the Gulf of Tonkin Resolution (6 August 1964)

SENATOR MORSE: I am unalterably opposed to this course of action which, in my judgment, is an aggressive course of action on the part of the United States. . . .

I think what happened is that [South Viet Nam Premier Nguyen] Khanh got us to backstop him in open aggression against the territorial integrity of North Vietnam. I have listened to briefing after briefing and there isn't a scintilla of evidence in any briefing yet that North Vietnam engaged in any military aggression against South Vietnam either with its ground troops or its navy. I shall vote against the resolution.

SECRETARY RUSK: I feel compelled to make a brief comment on what the distinguished Senator from Oregon has just said.

Since 1954 the North Vietnamese have been undertaking to undermine and take over the Government of South Vietnam. There was some surcease from those depredations during the years about 1956 to 1958, but in 1959 the North Vietnamese again came back to it, made a decision to step up their activities, and in 1960 publicly proclaimed their purpose.

Now, the shape and form of armed attack and of aggression have been changing in this Postwar world. I cannot, myself, see any lack of aggressiveness or any lack of military action in the infiltration of parties of individuals, some of them running up to 150 and 200 at a time, infiltrating through Laos, contrary to agreements, into South Vietnam contrary to their obligations, for the purpose of carrying on armed action against the authorities and the people of South Vietnam. . . .

SENATOR MORSE: I don't propose to engage in a debate with the Secretary of State here. I disagree on the basis of the many replies presented, on the basis of his own testimony before this committee when we have asked time after time for evidence from the Secretary of State and the Pentagon Building of any proof of any organized military operation of North Vietnam going into South Vietnam.

Source: Pentagon Papers, Gravel Edition, 2:681–84.

DOCUMENT 225: Gulf of Tonkin Resolution Empowering the President to Use American Forces in Southeast Asia (7 August 1964)

Resolved by the Senate and House of Representatives of the United States of America in Congress assembled,

That the Congress approves and supports the determination of the President, as Commander in Chief, to take all necessary measures to repel any armed attack against the forces of the United States and to prevent further aggression.

Sec. 2. The United States regards as vital to its national interest and to world peace the maintenance of international peace and security in southeast Asia. Consonant with the Constitution of the United States and the Charter of the United Nations and in accordance with its obligations under the Southeast Asia Collective Defense Treaty, the United States is, therefore, prepared, as the President determines, to take all necessary steps, including the use of armed force, to assist any member or protocol state of the Southeast Asia Collective Defense Treaty requesting assistance in defense of its freedom.

Sec. 3. This resolution shall expire when the President shall determine that the peace and security of the area is reasonably assured by international conditions created by action of the United Nations or otherwise, except that it may be terminated earlier by concurrent resolution of the Congress.

Source: Pentagon Papers, Gravel Edition, 2:702–4.

DOCUMENT 226: "May 2nd Movement" and Student Opposition to War (August 1964)

The war in Vietnam is not a war for freedom or democracy. It is a war against the people of Vietnam.

The government has no right to draft any citizen to participate in such a war.

We, the students of the United States, refuse to be drafted. We do not recognize the right of the government to draft our fellow students. We refuse to be turned into killers and corpses for a war that is not ours. (Collected August 10, 1964)

Source: G. Louis Heath, ed., *Mutiny Does Not Happen Lightly: The Literature of the American Resistance to the Vietnam War* (Metuchen, N.J.: Scarecrow Press, 1976), 20.

DOCUMENT 227: North Vietnam's Foreign Minister Xuan Thuy Responds to U.S. Complaint at the United Nations (19 August 1964)

The Government of the Democratic Republic of Viet Nam holds that the "complaint" lodged by the U.S. Government with the U.N. Security Council is a slander, an act contrary to the 1954 Geneva Agreements on Viet Nam, and should be rejected. . . .

Exercising their legitimate and sacred right of self-defence, the Vietnamese people dealt the U.S. aggressors telling blows.

The acts of war by the U.S. Government against the Democratic Republic of Viet Nam have aroused a powerful wave of indignation all over the world, and continue to be vigorously opposed and sternly condemned by peace-loving world opinion, including progressive opinion in the United States. Although the U.S. Government has set moving its entire propaganda machine about the so-called "second incident in the Tonkin Gulf", public opinion in the world, and even in Western countries, is sceptical, and has questioned the U.S. allegations. Washington rulers, increasingly embarrassed, are unable to cover up a far too obvious truth.

Source: FRUS, VN-1964, 484–87.

DOCUMENT 228: The North Vietnamese Article "Facing the Skyhawks" Reports the Capture of One of the First American Prisoners of War in Vietnam (1964)

Great surprise was in store for the Yankee airmen on that day of August 5, 1964. . . .

The airmen of the Seventh Fleet had thought that they would have to deal with poor creatures, frightened out of their wits, who would start scampering off like mice when they saw Skyhawks coming down on them, spitting fire and death. They had instead run into real men.

A big surprise was in store for lieutenant Everett Alvarez: before one could say Jack Robinson, his plane was hit smack on the nose and he had to bail out and make a parachute descent over this famous Ha Long Bay whose marvels he could admire for the first time. Another surprise was awaiting him when he found himself in the water: hardly had he time to recover himself when a boat was on him, with armed people shouting to him to surrender. Everywhere people were ready. Here, even fishermen carry weapons and stand ready to shoot at and to jump on the first enemy to appear. Fishermen who, rather than run for shelter when he, Alvarez, and his colleagues showered bombs and rockets on Hong Gai, had stayed at their posts, and fired on ultra-modern planes with their rifles!

Poor Alvarez! He had thought he would come back a hero, and here he was, a prisoner.

Source: "Facing the Skyhawks," by Nguyen Nghe, 20 September 1964, in John Galloway, *The Gulf of Tonkin Resolution* (Rutherford, N.J.: Fairleigh Dickinson University Press, 1970), 538–45.

DOCUMENT 229: Senate Majority Leader Mike Mansfield's "Sagging Limb" Memo to President Johnson (9 December 1964)

We remain on a course in Viet Nam which takes us further and further out on the sagging limb. That the Viet Cong, a few weeks ago, pinpointed a major raid at Bien Hoa on an American installation and American personnel scarcely a dozen miles from Saigon may be indicative of a graver deterioration in the general military situation than has heretofore been apparent. It is also indicative of a growing boldness in the Viet Cong. . . .

Policy Suggestions

1. Avoid United States military action beyond the borders of South Viet Nam, especially if the primary purpose of such action is to demonstrate the firmness of our will or our capacity to inflict damage. . . .

2. Keep United States forces clear of the Cambodian border and consider dispatching a special mission to Phom Penh [*sic*] in an effort to negotiate differences and to reduce the very high level of mutual hostility which now prevails. . . .

3. Continue and intensify tangible encouragement to Souvanna Phouma, above all other Laotian leaders, in his efforts to keep some semblance of order and unity in Laos. Ask him what needs to be done rather than suggest to him what to do. Let the initiative be his totally and provide any reasonable support which he asks.

4. Place no obstacles in the way of the Western European countries, Japan, India, and others, who might seek to establish commercial and other contacts with Hanoi. This might help to reduce the heavy Chinese domination of that area and in so doing, perhaps, begin to lay the groundwork for negotiation of a peaceful settlement when conditions in South Viet Nam permit it.

5. Begin to think and act in a political sense in South Viet Nam in terms of assisting in evolving a government which can speak with some native validity and authority for that section should the time come when negotiation of a bonafide peaceful settlement, perhaps on the basis of confederation, is possible. . . .

6. If some such course as the above is not practical we had better begin now to face up to the likelihood of years and years of involvement and a vast increase in the commitment, and this should be spelled out in no uncertain terms to the people of the nation.

7. Thinking further ahead, opportunities should be sought to explore Chinese intentions in Viet Nam and elsewhere in face-to-face confrontations in some setting other than Warsaw and by means other than routine diplomatic exchanges.

Source: Porter, *Vietnam: Definitive Documentation*, 2:333–35.

DOCUMENT 230: U.S. Secretary of State Dean Rusk's Conversation with Soviet Foreign Minister Gromyko on U.S.-USSR Relations in Southeast Asia (9 December 1964)

In response to the Secretary's remark that he wished to discuss the situation in South East Asia . . . Mr. Gromyko said he wished to ask what intentions the U.S. had in that area. As the Soviet Union had stated on a number of earlier occasions, it believed that the U.S. had made a great mistake by getting involved in South Vietnam, because there were no U.S. interests involved in that area. But the U.S. had its troops in South Vietnam and was now increasing them. This was not in accord with the U.S.-expressed desire to reduce tensions in the area. Consequently, the question arose as to what the real U.S. intentions were. The Soviet Union had no troops or experts in the area and had taken no action similar to the actions taken by the U.S.

The Secretary observed that on the basis of Mr. Gromyko's remarks, it appeared that there was no problem between the U.S. and the U.S.S.R. in South East Asia. Unfortunately, Hanoi and Peiping were very active in that area. Our position was very simple: if Peiping and Hanoi left their neighbors alone, there would be no U.S. troops in that area. We had no interests and we sought no bases there, and all we were doing was because of Hanoi and Peiping. The Secretary hoped that there was no difference between our two countries as to the facts of the situation. . . . Perhaps some people on the Soviet side said that this was a war of liberation, but we regarded the situation as pure aggression. The Secretary repeated that if Hanoi and Peiping left their neighbors alone, we would not be there; otherwise, he stressed, we were in a serious situation. He hoped the Soviet Union would in no way encourage Hanoi and Peiping and would use its influence to restrain them.

Source: FRUS, VN-1964, 990–93.

DOCUMENT 231: Hanoi's Four Point Negotiating Position (8 April 1965)

The unswerving policy of the DRV Government is to respect strictly the 1954 Geneva agreements on Vietnam and to implement correctly their basic provisions as embodied in the following points:

1. Recognition of the basic national rights of the Vietnamese people—peace, independence, sovereignty, unity, and territorial integrity. According to the Geneva agreements, the U.S. Government must withdraw from South Vietnam U.S. troops, military personnel, and weapons of all kinds, dismantle all U.S. military bases there, and cancel its military alliance with South Vietnam. According to the Geneva agreements, the U.S. Government must stop its acts of war against North Vietnam and completely cease all encroachments on the territory and sovereignty of the DRV.

2. Pending the peaceful reunification of Vietnam, while Vietnam is still temporarily divided into two zones the military provisions of the 1954 Geneva agreements on Vietnam must be strictly respected. . . .

3. The internal affairs of South Vietnam must be settled by the South Vietnamese people themselves in accordance with the program of the National Liberation Front of South Vietnam without any foreign interference.

4. The peaceful reunification of Vietnam is to be settled by the Vietnamese people in both zones, without any foreign interference.

Source: Marvin E. Gettleman, Jane Franklin, Marilyn B. Young, and H. Bruce Franklin, *Vietnam and America: A Documented History*, 2nd ed. (New York: Grove Press, 1995), 276–78.

DOCUMENT 232: Undersecretary of State George Ball Argues Against Escalating U.S. Involvement (18 June 1965)

Beginning in the fall of 1961, one key State Department officer, Undersecretary of State George W. Ball, had advised both Presidents Kennedy and Johnson that military recommendations for more troops in South Vietnam would not solve America's predisposed dilemma in Southeast Asia. He became the primary spokesperson within the administration who continually advised against any escalated U.S. military involvement in Vietnam. In mid-June 1965 Secretary of Defense Robert McNamara proposed to President Johnson that a sudden and massive buildup of some 395,000 personnel be deployed to South Vietnam by the end of the year. In an important memorandum of 18 June 1965, however, Ball vainly sought to forestall the deployment of more American combat troops to the region. Sensitive to President Johnson's determination to command, Undersecretary Ball entitled his memo "Keeping the Power of Decision in the South Vietnam Crisis."

"Your most difficult continuing problem in South Vietnam," I wrote the President, "is to prevent 'things' from getting into the saddle or, in other words, finding a way to keep control of policy and prevent the momentum of events from taking over."

The best formula for maintaining freedom of decision is (a) to limit our commitments in time and magnitude and (b) to establish specific time schedules for the selection of optional courses of action on the basis of pre-established criteria.

Before we commit an endless flow of forces to South Vietnam we must have more evidence than we now have that our troops will not bog down in the jungles and rice paddies—while we slowly blow the country to pieces.

The French fought a war in Viet-Nam, and were finally defeated— after seven years of bloody struggle and when they still had 250,000 combat-hardened veterans in the field, supported by an army of 205,000 Vietnamese.

To be sure, the French were fighting a colonial war while we are fighting to stop aggression. But when we have put enough Americans on the ground in South Viet-Nam to give the appearance of a white man's war, the distinction as our ultimate purpose will have less and less practical effect.

Ever since 1961—the beginning of our deep involvement in South Viet-Nam—we have met successive disappointments. We have tended to overestimate the effectiveness of our sophisticated weapons under jungle conditions. We have watched the progressive loss of territory to Viet Cong control. We have been unable to bring about the creation of a stable political base in Saigon. . . .

We have not so far seen enough evidence to be sure that the South Vietnamese forces will stand up under the heightening pressure—or, in fact, that the Vietnamese people really have a strong will to fight after twenty years of struggle. We cannot be sure how far the cancer has infected the whole body politic of South Viet-Nam and whether we can do more than administer a cobalt treatment to a terminal case.

Yet the more forces we deploy in South Viet-Nam—particularly in combat roles—the harder we shall find it to extricate ourselves without unacceptable costs if the war goes badly.

Source: George W. Ball, *The Past Has Another Pattern* (New York: Norton, 1982), 395–96.

DOCUMENT 233: Undersecretary of State Ball Recalls His "Compromise Solution" (1 July 1965)

The war was rapidly careening out of control, and I was less and optimistic that I could deflect the strong forces steadily gaining momentum. Nevertheless, on July 1, I sent the President a memorandum entitled "A Compromise Solution for South Vietnam." As the following excerpts make clear, it once again expressed my pessimism:

A Losing War: The South Vietnamese are losing the war to the Viet Cong. No one can assure you that we can beat the Viet Cong or even force them to the conference table on our terms no matter how many hundred thousand white *foreign* (US) troops we deploy.

No one has demonstrated that a white ground force of whatever size can win a guerrilla war—which is at the same time a civil war between Asians—in jungle terrain in the midst of a population that refuses cooperation to the white forces (and the SVN) and thus provides a great intelligence advantage to the other side.

The decision you face now, therefore, is crucial. Once large numbers of US troops are committed to direct combat they will begin to take heavy casualties in a war they are ill-equipped to fight in a noncooperative if not downright hostile countryside.

Once we suffer large casualties we will have started a well-nigh irreversible process. Our involvement will be so great that we cannot—without national humiliation—stop short of achieving our complete objectives. *Of the two possibilities I think humiliation would be more likely than the achievement of our objective—even after we had paid terrible costs.*

Source: Ball, *The Past Has Another Pattern*, 398–99.

DOCUMENT 234: U.S. Commanding General in Vietnam William Westmoreland Recommends a Buildup of U.S. Troops (June–July 1965)

As the result of yet another military coup d'état in Saigon in May 1965, and U.S. recognition of the new Thieu-Ky government on 19 June, the commanding General of all U.S. forces in Vietnam, General William C. Westmoreland, observed that a military crisis had begun throughout South Vietnam. He notified his superiors in Washington that if the United States intended to achieve its goal of denying the enemy a victory in South Vietnam, it had to provide substantial American ground combat troops to South Vietnam to withstand the pressure from combined Viet Cong and North Vietnamese forces.

[On 12 June] I made clear my view that an enclave strategy was no answer. If South Vietnam was to survive, I cabled, we had to have "a substantial and hard-hitting offensive capability on the ground to convince the VC that they cannot win." The United States had to make an "active commitment" with troops that could "be maneuvered freely." . . .

It was virtually impossible to provide Secretary [McNamara] with a meaningful figure [during the secretary's visit to Vietnam in mid-July]. In the end I told him only that I thought twenty-four more battalions in addition to the forty-four under consideration, plus more combat support and logistical troops, would put us in a position to *begin* the "win phase" of our strategy. That meant about 175,000 American troops at the start, followed by about 100,000.

Source: William C. Westmoreland, *A Soldier Reports* (Garden City, N.Y.: Doubleday, 1976), 140–42.

DOCUMENT 235: Undersecretary of State Ball Recalls the National Security Meeting at Which President Johnson Decided on Massive Troop Deployment to Vietnam (21 July 1965)

On the morning of 21 July 1965 President Johnson convened a meeting of his national security advisers. The war was going badly. As the advisers assembled at the White House, they were given a memorandum from the Joint Chiefs of Staff. The memo stressed that only the prompt deployment of massive numbers of American troops could save the situation. Undersecretary of State George Ball foresaw that this deployment meant committing thousands of American troops to aggressive combat roles and that the war would then become unequivocally an American enterprise.

The President began with searching questions. Could we get more soldiers from our allies? What had altered the situation to the present point of urgency? McNamara produced a map. The Viet Cong, it showed, controlled about 25 percent of the South. United States forces would not be committed in those areas; they would be deployed "with their backs to the sea, for protection." They would conduct search and destroy operations against large-scale units.

"Why," I asked, "does anyone think that the Viet Cong will be so considerate as to confront us directly? They certainly didn't do that for the French." General Wheeler, the chairman of the Joint Chiefs of Staff, replied, "We can force them to fight by harassment."

After the others had expressed support for the proposed new escalation, the President asked whether any of us opposed it, looking directly at me. I made my usual speech, pointing out that we would be embarking on "a perilous voyage" and could not win. But, he asked, what other courses were available? We must, I replied, stop deceiving ourselves, face reality, and cut our losses. "If we get bogged down, the costs will be far greater than a planned withdrawal, while the pressures to create a larger war could become irresistible. We must stop propping up that absurd travesty of a government in Saigon. Let's let it fall apart and negotiate a withdrawal, recognizing that the country will face a probable take-over by the Communists."

The President replied, "You've pointed out the dangers but you've not really proposed an alternative."

After others had expressed similar sentiments, the President once more turned to me. "George," he asked, "do you think we have another course?" I answered, "I certainly don't agree with the course Bob McNamara's recommending." "All right," said the President, "we'll hear you out; then I can determine if any of your suggestions are sound and can be followed. I'm prepared to do that if convinced."

I could, I said, present to him only "the least bad of two courses." The course I could recommend was costly, but we could at least limit the cost to the short-term. At that point—just as I was beginning to speak—the President interrupted. "We'll have another meeting this afternoon where you can express your views in detail." Meanwhile, he wanted further justification for the introduction of one-hundred-thousand more troops. In response to the President's concern about increased losses, General Taylor directly contradicted a view expressed earlier by Secretary McNamara that our losses in Vietnam would be proportional to the number of our men in that country. "The more men we have," the General now declared, "the greater the likelihood of smaller losses."

When we reconvened at 2:30 that afternoon, the President asked me to explain my position. I outlined why, in my view, we could not win. Even after a protracted conflict the most we could hope to achieve was "a messy conclusion" with a serious danger of intervention by the Chinese. In a long war, I said, the President would lose the support of the country. I showed him a chart I had prepared showing the correlation between Korean casualties and public opinion. As our casualties during the Korean War had increased from 11,000 to 40,000, the percentage of those Americans who thought that we had been right to intervene had diminished from 56 percent in 1950 to a little more than 30 percent in 1952. Moreover, as our losses mounted, many frustrated Americans would demand that we strike at the "very jugular of North Vietnam" with all the dangers that entailed. Were it possible for us to win decisively in a year's time, friendly nations might continue to support us. But that was not in the cards.

"No great captain in history ever hesitated to make a tactical withdrawal if conditions were unfavorable to him," I argued. "We can't even find the enemy in Vietnam. We can't see him and we can't find him. He's indigenous to the country, and he always has access to much better intelligence. He knows what we're going to do but we haven't the vaguest clue as to his intentions. I have grave doubts that any Western army can successfully fight Orientals in an Asian jungle." . . .

Since our main concern was to avoid undermining our credibility, we would shift the burden to the South Vietnamese government. We should insist on reforms that it would never undertake, which would impel it to move toward a neutralist position and ask us to leave. "I have no illusions," I said, "that after we were asked to leave South Vietnam, that country would soon come under Hanoi's control. That's implicit in our predicament." I then discussed the effect on other nations in the area.

The President then asked the question most troubling him. "Wouldn't we lose all credibility by breaking the word of three Presidents?" I replied, "We'll suffer the worst blow to our credibility when it is shown that the mightiest power on earth can't defeat a handful of miserable guerrillas."

Then, asked the President, "aren't you basically troubled by what the world would say about our pulling out?"

"If we were helping a country with a stable, viable government, it would be a vastly different story. But we're dealing with a revolving junta. How much support," I asked rhetorically, "do we really have in South Vietnam?"

The President then mentioned two of my points that particularly troubled him. One was that Westerners could never win a war in Asia; the other was that we could not successfully support a people whose government changed every month. He then asked, "What about the reaction of the Europeans? Wouldn't they be shaken in their reliance on us if we pulled out of Vietnam?"

"That idea's based on a complete misunderstanding of the way the Europeans are thinking," I said. "They don't regard what we are doing in Vietnam as in any way comparable to our involvement in Europe. Since the French pulled out of Vietnam, they can hardly blame us for doing the same thing; they cut their losses, and de Gaulle is urging us to follow suit. . . . They only care about one thing. They're concerned about their own security. Troops in Berlin have real meaning; troops in Vietnam have none."

I then summarized the alternatives. "We can continue a dragged out, bitterly costly, and increasingly dangerous war, with the North Vietnamese digging in for a long term since that's their life and driving force."

Or "we can face the short-term losses of pulling out. It's distasteful either way; but life's full of hard choices."

Source: Ball, *The Past Has Another Pattern*, 399–402.

DOCUMENT 236: Senator Mansfield Urges President Johnson Not to Get Enmeshed in Vietnam (27 July 1965)

Subsequent to our telephone conversation, I met with the following Senators in my office this afternoon: Aiken . . . Cooper . . . Russell . . . Fulbright . . . Sparkman.

I opened the meeting by reporting fully on the Leadership discussion of Vietnam this morning. There was a general sense of reassurance that your objective was not to get in deeply and that you intended to do only what was essential in the military line until January, while Rusk and Goldberg were concentrating to get us out. A general desire to support you in this course was expressed. . . .

Among the major points which were raised . . . were the following: . . .

4. Bridges to Eastern Europe need to be kept open and continued encouragement of the evolution of these nations (Yugoslavia, in particular) towards full independence, political and economic, under their own unique organization is of the greatest importance.

5. The Russians are deeply concerned that we are abandoning the policy of peaceful co-existence; some tangible reassurance that we are not, perhaps through the consular convention, is desirable.

6. The country is backing the President on Viet-Nam primarily because he is President, not necessarily out of any understanding or sympathy with policies on Viet Nam; beneath the support, there is deep concern and a great deal of confusion which could explode at any time; in addition racial factors at home could become involved.

7. The main perplexity in the Vietnamese situation is that even if you win, totally, you still do not come out well. What have you achieved? It is by no means a "vital" area of U.S. concern as it was described by Lodge at a hearing this morning. . . .

It should be noted that there was obviously not a unanimity among the Members present on all of the points listed. But there was a very substantial agreement on many of them. Moreover, there was full agreement that insofar as Viet Nam is concerned we are deeply enmeshed in a place where we ought not to be; that the situation is rapidly going out of control; and that every effort should be made to extricate ourselves.

Source: Porter, *Vietnam: Definitive Documentation*, 2:391–92.

DOCUMENT 237: President Johnson Confers with Congressional Leaders (27 July 1965)

Before making his decision on deploying U.S. combat troops to Vietnam, President Johnson asked several congressional leaders to meet with him at the White House during the evening of 27 July 1965. Among the congressional leaders were Senators Mansfield, Dirksen, Hickenlooper, Kuchel, Long, and Smathers and Representatives Mc-Cormack, Albert, Arends, Boggs, and Ford. Johnson said that the Viet Cong were increasing their efforts to take over South Vietnam and that the United States was stepping up its measures to prevent such an outcome. President Johnson emphasized that U.S. policy was unchanged: protect the South Vietnamese government from a communist take-over.

In the entire group the only expression of serious doubt and opposition to the proposed course again came from Mike Mansfield. As always, he expressed his opinion candidly. He spoke of the deepening discontent in the country. He thought the best hope was "a quick stalemate and negotiations." But he concluded by saying that as a Senator and Majority Leader he would support the President's position.

Speaker McCormack closed the meeting by assuring me that I would have united support. "This was an historic meeting," he said. "The President will have the support of all true Americans."

Source: Lyndon B. Johnson, *The Vantage Point: Perspectives of the Presidency, 1963–1969* (New York: Holt, Rinehart and Winston, 1971), 150–51.

DOCUMENT 238: President Johnson Recalls His Vantage Point for Decision (July 1965)

A President searches his mind and his heart for the answers, so that when he decides on a course of action it is in the long-range best interests of the country, its people, and its security. . . .

This is what I could foresee: First, from all the evidence available to me it seemed likely that all of Southeast Asia would pass under Communist control, slowly or quickly, but inevitably, at least down to Singapore but almost certainly to Djakarta. I realize that some Americans believe they have, through talking with one another, repealed the domino theory. In 1965 there was no indication in Asia, or from Asians, that this was so. On both sides of the line between Communist and non-Communist Asia the struggle for Vietnam and Laos was regarded as a struggle for the fate of Southeast Asia. . . .

Second, I knew our people well enough to realize that if we walked away from Vietnam and let Southeast Asia fall, there would follow a divisive and destructive debate in our country. This had happened when the Communists took power in China. But that was very different from the Vietnam conflict. We had a solemn treaty commitment to Southeast Asia. We had an international agreement on Laos made as late as 1962 that was being violated flagrantly. We had the word of three Presidents that the United States would not permit this aggression to succeed. A divisive debate about "who lost Vietnam" would be, in my judgment, even more destructive to our national life than the argument over China had been. It would inevitably increase isolationist pressures from the right and the left and cause a pulling back from our commitments in Europe and the Middle East as well as in Asia.

Third, our allies not just in Asia but throughout the world would conclude that our word was worth little or nothing. Those who had counted so long for their security on American commitments would be deeply shaken and vulnerable.

Fourth, knowing what I did of the policies and actions of Moscow and Peking, I was as sure as a man could be that if we did not live up to our commitment in Southeast Asia and elsewhere, they would move to exploit the disarray in the United States and in the alliances of the Free World.

Source: Johnson, *Vantage Point*, 151–52.

DOCUMENT 239: President Johnson's Decision for Massive American Effort (July 1965)

My generation had lived through the change from American isolationism to collective security in 1940–1941. I had watched firsthand in Congress as we swerved in 1946–1947 from the unilateral dismantling of our armed forces to President Truman's effort to protect Western Europe. I could never forget the withdrawal of our forces from South Korea and then our immediate reaction to the Communist aggression of June 1950.

As I looked ahead, I could see us repeating the same sharp reversal once again in Asia, or elsewhere—but this time in a nuclear world with all the dangers and possible horrors that go with it. . . .

This was the private estimate that brought me to the hard decision of July 1965. None of the very few who opposed the decision gave me facts or arguments that broke or even weakened this chain of conclusions. These were the thoughts . . . that were in my mind when I went to meet the White House press corps on July 28, 1965, and opened the press conference by saying:

> I have today ordered to Vietnam the Air Mobile Division and certain other forces which will raise our fighting strength from 75,000 to 125,000 men almost immediately. Additional forces will be needed later, and they will be sent as requested.

Source: Johnson, *Vantage Point*, 152–53.

DOCUMENT 240: Secretary of Defense Robert McNamara Evaluates the Bombing Program Against North Vietnam for President Johnson (30 July 1965)

1. Rationale for bombing the North.

The program of bombing RVN began in an atmosphere of reprisal. We had had the August Tonkin Gulf episode; we had absorbed the November 1 attack on Bien Hoa Airfield and the Christmas Eve bombing of the Brinks Hotel in Saigon. The attacks at U.S. installations at Pleiku on February 7 and Qui Nhon on February 10 were the immediate causes of the first strikes against North Vietnam. The strike following Pleiku was announced as a "response"—a "reprisal"; our strike following Qui Nhon was called a response to more generalized VC terrorism. The major purposes of the bombing program, however, were:

   a. To promote a settlement. The program was designed (1) to influence the DRV to negotiate (explicitly or otherwise), and (2) to provide us with a bargaining counter within negotiations.

   b. To interdict infiltration. The program was calculated to reduce the flow of men and supplies from the North to the South—at the least, to put a ceiling on the size of war that the enemy could wage in the South. Supplemental purposes of the program were (c) to demonstrate to South Vietnam, North Vietnam and the world the U.S. commitment to see this thing through, (d) to raise morale in South Vietnam by punishing North

Vietnam, the source of the suffering in the South, and (e) to reduce criticism of the Administration from advocates of a bombing program.

Source: Pentagon Papers, Gravel Edition, 3:395.

DOCUMENT 241: Secretary of Defense McNamara Encourages President Johnson to Escalate the War (30 November 1965)

2. We have but two options, it seems to me. One is to go now for a compromise solution . . . and hold further deployments to a minimum. The other is to stick with our stated objectives and with the war, and provide what it takes in men and materiel. If it is decided not to move now toward a compromise, I recommend that the US both send a substantial number of additional troops and very gradually intensify the bombing of NVN. Amb. Lodge, Wheeler, Sharp and Westmoreland concur in this prolonged course of action, although Wheeler and Sharp would intensify the bombing of the North more quickly. . . .

3. Bombing of NVN . . . over a period of the next six months we gradually enlarge the target system in the northeast (Hanoi-Haiphong) quadrant until, at the end of the period, it includes "controlled" reconnaissance of lines of communication throughout the area, bombing of petroleum storage facilities and power plants, and mining of the harbors. (Left unstruck would be population targets, industrial plants, locks and dams.)

Source: Pentagon Papers, Gravel Edition, 4:622–23.

DOCUMENT 242: Assistant Secretary of Defense John T. McNaughton's Memorandum that U.S. Objective Is to Avoid Humiliation (19 January 1966)

We . . . have in Vietnam the ingredients of an enormous miscalculation. . . .

The ARVN is tired, passive and accommodation-prone. . . . The PAVN/VC are effectively matching our deployments. . . . The bombing of the North . . . may or may not be able effectively to interdict infiltration. . . . Pacification is stalled despite efforts and hopes. The GVN political infrastructure is moribund and weaker than the VC infrastructure among most of the rural population. . . . South Vietnam is near the edge of serious inflation and economic chaos.

C. *The present U.S. objective in Vietnam is to avoid humiliation.* The reasons why we *went into* Vietnam to the present depth are varied; but they are now largely academic. Why we have *not withdrawn* from Vietnam is, by all odds, *one* reason: (1) to preserve our reputation as a guarantor, and thus to preserve our effectiveness in the rest of the world. We have not hung on (2) to save a friend, or (3) to deny the Communists the added acres and heads (because the dominoes don't fall for that reason in this case), or even (4) to prove that "wars of national liberation" won't work (except as our reputation is involved). At each decision point we have gambled; at each, to avoid the damage to our effectiveness of defaulting on our commitment, we have upped the ante. We have not defaulted, and the ante (and commitment) is now very high. It is important that we behave so as to protect our reputation. At the same time, since it is our *reputation* that is at stake, it is important that we not construe our obligation to be more than do the countries whose opinions of us *are* our reputation. . . .

We are in a dilemma. It is that the situation may be "polar." That is, it may be that while going for victory we have the strength for compromise, but if we go for compromise we have the strength only for defeat— this because a revealed lowering of sights from victory to compromise (a) will unhinge the GVN and (b) will give the DRV the "smell of blood." The situation therefore requires a thoroughly loyal and disciplined U.S. team in Washington and Saigon and great care in what is said and done. It also requires a willingness to escalate the war if the enemy miscalculates, misinterpreting our willingness to compromise as implying we are on the run.

Source: The Pentagon Papers as published by the *New York Times* (New York: Bantam, 1971), 491–92.

DOCUMENT 243: Ambassador Henry Cabot Lodge's Telegram to Secretary of State Rusk on Failure of Italian-Polish Diplomatic Channel of Talks ("Marigold") with Hanoi (24 July 1966)

1. [Italian Ambassador in Saigon Giovanni] D'Orlandi, [Geneva Conference's International Control Commission Representative Janusz] Le-

wandowski and I met at D'Orlandi's office at 4:30. The meeting lasted for twenty minutes. Lewandowski talked as follows:

2. "I have the following instructions from Warsaw which I have been asked to transmit to Ambassador Lodge:

A. "It is difficult to discuss any proposition during the current important escalation of war activities in the South, and of the bombing in the North.

B. "To hold such discussion could be looked upon as a maneuver to force the DRV to negotiate under American conditions.

C. "We know very well that the DRV will not give up the fight while the United States pursues its present policy of military pressure.

D. "We have reasons to state that no proposition without the cessation of the bombing of the DRV will produce results.

E. "United States Government has no right to bomb the DRV and no right to propose conditions for its cessation.

F. "If the United States desires a peaceful solution, it must recognize the four points proposed by the DRV and prove it in practice.

G. "The United States must stop bombing and other military activity against North Viet-Nam. Only then can a political solution be expected."

Source: Porter, *Vietnam: Definitive Documentation*, 2:427.

DOCUMENT 244: Martin Luther King, Jr.'s "Declaration of Independence from the War in Vietnam" and the Growing Cynicism of American Troops (4 April 1967)

I come to this platform to make a passionate plea to my beloved nation. This speech is not addressed to Hanoi or to the National Liberation Front. It is not addressed to China or to Russia. . . .

Since I am a preacher by trade, I suppose it is not surprising that I have seven major reasons for bringing Vietnam into the field of my moral vision. There is at the outset a very obvious and almost facile connection between the war in Vietnam and the struggle I, and others, have been waging in America. A few years ago there was a shining moment in that struggle. It seemed as if there was a real promise of hope for the poor— both black and white—through the Poverty Program. Then came the build-up in Vietnam, and I watched the program broken and eviscerated as if it were some idle political plaything of a society gone mad on war, and I knew that America would never invest the necessary funds or energies in rehabilitation of its poor so long as Vietnam continued to draw men and skills and money like some demonic, destructive suction tube. So I was increasingly compelled to see the war as an enemy of the poor and to attack it as such.

Perhaps the more tragic recognition of reality took place when it became clear to me that the war was doing far more than devastating the hopes of the poor at home. It was sending their sons and their brothers and their husbands to fight and to die in extraordinarily high proportions relative to the rest of the population. We were taking the young black men who had been crippled by our society and sending them 8000 miles away to guarantee liberties in Southeast Asia which they had not found in Southwest Georgia and East Harlem. So we have been repeatedly faced with the cruel irony of watching Negro and white boys on TV screens as they kill and die together for a nation that has been unable to seat them together in the same schools. So we watch them in brutal solidarity burning the huts of villages, but we realize that they would never live on the same block in Detroit. I could not be silent in the face of such cruel manipulation of the poor. . . .

At this point, I should make it clear that while I have tried here to give a voice to the voiceless of Vietnam and to understand the arguments of those who are called enemy, I am as deeply concerned about our own troops there as anything else. For it occurs to me that what we are submitting them to in Vietnam is not simply the brutalizing process that goes on in any war where armies face each other and seek to destroy. *We are adding cynicism to the process of death, for our troops must know after a short period there that none of the things we claim to be fighting for are really involved.* Before long they must know that their government has sent them into a struggle among Vietnamese, and the more sophisticated surely realize that we are on the side of the wealthy and the secure while we create a hell for the poor.

Somehow this madness must cease. I speak as a child of God and brother to the suffering poor of Vietnam and the poor of America who are paying the double price of smashed hopes at home and death and corruption in Vietnam. I speak as a citizen of the world, for the world as it stands aghast at the path we have taken. I speak as an American to the leaders of my own nation. The great initiative in this war is ours. The initiative to stop must be ours.

Source: Gettleman et al., *Vietnam and America: A Documented History,* 1st ed., 306–14.

DOCUMENT 245: President Johnson's "San Antonio Formula" (September–October 1967)

On 29 September 1967 President Johnson delivered a speech before the National Legislative Conference in San Antonio, Texas. In this speech he publicly offered to negotiate with the North Vietnamese in Paris to end hostilities in Southeast Asia.

The United States is willing to stop all aerial and naval bombardment of North Vietnam when this will lead promptly to productive discussions. We, of course, assume that while discussions proceed, North Vietnam would not take advantage of the bombing cessation or limitation.

From that date on the offer came to be known as "the San Antonio formula." It relaxed somewhat the proposal we had made to Ho Chi Minh in February. We were not asking him to restrict his military actions before a bombing halt, and once the bombing ended we were not insisting that he immediately end his military effort, only that he not increase it. Since the leaders in Hanoi seemed to be having difficulty with the idea of making any military commitments prior to a bombing halt, we made it clear that we were prepared to "assume" they would not take advantage of the cessation. All we asked was that a cessation of bombing would lead promptly to peace talks and that those talks would be "productive."

Despite continued lack of movement in the Paris channel, we kept it open and exchanges continued well into October through the French go-betweens. Finally, on October 17, we received the following message from Mai Van Bo:

At the present time, the United States is continuing the escalation of the war in an extremely grave manner. In these conditions, words of peace are only trickery. At a time when the United States continues the escalation we can neither receive Mr. Kissinger nor comment on the American views transmitted through this channel. . . .

The North Vietnamese representative said that discussions could take place only when bombing of the North had ended "without condition." With this statement, I became convinced again that Hanoi had no interest in serious talk about peace except, as always, on its own stiff terms.

Source: Johnson, *Vantage Point*, 266–68.

DOCUMENT 246: Secretary of State Rusk's Remarks on Containment of China (16 October 1967)

Secretary Rusk: In my press conference I pointed the finger at what I called Asian communism because the doctrine of communism as announced and declared in Peking has a special quality of militancy, a militancy which has largely isolated Peking within the Communist world, quite apart from the problem it has created with many other countries. . . .

Mr. Barnett: Mr. Secretary, since your last press conference, some of your critics have accused you of using the threat of "yellow peril" to justify the allied forces' presence in South Viet-Nam. And, related to that also is the fact that many people have seen what they consider a shade different emphasis in your approach to this, that at one time American forces were there to justify the self-determination of South Viet-Nam, and now you're talking more in terms of giving strength to the non-communist nations in Asia as a defense against Peking. Could you clarify this?

Secretary Rusk: Yes. In the first place, I put out a statement [on October 16] in which I rejected categorically any effort to put into my mouth the concept of "the yellow peril," which was a racial concept of 60 or 70 years ago fostered by extreme journalism of those days. This is not in my mind.

I pointed out that other Asian nations, ranging from Korea and Japan on the one side around to the subcontinent of India on the other, are concerned about their own safety over against the things which are being said and done in Peking and by Peking. These free nations of Asia also are of Asian races. So that to me, this has nothing whatever to do with the sense of "yellow peril" that was built upon a racial fear and hostility 60 or 70 years ago in which the hordes of Asia were going to overrun the white race as a racial matter. . . .

Mr. De Segonzac: But by injecting the Chinese question in the whole affair of Viet-Nam as you have in your last press conference, aren't you making it more difficult to come to some form of solution, because you're giving the impression now that the whole question of Viet-Nam is not so much to help a small power, as was explained previously, to come to its self-decisions, but now you're putting it as a problem of China and the dangers of China in the Far East?

Secretary Rusk: Well, this is not something that is an opinion solely of my own. There are many countries in Asia who are concerned about

Peking and their attitude. I have no doubt that if Peking were strongly to support the reconvening of a Geneva conference that there might well be a Geneva conference, for example. At the present time, they bitterly oppose such a conference. . . .

I don't think that we can pretend that the policies of China and some of the actions being taken by China are a contribution toward peace in Asia. At least our Asian friends don't think so.

Mr. Ruge: Mr. Secretary, if the aim of U.S. policy is now mainly containment of China, how do you envision the future of Asia? Do you expect to have all the other Asian countries armed to the point where they're strong enough to resist China, or is that a permanent role for the United States in the Pacific as the gendarmes for a couple of billions?

Secretary Rusk: Well, I myself have not used that term "containment of China." It is true that at the present time we have an alliance with Korea, Japan, the Republic of China on Taiwan, the Philippines, Thailand, Australia, and New Zealand. Now, does that system of alliances add up to containment? That is something one can judge.

Source: Pentagon Papers, Gravel Edition, 4:682–84.

THE TET OFFENSIVE AND THE CHANGE OF COURSE, JANUARY–DECEMBER 1968

DOCUMENT 247: Senator Robert Kennedy Comments During Interview that U.S. Security Is Independent of Any Victory Against the "Great Threat of Asian Communism" (26 November 1967)

Now we're saying we're going to fight there [Vietnam] so that we don't have to fight in Thailand, so that we don't have to fight on the west coast of the United States, so that they won't move across the Rockies. . . . Maybe [the people of South Vietnam] don't want it, but we want it, so we're going in there and we're killing South Vietnamese, we're killing children, we're killing women, we're killing innocent people . . . because [the Communists are] 12,000 miles away and they might get to be 11,000 miles away. . . .

Do we have a right here in the United States to say that we're going to kill tens of thousands, make millions of people, as we have . . . refugees, kill women and children? . . . I very seriously question whether we have that right. . . . Those of us who stay here in the United States, we must feel it when we use napalm, when a village is destroyed and civilians are killed. This is also our responsibility. . . . The picture last week of a paratrooper holding a rifle to a [Vietnamese] woman's head, it must trouble us more than it does. . . .

We love our country for what it can be and for the justice it stands for and what we're going to mean to the next generation. It is not just the land, it is not just the mountains, it is what this country stands for. And that is what I think is being seriously undermined in Vietnam.

. . . [There is] an unhappiness and an uneasiness within the United States at the moment, and there has to be an outlet for it.

Source: Face the Nation, 26 November 1967, quoted in Arthur M. Schlesinger, Jr., *Robert Kennedy and His Times* (Boston: Houghton Mifflin, 1978), 824.

DOCUMENT 248: President Johnson Remembers the Tet Offensive (January 1968)

The year 1968 was a major turning point in the Vietnam war. In late January the USS *Pueblo* and its crew were seized by North Korean patrol boats off the coast of North Korea. A few days later the North Vietnamese launched a surprise major offensive against U.S. and South Vietnamese forces. This "New Year" (Tet) offensive even threatened the compound of the U.S. Embassy in Saigon. Up to this point, President Johnson had claimed that the war was wearing down the communists and that Americans could see "light at the end of the tunnel." The Tet offensive, however, shattered the illusion that the war would soon be won. Although the North Vietnamese offensive was a military disaster for the communists, it triggered increased pressures within the United States to terminate U.S. involvement. In March of that year President Johnson also decided not to seek reelection and, on the counsel of his closest advisers, began moving toward a negotiated settlement.

There is no doubt in my mind that the Tet offensive was a military debacle for the North Vietnamese and the Viet Cong. I am convinced that historians and military analysts will come to regard that offensive and its aftermath as the most disastrous Communist defeat of the war in Vietnam. Indeed, some analysts have already reached that conclusion. But the defeat the Communists suffered did not have the telling effect it should have had largely because of what we did to ourselves.

There was a great deal of emotional and exaggerated reporting of the Tet offensive in our press and on television. The media seemed to be in competition as to who could provide the most lurid and depressing accounts. Columnists unsympathetic to American involvement in Southeast Asia jumped on the bandwagon. Some senatorial critics and numerous opponents of America's war effort added their voices to the chorus of defeatism. The American people and even a number of officials in government, subjected to this daily barrage of bleakness and near panic, began to think that we must have suffered a defeat.

Source: Johnson, *Vantage Point*, 383–84.

DOCUMENT 249: Secretary of State Dean Rusk and the Tet Offensive as a Turning Point in America's Policy Toward Vietnam (31 January 1968)

Tet was a major military victory for allied forces, but it quickly proved to be a political loss. In the days and weeks after the offensive, opinion remained divided within the administration and the nation at large over the meaning of the Tet offensive. From a purely military point of view, it reminded me of Germany's Battle of the Bulge in World War II—a last-ditch offensive. North Vietnamese strategists committed all their available manpower, apparently hoping that their offensive would spark a general uprising among the South Vietnamese people, but this did not occur. For us and our South Vietnamese allies, these were indeed rough days, and we suffered substantial casualties. The Tet offensive severely disrupted the pacification program in the countryside, and South Vietnamese forces were drawn back to defend provincial capitals, towns, and populated areas, leaving much of the countryside exposed to the enemy. But overall the Tet offensive was a severe military setback for the enemy. He took terrible losses.

And yet what was a striking military defeat for Hanoi was turned into a brilliant political victory in the United States because of Tet's effects upon the American people. How that came about is a very interesting question. The media's portrayal of the Tet offensive was certainly a factor.

Source: Dean Rusk, *As I Saw It* (New York: Norton, 1990), 477–78.

DOCUMENT 250: Senator Eugene McCarthy Advocates a Greater Emphasis on U.S. Social Problems than on Military Action in Vietnam (March 1968)

The most important struggle for the future welfare of America is not in the jungles of Vietnam; it is in the streets and schools and tenements of our cities. Yet the commitment of resources and moral energy to the problems of our cities has been but a fraction of the amount committed to the Saigon regime.

Source: Eugene McCarthy, *First Things First: New Priorities for Americans* (New York: New American Library, 1968), 20.

DOCUMENT 251: Clark Clifford Recalls "the Tuesday Lunch" with President Johnson and the Decision to Call Together "the Wise Men" (19 March 1968)

I looked for allies to help convince him to turn toward de-escalation or disengagement. When I realized the degree to which Dean Acheson had become disillusioned with the war, it occurred to me that, if presented in the right manner, a shift in the views of some of the other Wise Men, who had given the President such strong support in November 1967, might make an impression on President Johnson. . . . [A]t the Tuesday Lunch on March 19, I suggested that the President reconvene his senior advisory group. . . . [T]he President agreed, and we decided to convene the group on March 25, six days before his speech to the nation on Vietnam.

Source: Clark Clifford, *Counsel to the President* (New York: Random House, 1991), 507–8.

DOCUMENT 252: Secretary of Defense Clark Clifford Recalls the "Most Distinguished Dinner Party" at the U.S. State Department (25–26 March 1968)

On 25–26 March a gathering of President Johnson's senior advisers, a group which became known as "the Wise Men," convened at the president's behest to make recommendations to him about America's involvement in Vietnam. This "Cold War Knighthood" of elder statesmen met late into the night in what became known as "possibly the most distinguished dinner party of the American Establishment ever held." At its conclusion they made an initial recommendation to President Johnson that American forces be slowly withdrawn from South Vietnam.

[T]here could be no pleasure in participating in an event that required its participants to admit that their previous advice had been wrong, and that the President must change course, no matter what the consequences. . . .

The most important briefing came from Phil Habib [State Department Political Counsellor]. . . . He presented a bleak but balanced picture of a South Vietnamese government unlikely to pull itself together. . . .

[T]he President [arrived and] asked McGeorge Bundy to summarize the group's views. Bundy began with a blunt statement that seemed to shock the President:

> Mr. President, there has been a very significant shift in most of our positions since we last met. . . . On the question of troop reinforcements the dominant sentiment was that . . . there should not be a substantial escalation, nor an extension of the conflict.

Source: Clifford, *Counsel to the President*, 511–16.

DOCUMENT 253: President Johnson Decides Not to Seek Reelection (31 March 1968)

Tonight, I renew the offer I made last August—to stop the bombardment of North Vietnam. We ask that talks begin promptly, that they be serious talks on the substance of peace. We assume that during those talks Hanoi will not take advantage of our restraint.

We are prepared to move immediately toward peace through negotiations. . . .

Now, as in the past, the United States is ready to send its representatives to any forum, at any time, to discuss the means of bringing this ugly war to an end. . . .

I call upon President Ho Chi Minh to respond positively, and favorably, to this new step toward peace.

But if peace does not come now through negotiations, it will come when Hanoi understands that our common resolve is unshakable, and our common strength is invincible. . . .

But the heart of our involvement in South Vietnam—under three different Presidents, three separate administrations—has always been America's own security.

And the larger purpose of our involvement has always been to help the nations of Southeast Asia become independent and stand alone, self-sustaining, as members of a great world community—at peace with themselves, and at peace with all others. . . .

Of those to whom much is given, much is asked. I cannot say and no man could say that no more will be asked of us.

Yet I believe that now, no less than when the decade began, this generation of Americans is willing to "pay any price, bear any burden, meet any hardship, support any friend, oppose any foe to assure the survival and the success of liberty."

Since those words were spoken by John F. Kennedy, the people of America have kept that compact with mankind's noblest cause. And we shall continue to keep it. . . . I have concluded that I should not permit the Presidency to become involved in the partisan divisions that are developing in this political year. . . . Accordingly, I shall not seek, and I will not accept, the nomination of my Party for another term as your President.

Source: Papers of the Presidents: Lyndon B. Johnson, 1968 (Washington: GPO, 1970); also see Janet Podell and Steven Anzovin, eds., *Speeches of the American Presidents* (New York: H. W. Wilson, 1988), 649–55.

DOCUMENT 254: Inquiry into the Massacre at My Lai, Vietnam (16–19 March 1968)

In a November 1969 news series by *New York Times* reporter Seymour Hersh, the American public learned that, in mid-March 1968, a platoon of U.S. soldiers cold-bloodedly killed virtually the entire population of the South Vietnamese village of My Lai. In an investigation conducted almost two years later by the U.S. Army, it was learned that not a single shot had been fired from the village upon the American servicemen, and that the Army had systematically covered up the massacre for over a year.

I. Findings of the Inquiry:

1. During the period 16–19 March 1968, US Army troops of Barker, 11th Brigade, Americal Division, massacred a large number of noncombatants in two hamlets of Son My Village, Quang Ngai Province, Republic of Vietnam. The precise number of Vietnamese killed cannot be determined but was at least 175 and may exceed 400.

2. The massacre occurred in conjunction with a combat operation which was intended to neutralize Son My Village as a logistical support base and staging area, and to destroy elements of an enemy battalion thought to be located in the Son My area.

3. The massacre resulted primarily from the nature of the orders issued by persons in the chain of command within TF Barker.

4. The task force commander's order and the associated intelligence estimate issued prior to the operation were embellished as they were disseminated through each lower level of command, and ultimately presented to the individual soldier a false and misleading picture of the Son My area as an armed enemy camp, largely devoid of civilian inhabitants.

5. Prior to the incident, there had developed within certain elements of the 11th Brigade a permissive attitude toward the treatment and safeguarding of noncombatants which contributed to the mistreatment of such persons during the Son My operation.

6. The permissive attitude in the treatment of Vietnamese was, on 16–19 March 1968, exemplified by an almost total disregard for the lives and property of the civilian population of Son My Village on the part of commanders and key staff officers of TF Barker.

7. On 16 March, soldiers at the squad and platoon level, within some elements of TF Barker, murdered noncombatants while under the supervision and control of their immediate superiors.

8. A part of the crimes visited on the inhabitants of Son My Village included individual and group acts of murder, rape, sodomy, maiming, and assault on noncombatants and the mistreatment and killing of detainees. They further included the killing of livestock, destruction of crops, closing of wells, and the burning of dwellings within several sub-hamlets.

9. Some attempts were made to stop the criminal acts in Son My Vil-

lage on 16 March; but with few exceptions, such efforts were too feeble or too late.

10. Intensive interrogation has developed no evidence that any members of the units engaged in the Son My operation was under the influence of marijuana or other narcotics. . . .

Omissions and Commissions by Individuals . . .

23. 1LT (then 2LT) William L. Calley

a. He ordered the execution by his platoon of an unlawful operation against inhabited hamlets in Son My Village, which included the destruction of houses by burning, killing of livestock, the destruction of crops and other foodstuffs, and the closing of wells; and expressly ordered the killing of persons found there.

b. He directed and supervised the men of his platoon in the systematic killing of many noncombatants in and around My Lai.

c. He personally participated in the killing of some noncombatants in and around My Lai.

d. He failed to report the killings of noncombatants in and around My Lai as a possible war crime as required by MACV Directive 20–4.

Source: U.S. Department of Army Review, *Report of Preliminary Investigations into My Lai Incident,* "General William R. Peers' Report to Secretary of the Army, 14 March 1970" (Washington: GPO, 1976), sec. 12, pp. 1–5. Also see Joseph Goldstein, Burke Marshall, and Jack Schwartz, *The My Lai Massacre and Its Cover-Up: Beyond the Reach of Law* (New York: Free Press, 1976), 314–45.

DOCUMENT 255: An Infantryman's Cynical Perspective of the War (1968)

As infantrymen learned to cope with the dangers of their occupation, they also began to develop a cynicism that changed their commitment to the war itself. Although their combat efficiency increased during the first three months, their commitment to the stated aims and goals of the war began to slide in the opposite direction.

Disenchantment had always existed, even in the first years of America's involvement in Vietnam, but it became more obvious and widespread by mid-1968, when the undeclared war grew ever more unpopular in the wake of the Tet offensive and the presidential election campaigns. The actual experience of fighting laid the groundwork for changes in the attitudes of American combat soldiers toward their government's stated objectives in Vietnam and toward the government of

South Vietnam. These attitudes were passed on from veterans to new guys, resulting in a slowly maturing pessimism that was inherited and inculcated in the squads and fire teams—where it really mattered. At what was literally the grass roots level, soldiers knew exactly what they were fighting for; being shot at made that obvious. What became obscure in the daily attrition was the purpose: what they were hoping to achieve for all the effort. Unfortunately, most soldiers were unable to find any apparent purpose for the sacrifices they had witnessed or made. The cause in Vietnam that had seemed so necessary and immediate in 1965 was remarkably devoid of genuine meaning after only a few lives or enemy contacts or rotations. Commitment to the war and its ideals was replaced by practical considerations that were, of necessity, self-centered.

Although most soldiers in Vietnam wanted to "win" in some ultimate sense, the goal of the man in the field was to simply survive to make it home again. That thought came to dominate the actions of nearly every soldier. The realization that they were fighting to get home again put an end to many of the predilections they entertained when they went overseas. Some veterans say that they fought for God and country and to stop the spread of communism. Far more fought because their pride, self-respect, and sense of self-preservation demanded it. For most, there did not seem to be any loftier concerns than those.

Source: James R. Ebert, *A Life in a Year: The American Infantryman in Vietnam, 1965–1972* (Novato, Calif.: Presidio Press, 1993), 232–35.

DOCUMENT 256: Flyer Distributed to Demonstrate Against the War at the Democratic National Convention in Chicago (28 August 1968)

The majority of the American people want the United States to stop the bombing and get out of Vietnam. The politicians are in Chicago threatening to continue the war and to suppress opposition. This is the only demonstration for which the city has issued a permit despite repeated requests by many groups.

The political bosses at the Democratic Convention and the political boss of Chicago, Richard J. Daley, are obviously afraid to hear what the people want. They have turned Chicago into an armed camp and have tried to scuttle free speech so that they wouldn't have to listen to the innumerable Americans WHO WANT THE UNITED STATES TO GET OUT OF VIETNAM. . . .

We urge all Chicagoans to join with the thousands coming from across the country in a massive antiwar demonstration at Grant Park, Wednesday from 1 to 4 P.M.

Source: Heath, *Mutiny Does Not Happen Lightly*, 23.

THE NIXON-KISSINGER STRATEGY FOR THE VIETNAMIZATION OF THE WAR, 1969–1972

President Nixon and his National Security Adviser Henry Kissinger believed continued American involvement in Vietnam a mistake. To defuse criticism within the United States and yet maintain U.S. credibility they began "Vietnamizing" the war, that is, withdrawing American troops and turning the war over increasingly to the South Vietnamese, while trying to put in place a "large policy" of new relations with China and the Soviet Union. Their efforts resulted in a peace agreement in January 1973, but it came only after four more years of terrible bloodshed and sacrifice.

DOCUMENT 257: President Nixon's Eight-Point Strategy to End the War (14 May 1969)

I know that some believe that I should have ended the war immediately after the inauguration by simply ordering our forces home from Vietnam.

This would have been the easy thing to do. It might have been a popular thing to do. But I would have betrayed my solemn responsibility as President of the United States if I had done so.

I want to end this war. The American people want to end this war. The people of South Vietnam want to end this war. But we want to end it permanently so that the younger brothers of our soldiers in Vietnam will not have to fight in the future in another Vietnam someplace else in the world. . . .

Against that background, let me discuss first, what we have rejected, and second, what we are prepared to accept.

We have ruled out attempting to impose a purely military solution on the battlefield.

We have also ruled out either a one-sided withdrawal from Vietnam, or the acceptance in Paris of terms that would amount to a disguised American defeat.

When we assumed the burden of helping defend South Vietnam, millions of South Vietnamese men, women, and children placed their trust in us. To abandon them now would risk a massacre that would shock and dismay everyone in the world who values human life.

Abandoning the South Vietnamese people, however, would jeopardize more than lives in South Vietnam. It would threaten our long-term hopes for peace in the world. A great nation cannot renege on its pledges. A great nation must be worthy of trust. . . .

—As soon as agreement can be reached, all non-South Vietnamese forces would begin withdrawals from South Vietnam.

—Over a period of 12 months, by agreed-upon stages, the major portions of all U.S., allied, and other non-South Vietnamese forces would be withdrawn. At the end of this 12-month period, the remaining U.S., allied, and other non-South Vietnamese forces would move into designated base areas and would not engage in combat operations.

—The remaining U.S. and allied forces would complete their withdrawals as the remaining North Vietnamese forces were withdrawn and returned to North Vietnam.

—An international supervisory body, acceptable to both sides, would be created for the purpose of verifying withdrawals, and for any other purposes agreed upon between the two sides.

—This international body would begin operating in accordance with an agreed timetable and would participate in arranging supervised cease-fires in Vietnam.

—As soon as possible after the international body was functioning, elections would be held under agreed procedures and under the supervision of the international body.

—Arrangements would be made for the release of prisoners of war on both sides at the earliest possible time.

—All parties would agree to observe the Geneva Accords of 1954 regarding South Vietnam and Cambodia, and the Laos Accords of 1962.

Source: Papers of the Presidents: Richard M. Nixon, 1969 (Washington: GPO, 1971), 369–73.

DOCUMENT 258: President Nixon's Speech Calling for the "Vietnamization" of the War and His Appeal to "the Great Silent Majority" (3 November 1969)

We have taken . . . significant initiatives which must remain secret to keep open some channels of communication which may still prove to be productive.

But the effect of all the public, private, and secret negotiations which have been undertaken since the bombing halt a year ago and since this administration came into office on January 20, can be summed up in one sentence: No progress what-ever has been made except agreement on the shape of the bargaining table. . . .

Now let me turn, however, to a more encouraging report on another front.

At the time we launched our search for peace I recognized we might not succeed in bringing an end to the war through negotiation. I, therefore, put into effect another plan to bring peace—a plan which will bring the war to an end regardless of what happens on the negotiating front.

It is in line with a major shift in U.S. foreign policy which I described in my press conference at Guam on July 25. Let me briefly explain what has been described as the Nixon Doctrine—a policy which not only will help end the war in Vietnam, but which is an essential element of our program to prevent future Vietnams.

We Americans are a do-it-yourself people. We are an impatient people. Instead of teaching someone else to do a job, we like to do it ourselves. And this trait has been carried over into our foreign policy.

In Korea and again in Vietnam, the United States furnished most of the money, most of the arms, and most of the men to help the people of those countries defend their freedom against Communist aggression.

Before any American troops were committed to Vietnam, a leader of another Asian country expressed this opinion to me when I was traveling in Asia as a private citizen. He said: "When you are trying to assist another nation defend its freedom, U.S. policy should be to help them fight the war but not to fight the war for them."

Well, in accordance with this wise counsel, I laid down in Guam three principles as guidelines for future American policy toward Asia:

—First, the United States will keep all of its treaty commitments.

—Second, we shall provide a shield if a nuclear power threatens the freedom of a nation allied with us or of a nation whose survival we consider vital to our security.

—Third, in cases involving other types of aggression, we shall furnish military and economic assistance when requested in accordance with our treaty commitments. But we shall look to the nation directly threatened to assume the primary responsibility of providing the manpower for its defense. . . .

The defense of freedom is everybody's business—not just America's business. And it is particularly the responsibility of the people whose freedom is threatened. In the previous administration, we Americanized the war in Vietnam. In this administration, we are Vietnamizing the search for peace.

The policy of the previous administration not only resulted in our assuming the primary responsibility for fighting the war, but even more significantly did not adequately stress the goal of strengthening the South Vietnamese so that they could defend themselves when we left.

The Vietnamization plan was launched following Secretary [of Defense Melvin] Laird's visit to Vietnam in March. Under the plan, I ordered first a substantial increase in the training and equipment of South Vietnamese forces.

In July, on my visit to Vietnam, I changed General Abrams' orders so that they were consistent with the objectives of our new policies. Under the new orders, the primary mission of our troops is to enable the South Vietnamese forces to assume the full responsibility for the security of South Vietnam. . . .

My fellow Americans, I am sure you can recognize from what I have said that we really only have two choices open to us if we want to end this war.

—I can order an immediate, precipitate withdrawal of all Americans from Vietnam without regard to the effects of that action.

—Or we can persist in our search for a just peace through a negotiated settlement if possible, or through continued implementation of our plan for Vietnamization if necessary—a plan in which we will withdraw all our forces from Vietnam on a schedule in accordance with our program, as the South Vietnamese become strong enough to defend their own freedom.

I have chosen this second course. . . .

I know it may not be fashionable to speak of patriotism or national destiny these days. But I feel it is appropriate to do so on this occasion. And so tonight—to you, the great silent majority of my fellow Americans—I ask for your support. . . .

The more support I can have from the American people, the sooner that pledge can be redeemed; for the more divided we are at home, the less likely the enemy is to negotiate at Paris. Let us be united for peace. Let us also be united against defeat. Because let us understand: North Vietnam cannot defeat or humiliate the United States. Only Americans can do that.

Source: Papers of the Presidents: Nixon, 901–9.

DOCUMENT 259: President Nixon Decides to Invade Cambodia (26 April 1970)

In April 1970 President Nixon received intelligence reports that the Vietnamese communists had two sanctuaries in neighboring Cambodia. The first, called "Parrot's Beak," was a sliver of land that pushed into South Vietnam and reached within thirty-three miles of Saigon. The South Vietnamese Army (ARVN) had a sizeable force stationed near this border area. President Nixon's reports indicated, however, that the heaviest communist concentration was in another border area, the "Fishhook," a curving piece of Cambodian territory that jutted into South Vietnam some fifty miles northwest of Saigon. According to these reports this was the primary area of operation for the COSVN—the Central Office of South Vietnam. COSVN was the communists' floating command post for supplies, food, and medical facilities.

The Fishhook was the nerve center of the Communist forces in the sanctuaries, and it would be strongly defended. The initial intelligence estimates projected that . . . the concentration of Communist troops in the area might result in very high casualties in the first week of the operation.

I began to consider letting the ARVN go into the Parrot's Beak and sending a mixed force of American and South Vietnamese troops into the Fishhook. Giving the South Vietnamese an operation of their own would be a major boost to their morale as well as provide a practical demonstration of the success of Vietnamization. It would also be a good diversionary cover for the . . . more difficult Fishhook operation.

I never had any illusions about the shattering effect a decision to go into Cambodia would have on public opinion at home. I knew that opinions among my major foreign policy advisers were deeply divided over the issue of widening the war, and I recognized that [it could mean] personal and political catastrophe for me and my administration.

On Sunday night, April 26, I reached my decision. We would go for broke. The ARVN would go into the Parrot's Beak and a joint ARVN-U.S. force would go into the Fishhook.

Source: Richard Nixon, *RN: The Memoirs of Richard Nixon* (New York: Grosset and Dunlap, 1978), 449–50.

DOCUMENT 260: The Vietnam Veterans Memorial Wall, Panel 10W, Line 3 (11 November 1982)

Thomas G. Standley, a U.S. Army infantryman from Nashville, Tennessee, was killed in May 1970 during the U.S. operation in Cambodia. His name and the names of over 58,000 other soldiers, sailors, and airmen are engraved upon the mirrorlike-granite Vietnam Veterans

Memorial Wall in Washington. At the time of his death, twenty-year-old "Tommy" was just a few weeks older than his cousin, Gary D. Vaughan, my research assistant for the last five years.

In honor of the men and women of the Armed Forces of the United States who served in the Vietnam War. The names of those who gave their lives and of those who remain missing are inscribed in the order they were taken from us.

◆ THOMAS G STANDLEY ◆

Our Nation honors the courage, sacrifice and devotion to duty and country of its Vietnam Veterans. This Memorial was built with private contributions from the American People. November 11, 1982.

Source: Vietnam War Memorial Wall, Panel 10W, Line 3, Washington, D.C.

DOCUMENT 261: The Student Mobilization Committee Platform (22 November 1970)

The Student Mobilization Committee to End the War in Vietnam is the mass national organization of American youth united in uncompromising struggle against the war in Vietnam.

Our program is simple. We fight for the immediate and unconditional withdrawal of all U.S. troops and material from Vietnam, for abolition of the draft, against all forms of campus complicity with the war in Vietnam, for self-determination for Vietnam, women, and Black and Third-World America, for constitutional rights for GIs and high school students.

We are an action organization, with a strategy of building mass actions of the kind that have already brought millions of Americans into the streets in opposition to the war. We intend to continue uniting even larger and broader sections of the student and academic community and GIs than ever before.

As part of this strategy, we have always participated as fully as possible in the broad adult antiwar coalitions that have initiated mass demonstrations and will continue to do so, urging these coalitions to extend organized antiwar sentiment through massive, independent actions like November 15.

Source: Heath, *Mutiny Does Not Happen Lightly,* 28–33.

DOCUMENT 262: John Kerry's Testimony of the "Winter Soldier Investigation" for the Vietnam Veterans Against the War (VVAW) Before the Senate Foreign Relations Committee (22 April 1971)

As a Navy lieutenant in Vietnam, John Kerry had been awarded the Silver Star, the Bronze Star with oak leaf cluster, and three Purple Hearts. In 1984 he was elected to the U.S. Senate from Massachusetts.

I would like to say for the record, and also for the men behind me who are also wearing the uniform and their medals, that my sitting here is really symbolic. I am not here as John Kerry. I am here as one member of the group of 1,000 which is a small representation of a very much larger group of veterans in this country, and were it possible for all of them to sit at this table they would be here and have the same kind of testimony. . . .

I would like to talk on behalf of all those veterans and say that several months ago in Detroit we had an investigation at which over 150 honorably discharged, and many very highly decorated, veterans testified to war crimes committed in Southeast Asia. These were not isolated incidents but crimes committed on a day to day basis with the full awareness of officers at all levels of command.

It is impossible to describe to you exactly what did happen in Detroit—the emotions in the room and the feelings of the men who were reliving their experiences in Vietnam. They relived the absolute horror of what this country, in a sense, made them do.

They told stories that at times they had personally raped, cut off ears, cut off heads, taped wires from portable telephones to human genitals and turned up the power, cut off limbs, blown up bodies, randomly shot at civilians, razed villages in [a] fashion reminiscent of Genghis Khan, shot cattle and dogs for fun, poisoned food stocks, and generally ravaged the countryside of South Vietnam in addition to the normal ravage of war and the normal and very particular ravaging which is done by the applied bombing power of this country.

We call this investigation the Winter Soldier Investigation. The term Winter Soldier is a play on words of Thomas Paine's in 1776 when he spoke of the Sunshine Patriots and summer time soldiers who deserted at Valley Forge because the going was rough.

We who have come here to Washington have come here because we feel we have to be winter soldiers now. We could come back to this country, we could be quiet, we could hold our silence, we could not tell what went on in Vietnam, but we feel because of what threatens this country, not the reds, but the crimes which we are committing that threaten it, that we have to speak out.

I would like to talk to you a little bit about what the result is of the feelings these men carry with them after coming back from Vietnam. The country doesn't know it yet but it has created a monster, a monster in the form of millions who have been taught to deal and to trade in violence and who are given the chance to die for the biggest nothing in history; men who have returned with a sense of anger and a sense of betrayal which no one has yet grasped.

As a veteran and one who feels this anger I would like to talk about it. We are angry because we feel we have been used in the worst fashion by the administration of this country.

In 1970 at West Point Vice President Agnew said "some glamorize the criminal misfits of society while our best men die in Asian rice paddies to preserve the freedom which most of those misfits abuse," and this was used as a rallying point for our effort in Vietnam.

But for us, as boys in Asia whom the country was supposed to support, his statement is a terrible distortion from which we can only draw a very deep sense of revulsion, and hence the anger of some of the men who are here in Washington today. It is a distortion because we in no way consider ourselves the best men of this country; because those he calls misfits were standing up for us in a way that nobody else in this country dared to; because so many who have died would have returned to this country to join the misfits in their efforts to ask for an immediate withdrawal from South Vietnam; because so many of those best men have returned as quadriplegics and amputees—and they lie forgotten in Veterans Administration Hospitals in this country which fly the flag which so many have chosen as their own personal symbol—and we cannot consider ourselves America's best men when we are ashamed of and hated for what we were called on to do in Southeast Asia.

In our opinion, and from our experience, there is nothing in South Vietnam which could happen that realistically threatens the United States of America. And to attempt to justify the loss of one American life in Vietnam, Cambodia or Laos by linking such loss to the preservation of freedom, which those misfits supposedly abuse, is to us the height of criminal hypocrisy, and it is that kind of hypocrisy which we feel has torn this country apart. . . .

We found most people didn't even know the difference between communism and democracy. They only wanted to work in rice paddies without helicopters strafing them and bombs with napalm burning their villages and tearing their country apart. They wanted everything to do with the war, particularly with this foreign presence of the United States of America, to leave them alone in peace, and they practiced the art of survival by siding with whichever military force was present at a particular time, be it Viet Cong, North Vietnamese or American.

We found also that all too often American men were dying in those rice paddies for want of support from their allies. We saw first hand how monies from American taxes were used for a corrupt dictatorial regime. We saw that many people in this country had a one-sided idea of who was kept free by our flag, and blacks provided the highest percentage of casualties. We saw Vietnam ravaged equally by American bombs and search and destroy missions, as well as by Viet Cong terrorism, and yet we listened while this country tried to blame all of the havoc on the Viet Cong.

We rationalized destroying villages in order to save them. We saw America lose her sense of morality as she accepted very coolly a My Lai and refused to give up the image of American soldiers who hand out chocolate bars and chewing gum.

We learned the meaning of free fire zones, shooting anything that moves, and we watched while America placed a cheapness on the lives of orientals.

We watched the United States falsification of body counts, in fact the glorification of body counts. We listened while month after month we were told the back of the enemy was about to break. We fought using weapons against "oriental human beings." We fought using weapons against those people which I do not believe this country would dream of using were we fighting in the European theater. We watched while men charged up hills because a general said that hill has to be taken, and after losing one platoon or two platoons they marched away to leave the hill for reoccupation by the North Vietnamese. We watched pride allow the most unimportant battles to be blown into extravaganzas, because we couldn't lose, and we couldn't retreat, and because it didn't matter how many American bodies were lost to prove that point, and so there were Hamburger Hills and Khe Sanhs and Hill 81s and Fire Base 6s, and so many others. . . .

We are asking here in Washington for some action; action from the Congress of the United States of America which has the power to raise and maintain armies, and which by the Constitution also has the power to declare war.

We have come here, not to the President, because we believe that this body can be responsive to the will of the people, and we believe that the will of the people says that we should be out of Vietnam now.

We are here in Washington also to say that the problem of this war is not just a question of war and diplomacy. It is part and parcel of everything that we are trying as human beings to communicate to people in this country—the question of racism which is rampant in the military, and so many other questions such as the use of weapons; the hypocrisy in our taking umbrage at the Geneva Conventions and using that as justification for a continuation of this war when we are more guilty than any other body of violations of those Geneva Conventions; in the use of free fire zones, harassment interdiction fire, search and destroy missions, the bombings, the torture of prisoners, the killing of prisoners, all accepted policy by many units in South Vietnam. That is what we are trying to say. It is part and parcel of everything. . . .

We are also here to ask, and we are here to ask vehemently, where are the leaders of our country? Where is the leadership? We are here to ask where are McNamara, Rostow, Bundy, Gilpatric and so many others? Where are they now that we, the men whom they sent off to war, have returned? These are commanders who have deserted their troops, and there is no more serious crime in the laws of war. The Army says they never leave their wounded. The Marines say they never leave even their dead. These men have left all the casualties and retreated behind a pious shield of public rectitude. They have left the real stuff of their reputations bleaching behind them in the sun in this country.

Source: Gettleman et al., *Vietnam and America: A Documented History,* 1st ed. 453–58.

DOCUMENT 263: Tape Recordings by President Nixon's Chief of Staff, H. R. Haldeman, Reveal Nixon's Reaction to "The Pentagon Papers" (13–15 June 1971)

Sunday, June 13, 1971

The big deal today was a break in *The New York Times* of the reprinting of the 40-volume Vietnam Papers, that covered the whole McNamara operation. . . . It really blasts McNamara and Kennedy and Johnson. . . . The point is that it's criminally traitorous that the documents got to *The New York Times,* and even more so that *The Times* is printing them. The *Times* says they plan to print the whole series of articles. The key now is for us to keep out of it and let the people that are affected cut each other up on it.

14 June

The P [President Nixon] called me in [and] raised the point that there's cause in this for everyone to be concerned, especially regarding foreign policy. As to staff leakage, etc., the P is especially concerned about Henry's [Kissinger] staff. He thinks that we should get the story out on

... at Brookings [Institution, a liberal think tank in Washington], who is the suspected villain.

15 June

The big thing today was still the *New York Times* story follow-up, as they go on running it and the whole thing builds substantively. [Attorney General John] Mitchell went ahead last night with his request of them to cease publication; they refused. So today he went for an injunction, got a temporary restraining order, and probably will be able to get an injunction. After meeting with the P this afternoon, decided to file criminal charges. So we're pretty much in the soup on the whole thing now. The real problem is to try to establish clearly that the Administration's interest here is in the violation of Top Secret classifications rather than in the release of this particular material. The problem otherwise is that we're going to be tied into it and get blamed for the same kind of deception that was practiced by the Johnson Administration.

Source: H. R. Haldeman, *The Haldeman Diaries: Inside the Nixon White House* (New York: G. P. Putnam's Sons, 1994), 299–301.

DOCUMENT 264: Henry Kissinger Remembers President Nixon's "China Initiative" and Exigencies of *Realpolitik* in Negotiations with Hanoi (January–February 1972)

China was not important to us because it was physically powerful. . . . We needed China to enhance the flexibility of our diplomacy. Gone were the days when we enjoyed the luxury of choosing the moment to involve ourselves in world affairs. We were permanently involved but not so physically or morally predominant as before. We had to take account of other power centers and strive for an equilibrium among them. The China initiative also restored perspective to our national policy. It reduced Indochina to its proper scale—a small peninsula on a major continent. Its drama eased for the American people the pain that would inevitably accompany our withdrawal from Southeast Asia. And it brought balance into the perceptions of our friends around the world.

Source: Henry A. Kissinger, *The White House Years* (Boston: Little, Brown, 1979), 1049.

DOCUMENT 265: Henry Kissinger's "Peace Is at Hand" Statement (October 26, 1972)

We have now heard from both Vietnams and it is obvious that the war that has been raging for 10 years is drawing to a conclusion, that this is a traumatic experience for all of the participants.

The President thought that it might be helpful if I came out here and spoke to you about what we have been doing, where we stand, and to put the various allegations and charges into perspective.

First, let me talk about the situation in three parts: where do we stand procedurally; what is the substance of the negotiations and where do we go from here?

We believe peace is at hand. We believe that an agreement is within sight on the May 8 proposals of the President and some adaptations of our Jan. 25 proposals, which is just to all parties.

It is inevitable that in a war of such complexity that there should be occasional difficulties in reaching a final solution. But we believe that by far the longest part of the road has been traversed and what stands in the way of an agreement now are issues that are relatively less important than those that have already been settled.

Source: Russell D. Buhite, ed., *The Dynamics of World Power: A Documentary History of United States Foreign Policy, 1945–1973*, Vol. 4, *The Far East* (New York: Chelsea House, 5 vols., 1973), 795–800.

PARIS PEACE AGREEMENT AND FALL OF SAIGON

Through the efforts of Secretary of State Henry Kissinger in Paris, the Nixon Administration had reached a preliminary agreement with the North Vietnamese. However, they still had to persuade, South Vietnamese President Thieu to join in signing the final document. President Nixon relied on President Thieu's "common sense and patriotism—if not his instinct for survival"—to conclude that the agreement reached in Paris by American and North Vietnamese negotiators was the best he could hope for and that the conduct of the war was out of his hands. Recognizing Thieu's reluctance to accept the Paris Peace Accords, President Nixon sent his National Security Aide General Alexander Haig to Saigon to meet with Thieu on 16 January.

President Thieu finally decided to accept the agreement. On 20 January Richard Nixon was sworn in for his second term as the thirty-seventh president of the United States.

DOCUMENT 266: President Nixon Urges South Vietnamese President Thieu to Accept the Inescapable Conclusion of the War by Jointly Signing the Paris Peace Agreement (January 1973)

[General Haig] met with Thieu and handed him a letter from me. In it I said that I had irrevocably decided to initial the agreement on January 23 and sign it on January 27. "I will do so," I wrote, "if necessary, alone." I continued:

> In that case I shall have to explain publicly that your government obstructs peace. The result will be an inevitable and immediate termination of U.S. economic and military assistance which cannot be forestalled by a change of personnel in your government. I hope, however, that after all our two countries have shared and suffered together in conflict, we will stay together to preserve peace and reap its benefits. . . .
>
> Finally, I want to emphasize my continued commitment to the freedom and progress of the Republic of Vietnam. It is my firm intention to continue full economic and military aid.

Source: Nixon, *RN,* 749–51.

DOCUMENT 267: Paris Peace Agreement to End Hostilities in Vietnam (27 January 1973)

With a view to ending the war and restoring peace in Viet-Nam on the basis of respect for the Vietnamese people's fundamental national rights and the South Vietnamese people's right to self-determination, and to contributing to the consolidation of peace in Asia and the world,

The parties to the agreement: The Republic of Vietnam, the Provisional Revolutionary Government of South Vietnam, the United States and the Democratic Republic of Vietnam,

Have agreed on the following provisions and undertake to respect and to implement them:

Article 1

The United States and all other countries respect the independence, sovereignty, unity, and territorial integrity of Viet-Nam as recognized by the 1954 Geneva Agreements on Viet-Nam.

Article 2

A cease-fire shall be observed throughout South Viet-Nam as of 2400 hours G.M.T., on January 27, 1973. . . .

The complete cessation of hostilities mentioned in this Article shall be durable and without limit of time. . . .

Article 3

The parties undertake to maintain the cease-fire and to ensure a lasting and stable peace.

As soon as the cease-fire goes into effect:

(a) The United States forces and those of the other foreign countries allied with the United States and the Republic of Viet-Nam shall remain in-place pending the implementation of the plan of troop withdrawal. . . .

(c) The regular forces of all services and arms and the irregular forces of the parties in South Viet-Nam shall stop all offensive activities against each other and shall strictly abide by the following stipulations:

All acts of force on the ground, in the air, and on the sea shall be prohibited;

All hostile acts, terrorism and reprisals by both sides will be banned.

Article 4

The United States will not continue its military involvement or intervene in the internal affairs of South Vietnam.

Article 5

Within 60 days of the signing of this agreement, there will be a total withdrawal from South Vietnam of troops, military personnel, including technical military personnel and military personnel associated with the pacification program, armaments, munitions and war material of the United States and those of the other foreign countries mentioned in Article 3 (a). . . .

Article 6

The dismantlement of all military bases in South Vietnam of the United States and of the other foreign countries mentioned in Article 3 (a) shall be completed within 60 days of the signing of this agreement. . . .

Article 8

(a) The return of captured military personnel and foreign civilians of the parties shall be carried out simultaneously with and completed not later than the same day as the troop withdrawal mentioned in Article 5. The parties shall exchange complete lists of the above-mentioned captured military personnel and foreign civilians on the day of the signing of this agreement.

(b) The parties shall help each other to get information about those military personnel and foreign civilians of the parties missing in action, to determine the location and take care of the graves of the dead so as to facilitate the exhumation and repatriation of the remains, and to take any such other measures as may be required to get information about those still considered missing in action.

Source: U.S. State Department, *United States Treaties and Other International Agreements*, Vol. 24, part 1, 1973 (Washington: GPO, 1974), 1–224 passim.

DOCUMENT 268: Secretary of State Kissinger Recalls President Nixon's Promise of Economic Reconstruction Aid for North Vietnam after Peace Accord (1 February 1973)

[I]n the summer of 1971 during my secret negotiations with Le Duc Tho, we proposed yet another reconstruction scheme. Le Duc Tho noted it without any show of interest. Nixon reiterated the offer publicly as part of a comprehensive proposal on January 25, 1972. Briefing the press the next day, I explained that we were prepared to contribute several billion dollars to the reconstruction of Indochina, including North Vietnam. The President's Foreign Policy Report issued on February 9, 1972, was even more specific: "We are prepared to undertake a massive, 7.5 billion dollar five-year reconstruction program in conjunction with an overall agreement in which North Vietnam could share up to two and a half billion dollars." In my "peace is at hand" press conference of October 26, 1972, I repeated this theme. And I did so again in a press conference on January 24, 1973, as did Nixon on January 31, 1973.

By then Hanoi's interest in the proposition had quickened. It would not admit that it would end the war for economic reasons. But once it had decided on a cease-fire out of military necessity, it was ready, if not eager, to extract the maximum aid from us. Characteristically, Hanoi couched this not in terms of an acceptance of our offer but as a demand for reparations. Nor were Hanoi's ideas of the appropriate aid level characterized by excessive modesty; Le Duc Tho simply demanded for Hanoi the entire package of $7.5 billion that we had earmarked for *all* of Indochina. We were prepared to accept neither of these propositions. We were willing to extend aid because it had been promised by two administrations and especially because we thought it useful as one of the inducements to encourage observance of the Agreement. But we insisted that our offer was an application of traditional American principles; it was a voluntary act, not an "obligation" to indemnify Hanoi. It may have been hairsplitting but to us it involved a point of honor. Through weeks of weary haggling we managed to reduce Hanoi's demand to

$3.25 billion, which was put forward as a target figure subject to further discussion and Congressional approval.

The relevant documents were the Paris Agreement and a Presidential message. Article 21 of the Paris Agreement stated:

> The United States anticipates that this Agreement will usher in an era of reconciliation with the Democratic Republic of Vietnam as with all the peoples of Indochina. In pursuance of its traditional policy, the United States will contribute to healing the wounds of war and to postwar reconstruction of the Democratic Republic of Vietnam and throughout Indochina.

It was a promise given in the expectation that the war was ending and an era of reconciliation would then be possible. And I repeatedly emphasized to Le Duc Tho that any aid presupposed both Congressional approval and Hanoi's living up to the Paris Agreement.

Our intention to extend aid and even its order of magnitude were well known and had been stated many times on the public record. What was kept secret at the time was a cabled message from Nixon to Premier Pham Van Dong spelling out the procedures for implementing Article 21. In order to underline the fact that it was voluntary and distinct from the formal obligations of the Agreement, Le Duc Tho and I had agreed that the message would be delivered on January 30, 1973, three days after the Agreement was signed, in exchange for a list of American prisoners held in Laos. When on the appointed day the North Vietnamese failed to provide a list of the American prisoners of war held in Laos, we instructed our representative in Paris to delay handing over the note. This produced immediate action: The Laotian POW list was handed over on the afternoon of February 1; as agreed, we gave the North Vietnamese the Nixon message to Pham Van Dong at the same time.

Source: Henry A. Kissinger, *Years of Upheaval* (Boston: Little, Brown, 1982), 38–40.

DOCUMENT 269: Public Law 93-52, the Fulbright-Aiken Amendment Prohibiting U.S. Military Activity in Indochina (1 July 1973)

SEC. 108. Notwithstanding any other provision of law, on or after August 15, 1973, no funds herein or heretofore appropriated may be obligated or expended to finance directly or indirectly combat activities by United States military forces in or over or from off the shores of North Vietnam, South Vietnam, Laos or Cambodia.

Source: Public Law 93-52 section 108, July 1, 1973, U.S. Congress, Senate Committee on Foreign Relations, *Background Information Relating to Southeast Asia and Vietnam*, 7th rev. ed. (Washington: GPO, 1975), 577.

DOCUMENT 270: War Powers Resolution of the U.S. Congress (7 November 1973)

Policy and Purpose

(a) *Congressional declaration*: It is the purpose of this chapter to fulfill the intent of the framers of the Constitution of the United States and insure that the collective judgment of both the Congress and the President will apply to the introduction of United States Armed Forces into hostilities, or into situations where imminent involvement in hostilities is clearly indicated by the circumstances, and to the continued use of such forces in hostilities or in such situations.

(b) *Congressional legislative power under necessary and proper clause*: Under article 1, section 8, of the Constitution, it is specifically provided that the Congress shall have the power to make all laws necessary and proper for carrying into execution, not only its own powers but also all other powers vested by the Constitution in the Government of the United States, or in any department or officer hereof.

(c) *Presidential executive power as Commander-in-Chief, limitation*: The constitutional powers of the President as Commander-in-Chief to introduce United States Armed Forces into hostilities, or into situations where imminent involvement in hostilities is clearly indicated by the circumstances, are exercised only pursuant to (1) a declaration of war, (2) specific statutory authorization, or (3) a national emergency created by attack upon the United States, its territories or possessions, or its armed forces. . . .

Consultation; initial and regular consultations

The President in every possible instance shall consult with Congress before introducing United States Armed Forces into hostilities or into situations where imminent involvement in hostilities is clearly indicated by the circumstances, and after every such introduction shall consult regularly with the Congress until United States Armed Forces are no longer engaged in hostilities or have been removed from such situations.

Reporting requirement

(a) *Written report; time of submission; circumstances necessitating submission; information reported.* . . . In the absence of a declaration of war, in any case in which United States Armed Forces are introduced—(1) into hostilities or into situations where imminent involvement in hostilities is clearly indicated by the circumstances; (2) into the territory, airspace or waters of a foreign nation, while equipped for combat, except for deployments which relate solely to supply, replacement, repair or training of such forces; or (3) in numbers which substantially enlarge United States Armed Forces equipped for combat already located in a foreign nation; the President shall submit within 48 hours to the Speaker of the House of Representatives and to the President, pro tempore of the Senate a report, in writing, setting forth: (A) the circumstances necessitating the introduction of United States Armed Forces; (B) the constitutional and legislative authority under which such introduction took place; and (C) the estimated scope and duration of the hostilities or involvement.

Source: United States Code, 1976 ed., Vol. 11, Title 50, Ch. 33 (Washington: GPO, 1977), 1926–29.

DOCUMENT 271: U.S. Defense Attaché's Report of Fall of South Vietnam (May 1975)

2. There are certain retrospective thoughts and ideas which most probably contributed to the situation which led up to the final evacuation of the Defense Attache Office (DAO) and the remainder of the American Mission from Saigon.

a. There is no question but what the action of the United States Congress to appropriate only $700 million of the $1 billion authorized for the Defense Assistance Vietnam (DAV) program had an erosive effect on the morale of the Republic of Vietnam Armed Forces (RVNAF) and probably upon certain other elements of the national administration such as the Ministry of National Defense (MOND). The erosion, although gradual, was enough to set the stage for much further erosion in connection with the later proposed supplemental appropriation. . . .

d. The evacuation began on Saturday, 15 March 1975, a fateful day in the history of the Republic of Vietnam. . . .

e. As the withdrawal developed further, and as it became more and more clear that it would indeed be a debacle, President Thieu made still another decision which, as later proved, would further debilitate the situation. At another meeting with his senior military leaders and advisors, he decided to move the Airborne Division, in the line south and west of Da Nang, down to the Saigon area as a strategic reserve. . . .

f. Upon the withdrawal of one airborne brigade, [Lt. General] Truong ordered one marine brigade out of the lines at Quang Tri. . . . Reportedly, the province chief advised his own people to evacuate their families south and within hours there was a general evacuation of the civilian populace from Quang Tri. The NVA [North Vietnamese Army] attacked out of Quang Tri . . . and the city itself fell. . . . The general populace of the city joined [the evacuation] and the highway [south to Da Nang] became choked with people and vehicles. . . . Truong intended to defend the Hue enclave at least long enough to get the bulk of his materiel out and moved south. It was then that the "family syndrome" manifested itself.

g. Although the marine and airborne elements had their families in the Saigon area, ARVN all had their families in close proximity to where their areas of operation were. Consequently, as the chances for egress lessened, ARVN soldiers and officers became increasingly apprehensive about the welfare of their families. The famous ARVN 1st Division first fell prey to this condition. As it became evident that the NVA buildup was cutting them off from access to Da Nang except by sea, ARVN pulled out of the line to get their families to safety. Suddenly, LTG Truong lost a significant part of his fighting strength. Where he had planned to defend Hue, he found that he could no longer do it. Accordingly, another quick switch in plans was made with the result that another two division sets of equipment and significant tonnages of ammunition and POL [petroleum, oil, lubricants] were lost to the enemy. . . .

l. In retrospect, had the one million refugees been successfully evacuated south, the RVN would have had an insurmountable problem with their relocation. As it was, they experienced great difficulties in assimilating the less than 100,000 that did escape.

m. The pandemonium which overtook reason in Da Nang literally wrested control of the city from all official presence. The last Americans out of the city escaped over the beach onto Vietnamese naval craft along with the military hierarchy. Later in the evacuation of Saigon, the reverse would be true. The experience was shattering to all who participated. . . . All were in a daze for days thereafter and some had not fully recovered as late as 29 April when Saigon was evacuated.

Source: Porter, *Vietnam: Definitive Documentation*, 659–63.

VIETNAM RETROSPECTIVES, 1976–1995

With the fall of South Vietnam in April 1975 came the postmortem debate in the United States. Who "lost" the war in Vietnam? Why did the United States, its leaders, and its citizenry commit so much in men, material, and prestige in a civil war thousands of miles from its borders? How did the war fundamentally change America's view of itself and its relationship with the rest of the world? These and many other questions remain for future generations to reflect and act upon.

DOCUMENT 272: General Westmoreland Blames the Press, Student Protestors, Domestic Politics, and Flawed Military Strategy for U.S. Defeat in Vietnam (1976)

Even after introduction of American combat troops into South Vietnam in 1965, the war still might have been ended within a few years except for the ill-considered policy of graduated response against North Vietnam. Bomb a little bit, stop it a while to give the enemy a chance to cry uncle, then bomb a little bit more but never enough to really hurt. That was no way to win.

Yet even with the handicap of graduated response, the war still could have been brought to a favorable end following defeat of the enemy's Tet offensive in 1968. The United States had in South Vietnam at that time the finest military force—though not the largest—ever assembled. Had President Johnson changed our strategy and taken advantage of the enemy's weakness to enable me to carry out the operations we had planned over the preceding two years in Laos and Cambodia and north of the DMZ, along with intensified bombing and the mining of Haiphong Harbor, the North Vietnamese doubtlessly [*sic*] would have broken. But that was not to be. Press and television had created an aura not of victory but of defeat, which, coupled with the vocal antiwar elements, profoundly influenced timid officials in Washington.

Source: Westmoreland, *A Soldier Reports*, 410.

DOCUMENT 273: Secretary Kissinger's Lessons for America from the Vietnam War (1994)

America, at any rate, paid a price for its adventure in Vietnam that was out of proportion to any conceivable gain. It was clearly a mistake to have staked so much on such ill-defined causes. America had become involved in the first place because it applied literally the maxims of its successful European policy to a region with radically different political, social, and economic conditions. Wilsonian idealism permitted no cultural differentiation, while the theory of collective security held that, security being indivisible, the fabric of the entire international order would unravel if even one strand were pulled out.

Too idealistic to base its policy on national interest, and too focused on the requirements of general war in its strategic doctrine, America was unable to master an unfamiliar strategic problem in which the political and military objectives were entwined. Imbued with the belief in the universal appeal of its values, America vastly underestimated the obstacles to democratization in a society shaped by Confucianism, and among a people who were struggling for political identity in the midst of an assault by outside forces.

Perhaps the most serious, and surely the most hurtful, domino which fell as a result of the Vietnam War was the cohesion of American society. American idealism had imbued both officials and critics with the misconception that Vietnamese society could be transformed relatively easily and quickly into an American-style democracy. When that optimistic proposition collapsed and it became apparent that Vietnam was far from being a democracy, disillusionment was inevitable. There was also a nearly incomprehensible misconception about the nature of the military problem. Lacking criteria for judgment, officials often misunderstood, and therefore often misstated, the issues.

Source: Henry A. Kissinger, *Diplomacy* (New York: Simon and Schuster, 1994), 698–99.

DOCUMENT 274: Dean Rusk's and Robert McNamara's Retrospective Memoirs (1990, 1995)

Dean Rusk in 1990: I have been offered many chances to present a *mea culpa* on Vietnam, but I have not availed myself of those opportunities. I thought the principal decisions made by President Kennedy and President Johnson were the right decisions at the time they were made. I supported their decisions. There is nothing I can say now that would diminish my share of responsibility for the events of those years. I live with that, and others can make of it what they will.

I have not apologized for my role in Vietnam, for the simple reason that I believed in the principles that underlay our commitment to South Vietnam and why we fought that war....

... I have not tried to play the role of grandstand quarterback or participate actively in postmortem discussions of our Vietnam policy. We all made mistakes of judgment and decisions we came to regret. There is blame enough. But I feel that I owe my primary allegiance to my two presidents, to the men and women we sent to South Vietnam, and to the cause they tried their best to serve....

In Vietnam the decisive issue was the fidelity of the United States to collective security and its treaty commitments.

* * * * *

Robert McNamara in 1995: Some argue that [the Vietnam War] hastened the end of the Cold War. But I also know that the war caused terrible damage to America. No doubt exists in my mind about that. None. I want to look at Vietnam in hindsight, not in any way to obscure my own and others' errors of judgment and their egregious costs but to show the full range of pressures and the lack of knowledge that existed at the time.

I want to put Vietnam in context.

We of the Kennedy and Johnson administrations who participated in the decisions on Vietnam acted according to what we thought were the principles and traditions of this nation. We made our decisions in light of those values.

Yet we were wrong, terribly wrong. We owe it to future generations to explain why.

I truly believe that we made an error not of values and intentions but of judgment and capabilities. I say this warily, since I know that if my comments appear to justify or rationalize what I and others did, they will lack credibility and only increase people's cynicism. It is cynicism that makes Americans reluctant to support their leaders in the actions necessary to confront and solve our problems at home and abroad.

Sources: Rusk, *As I Saw It,* 492–95; Robert McNamara, *In Retrospect: The Tragedy and Lessons of Vietnam* (New York: Times Books, 1995), xvi–xvii.

DOCUMENT 275: Following the Persian Gulf War Against Iraq, President George Bush Declares that America Has Kicked the "Vietnam Syndrome" (1–4 March 1991)

"It's a proud day for America. By God, we've kicked the Vietnam syndrome once and for all!" [1 March]

I made a comment . . . the other day about shedding the divisions that incurred from the Vietnam war. I want to repeat and say especially to the Vietnam veterans that . . . it's long overdue. It is long overdue that we kicked the Vietnam syndrome, because many veterans from that conflict came back and did not receive the proper acclaim that they deserve—that this nation was divided and we weren't as grateful as we should be. So somehow, when these [Persian Gulf veterans of Operation Desert Storm] come home, I hope that message goes out to those that served this country in the Vietnam war that we appreciate their service as well. [4 March]

Source: Public Papers of the Presidents: George Bush, 1991 Book 1 (Washington: GPO, 1992), 197, 209. Also see "Kicking the 'Vietnam Syndrome,' " *Washington Post*, 4 March 1991.

FURTHER READING

Baritz, Loren. *Backfire: A History of How American Culture Led Us into Vietnam* (1985).
Berman, Larry. *Lyndon Johnson's War* (1989).
Berman, William C. *William Fulbright and the Vietnam War* (1988).
De Mark, Brian. *Into the Quagmire* (1991).
DiLeo, David. *George Ball* (1991).
Duiker, William. *U.S. Containment Policy and the Conflict in Indochina* (1994).
Franklin, H. Bruce. *M.I.A. or Mythmaking in America* (1993).
Herring, George. *America's Longest War* (1987).
Holsti, Ole, and James Roseneau. *American Leadership in World Affairs* (1984).
Lomperis, Timothy J. *The War Everyone Lost—and Won* (1984).
Small, Melvin. *Johnson, Nixon, and the Doves* (1988).
Smith, R. B. *An International History of the Vietnam War* (1986).
Summers, Harry. *On Strategy* (1981).
Young, Marilyn B. *The Vietnam Wars, 1945–1990* (1991).

Part VII

The Iranian Revolution and Hostage Crisis, 1978–1981

The Iranian hostage crisis can only be understood against the background of American support for the government of Shah Reza Pahlavi, an association that began during World War II and continued, with varying degrees of intensity, until 1979. Although the British and Soviets played the dominant role by occupying Iran between 1941 and 1945, the United States sent troops there during the war, partly to assist in the delivery of Lend-Lease supplies to the Soviet Union and partly to ensure American access to Iranian oil at war's end. It was to further the goal of access that the United States sponsored the Iranian Declaration of 1943 urging respect for Iran's territorial and administrative integrity. In 1946 the United States applied pressure on the Soviet Union to withdraw its troops, again partly because of its desire for continued American access to the country.

Between 1951 and 1953 the United States became more directly involved in Iranian affairs. Because it worried about the growing power within the government of Mohammad Mossadegh, who as prime minister seemed intent on appropriating Western oil interests and allying with the communists, the United States in 1953 participated in a coup that restored the shah to supreme authority. The Central Intelligence Agency (CIA) played a major role in this operation, but could not have succeeded had not a large sector of Iranian opinion turned against Prime Minister Mossadegh.

With American encouragement and assistance, the shah made major steps toward "Westernizing" Iranian society from 1953 through the early 1970s. In addition to initiating such political reforms as suffrage for Iranian women, he accepted various aspects of Western popular culture into Iran's Islamic society. Simultaneously with these political and cultural changes, the shah used American technology and equipment to build up a massive military regime that tied the shah to the American position in the Cold War.

This combination of the Westernization and militarization of Iran brought intense domestic criticism upon the shah's regime during the mid-1970s. Cultural nationalists and Islamic fundamentalists increasingly condemned the shah for selling out the nation's values—and for squandering its enormous petroleum revenues. By 1978 massive demonstrations, many of them led by prominent Islamic religious leaders, or ayatollahs, broke out in major cities across the country. These early riots in Iran were brutally repressed by the shah's secret police. When revolutionary turmoil became too widespread, the shah, rather than militarily occupying his own homeland, fled the country in January 1979. The Ayatollah Ruholla Khomeini, whom the shah had driven into exile, returned several weeks later to take the reins of power of a militant, revolutionary, and intolerant theocratic government.

Among American officials, President Nixon and his National Security Adviser/Secretary of State Henry Kissinger had been particularly devoted to the shah's regime. Thinking it essential in the ultimate effort to contain the Soviet Union, President Jimmy Carter continued the decades-long American commitment to the shah. Both the Nixon and Carter Administrations maintained the special relationship not oblivious to, but generally unwilling to acknowledge, the growing power of the Iranian opposition. Carter's decision to allow the shah to enter the United States for cancer treatment in the fall of 1979, however, galvanized the mass hatred of America within Iran and led to the occupation of the U.S. Embassy in Tehran on 4 November. The resulting crisis over Americans held hostage in Iran was to last for 444 days.

CHRONOLOGY

1953

August. CIA Operation Ajax to install Reza Pahlavi as shah

1976

November. Jimmy Carter elected president

1977

May. Sec. of State Vance visits Shah in Tehran

July. Panama Canal Treaty

December. Carter toasts the shah as "island of stability"

1978

September. Camp David Accords

November. Revolution in Iran topples the shah; U.S. recognizes People's Republic of China

1979

January 16–23. Shah and his family flee to exile in Egypt

January 31. Ayatollah Khomeini assumes power in Iran

April. Kissinger and Rockefeller request American asylum for shah

November 4. American hostages seized at U.S. Embassy

November 9. U.S. halts shipment of military parts to Iran

November 14. Carter freezes Iranian assets in American banks

November 17. Khomeini orders release of female and African-American hostages

November 23. Bani-Sadr ousted and replaced by Ghotbzadeh

November 29. U.S. petitions The Hague's International Court of Justice

December 2. Shah is flown to U.S. facility at San Antonio

December 11. Hamilton Jordan gets Panama asylum for shah

December 25–26. Soviet Union invades Afghanistan

1980

January. Carter applies sanctions against USSR

January 19. Secret negotiations in London with go-betweens

January 23. Carter Doctrine to protect Persian Gulf oil supply

January 25. Bani-Sadr becomes president in Iran

January 26–27. Canadian Embassy helps Americans to flee Iran

April 25. Rescue attempt fails and eight crew members killed

September 19–21. Iran-Iraq border war begins

November. Ronald Reagan elected president

1981

January 20. Iran releases American hostages

EISENHOWER-NIXON LEGACY, 1953–1976

The documents below indicate American involvement in the Iranian coup of 1953 and show how the United States became so closely tied to the shah's regime from that time onward. It is particularly noteworthy that during this period Iran became an American client state in the Cold War against the Soviet Union, a significant factor in the revolution of the late 1970s.

DOCUMENT 276: National Security Council's Discussion of Iranian Oil, National Prestige, and Effects on U.S. Security (11 March 1953)

3. Developments in Iran Affecting U.S. Security

[Presidential Assistant Robert] Cutler briefed the Council on the latest available information on Iran, which included the probability that [Iranian Prime Minister Mohammad] Mossadegh was about to turn down the latest plan for settlement of the oil controversy. . . .

Secretary [of State John Foster] Dulles then stated that . . . any proposal that the United States purchase Iranian oil at this time would constitute a terrific blow to the British. In discussing this idea with him during his visit, Foreign Secretary [Anthony] Eden had told Secretary Dulles that if we even sent technicians to assist in reopening the Abadan refinery, Eden would be unable to survive as Foreign Secretary. . . . It was the feeling generally in the State Department, continued Secretary Dulles, that we should not encourage the Iranian Government as to any hope of reactivating the refinery or of buying Iranian oil. . . .

The President [Dwight Eisenhower] said that he had very real doubts whether, even if we tried unilaterally, we could make a successful deal with Mossadegh. He felt that it might not be worth the paper it was written on, and the example might have very grave effects on United States oil concessions in other parts of the world.

Source: U.S. Department of State, *Foreign Relations of the United States, 1952–1954*, Vol. 10, *Iran, 1951–1954* (hereafter *FRUS, Iran*) (Washington: GPO, 1989), 711–13.

DOCUMENT 277: Operation Ajax as CIA Countercoup for "Boy Scout" (3 August 1953)

During a clandestine meeting in Tehran on 2 August 1953, Central Intelligence Agency Officer Kermit Roosevelt told the shah he represented both President Eisenhower and Prime Minister Churchill in planning a coup attempt, Operation Ajax, against Prime Minister Mossadegh's government. The shah and the CIA officer met again late the next night.

The shah told me, "we *must* make some plans." . . .

"This reminds me, as a good Moslem, of Mohammed's Hegira in 622 A.D. . . . He 'fled' purely to dramatize his situation. I could do the same."

[The shah continues.] "Once we've made the final arrangements, and I have signed the *firmans* [royal decrees], dismissing Mossadegh and appointing Zahedi, I'll fly up to the Caspian. If by any horrible chance things go wrong, the Empress and I . . . will take our plane straight to Baghdad. From there we can look the situation over and decide to what place we should return."

Without further discussion, this became the plan. . . .

In the meantime we continued to explore four lines of attack that had been planned. But first . . . I explained one of the security practices we followed. . . .

"There is one routine precaution we are taking. Everyone involved is assigned a 'cryptonym' and . . . a nickname. . . . My cryptonym is RNMAKER. Yours is KGSAVOY. Your nickname . . . is 'Boy Scout.' " . . .

I returned to the "four lines of attack."

"The first would be an alliance with the mullahs. . . . So far all we got from them are demands for huge sums of money." . . .

". . . The second is your military support. We are agreed that except for General Riahi and a few officers very close to him, the armed forces are devotedly loyal to you." . . .

". . . All that we need to do is to make sure that they see the realities of the situation—that Mossy, the old bugger, smart-ass Riahi, the Tudeh and the Russians are trying to do you in. We get that across and we've nothing to worry about." . . .

"Now, I've already mentioned our Iranian allies, or agents . . . Boscoe One and Two. They are extremely competent, professional 'organizers' who have already demonstrated their competence. . . . They have a strong team under them. . . . They can distribute pamphlets, organize mobs, keep track of the opposition." . . .

". . . We have a gigantic safe . . . jam-packed with stacks of rial [Iranian currency] notes. . . . We have the equivalent of about one million dollars in that safe." [Roosevelt estimated Operation Ajax cost less than $100,000.]

. . . The fourth and final line of attack—what the Zahedis, father and son, had to contribute. The general was still hiding in the mountains east of Tajrish.

Source: Kermit Roosevelt, *Countercoup* (New York: McGraw-Hill, 1979), 156–67.

DOCUMENT 278: Shah Asserts Countercoup Was Popular Mandate for His Monarchy (13–19 August 1953)

I had already made contingency plans with the help of my American friends, who in those days included Kermit Roosevelt of the CIA and the U.S. ambassador in Teheran, Lloyd [Loy] Henderson. We had agreed that should Mossadegh use force to resist his ouster, I would temporarily leave the country. We felt my departure would crystallize the situation by forcing Mossadegh to show his true colors and thus rally public opinion behind the throne. . . .

The tide had begun turning on August 18. Anti-Mossadegh newspapers managed to publish my decree naming Zahedi Prime Minister. . . . Later that day the first anti-government demonstrators took to the streets. Nationalists and soldiers moved to break up Tudeh [Iranian Communist Party] demonstrations. . . .

I returned to Teheran where I was greeted with popular enthusiasm. Throughout Iran the people were undeniably behind the crown. Before, I had been no more than a hereditary sovereign, but now I had truly been elected by the people.

Source: Mohammad Reza Pahlavi, *Answer to History* (New York: Stein and Day, 1980), 89–90.

DOCUMENT 279: Message from President Eisenhower to the Shah (24 August 1953)

In the spirit of friendliness which has always been the basis for the relations of our two countries, I offer you my sincere felicitations on the occasion of your happy return to your country, and my continuing good wishes for every success in your efforts to promote the prosperity of your people and to preserve the independence of Iran.

Source: FRUS, Iran, 766.

DOCUMENT 280: U.S. Foreign Service Officer's Dispatch from Tehran (15 June 1964)

What is Holding [the Shah] Up? Since the regime is at present reluctant to mobilize the peasantry as a political force and since it is lacking support, by and large, from the intelligentsia and the urban middle class in general, since it has disappointed the workers and continues at odds with the Moslem clergy, and since its supporters seem to be lacking in conviction and ideology, one may wonder what is sustaining it so long in power. Here tangibles as well as intangibles are involved. The regime derives support from the reform-minded and loyal portion of the intelligentsia, from important elements of the bureaucracy, from elements of the business and professional class associated with the Progressive Center and the New Iran Party, from some peasant representatives, and, most important, from the extremely effective internal security services and the armed forces which receive special benefits and who constitute the true basis of power of the Shah. In time, the Shah expects to develop a sound and fairly democratic basis of support for his regime on the basis of the accomplishments of his reform program, the increasing wealth of the country, and the abatement of social tensions resulting therefrom. But if one asks an intelligent Iranian about the basis of the Shah's power the reply is apt to be quite different, and indeed quite amazing. He will perhaps first talk about SAVAK and about the useful margin for error that is provided by Iran's oil revenues. But then he soars into the wild blue yonder.

It is the Americans, he is apt to say, who are propping up the regime, implying (or stating outright) that without our support the Shah and his government would be swept away in short order. While this is fantastic oversimplification of the situation, it is an important intangible factor in the present political equation in Iran. We are not referring here to the perennial accusations we hear from opposition elements who wish the United States to fight their battles for them. There is good reason to believe that the Shah himself occasionally believes this myth. . . . Prime Ministers are widely believed to be chosen by the United States, and even otherwise well-informed Iranians . . . have entirely exaggerated notions about the extent of American military assistance to the Shah's regime.

Source: Institute for the Study of Diplomacy, "A View from Tehran: A Diplomatist Looks at the Shah's Regime," [Political Counselor] Martin F. Herz's "Some Intangible Factors in Iranian Politics," dispatch of 15 June 1964 (Washington: Institute for the Study of Diplomacy, 1981), 7–8.

DOCUMENT 281: Secretary of State Henry Kissinger Links the Strategy of Selling American Weaponry to Iran as Counterbalance to Soviet-Iraqi Treaty (1972)

For what [President Richard] Nixon faced in 1972 was not a theory but a reality. Britain's withdrawal from the Gulf at the end of 1971 had been followed in April 1972 by a Friendship Treaty between Iraq and the Soviet Union, which led to the heavy supply of modern military equipment to that then most radical of Arab states. To keep Iraq from achieving hegemony in the Persian Gulf, we had either to build up American power or to strengthen local forces. America's eagerness to forget Vietnam, and the later conservative resurgence, have obliterated the mood of that period. That America had to reduce its foreign involvements was the universal wisdom. . . . Creating a credible military capability for the defense of the Persian Gulf by America alone is a task of enormous, perhaps insuperable, practical and logistical difficulty in the best of circumstances. Our choice in 1972 was to help Iran arm itself or to permit a perilous vacuum. Nor did the Nixon doctrine ever look to any country to defend itself alone against a superpower; it explicitly offered assistance if a nuclear power—a euphemism for the USSR—attacked an ally willing to defend itself. For decades, Iran under the Shah contributed importantly to the stability of the region and to international security.

Source: Henry A. Kissinger, *Years of Upheaval* (Boston: Little, Brown, 1982), 669.

CARTER ADMINISTRATION AND FALL OF THE SHAH, 1977–1978

Despite President Carter's commitment to human rights and his aversion to continued arms sales, he did not reverse the American policy of support for the shah. Indeed, he approved the sale of high technology weaponry, including AWACS (Airborne Warning and Control System) aircraft to Iran, and he developed a close personal relationship with the Iranian leader. By the summer and fall of 1978, however, it had become increasingly clear to Carter Administration officials that the U.S.-backed regime was in deep trouble. How to respond to the revolutionary situation inside Iran became a major U.S. policy issue at the end of 1978.

DOCUMENT 282: National Security Adviser Zbigniew Brzezinski Links the Nixon-Kissinger Persian Gulf Strategy with Carter Administration's Objectives (1977–1978)

During the sixties Iran became our major strategic asset in the wake of the British disengagement from "east of Suez." That pull-out created a power vacuum in the Persian Gulf region, and American policy was to fill it by building up the military capability first of Iran, then of Saudi Arabia, and by enhancing their political status as the two American-backed pillars of regional security. The rivalry between Iran and Saudi Arabia over the Persian (or, symptomatically, Arabian) Gulf notwithstanding, American policy was based on the premise that close collaboration with both of these states was possible, given their fear of Soviet Communism and their related desire to contain the more pro-Soviet tendencies in the pan-Arab circles, notably manifest in Iraq. The high point of that policy was the decision made by President Nixon and Henry Kissinger to gratify the Shah's desire for a rapid military buildup through massive U.S. arms transfers to Iran.

Recognizing Iran's strategic centrality, we chose to continue that policy, approving major sales of arms to Iran in the course of 1978, but we also encouraged the Shah to couple his extraordinarily ambitious efforts to modernize his country with more rapid progress toward constitutional rule.

Source: Zbigniew Brzezinski, *Power and Principle: Memoirs of the National Security Adviser, 1977–1981* (New York: Farrar, Straus & Giroux, 1983), 356–57.

DOCUMENT 283: Secretary of State Cyrus Vance Discusses the Carter Administration's Review of Human Rights in Iran (1977)

During the presidential election of 1976, candidate Jimmy Carter placed great emphasis on human rights as a guiding principle of U.S. foreign policy. During the early days of his administration, President Carter disturbed some U.S. allies whose human rights records were poor. In major speeches in 1977, Secretary of State Cyrus Vance and Undersecretary of State Warren Christopher reiterated the universality of human rights to relations with the United States: while the issue of human rights was not to be used as an ideological weapon, it remained a basic element of U.S. foreign policy.

It was clear that it would be hard to maintain public support for our strategic relationship with Iran if the shah failed to pay more attention to human rights. I was aware that the shah would be anxious about our policies on these two matters. Neither the president nor I, however, believed that the maintenance of a stable relationship with Iran precluded encouragement of improvement in its human rights policy and the development of a practical method of identifying and meeting its military needs.

Source: Cyrus Vance, Hard Choices: Critical Years in America's Foreign Policy (New York: Simon and Schuster, 1983), 316.

DOCUMENT 284: President Carter and Shah Teargassed on South Lawn of White House (15 November 1977)

On the south lawn of the White House, I stood and wept. Tears were streaming down the faces of more than two hundred members of the press. It was a memorable moment. In the distance we could hear the faint but unmistakable sounds of a mob, shouting at the mounted police who had just released canisters of tear gas to disperse them. Unfortunately, an ill wind seemed to have been blowing directly toward us as we greeted the leader of Iran, and the gas fumes had engulfed us all.

With the television cameras focused on me as I welcomed the Shah to our country, I tried to pretend that nothing was wrong. So, with difficulty, I refrained from rubbing my eyes and avoided the extreme irritation that afflicted most of the others. The Shah and his wife, Farah, were deeply embarrassed, and apologized several times to Rosalynn and me for having been the object of the Iranian student demonstrations. . . .

That day—November 15, 1977—was an augury. The tear gas had created the semblance of grief. Almost two years later, and for fourteen months afterward, there would be real grief in our country because of Iran.

Source: Jimmy Carter, Keeping Faith: Memoirs of a President (New York: Bantam Books, 1982), 433–34; paperback edition, University of Arkansas Press, 1995.

DOCUMENT 285: Shah Recalls President Carter's Remark that Iran Was an "Island of Stability" (31 December 1977)

My talks with President Carter had gone well. Iran's relationship with the U.S. had been so deep and so friendly during the last three Administrations—I had counted Lyndon Johnson, Richard Nixon and Gerald Ford among my friends—that it seemed only natural that our friendship would continue. After all, good relations were in the best interests of both nations. Carter appeared to be a smart man.

My favorable impression of the new American President deepened when he visited Teheran to spend New Year's Eve with us at Niavaran Palace. I have never heard a foreign statesman speak of me in quite such flattering terms as he used that evening. "Iran, because of the great leadership of the Shah, is an island of stability in one of the more troubled areas of the world."

Source: Mohammad Reza Pahlavi, *Answer to History*, 152–53.

DOCUMENT 286: Empress Farah's Private Secretary Recalls the Spark that Ignited the Revolution and the Symbolism of the *Chador* (January 1978)

Since the mid-1970s, the Ayatollah Ruholla Khomeini had been announcing his religious teachings and his hate for the shah's secular Iran on inflammatory, smuggled tapes broadcast to the orthodox Muslim (Shia) sections of the Iranian population. In January 1978 the publication of a provocative article by the shah's minister of information in a respected Iranian newspaper raised the aging Ayatollah to the rank of savior to many of the country's Shia people.

The hypocrites advising the Shah aggravated a delicate situation and rocked his throne more and more. Then, an irrevocable provocation of the religious sensibilities of the people, which finally opened the floodgates to bloody revolution, resulted from a leading article published in the newspaper *Keyhan* in January 1978 on the instructions of the Shah's Minister of Information and spokesman for Rastakhiz. In this article Ayatollah Khomeini, then in exile in Iraq, was accused of being a British agent of Indian, not Iranian, origin. He was also charged quite openly with immorality. In the resultant violent disturbances [on 7 January] about thirty people were killed in Qom, the holy pilgrimage city of the Shias.... The Revolution had started. Public insurrection broke out when theology students there were shot by the regime's security police as they protested in the seminary grounds. Demonstrations and impassioned funeral processions followed in Qom and other cities in memory of the religious martyrs....

As a symbol of protest, the *chador* (Islamic veil) played a decisive part in the whole process of the Revolution. Veiled working-class women, whose young sons had been killed in street battles, marched in huge demonstrations. In chorus with their menfolk they shouted slogans against the regime and condemned the Shah and his family. But these women were now joined in sympathy by veiled women students, housewives, professional women and other Westernized, educated Iranian women from the middle classes. . . . Their strong presence in the demonstrations allowed them to form a sort of protective barrier for the male demonstrators. And from the time that these women joined it, the Revolution gained increasingly in religious fervour.

Source: Minou Reeves, *Behind the Peacock Throne* (London: Sidgwick and Jackson, 1986), 169–72.

DOCUMENT 287: Shah Blames "the Unholy Alliance of Red and Black" for Collapse of His Monarchy (January–February 1978)

On 7 January 1978, the first riots erupted in which the clergy were suspected as the major source of the agitation. Demonstrators surged through the streets of the holy city of Qom, where thousands of pilgrims annually visit the tomb of Massoumeh, the sister of Imam Reza. The next wave of violence hit the city of Tabriz on 18 February, and soon reached the Islamic holy cities of Qom and Meshed.

There is little doubt in my mind that communist elements had infiltrated the 4,000 religious students and their supporters who took part in the protest. I am equally certain that rebellious and dissatisfied mullahs were at the center of the unrest. . . . The renewal of violence after a year's calm troubled me. I realized that political agitation in Iran was entering a new phase, that the conspirators, whatever their origins, had changed their tactics and we were now faced with organized violence. . . .

These were contained, but it took considerable force to do so, perhaps too much force. . . . As the riots spread, underlying social issues began to emerge. The unholy alliance of red and black was beginning to solidify. Looking back, the uprisings in Tabriz marked the beginning of efforts to reduce my authority, to turn me into a weak and ineffectual "constitutional" monarch, and finally to oust me.

Source: Mohammad Reza Pahlavi, *Answer to History*, 153–56.

DOCUMENT 288: Shah's Twin Sister Recalls Her Brother's Restraint in the Use of Force to Quell the Rioting in Iran (February 1978)

On February 18 there were serious riots in Tabriz, during which about 100 people were killed. Critics accused my brother of condoning this bloodshed, but they did so with little firsthand information of what the actual conditions are when troops are sent to restore order (even when those troops have been instructed to exercise restraint) among a howling mob that has been put into motion by professional agitators and terrorists, many of whom are armed and dangerous. In the heat and hysteria of the moment it is very difficult for the average soldier to differentiate between the unarmed civilian and the professional terrorist. . . .

If my brother had indeed been willing to keep his throne at any price, I think he would have ordered a massive show of force at Tabriz and a severe curtailment of personal liberties—but he chose to do neither of these. After the Tabriz riot, I said to Prime Minister Amouzegar: "I think you must be careful that this doesn't snowball into something more serious." He seemed to feel that he had the situation well in hand. He was, of course, mistaken. Similar incidents followed, in Qom and Meshed and Teheran. These riots took place during a steady campaign of biased anti-Shah news reports by the BBC [British Broadcasting Corporation].

Source: Ashraf Pahlavi, *Faces in a Mirror: Memoirs from Exile* (Englewood Cliffs, N.J.: Prentice-Hall, 1980), 199–200.

DOCUMENT 289: The Shah Uses SAVAK Against the Growing Strength of Islamic Fundamentalists in Iran (1978)

As the shah continued to placate the fractured opponents to his government with minor administrative changes, a revolutionary Islamic faction grew increasingly vocal and organized. Much of the press coverage of early 1978, however, focused on the methods employed by the Iranian Secret Police—SAVAK—to combat and squelch dissent within Iran.

The name SAVAK comes from the initials in Persian of the Organization for State Security and Information. Similar organizations exist worldwide since every country is obliged to protect its populace from subversion. Accordingly they are called KGB, CIA or FBI. . . .

SAVAK was instituted in Iran to combat communist subversion after the disastrous Mossadegh episode. It is not for me to judge the attitude adopted by Western countries towards their communists. However, a common frontier with the Soviet Union tends to sharpen one's perceptions of their activities. . . .

I cannot defend SAVAK's every action and will not attempt to do so here. There were people arrested and abused. Unfortunately, this is not a perfect world. Worldwide police brutality exists. Inherent in police work is the potential for abuse and cruelty. My country, too, fell victim to such excesses.

Source: Mohammad Reza Pahlavi, *Answer to History*, 156–58.

DOCUMENT 290: British Ambassador to Iran Anthony Parsons Describes the Shah's Loss of Morale (October 1978)

In mid-October, [U.S. Ambassador William H.] Sullivan and I called on General [Gholamali] Oveissi, the Martial Law Commander, with the approval and support of the Prime Minister. We told him that rumours were circulating in the officer corps that Britain and America would favour a military takeover of the government. We wanted him to know that these rumours were baseless. Both our governments favoured progressive democratisation as the only way to solve the crisis. A reversal of this process would face us with severe problems of domestic opinion in our own countries. . . .

Another negative factor in the equation was the public effect of the Shah's loss of morale. He made two good speeches on Iran television during October, one about liberalisation and the other about the legitimacy of the monarchy. What he said was cogent and well thought out, but his listless and dispirited manner created a poor impression. Respect for and awe of him evaporated and I concluded towards the middle of the month that the best that could possibly be expected was that he might, if everything went well, recover enough prestige to act as a purely constitutional monarch—no more.

Source: Anthony Parsons, *The Pride and the Fall: Iran 1974–1979* (London: Jonathan Cape, 1984), 84–85.

DOCUMENT 291: U.S. Ambassador to Iran William Sullivan Transmits His "Thinking the Unthinkable" Cable to Washington (November 1978)

On 9 November 1978 the U.S. Ambassador to Iran, William Sullivan, wrote a cable back to his superiors at the State Department setting forth some fundamental considerations and making recommendations for future U.S. policy toward Iran. He had reached the conclusion that the newly installed military government of General Azhari represented the shah's last chance for survival. Sullivan cabled that if it failed to restore law and order, the success of the Islamic revolution was inevitable. In this cable, which he entitled "Thinking the Unthinkable," Sullivan argued that some fundamental clichés about Iran were no longer valid. He pointed out, for example, that since the 1950s stability in Iran had rested on two pillars—the monarchy and the Shia religion. He especially noted that the religious pillar had been largely subordinate to the monarchic during this period, but now the roles were reversing in a dramatic and sudden fashion.

Years after leaving Tehran, Sullivan complained about the lack of guidance from the State Department or from the Carter Administration during the critical months of November and December 1978. Repeated public assertions by State Department officers and President Carter himself of support for the shah became something of a joke among the American news media. The shah, in fact, later expressed to Sullivan that these constant "feel good" pronouncements of public support for the shah were actually an embarrassment to him. They made him look like a puppet of the United States and undermined the credibility of his independence from Washington.

It was clear that the shah's public support had shrunk dramatically. His only real strength came from the military. This change had been so widely noted that it had become commonplace among most observers to refer to the monarchic pillar as the shah—supported by the military.

However, I went on, even that relationship had changed with the installation of a military government. It had been converted into a situation that reflected the strength of the military "which currently supports the shah." I felt that these altered circumstances required us to examine the relationship, both actual and potential, between the military and the religious. . . .

I therefore suggested we begin to "think the unthinkable" and prepare for this contingency. . . .

Whatever the situation in Washington, and whatever the motivations of the individuals involved, I did not seem able to get any serious "thinking the unthinkable" by those responsible for policy formulation. My normal experience with cables of this sort led me to expect that a significant review of our policy would take place in Washington and that I would receive some guidance concerning the attitudes of our administration toward my recommendations. I waited in vain for any such response. In fact, the cable was never answered by Washington.

Source: William H. Sullivan, *Mission to Iran* (New York: Norton, 1981), 200–204.

DOCUMENT 292: National Security Adviser Brzezinski Recalls Overload on Decision-Making Circuits (Fall 1978)

Until the crisis became very grave, the attention of the top decision makers, myself included, was riveted on other issues, all extraordinarily time-consuming, personally absorbing, and physically demanding.

Our decision-making circuits were heavily overloaded. The fall of 1978 was the time of the Camp David process and its aftermath. This was also the time of the stepped-up SALT negotiations, and during the critical December days we would literally rush from one meeting, in which the most complex positions on telemetry encryption or cruise missile definition would be hammered out, to another meeting on the fate of Iran. The fall, and especially November–December, was also the period of the critical phase in the secret U.S.-Chinese negotiations, and those took up some of the President's and much of my own time. In addition, the crisis in Nicaragua was beginning to preoccupy and absorb us. Finally, Cy Vance was heavily involved in key negotiations abroad, notably in the Middle East, while for Harold Brown this was the period of most difficult battles with the President over the defense budget, which he conducted with great energy and at the cost of some personal friction with Carter. It was unfortunately not a time in which undivided attention could be focused easily and early on what became a fatal strategic and political turning point.

Source: Brzezinski, *Power and Principle*, 358.

DOCUMENT 293: Ambassador Sullivan Recommends a Voluntary Exodus of Americans from Iran (December 1978)

While political decisions back in Washington were confused and muffled in late 1978, the U.S. Embassy in Tehran was increasingly occupied with the protection of Americans from acts of violence and revenge. At the beginning of 1978, approximately 35,000 Americans lived in Iran. During the year there were some limited reductions of Americans in-country, primarily families of American business executives working in Iran. After a number of business offices were burned on 4 November, that trickle of departures turned into a flood of evacuees. By the beginning of December an informal census by the embassy indicated that there were still nearly 20,000 Americans scattered throughout Iran.

At this stage the choice concerning departure was left on a voluntary basis, both in the official and the business community. Our census at the time of Ashura indicated that the American presence had been reduced to approximately twelve thousand people as the result of the voluntary exodus. This still left us a considerable problem to cope with in the protection of American citizens.

Source: Sullivan, *Mission to Iran*, 209.

DOCUMENT 294: Presidential Adviser George Ball's Reproach of the NSC and His Recommendation to President Carter to Retract U.S. Support of Shah (December 1978)

On 30 November 1978 former State Department officer George Ball was summoned to Washington to review the Iranian situation. He was given an office with the staff of the National Security Council and worked with United States Navy Captain Gary Sick, an expert on the Persian Gulf.

On 11 December 1978 Ball wrote a memorandum to President Carter and to key members of the National Security Council: the Acting Secretary of State, the Secretary of Defense, the Secretary of the Treasury, the chairman of the Joint Chiefs of Staff, and the head of the CIA.

This group, whom Ball met on the morning of 12 December greeted his report with mixed reactions. Though Acting Secretary of State Warren Christopher expressed his support, the views of most of the others tended to be either qualified or negative. For his part, Ball was depressed by the group's unwillingness to act on his recommendations. President Carter did not take Ball's advice about advising the shah to transfer his power, nor did he authorize any contact with Khomeini.

In spite of Captain Sick's friendliness, insight, patience, and excellent guidance, I felt depressed by the conditions I now found—particularly the distorted role of the National Security Council (the NSC). . . . I found President Carter's National Security Assistant, Zbigniew Brzezinski, trying to emulate Kissinger's rise to prominence by inflating and manipulating the NSC. He was operating in a free-wheeling manner, calling in foreign ambassadors, telephoning or sending telegrams to foreign dignitaries outside State Department channels, and even hiring a press adviser so he could compete with the Secretary of State as the enunciator of United States foreign policy.

That Brzezinski had the President's ear and wielded significant influence seemed clear enough. He possessed the same facility as Walt Rostow for inventing abstractions that sounded deceptively global and profound—at least to Presidents not inoculated by early exposure to the practice. As Scotty Reston had said of another academic diplomat, he "delighted in flinging continents about." My father had once described that facility as "a flair for making little fishes talk like whales." . . .

The Shah's regime, I wrote, "is on the verge of collapse." That "collapse is far more significant than a localized foreign policy crisis with exceptionally high stakes; it challenges the basic validity of the Nixon Doctrine." We had no one but ourselves to blame for the situation in which we were now confronted, for

> we made the Shah what he has become. We nurtured his love for grandiose geopolitical schemes and we supplied him the hardware to indulge his fantasies. Once we had anointed him as protector of our interests in the Persian Gulf, we became dependent on him. Now that his regime is coming apart under the pressure of imported modernization, we have so committed ourselves as to have no ready alternative.
>
> Meanwhile, we must deal with the realities of the Shah's precarious power position and help him face it. We must make clear that, in our view, his only chance to save his dynasty (if indeed that is still possible) and retain our support is for him to transfer power to a government responsive to the people. Only if he takes that action can Iran hope to avoid continued disaffection followed by a cumulative economic paralysis.

So long as we continued to express our unqualified support for the Shah, he would, I wrote, try to hang on to his full power and avoid the "hard decisions and . . . difficult actions required even for his own survival." He had so far given no indication that he might abdicate, yet he could not be sure of his army's loyalty were it used against the people. Though, I wrote, "the older hard-line officers in the top military command are likely to remain loyal to the Shah and if necessary to use brutal force to keep him in power," there is "growing discontent particularly among the junior officers." The worst thing that could happen would be for the Shah to try to save himself by turning his army against the people and having it disintegrate. If his troops refused to fire on their own fathers and brothers, that would mean mutiny and civil war and the Soviets could well be the largest gainer.

Source: George W. Ball, *The Past Has Another Pattern* (New York: Norton 1982), 457–61.

DOCUMENT 295: In an Interview with an Iranian Reporter, the Shah Blames British and American Oil Companies for the Iranian Revolution (25 December 1978)

Q: There was an article by [former CIA director and, from 1974 to 1977, ambassador to Iran] Richard Helms in *Time* magazine on December 18 which clearly illustrates the consequences of this excessive trust [in U.S. and U.K. support]. If you read the article you might believe that Helms is rushing to your defense; but in reality he has done you great harm. He criticizes Jimmy Carter for his suggestion that he did not believe that His Majesty would emerge unscathed from the current crisis, but adds that the United States should not allow you to fail since you have been upholding American interests. He states that during the Arab-Israeli conflict of 1973 you hastily sent an envoy to Egypt and Saudi Arabia to try to prevent the imposition of an oil embargo against the United States. He also reveals hitherto secret information, according to which you're said to have sent a squadron of F-5 combat planes to help the Americans during the Vietnam War. I'm sure you can imagine the disastrous effects of such an article in our current volatile political climate.

SHAH: Suggestions of this kind are certainly not aimed at defending us; quite the reverse! It was exactly the same when the British foreign minister declared two months ago that I had to be supported because I had defended British interests in the region. These gentlemen are determined to go out of their way to persuade my people that I was at the service of foreigners. Instead of really supporting me, they malign me. Their treachery is without limit.

Q: Everyone imagined that the British and the Americans were your friends?

SHAH: Not at all. The British never sincerely supported me, and for about a year now the Americans haven't been supporting me either. It's exactly as if they'd agreed between themselves to do away with me.

Q: Why would they adopt such a policy?

SHAH: I have no idea. Maybe because they don't want to see a strong country in this region. I have the impression that they're worried about their interests in the long term.

Source: Ehsan Naraghi, *From Palace to Prison: Inside the Iranian Revolution*, translated by Nilou Mobasser (Chicago: Ivan R. Dee, 1994), 123–24.

CRISIS SWELLS IN ADVERSARIAL IRAN, JANUARY–NOVEMBER 1979

The year 1979 was a fateful one in Iran and for American policy. In January the shah and his family fled the country; on 1 February the Ayatollah Khomeini returned to take command of the revolutionary forces; in mid-February the U.S. Embassy was seized briefly by Iranian militants; in October President Carter approved the shah's entry into the United States for medical treatment; and on 4 November Iranian students took over the U.S. Embassy in Tehran.

DOCUMENT 296: NSC Adviser Brzezinski Writes Memo with Plan "C" Calling for Iranian Military Coup (18 January 1979)

On 18 January National Security Adviser Brzezinski wrote a long and personal memo to President Carter. In the memo he argued that the United States did not have the luxury of a simple alternative in Iran, but rather was faced with a gradual deterioration that would produce disastrous international consequences. He warned that the Iranian military would become more politicized, demoralized, and fragmented. He argued that Iran was likely to shift piecemeal to an orientation similar to that of Libya or into anarchy, with the result that the U.S. position in the Gulf would be undermined. He feared that America's standing throughout the Arab world would decline and that the Israelis would become more security-oriented and hence less willing to compromise. He was also concerned that the Soviet influence in southwestern Asia would grow, that U.S. allies would see the Carter Administration as impotent, that the price of oil would increase, and that the United States would likely lose some sensitive equipment and intelligence capabilities germane to the Strategic Arms Limitation Talks (SALT). He even projected that there would be severe domestic political repercussions from the "loss" of Iran.

I outlined alternative courses of action, which I defined essentially as: to continue as at present, to push more actively for a coalition, or to stage a military coup. I argued that the second alternative simply would produce all of the negative consequences I had outlined, and that was also likely to be the effect of pursuing our present course of action. I told the President that I was not arguing for an immediate decision to stage a coup, but that I felt that within the next two weeks we would have to make a deliberate choice to that effect.

Source: Brzezinski, *Power and Principle*, 385–86.

DOCUMENT 297: U.S. Embassy in Tehran and Consulate in Tabriz Seized (14 February 1979)

Valentine's Day began normally enough. However, about 9:30 there was steady gunfire outside the embassy walls and gradually the shooting was concentrated on the building itself. Ambassador Sullivan ordered the 20 marine guards to fire tear gas and to shoot only in self defense, and even then to use only birdshot. Groups of militants began trying to climb over the 9-to-12 feet high brick walls at the front and sides of the 27-acre embassy compound. Snipers appeared on all the surrounding rooftops and poured down gunfire, making it impossible for anyone inside the grounds to move. . . .

Seeing the mass of insurgents grow to 200 and then to 400, over the walkie-talkie network Ambassador Sullivan ordered the marines to surrender in order to avoid bloodshed. As the attack on the outlying buildings intensified, Americans in the chancery began locking it up. Sullivan told his staff aide, Ralph Boyce, and another embassy officer, David Patterson, to call for military support and protection. Patterson reached Ayatollah Taleqani's lieutenants promptly, but it took nearly 30 minutes to get through to the government—first because the phone lines were busy and then because no one answered. A call finally reached the prime minister's office around 10:45. Immediate help was promised. But by then marines in the ambassador's residence and the restaurant already had surrendered and the main building was heavily besieged. . . .

Safely hidden away about two miles from the embassy, I began trying to contact other Americans by telephone. . . . By noon I had alerted the American consulates in Shiraz and Isfahan. They had heard nothing about the trouble in Tehran; everything was tense but peaceful in those cities. These consulates radioed the news of the takeover to nearby U.S. embassies in the Persian Gulf. The third consulate, in Tabriz, did not answer its phone; it was under attack as well.

Source: John Stempel, *Inside the Iranian Revolution* (Bloomington: Indiana University Press, 1981), 184–87.

DOCUMENT 298: A U.S. Intelligence Official Links the Iranian Revolution with Collapse of SALT II (March 1979)

One almost immediate consequence of the fall of the shah and Bakhtiar was the loss of the NSA [National Security Agency] listening posts in Iran that had monitored Soviet missile testing and development. On January 31 American personnel abandoned the Behshahr station, though it continued for some time to relay SIGINT automatically via satellite to the United States. On March 1 the Kabkan listening post was also abandoned. The loss of the two Iranian SIGINT stations added to Carter's difficulties in gaining congressional support for the conclusion of SALT II, which he described as "among our top priorities." In his State of the Union message at the beginning of the year, he had insisted that SALT II would be fully verifiable. . . . Immediately after the loss of the Kabkan listening post, however, an unidentified official told [the] *New York Times*:

> Kabkan is not replaceable. No tricks are going to overcome that in the short run, and the short run could be three or four years. It is going to affect our capability on verification. I don't think people realize how important that base was, not just for SALT, but generally for keeping up with the Soviet missile program.

Source: Christopher Andrew, *For the President's Eyes Only: Secret Intelligence and the American Presidency from Washington to Bush* (New York: HarperCollins, 1995), 442.

DOCUMENT 299: Rosalynn Carter Recalls Pressure for an Entry Visa for "Mr. Pahlavi" (April–October 1979)

The turmoil didn't die down, and the pressure on Jimmy to bring the shah to our country mounted, mostly from people who were trying to protect financial investments or who felt indebted to him for being such a good friend of the United States. But Jimmy resisted. On April 19, 1979, I wrote in my diary: "We can't get away from Iran. Many people— Kissinger, David Rockefeller, Howard Baker, John McCloy, Gerald Ford—all are after Jimmy to bring the shah to the United States, but Jimmy says it's been so long, and anti-American and anti-shah sentiments have escalated so that he doesn't want to. Jimmy said he explained to all of them that the Iranians might kidnap our Americans who are still there and also destroy our satellite observation stations in northern Iran."

There it was, without the comforting luxury of hindsight, seven months before the Iranians made good Jimmy's fears. In the meantime the shah had moved from Morocco to the Bahamas, then on to Mexico. . . .

One day we were at Camp David, having just returned from Boston and the dedication of the Kennedy Library. . . . The date was October 20, 1979. We had just changed into comfortable clothes when the telephone rang. It was a long call and to my astonishment, I heard Jimmy say, "Let him come on in, and instruct our embassy in Tehran to notify the Iranian prime minister."

"Who? Let who come in?" I asked.

"The shah," Jimmy said. "He's got cancer and the State Department says he requires treatment that he can only get in our country. I just can't keep him out and let him die. He's been our friend too long to turn our backs on him now."

Source: Rosalynn Carter, *First Lady from Plains* (Boston: Houghton Mifflin, 1984), 308–9.

DOCUMENT 300: Adviser Brzezinski Describes Iranian Revolution's Impact on U.S. Security (1979)

The crisis in Iran confronted U.S. decision makers with two fundamental questions: (1) What was the United States' central interest in

Iran, and thus what must be protected as our first priority?, and (2) How could political stability be maintained in a traditional but rapidly modernizing state, in which the ruler's absolute personal power was challenged by an escalating revolutionary situation? These two issues were at the heart of the internal debate at the Carter White House, and the disagreements over viable options were derived largely from differing answers to these central questions.

My answer to the first question was a largely geopolitical one, which focused on the central importance of Iran to the safeguarding of the American and, more generally, Western interest in the oil region of the Persian Gulf. My concerns were shared most strongly by Jim Schlesinger and Charles Duncan. I often felt during our debates that Secretary Vance or Deputy Secretary Christopher or Under Secretary David Newsom, while certainly not inclined to reject that view, were much more preoccupied with the goal of promoting the democratization of Iran and feared actions—U.S. or Iranian—that might have the opposite effect. When the crisis became acute, the focus of these State Department officials shifted to a primary preoccupation with the evacuation of Americans from Iran rather than to a mounting concern over the American position in Iran. To be sure, I shared their humane concerns, but I did not agree with their priorities. The President was thus clearly pulled in opposite directions by his advisers and perhaps even by a conflict between his reason and his emotions.

Source: Brzezinski, *Power and Principle,* 354–56.

EMBASSY SEIZURE AND REACTIONS, NOVEMBER 1979

The first days and weeks after the embassy's seizure brought frantic deliberation in Washington on how best to respond. Discussions centered on economic sanctions and a possible rescue mission. Probably to the detriment of his political fortunes in the election of 1980, President Carter decided to focus national and international attention on the hostage incident and to stay close to the White House—to prove to the hostages' families as well as the American people that he was doing all that was possible to secure the liberation of the American hostages.

DOCUMENT 301: The Vienna Convention on Diplomatic Relations (18 April 1961)

The States Parties to the Present Convention,
   Recalling that peoples of all nations from ancient times have recognized the status of diplomatic agents, . . .
   Believing that an International convention on diplomatic intercourse, privileges and immunities would contribute to the development of friendly relations among nations, irrespective of their differing constitutional and social systems,
   Realizing that the purpose of such privileges and immunities is not to benefit individuals but to ensure the efficient performance of the functions of diplomatic missions as representing States, . . .
   Have agreed as follows: . . .

Article 22

1. The premises of the mission shall be inviolable. The agents of the receiving State may not enter them, except with the consent of the head of the mission.

2. The receiving State is under a special duty to take all appropriate steps to protect the premises of the mission against any intrusion or damage and to prevent any disturbance of the peace of the mission or impairment of its dignity. . . .

Article 26

Subject to its laws and regulations concerning . . . national security, the receiving State shall ensure to all members of the mission freedom of movement and travel in its territory. . . .

Article 29

The person of a diplomatic agent shall be inviolable. He shall not be liable to any form of arrest or detention. The receiving State shall treat him with due respect and shall take all appropriate steps to prevent any attack on his person, freedom or dignity. . . .

Article 31

1. A diplomatic agent shall enjoy immunity from the criminal jurisdiction of the receiving State. He shall also enjoy immunity from its civil and administrative jurisdiction, except in case[s] . . . relating to any professional or commercial activity exercised by the diplomatic agent in the receiving State outside his official functions.

Source: Robert A. Friedlander, *Terrorism: Documents of International and Local Control*, Vol. 3 (New York: Oceana Publications, 1981), 99–115.

DOCUMENT 302: U.S. Embassy-Tehran Informs State Department Ops Center that Compound Is under Siege (4 November 1979)

A few moments after 3:00 A.M. Washington time on Sunday, November 4, 1979, a call came to the State Department Operations Center from Embassy Tehran. Round the clock every day of the year, senior foreign service officers man the brightly lit "Ops Center" on the seventh floor, several dozen steps from the Secretary of State's suite of offices. From a panel of desks, by secure and open phones and by coded telegrams, they are a link between embassies around the world and action officers and senior policymakers in Washington. The phones ring constantly, and they work against the background chatter of the teletype machines and the whoosh of messages coming by pneumatic tube from the communications center several floors below.

This time it was Political Officer Ann Swift reporting that just before 10:30 A.M. Tehran time—Tehran then was seven and one-half hours later than Eastern Standard Time—a large mob of young Iranians had poured into the embassy compound, was then surrounding the chancery building, and was breaking into other buildings on the compound. Unlike the armed guerrillas who had overrun the embassy the previous February 14, shooting as they came, this mob appeared unarmed. Though technically not the senior officer in the embassy when the attack began, Swift as the senior political officer on the premises seemed to become the hub of a small leadership group that gathered quickly in the ambassador's suite on the second floor of the chancery. Chargé d'Affaires Bruce Laingen and Political Counsellor Victor Tomseth had gone with Security Officer Mike Howland to the Foreign Ministry on routine business. Swift and her colleagues had started to draft a flash telegram but decided to try to get through on the phone too.

Swift's phone call was immediately patched by the Ops Center watch officer to three Washington-area bedrooms. Having served since April 1978 as Assistant Secretary of State for Near Eastern and South Asian Affairs, I was the senior official in a bureau of 110 people in Washington and 1,000 in thirty-seven diplomatic and consular posts in twenty-four countries from Morocco to Bangladesh....

For the next two hours, the three of us shared a running conversation with Swift and her colleagues on the phone in the ambassador's outer office in Tehran. She stayed on the phone while others with her moved in and out of the office reporting what they saw through the windows or learned from the Marines on the lower floors. . . .

Meanwhile, Secretary Vance arrived at the department where he and his senior assistant Arnold Raphel worked from his outer office. Raphel was a career officer who, as it happened, had served in two posts in Iran and spoke Farsi. The Secretary depended on his commonsense judgments, and his colleagues respected his good-humored and highly competent way of handling our business with the Secretary when time prevented our doing it ourselves. The White House Situation Room alerted the President and key members of his staff. Other watch officers in Washington alerted their principal officials.

Source: Harold H. Saunders, "The Crisis Begins," in Warren Christopher et al., *American Hostages in Iran: The Conduct of a Crisis* (New Haven, Conn.: Yale University Press, 1985), 35–37.

DOCUMENT 303: President Carter's Crisis-Management and Decision-Making Process Within the Special Coordinating Committee (SCC) (November 1979)

There were so many conflicting questions and ideas during this time that we took extra steps to insure maximum harmony among the many agencies involved. At least once each day my top advisers—the Vice President, Secretaries of State, Defense, and Treasury, Attorney General, National Security Adviser, members of the Joint Chiefs of Staff, my Press Secretary, Legal Counsel, Director of the Central Intelligence Agency, and others as necessary—met in the Situation Room at the White House to discuss Iran. When I did not meet with them, they prepared written minutes almost immediately after they adjourned. Any question of policy was referred to me, either during the meeting or in a series of questions within the written report. I would answer the questions and give additional instructions, and then could feel reasonably confident that everyone would work by the same rules. In times of emergency or when there was an especially difficult decision, we met in the Oval Office or the Cabinet Room, so that I could participate in the full discussion. Throughout the long months of this ordeal, we maintained a remarkable degree of harmony and confidentiality among the disparate groups, with practically no damaging leaks. . . .

My decision to remain near Washington would become controversial, particularly because it coincided with the official beginning of the 1980

Democratic presidential campaign. . . . I decided that until the hostages were freed I would not make political appearances.

Source: J. Carter, *Keeping Faith,* 462–63.

DOCUMENT 304: National Security Council Aide Gary Sick Recalls the SCC Discussion on the Rescue or Military Retaliation Options (6 November 1979)

On November 6, the second day of the crisis, the Joint Chiefs of Staff presented to the Special Coordinating Committee (SCC) of the National Security Council (NSC) the general outlines of three potential courses of military action. These were: first, a possible rescue mission to extract the imprisoned Americans from the besieged embassy in downtown Tehran; second, a possible retaliatory strike that would cripple Iran's economy; and third, considerations of how the United States might be required to respond if Iran should disintegrate.

In the meetings of November 6, most attention was paid to the first two.

The possibility of a rescue mission was examined in considerable detail. However, even the most cursory analysis of the embassy complex, its location in the center of a large city whose population was inflamed, and the great distances between Tehran and facilities that might be available for U.S. military use suggested that such an operation would be enormously complicated and would involve unacceptably high risks.

The Chairman of the Joint Chiefs recommended against any immediate attempt at a rescue mission, since reliable intelligence was unavailable and a complex plan would require time to develop. His judgment was supported by the Secretary of Defense, who had discussed the prospects with a high Israeli military official intimately associated with the Entebbe operation.

After a careful review, President Carter ordered the Department of Defense to proceed with preparations and planning for a rescue mission, while postponing any such attempt for the time being. He recognized that even a high-risk rescue attempt might become necessary if it appeared that the hostages were going to be killed by the Iranians.

Also at the meeting on November 6, President Carter was presented with a preliminary analysis of possible targets for a retaliatory strike. It was obvious that a purely punitive strike would not set the hostages free. On the contrary, it might well result in some or all of them being killed by their captors. Thus a punitive strike was viewed as retribution in the event the hostages were harmed. The President ordered that planning for such a strike be perfected and held in reserve, stressing that the objective would be economic targets, with the minimum possible loss of life among Iranian civilians.

Two other alternatives were examined in the context of a possible military strike. The seizure of a discrete piece of Iranian territory, for example an island, was considered. However, it was estimated that taking and holding a significant piece of Iranian territory would risk incurring sizable casualties—Iranian, American, or both. It could set off a continuing naval and air battle in the Persian Gulf that would be enormously costly to the broader interests of the United States, its Western allies, and the oil-producing states of the Gulf. Moreover, it was not considered likely to produce the freedom of the hostages. Rather, it might incite Iran to unite in a nationalistic visceral response and turn to the Soviet Union for protection. As a consequence, this option was never pressed much beyond the conceptual stage.

The possibility of dropping naval mines in Iranian harbors or otherwise imposing a military blockade was given serious consideration from the very beginning. For a variety of reasons, the mining option came to be regarded as the most likely policy choice if a decision should be taken to use limited military force against Iran. Mines could be planted on very short notice by naval forces already in place in the region. They would impose very high economic costs on Iran with little or no loss of life on either side. And the process was reversible, either by setting the mines to deactivate after a specific period of time or, if necessary, by physically removing them. As U.S. policy moved progressively toward an embargo on all trade with Iran, the ability to mine one or more Iranian harbors was increasingly regarded as a potentially classic example of the extension of diplomatic strategy by military means. . . .

As a result of the NSC meeting of November 6, a number of guidelines were developed that served as the basis for U.S. policy throughout the crisis. Five of these guidelines were related to the question of the use of force:

• The United States would attempt to increase the cost to Iran of its illegal actions, until the costs outweighed whatever benefits it might hope to achieve.

• Peaceful means would be explored and exhausted before resort to violence.

• The United States would retaliate militarily if the hostages were put on trial or physically harmed.

• The U.S. government would make no threats it was unable or unwilling to carry out.

• No military action would be taken that was not reversible. Specifically, President Carter was determined to avoid a situation where a limited military action would trap the United States in an open-ended escalatory cycle leading to land combat in Iran.

These guidelines were never codified and were never intended as declaratory policy. Rather, they were articulated by President Carter as objectives and policy boundaries for his advisers in developing U.S. strategy. They established the framework for consideration of military options.

Source: Gary Sick, "Military Options and Constraints," in Christopher et al., *American Hostages in Iran*, 144–47.

DOCUMENT 305: President Carter Meets with Hostages' Families (9 November 1979)

On November 9, I went to the State Department to meet with the hostages' families. Although the building was only a few hundred yards from the White House, the trip seemed long to me. There was no way for me to know how the families would react, but when we finally met, it was obvious that they and I shared the same feelings of grief and alarm. Secretary Vance and I briefed them on what had occurred, and explained some of the steps we were taking to insure the safety of their loved ones in Iran. The conversation was emotional for all of us, and afterward I was pleased when the families issued a statement of support for me and called on the nation to remain calm. This meeting was the beginning of a close relationship between us, which never faltered during the succeeding months.

Source: J. Carter, *Keeping Faith*, 460.

DOCUMENT 306: A Hostage Assesses the Embassy Seizure by Militants (November 1979)

VICTOR TOMSETH (chief political officer, at the Iranian Foreign Ministry): There certainly was a wave of fear in Iran following the takeover. The Iranians were quite concerned about what might happen to them as a consequence of the seizure of the embassy. I felt very strongly from the beginning that the most critical and dangerous period was the initial ten days, and this had to do with the fear on the part of the Iranians that something very bad was going to happen to them. In those circumstances Iranian behavior was extremely unpredictable, and a heightening of the rhetoric from the United States might have served to exacerbate that tension and uncertainty. But once the initial period passed, and the students realized what a tremendous political asset they had within the Iranian political context, I became fairly confident they would never willingly harm the people they were holding, and that barring an accident, it would ultimately become possible to negotiate a settlement.

In assessing whether or not President Carter should have tried to exploit the fear within Iran, I think it is important to first determine what American priorities should have been. The Carter administration chose to make the release of the hostages its top priority. Speaking as one who had a vested interest in that decision, I am quite happy with the order of priorities President Carter chose. But I can also understand why others would have liked to have seen a different set of priorities. A number of people that I have talked to have suggested that America's primary objective should not have been the lives of the hostages, but rather should have been to punish the Iranians for taking our people captive. If that had been done, then I certainly think that most if not all of the hostages would have been killed. Further, I don't think that the United States would have gained any credit worldwide. Personally, I was glad that it was Jimmy Carter in the White House on November 4 and in the days immediately thereafter, and not someone like Richard Nixon. President Carter was not inclined to act rashly, whereas someone else might have. His caution in those initial stages may very well have saved all of our lives.

Source: Tim Wells, *444 Days: The Hostages Remember* (San Diego: Harcourt Brace Jovanovich, 1985), 228–29.

DOCUMENT 307: CIA Director Stansfield Turner Meets with Ross Perot Concerning Rescue Operation (10–12 November 1979)

On 10 November CIA Director Stansfield Turner received a phone call from Ross Perot, who several months earlier had rescued two of his own employees from bondage in Iran by Islamic fundamentalists. Thinking that he could provide the CIA with some information on how to rescue the embassy personnel, Perot offered to use his contacts in Iran to help. He also suggested that the CIA might be able to pull off a rescue effort similar to his, and offered to come to Washington to brief the director on how he had done it. Director Turner accepted Perot's offer to collect information but had been noncommittal on any briefing about rescue operations.

I called Ross back and arranged for him to come to Washington the next day, Sunday. Now that the SCC [Special Coordinating Committee] realized that the hostage problem would not be solved easily, we were working around the clock. Ross was more than willing to accommodate us. On Day 8, then, he and nine members of his staff met with me and a group of CIA operations experts in the Director's conference room at the CIA. All of the people Ross brought with him had in one way or another been involved in the release of his two employees. They stressed that it would be easy to get a rescue team into Iran without its being detected; the men would pose as businessmen and go in through the airport, or would come in by land over remote routes. Of course, when Ross's people had gone through the airport in February, American passports were still acceptable in Iran. It would be more complicated now, as those same passports would ring alarm bells.

Ross and his people thought that if we infiltrated a military team into Tehran, it could canvass the territory, purchase its weapons, and then wait for the right moment to storm the embassy and release the hostages. They had few suggestions, however, on how to move the hostages and a rescue team—a total of more than a hundred people—safely out of Tehran. They had smuggled their two hostages and five rescuers out over land, but a much larger group posed quite different problems. A convoy of cars or trucks was almost bound to be stopped before it got out of Tehran. And it was highly unlikely that so many Westerners could work their way four hundred miles across Iran to Turkey unnoticed, either individually or in small groups.

The meeting with Perot's people forced us at the CIA to consider the advantages of inserting the rescue force clandestinely. By coincidence, just as our meeting was winding down, Harold Brown and Dave Jones came on the phone together to tell me they were working on a rescue plan that required assistance from the CIA in infiltrating an assault force of forty to sixty men into Tehran and then hiding it. I told them that Ross Perot was in my office describing just such a rescue mission, and suggested that they take the opportunity to talk with him.

Source: Stansfield Turner, *Terrorism and Democracy* (Boston: Houghton Mifflin, 1991), 39–42.

DOCUMENT 308: President Carter Orders Economic Sanctions Against Purchase of Iranian Oil (12 November 1979)

[On 12 November] I ordered that the United States discontinue oil purchases from Iran. My proclamation described the action as a move against the criminal officials who were condoning kidnapping, and not as a means to encourage conservation in our country. At the same time, I instructed Secretary of Energy Charles Duncan to do everything possible to cut back on all American oil imports and total consumption. We urged other nations to do the same. The worldwide oil shortage was already driving prices sky high.

I began to consider freezing all of Iran's assets—primarily consisting of gold and cash deposits—held in American banks both in our country and abroad. I hesitated only because such action was likely to reflect adversely on us as a reliable trading partner and might frighten other major depositors and investors into a massive transfer of their funds to other countries. Also, it had to be legal, to avoid a federal court injunction that would embarrass our nation. I directed Treasury Secretary Bill Miller and my other advisers to research the law to see how much authority I had, and then prepare legal documents so that, if necessary, the decision could be put into effect without delay. Cy Vance and I also assessed the advisability of breaking diplomatic relations with Iran, but decided against it; we had to keep open every possible avenue of communication, and the diplomatic status of the hostages was one characteristic that provided them some possible immunity from additional harm.

Source: J. Carter, *Keeping Faith*, 462.

DOCUMENT 309: Iranian Captors Release Female and African-American Hostages (19 November 1979)

CHARLES JONES (communications officer): I was the only black the terrorists didn't release. I think the main reason for that was because the Iranians thought I was a CIA agent. On the day of the takeover, I was caught in the communications vault destroying documents. They considered that to be a very, very unfriendly act, and they thought we were all spies. I was also the head of the communications section, and they figured that covered CIA operations, which it didn't. I didn't have anything to do with the CIA, but the Iranians didn't believe that. It's sort of ironic that they kept me, because some of the people they let go had much more sensitive jobs than me. But the Iranians didn't know what the hell they were doing.

Source: Wells, *444 Days*, 165.

DOCUMENT 310: CIA Director Turner Remembers President Carter Calling an SCC Meeting at Camp David (23 November 1979)

We moved on to Khomeini's latest threat of putting the hostages on trial and the students' renewed threat of killing them if we took military action. Both were alarming. The President had already made up his mind on how he would respond. If our people went on trial, we would mine some or all of Iran's ports. If even one hostage was hanged, we would bomb the Abadan refinery. But how could we get this message to Khomeini with maximum impact? I suggested that CIA operatives find a behind-the-scenes emissary. Cy preferred using the Swiss ambassador in Tehran, as the Swiss were representing us there. The President concurred. Later that day, he made a public statement that if the hostages were put on trial or harmed in any way, the consequences for Iran would be "extremely grave." . . .

This led to a long discussion of what kind of insults and humiliations we would accept to get the hostages back. National honor, not just the release of the hostages, had become an issue, just as it had with Lyndon Johnson in considering what kind of confession he could sign in the *Pueblo* affair. We decided the United States could agree to a Waldheim suggestion for organizing a commission to investigate Iran's complaint about past American support for the Shah, but only simultaneously with the release of the hostages. We were, of course, concerned about whether such a commission would produce anti-American propaganda, but everyone agreed we would have to take the chance.

Source: Turner, *Terrorism and Democracy*, 55–57.

DOCUMENT 311: CIA Director Turner Lists President Carter's 2-2-2 Strategy (28 November 1979)

My view that we were not serving the President well was reinforced at an SCC meeting on November 28, Day 25, when Zbig read us a list, compiled by the President, of six approaches, in sequence of severity. Again, the President seemed to be the only one taking time to think about strategy. His list included two political, two economic, and two military initiatives.

1. Obtain condemnation from friendly countries and the United Nations of Iran's holding of hostages. The objective would be to make Iran feel isolated.

2. Effect earliest graceful and humane departure of the Shah from the United States.

3. Establish an economic embargo on Iran and request friendly nations to join us.

4. Ask the United Nations Security Council to impose economic sanctions on Iran under Article VII of the UN Charter.

5. Mine some of Iran's harbors and threaten stronger military punishments if any hostages were harmed, but promise to lift the blockade when the hostages were released.

6. Make visible preparations for punitive military action in case any of the hostages was harmed.

Source: Turner, *Terrorism and Democracy,* 74.

DOCUMENT 312: President Carter's News Conference with Comments on Terrorism and His "Rose Garden Strategy" (28 November 1979)

. . . This nation will never yield to blackmail. For all Americans our constant concern is the well being and the safety of our fellow citizens who are being held illegally and irresponsibly hostage in Iran.

The actions of Iran have shocked the civilized world. For a government to applaud mob violence and terrorism, for a government actually to support and in effect participate in the taking and the holding of hostages is unprecedented in human history.

This violates not only the most fundamental precepts of international law but the common ethical and religious heritage of humanity.

There is no recognized religious faith on earth which condones kidnapping. There is no recognized religious faith on earth which condones blackmail. There is certainly no religious faith on earth which condones the sustained abuse of innocent people.

We are deeply concerned about the inhuman and degrading conditions imposed on the hostages. From every corner of the world, nations and people have voiced their strong revulsion and condemnation of Iran and have joined us in calling for the release of the hostages. . . .

Q: Mr. President, we appear to be in a rather dangerous period of international tension and volatility, especially in the Islamic world, and it comes at a time when we're about to embark on our quadrennial election campaign and all that that will bring. Have you given any thought to whether, following examples of other national emergencies, it may be wise to try to mute the political fallout of this by trying to bring opponents in and outside of your party into some kind of an emergency coalition for this purpose?

P: We have attempted to keep the political leaders in our nation informed both publicly and through other channels. . . .

I, myself, in order to stay close to the scene here where constantly changing events could be handled by me as President, have eliminated the major portion of political-oriented activities. I don't think the identity of the Islamic world is a factor. We have the deepest respect and reverence for Islam and for all those who share the Moslem faith. I might say that so far as I know, all the Islamic nations have joined us in condemning the activities and the actions of the Government of Iran. So I don't think religious divisions are affected here at all. But I will have to continue to restrict my own political activities and call on those who might be opposing me in the future for President to support my position as President and to provide unity for our country and for our nation in the eyes of those who might be looking for some sign of weakness or division in order to perpetuate their abuse of our hostages.

Source: Congressional Quarterly, *President Carter: 1979* (Washington: Congressional Quarterly, 1980), 118–21A.

FAILED NEGOTIATIONS AND SOVIETS IN AFGHANISTAN, NOVEMBER 1979–MARCH 1980

Another administration approach to solving the crisis was negotiation with any party that might have influence with the new Iranian regime. These efforts all came to naught as Khomeini's motives proved complex and layered; at least as important to him as embarrassing the United States, for instance, was energizing and revitalizing his revolutionary followers.

DOCUMENT 313: Secretary of State Cyrus Vance's Application for Interim Measures of Protection with the International Court of Justice (29 November 1979)

Dear Sir Humphrey Waldock,
President, International Court of Justice, The Hague:

The Government of the United States is today filing with the Court an Application and a Request for Interim Measures of Protection in a case against the Government of Iran for the seizure, and holding as hostages, of members of the United States Embassy in Tehran. As you are aware, at least fifty United States nationals are being subjected to prolonged and inhumane detention. They have already been held hostage for more than three weeks, and threats have been made that they may be placed on trial. . . .

I have designated the Legal Adviser of the United States Department of State, the Honorable Robert B. Owen, as Agent of the United States in this case.

Source: U.S. State Department, *Bulletin* 80, no. 2034 (January 1980), 7–38.

DOCUMENT 314: State Department Legal Adviser Robert Owen's Arguments Before the International Court of Justice (29 November 1979)

Sir, I have the honor to refer to the following: . . .

I. Statement of Facts

At about 10:30 A.M., Tehran time, on November 4, 1979, during the course of a demonstration of approximately 3,000 persons, the United States Embassy compound in Tehran was overrun by several hundred of the demonstrators. The Iranian Government's Security personnel on duty at the Embassy compound apparently made no effort to deter or discourage the demonstrators from the takeover. . . . In the process the invaders took hostage the Embassy security officer, who had come out of the Chancery to negotiate with them, and four of the Embassy's Marine guards. . . .

About two hours after the beginning of the attack, and after the invaders had attempted to set fire to the Chancery building and to cut through the upstairs steel doors with a torch, the demonstrators gained entry to the upper floor and seized the remaining personnel. . . .

During this continuing ordeal, the Government of Iran is failing and refusing to make any effort to secure the release of the hostages and the return of the Embassy and consular premises to the United States' control. The Government has refused any direct substantive contact with the United States Government officials in Tehran or at the United Nations. It refused to admit the special emissaries sent to Iran by the Government of the United States. The United States Chargé d'Affaires, who was at the Foreign Ministry at the time the attack began, has been confined to the Foreign Ministry and denied free access both to his diplomatic colleagues from other Embassies and to senior Iranian officials.

Moreover, the Government of Iran, from an early stage of the crisis, has given direct support and encouragement to the group holding the Embassy. Members of that group have been permitted to come and go freely from the compound. The Government of Iran has refused or ignored the repeated requests of the Government of the United States to free the hostages and to restore the Embassy compound to the possession of the United States. The Government of Iran has supported the demands of those holding the hostages, has endorsed the charges of espionage leveled against Embassy personnel, and has threatened to place the personnel on trial for espionage.

II. The Jurisdiction of the Court

Under Paragraph I of Article 36 of the Statute of the Court, the jurisdiction of the Court encompasses "all matters specially provided for . . . in treaties and conventions in force." The United States and Iran are, as members of the United Nations, parties to the Statute, and are also parties to three international conventions, each of which independently establishes the Court's jurisdiction over the present dispute. . . .

III. The Claims of the United States

The Government of the United States, in submitting the dispute to the Court, claims as follows:

(a) Pursuant to Article 29 of the Vienna Convention on Diplomatic Relations, the Government of Iran is under an international legal obligation to the United States to ensure that the persons of United States diplomatic agents be kept inviolate from "any form of arrest or detention" and that every such diplomatic agent shall be treated "with due respect" and protected from "any attack on his person, freedom, or dignity." The Government of Iran has violated and is currently violating the foregoing obligations. . . .

IV. Judgment Requested

Accordingly, the United States requests the Court to adjudge and declare as follows:

(a) That the Government of Iran, in tolerating, encouraging, and failing to prevent and punish the conduct described in the preceding Statement of Facts, violated its international legal obligations to the United States as provided by

• Articles 22, 24, 25, 27, 29, 31, 37 and 47 of the Vienna Convention on Diplomatic Relations,

• Articles 28, 31, 33, 34, 36, and 40 of the Vienna Convention on Consular Relations,

• Articles 4 and 7 of the Convention on the Prevention and Punishment of Crimes Against Internationally Protected Persons, Including Diplomatic Agents, and

• Articles II (4), XIII, XVIII, and XIX of the Treaty of Amity, Economic Relations and Consular Rights Between the United States and Iran, and

• Articles 2(3), 2(4), and 33 of the Charter of the United Nations;

(b) That pursuant to the foregoing international legal obligations, the Government of Iran is under a particular obligation immediately to secure the release of all United States nationals currently being detained within the premises of the United States Embassy in Tehran and to assure that all such persons and all other United States nationals in Tehran are allowed to leave Iran safely;

(c) That the Government of Iran shall pay to the United States, in its own right and in the exercise of its right of diplomatic protection of its nationals, reparation for the foregoing violations of Iran's international legal obligations to the United States, in a sum to be determined by the Court; and

(d) That the Government of Iran submit to its competent authorities for the purpose of prosecution those persons responsible for the crimes committed against the premises and staff of the United States Embassy and against the premises of its Consulates.

Source: U.S. State Department, *Bulletin* 80, no. 2034 (January 1980), 38–41.

DOCUMENT 315: Stansfield Turner Remembers the Vance-Brzezinski "Two Horse" Policy Dispute (November 1979)

I kept asking myself why a country of our political influence and economic and military power was even considering making a deal with a nation like Iran. Perhaps there were no other solutions, but I wondered if it was because the Carter team was not working well together. At our SCC meetings the discussion often could not stay on track. . . . Stress accounted for some of this, but overactive egos played a bigger part than they should have. And the strong philosophical differences between Cy and Zbig were also a key factor. . . .

The fundamental reason, then, that we were not working well as a team was that Cy was pushing in one direction and Zbig in another. Cy believed in keeping the door open for Iran to engage us in reasonable discussions. The Iranians, after all, felt they had a legitimate grievance, and held us responsible for much of what they hated of the Shah's regime. Cy felt that if we antagonized or humiliated them, it would take longer for them to deal with us, even through intermediaries. He wanted to apply whatever pressures we could through third parties, like the United Nations, countries friendly to revolutionary Iran, or world leaders who had rapport with Khomeini. He hoped not to drive more of a wedge between us and the Iranians; rather, he wanted to make them realize the hostage issue could cause them harm by isolating Iran from the community of nations. Cy's approach required considerable patience.

Zbig and, I believe, most of the rest of us felt this instance of hostage taking was so heinous that it had to be solved before we could discuss Iran's perceived grievances. Because we were both the aggrieved party and a very powerful nation, we assumed we could find a way to apply the necessary amount of pressure to the Iranians. We did not want to wait for them to come to their senses; we wanted to act. That attitude was strengthened on Day 15, when the Iranians released the thirteen black and female hostages, who brought back appalling stories of the conditions of imprisonment: hostages in the same room not being allowed to talk to one another; people bound hand and foot, lacking food and news, and subjected to other psychological pressures. We wanted action—now.

There was a problem, though, in that we activists could not think of pressures that might be effective other than punitive military actions, and those could put the lives of the hostages at risk. We were almost forced to consider Cy's strategy of less obtrusive diplomatic pressures combined with patient negotiations, but that did not stop us from continuing to search for active options.

There was no way to stop riding two horses.

Source: Turner, *Terrorism and Democracy*, 58–60.

DOCUMENT 316: Iranian Foreign Minister Bani-Sadr's Memoirs on the Mullahs' Political Goals with American Hostages (November 1979)

After the fall of the Bazargan Government on November 6, 1979, I accepted the post of minister of foreign affairs. It was my first executive position since returning to Iran. My first priority was to solve the hostage problem to prevent it from becoming the pretext for a war of restoration. I was convinced that falling into the trap of hostility would open the door to counterrevolutionary action. Also, when the Revolutionary Council suggested that I take charge of this ministry, I immediately asked what was to be done with the hostages. I went to see the students occupying the U.S. embassy and told them, quite frankly, what I thought. "You think that you have taken America hostage. What a delusion! In fact, you have made Iran the hostage of the Americans."

The next day . . . I went to see Khomeini in Qom. . . . He could not have been more explicit: "They are not diplomats, but spies; they are being watched." Initially, however, the plan was to lock them up for a few days and then release them. In fact, the reason the hostages were taken was to get rid of Bazargan. Khomeini, who had chosen Bazargan, could not change his mind so soon after installing him. It was therefore necessary to find some indirect approach to depose Bazargan, and the embassy affair was the ideal pretext for getting rid of him by accusing him of being in sympathy with the United States. I should mention that I contacted Bazargan at the time and advised him not to resign. Nevertheless, we were not on good terms. He was surprised by the step I took. We saw each other later, and I asked him, "Why did you put yourself in that impossible situation with the Americans?" He answered, "The hostage-taking was nothing but a ploy to get rid of me, but I didn't realize it right away."

Ordinarily, I would have known who had decided to take the hostages because the students "of the Imam's line" were subject to a five-member council—of which I was a member— . . . and we certainly never contemplated any such action. Moreover, three of the five members never officially knew who organized this operation using the Revolutionary Guards as a cover. In fact, the decision to take the Americans hostage came from Khomeini's entourage, supported by certain members of the Islamic Republic Party. They wanted to use the hostages to create a climate favorable to their takeover of the government. It is inconceivable that the Guards would have taken such a step alone.

From the beginning, the hostage affair was handled illogically. When one is preparing for an enemy attack or has decided to conduct an internal policy of confrontation, care must be taken to provide the necessary means. How was it that Khomeini and his aides planned the embassy takeover without considering the internal, regional, and international contexts? They exhibited a rare lack of foresight by doing nothing to protect our resources or our money and by failing to import the spare parts already paid for and stockpiled at American airports first. There was no hurry. These basic precautions could have been taken and then, afterward, the embassy could have been seized to obtain the Shah's extradition. One did not have to be an expert to see that the hostage affair was going to paralyze us economically. Early in the revolution, Ibrahim Yazdi received a report from the United States calling for a blockade of Iran. When I arrived at the foreign affairs ministry, I found two very explicit memorandums on this subject.

Thus, we knew what was in store for us, yet no one did anything about it. Everything that happened as a result of the hostage affair occurred with the full knowledge of the Iranian authorities. Our spare parts and our funds were frozen in the United States. A child could have spotted the trap. We found a document in the U.S. embassy in Tehran outlining a plan to freeze Iranian funds. This plan, which predates the hostage affair, was developed by Chase Manhattan Bank, which feared that revolutionary Iran would not pay its debts. It sent experts to Iran to investigate the regime. Their report concluded that there was no government, no justice, and therefore no law in Iran. Since government by the mullahs was synonymous with anarchy, the U.S. courts could be petitioned to freeze Iranian funds. This initial maneuver failed because proving to a court that Iran was a lawless country was not an easy matter. The international jurists who advised the banks found the plan unworkable. They prepared a second plan that resulted in our funds being frozen by the president of the United States.

What a lack of foresight! Withdrawing our funds should have been our first reprisal against the Americans for harboring the Shah. We could have taken legal action to obtain delivery of our spare parts and, as a last resort, occupied the embassy. In this way, we would have placed ourselves in the best possible position in case of an Iraqi attack.

Apprised of these facts by the Americans, Saddam Hussein knew when he attacked that we lacked spare parts and that the few we had were stored haphazardly in warehouses. During the Shah's reign, the Americans had asked for $250 million to provide computer management of the spare parts inventories they had sold us. The Shah had agreed, but the revolution had prevented completion of the work. Our military depots were in an indescribable mess.

Source: Abol Hassan Bani-Sadr, *My Turn to Speak: Iran, the Revolution and Secret Deals with the United States* (Washington: Brassey's, 1991), 21–23.

DOCUMENT 317: American Hostage Moorhead Kennedy Recalls His Captors' Motives (December 1979)

They used to tell us: "We have nothing against you personally. We like Americans. It's the United States that we hate." Part of this split in their attitude toward the American people and the U.S. government was based on their perception of history. The U.S. government had supported the Shah, had helped to train Savak, had collaborated with Savak in monitoring dissident students in the United States, and, very important, had "waged war against the helpless people of Vietnam." It was, however, the American people who had forced the withdrawal from Indochina. This persuaded our captors that a fissure existed between the government and the American people, one which they hoped the hostage crisis would widen. Later some were disillusioned by the extent to which the hostage crisis had pulled the country together. But this did not diminish their professedly high regard for the American people, if only they could get to them with "the truth."

On a deeper level, the students were coping with highly ambivalent feelings about our country which are difficult for us to understand. They were reacting to our successful and dominant culture, which in fact pervaded every aspect of Iranian life and which was the target of the revolution that these students were the vanguard of. For all its great past, present-day Iranian culture offered little, especially in science and technology but in other fields as well, to compete with the West. . . . These were students at the cutting edge of a revolution whose goal was to expunge Westernizing influences from Iran, and they were internalizing those very influences.

Source: Moorhead Kennedy, *The Ayatollah in the Cathedral* (New York: Hill and Wang, 1986), 119–20.

DOCUMENT 318: Rosalynn Carter Recalls the 1980 Presidential Campaign (December 1979)

At first, the public supported Jimmy all the way. During any crisis, the incumbent President can almost count on a surge of approval, and the Iranian crisis was no exception. Within the first few weeks of the Embassy takeover, the country was caught up in an outpouring of patriotism and support for the president, just as the 1980 campaign was beginning. Unfortunately for Ted Kennedy and Jerry Brown, both announced their candidacy the same week the hostages were captured; they were then in a predicament, trying to decide how to attack Jimmy in the midst of the general approbation. And from that time on, our fortunes and theirs would be strongly affected by the hostage situation. . . .

In December, Jimmy announced his candidacy for a second term as President, and I was really looking forward to his campaigning again. He had been working on the crisis day and night, and I thought it would be a good change for him to get out in the countryside and feel the approval in the air for what he was doing. We had a big announcement party planned in Washington, with simultaneous ones to be held all over the country, followed by a week of travel and much-needed fundraising. But once more, Iran changed our plans.

Jimmy decided he couldn't leave the White House to barnstorm around the country as a candidate. He needed to stay near the Situation Room to respond instantly to any message from Iran. He also thought it important with the crisis at hand to continue in the role of a President representing all Americans and not move into a highly partisan political campaign just representing Democrats.

Source: R. Carter, *First Lady from Plains*, 312–14.

DOCUMENT 319: National Security Council's Gary Sick Stresses the Geopolitical Impact of the Soviet Invasion of Afghanistan (December 1979)

The Afghan invasion transformed the entire strategic environment in the region, and it provided a compelling set of reasons for seeking a negotiated settlement with Iran instead of pressing the situation toward possible conflict. The Soviets, by their actions, appeared to have provided renewed evidence that the United States and Iran shared fundamental security interests, regardless of how much their politics might diverge. Similarly, the Soviet invasion shocked the Islamic states of the Persian Gulf into awareness of their own vulnerability and opened up new possibilities for cooperation with the United States. To have launched military action against Iran at that moment would have contributed to the political destabilization of regional governments and interrupted U.S. efforts to develop a regional security framework.

Also, of course, it was at this critical moment that a new set of possible intermediaries appeared on the scene, credibly offering the possibility of initiating a dialogue with the revolutionary forces close to Khomeini. Consequently, military plans were shelved and a new round of secret negotiations was begun that lasted until April 1980.

Source: Gary Sick, *All Fall Down: America's Tragic Encounter with Iran* (New York: Random House, 1985), 282.

DOCUMENT 320: Address by President Carter Emphasizes Doctrine to Defend Persian Gulf Oil Supplies Following Soviet Invasion of Afghanistan (23 January 1980)

. . . This is a time of challenge to our interests and our values and it is a time that tests our wisdom and our skills.

At this time in Iran 50 Americans are still held captive, innocent victims of terrorism and anarchy.

Also at this moment, massive Soviet troops are attempting to subjugate the fiercely independent and deeply religious people of Afghanistan.

These two acts—one of international terrorism and one of military aggression—present a serious challenge to the United States of America. . . .

Three basic developments have helped to shape our challenges: the steady growth and increased projection of Soviet military power beyond its own borders; the overwhelming dependence of the western democracies on oil supplies from the Middle East; and the press of social and religious and economic and political change in the many nations of the developing world exemplified by the revolution in Iran.

Each of these factors is important in its own right. Each interacts with the others. . . .

We continue to pursue these specific goals: First, to protect the present and long-range interests of the United States. Secondly, to preserve the lives of the American hostages and to secure, as quickly as possible, their safe release. If possible, to avoid bloodshed which might further endanger the lives of our fellow citizens. To enlist the help of other nations in condemning this act of violence which is shocking and violates the moral and legal standards of a civilized world. And also to convince and to persuade the Iranian leaders that the real danger to their nation lies in the north, in the Soviet Union, and from the Soviet troops now in Afghanistan, and that the unwarranted Iranian quarrel with the United States hampers their response to this far greater danger to them.

If the American hostages are harmed, a severe price will be paid.

We will never rest until every one of the American hostages [is] released. . . .

The region which is now threatened by Soviet troops in Afghanistan is of great strategic importance: It contains more than two-thirds of the world's exportable oil. The Soviet effort to dominate Afghanistan has brought Soviet military forces to within 300 miles of the Indian Ocean and close to the Straits of Hormuz—a waterway through which most of the world's oil must flow. The Soviet Union is now attempting to consolidate a strategic position, therefore, that poses a grave threat to the free movement of Middle East oil. . . .

Let our position be absolutely clear:

An attempt by any outside force to gain control of the Persian Gulf region will be regarded as an assault on the vital interests of the United States of America and such an assault will be repelled by any means necessary, including military force.

Source: Congressional Quarterly, *President Carter: 1980* (Washington: Congressional Quarterly, 1981), 133–36.

DOCUMENT 321: Secretary Vance Communicates to UN Secretary-General Kurt Waldheim American Six-Point Diplomatic Position to Resolve Crisis (12 January 1980)

The Soviet Union's invasion of Afghanistan and the resulting vote of condemnation on 12 January by the United Nations apparently influenced Iranian leaders to make indirect contacts with American officials toward a resolution of the crisis. On the day of the UN vote, Secretary of State Vance, with President Carter's approval, presented the Iranians, through UN Secretary-General Kurt Waldheim, a six-point statement of the U.S. position, of which Points 1, 4, and 6 are most pertinent.

1. The safe and immediate departure from Iran of all U.S. employees of the Embassy in Tehran. . . .

4. Once the hostages are safely released, the United States is prepared to lift the freeze of Iranian assets and to facilitate normal commercial relations between the two countries. . . .

6. The U.S. Administration is prepared to make a statement . . . that it understands the grievances felt by the people of Iran, and that it respects

the integrity of Iran, and the right of the people of Iran to choose their own form of government.

Source: Vance, *Hard Choices*, 400–401.

DOCUMENT 322: Iranian Foreign Minister Ghotbzadeh Meets Secretly with Presidential Adviser Hamilton Jordan in Paris Concerning Plot to Assassinate the Exiled Shah (17 February 1980)

[Islamic Republic of Iran's Foreign Minister Ghotbzadeh] said, "I see your newspapers and replays of your television news, and all I have heard about the last three months is hostages, hostages, hostages. Your press does not tell the story of the Shah's crimes or the events leading to their seizure. . . . I disagree with what those students have done. It isolates and hurts our country and our Revolution. But holding fifty-three Americans is a slight injustice compared to the killing and torturing of thousands and thousands of Iranians by the criminal Shah!"

"The policy of our country for the past thirty years is not the fault or responsibility of this Administration," I responded, "nor is it the responsibility of the captured men and women."

"Mr. Jordan, it is hard for my people to separate the guilty from the innocent. Your country and your Presidents have made it possible for the Shah to rule. As far as the Ayatollah Khomeini is concerned, you all have blood on your hands."

Clearly, it was futile to argue about the past. I decided to be blunt. "How do we resolve this crisis peacefully, honorably, and quickly?"

The contact paused and smiled slyly. "It is easy to resolve the crisis."

"How?" I shot back.

"All you have to do is kill the Shah," he said in a quiet voice.

I was shocked. "You're kidding."

He stopped smiling. "I am very serious, Mr. Jordan. The Shah is in Panama now. I am not talking about anything dramatic. Perhaps the CIA can give him an injection or do something to make it look like a natural death. I'm only asking you to do to the Shah what the CIA did to thousands of innocent Iranians over the past thirty years!"

"That's impossible!" I told him. "It's totally out of the question!"

He smiled again. "You asked me how to quickly resolve the crisis. I want to remove this thorn from our side just as badly as you do, Mr. Jordan," the man said, "but for very different reasons. Your purpose is to have the President re-elected, and my purpose is to refocus the attention of the Iranian people on our Revolution and to keep the United States and the Soviets from subverting it. You think we hate the United States. The truth is we hate both the United States and the Soviet Union. Both countries have used and exploited Iran! Our hatred of the United States is simply more recent."

Source: Hamilton Jordan, *Crisis: The Last Year of the Carter Presidency* (New York: Putnam's, 1982), 164–66.

DOCUMENT 323: The Jordan-Ghotbzadeh Draft Agreement Between the Carter Administration and the Iranian Government of President Bani-Sadr (March 1980)

The United States and Iran agree:

I. Principles and Procedures

1) to accept the principle of the development of a scenario, the initial stages of which will be precisely defined and the following stages defined in detail on the basis of the progress of events;

2) to implement this scenario with the aid of persons approved by both parties.

II. Appointment of a Fact-finding Commission

1) It is specified in the approval of this scenario that the secretary general of the United Nations will appoint a fact-finding commission "to hear Iranian grievances, to find a solution to the crisis between the United States and Iran as quickly as possible" and that Iran wants this commission to talk with each of the hostages.

III. Work of the Commission

1) The commission will not leave New York for Tehran until the above announcement has been made by the United States. It will endeavor to commence its work in Tehran at the beginning of the following week.

2) The commission will hold its meetings in private and will receive evidence and documents submitted to it by the Iranian authorities.

IV. Final Stages

1) The transfer of the hostages under the protection of the Iranian government will be made either in a hospital or at the embassy, after the "students" have left the building (Day 1).

2) Return of the commission to New York (Day 1 + 1).

3) Submission to the secretary general of the commission's report,

which shall include proceedings and recommendations. Publication of the report in the form of a United Nations document. The report will express the following principle, among others, as a recommendation to all governments:

Governments must respect and guarantee the exercise, within the framework of their internal legislation, of the rights of Iran:

a) to institute proceedings against the Shah, his family, or his associates, on the grounds of grave suspicion of criminal acts brought to light in the report.

b) to institute proceedings to recover the assets which, in the report, are presumed to have been illegally removed from Iran by the Shah, his family, or his associates (Day 1 + 2).

4) Release of the hostages and their departure from Iran (Day 1 + 3). . . .

6) Formation of a joint commission to resolve outstanding bilateral problems. (On a date to be determined by Iran and the United States within a period of one month following Day 1.)

Source: Bani-Sadr, *My Turn to Speak*, 27–28.

MILITARY RESCUE, ECONOMIC SANCTIONS, AND THE 1980 ELECTION, MARCH–NOVEMBER 1980

When negotiations proved unsuccessful, President Carter moved to approve a rescue mission in April 1980. Equipment failure and command problems doomed this effort, to the acute embarrassment of the administration. Not until after the Iranian leadership had decided that holding the fifty-two Americans was availing them little and costing them much in international prestige did they move toward a settlement. Iraq's invasion was also a crucial factor in their thinking because after that they desperately needed access to frozen assets in the United States to purchase military weaponry.

DOCUMENT 324: NSC Aide Recalls When the Military Option Comes to Fore (22 March 1980)

On Saturday, 22 March 1980, an NSC meeting was scheduled at the president's Camp David retreat in the Catoctin Mountains of Maryland. On that date, eight senior officials—Vice President Walter Mondale,

Secretaries Vance and Brown, CIA Director Turner, NSC Adviser Brzezinski, and Generals Jones, Aaron, and Powell—met with President Carter for a complete review of U.S. strategy toward Iran. The subject of the meeting concerned the use of military means to free the hostages.

The first stage of the plan involved the prepositioning of men, matériel and support equipment at key locations in the Middle East and Indian Ocean. This movement had to be accomplished under the cover of other routinely scheduled activities to avoid signaling that an operation was being prepared. To preserve security, the bulk of this matériel had to be held back until political authorization was granted to proceed with the operation. One of the key purposes of the March 22 NSC meeting was to begin some of these preliminary steps in order to reduce the time lapse between a decision and the actual launching of the raid.

The insertion of the force into Iran was a grueling and technically difficult operation. Under cover of darkness, eight RH-53D helicopters and eight C-130 aircraft were to depart from different locations, fly at very low level beneath Iranian radar coverage across more than 500 miles of Iranian desert, and rendezvous at an airstrip that would be secretly prepared near the small town of Tabas—the site called "Desert One" in the plan. At Desert One, the helicopters were to be refueled and loaded with the men and equipment ferried in by the fixed-wing aircraft.

Following the refueling and loading, the C-130s would leave Iran. The team would conceal itself at a prepared location southeast of Tehran, and the helicopters, still under cover of darkness, would proceed to a remote site in the mountains above Tehran, where they would be camouflaged and remain in hiding throughout the following day. This delay was required in order to ensure that the assault on the embassy itself could be carried out under cover of darkness. Because of the distances involved, it was impossible to insert the necessary forces, release the hostages and depart in a single night.

For the nonspecialist, it is difficult to appreciate the demands that this critical first phase of the operation placed on men, equipment and technology. Simply flying 600 miles nonstop in a helicopter is a remarkable feat. To do so at night, without lights, in complete radio silence, and at very low altitude can only be regarded as a heroic achievement in its own right. Hence, many of those closely associated with the planning of the rescue mission believed—quite rightly as it turned out—that this was the most difficult segment of the entire operation. As Secretary of Defense Harold Brown remarked in his press conference after the mission failed, there was no other country in the world that had the resources even to attempt such an operation.

Assuming the successful insertion of the team, and its survival undetected during the following day, the actual rescue operation would have been conducted under cover of darkness on the second night. The entry of the team into Tehran would have been in local vehicles to attract minimum attention, with the helicopters making the briefest possible appearance to pick up the team and the hostages. The helicopters were then to fly to an abandoned airfield near Tehran where they would rendezvous with transport aircraft. The helicopters would be abandoned, and the Americans would be flown out of the country under heavy U.S. air cover. . . .

President Carter asked what steps had to be taken immediately in order to prepare the way for a rescue mission. He said he did not want to undertake a rescue operation unless there was no choice. He would prefer to wait another ninety days rather than conduct an operation that resulted in the deaths of the hostages. General Jones pointed out that the nights were becoming progressively shorter in Iran, thereby reducing the time available to insert the team and conduct the assault on the embassy. As time went on, it would be necessary to begin thinking about a three-day operation instead of the already complex two-day plan.

President Carter made it clear that he did not regard the negotiating track as finished. (Bani-Sadr's self-imposed time limit for transfer of the hostages to the government still had about a week to run at that point.) He was not prepared to make a decision on a high-risk rescue venture while there were still opportunities to work out a negotiated release. However, he authorized the taking of certain preparatory steps, including the covert flight of a small reconnaissance aircraft to the secret rendezvous site, necessary to lay the groundwork for a possible future operation.

Source: Sick, *All Fall Down*, 284–87.

DOCUMENT 325: President Carter Frustrated at Inability to Resolve Crisis by the Jordan-Ghotbzadeh Diplomatic Channel (30 March–11 April 1980)

I decided it was now time to put more pressure on Iran. We redoubled our efforts among our friends to use their strongest possible influence in Tehran and to let Bani-Sadr know that the United States was planning to impose much more stringent sanctions and possibly close the Iranian seaports if the hostages were not released by the first of April. I talked personally to the leaders of Great Britain, France, and Germany, and sent messages to the others, stressing that our patience had run out; only if

Iran were induced to release the hostages could another even more serious confrontation between the two countries be avoided.

These efforts paid off. For the first time, I felt that all our allies were really helping us to the maximum extent of their ability. As my April 1 deadline approached, I received a positive report from Iran.

About 1:45, Cy reported that Ghotbsadeh had sent word to us that Bani-Sadr will make a statement tomorrow at noon Tehran time [4:30 A.M. in Washington], saying that the Revolutionary Council with Khomeini's approval had decided to transfer the hostages away from the students to the government on Tuesday. This story was already leaking from the Revolutionary Council. They asked the United States to acknowledge this move as being constructive, and also to point out that the Iranians had said the Majlis [the Iranian parliament] would make a decision on the full release of the hostages and call on them to expedite this process. If this develops to be a true report, it would be the most encouraging thing we've had lately out of Iran. . . .

To my dismay and bewilderment, some news stories accused me of arranging a phony exchange of messages with the Iranian leaders so as to affect the outcome of the Wisconsin primary which was held on this same day. These false reports grew into a refrain that was sung over and over during the months ahead, and eventually became accepted as the truth by many political commentators. . . .

On April 3, after meeting with the militants, two members of the Revolutionary Council announced that the hostages would be turned over to the government on Saturday, April 5; the militants said they would accede to the request of the government. Bani-Sadr announced once more that the hostages would be transferred, but added that the Council would take no action without Khomeini's approval. In an interview with ABC he said, "Don't worry, the transfer will be carried out." But experience dictated caution and doubt. We mixed in a little hope and prayer.

Friday, April 4, brought nothing but bad news. All during the day we communicated with the Iranians, either directly through [Christian] Bourguet and [Hector] Villalon or through Swiss Ambassador [Erik] Lang. They were joined in the effort by Archbishop [Hilarion] Capucci, who is a hero in the Revolutionary Council because he was convicted in Israel for smuggling weapons to the Palestinians. He tried to convince the terrorists to turn over the hostages to the government because holding them was damaging the revolutionary government structure in Iran.

Bani-Sadr and Ghotbsadeh were apparently convinced from the beginning. The Revolutionary Council varied between voting unanimously to move ahead with the transfer, or at times with 2 votes against it and 3 abstentions [out of a total of 25]. It was a comedy of errors, and eventually, because the Council was not unanimous, Bani-Sadr took the case to Khomeini, who decided against the transfer. . . .

It was obvious to me that the Revolutionary Council would never act. ... I decided to move ahead on additional economic sanctions, an embargo against the shipment of any goods to Iran except food and medicines, breaking off diplomatic relations and the expulsion of all Iranian diplomats, and a census of all financial claims against Iran. We again asked all our allies and other countries to join us in these actions, and to consider breaking diplomatic relations with Iran at an early date if the hostages continued to be held. Cy Vance met with more than twenty ambassadors in Washington to explain our decision and to seek the support of their countries. I also discussed various possible military operations with my most senior advisers.

Source: J. Carter, *Keeping Faith*, 501–5.

DOCUMENT 326: Press Secretary Jody Powell Comments on Charges that Carter Administration Played Domestic Politics with the Hostage Crisis (1 April 1980)

Tuesday [1 April] was also the day of the Wisconsin primary. It was important to us, because we had lost badly to [Senator Edward] Kennedy in New York the week before, after a humiliating mix-up in communications on a UN vote. But constant polling over the weekend had substantially relieved our concerns. Pat Caddell [Carter campaign's polling researcher] was predicting a big victory. His last run of numbers on Sunday showed Carter with a solid 15-point lead that could go as high as 25.

We gathered in the Oval Office in the early hours of Tuesday morning to await the first reports on Bani-Sadr's speech. It would require a response of some sort. A message from Iranian Foreign Minister Sadegh Ghotbzadeh on Monday had specifically requested that the President acknowledge the announcement as a "constructive step."

The primary in Wisconsin was far from our minds as we waited for the first wire service reports to come in, since we had no diplomats in positions who could cable us a report. As things turned out, we would have been better off to have given some thought to the political events of the day, and to the cynicism with which the press viewed the President's every action.

When the first English translation of Bani-Sadr's speech was received, about 5:30 A.M., it was almost, but not quite, what we were looking for. It promised to transfer the hostages, but there were conditions. The most troublesome was the last. It demanded that we recognize the right of the Majlis, the Iranian parliament, to decide the fate of the hostages. This was not acceptable. The words "Iranian parliament" were a contradiction in terms. We could not be in a position of appearing to give advance approval to whatever this yet-to-be-convened legislative assemblage of a seriously unstable government might decide to do.

In the end, however, we agreed that we had no choice but to respond positively. If we said nothing, or responded negatively, the arrangement would certainly collapse. We would react positively, announce a hold on additional sanctions, attempt to finesse the Majlis question with a comment about the competence of the institution to deal with the question, and hope for the best.

We also agreed unanimously that the President's response should not be delayed. It was now approaching mid-afternoon in Iran. Knowing the fragile nature of all agreements in that country, we did not want to let the situation sit overnight.

A presidential statement was agreed upon. I asked, without giving the question much thought, whether the President would prefer to go to the briefing room or invite the press into the Oval Office. He said it would be all right to bring them into his office. That suited me fine, since the network correspondents had said just a few minutes earlier that the Oval Office would be their preference.

At 7:20 A.M. the President made his statement, a few questions were asked, and the press scurried out to file their stories.

Later, some would accuse the President of injecting too much optimism into his comments, of hyping his reaction beyond what the facts would support. That charge simply will not stand up to a reading of the transcript of what he actually said. He stated clearly that we had no reason to expect that the hostages would actually be transferred except for Bani-Sadr's statement.

Source: Jody Powell, *The Other Side of the Story* (New York: William Morrow, 1984), 215–16.

DOCUMENT 327: President Carter Announces Sanctions Against Iran (7 April 1980)

Ever since Iranian terrorists imprisoned American Embassy personnel in Tehran early in November, these 50 men and women—their safety, their health, and their future—have been our central concern. We've made every effort to obtain their release on honorable, peaceful, and humanitarian terms, but the Iranians have refused to release them or even to improve the inhumane conditions under which these Americans are being held captive.

The events of the last few days have revealed a new and significant dimension in this matter. The militants controlling the Embassy have stated they are willing to turn the hostages over to the Government of Iran, but the Government has refused to take custody of the American hostages. This lays bare the full responsibility of the Ayatollah Khomeini and the Revolutionary Council for the continued illegal and outrageous holding of the innocent hostages. . . .

It must be made clear that the failure to release the hostages will involve increasingly heavy costs to Iran and to its interests. I have today ordered the following steps.

First, the United States of America is breaking diplomatic relations with the Government of Iran. The Secretary of State has informed the Government of Iran that its Embassy and consulates in the United States are to be closed immediately. . . .

Second, the Secretary of the Treasury will put into effect official sanctions prohibiting exports from the United States to Iran, in accordance with the sanctions approved by 10 members of the United Nations Security Council on January 13 in the resolution which was vetoed by the Soviet Union. . . .

Third, the Secretary of the Treasury will make a formal inventory of the assets of the Iranian Government, which were frozen by my previous order, and also will make a census or an inventory of the outstanding claims of American citizens and corporations against the Government of Iran. This accounting of claims will aid in designing a program against Iran for the hostages, for the hostage families, and other U.S. claimants. . . .

Fourth, the Secretary of Treasury [State] and the Attorney General will invalidate all visas issued to Iranian citizens for future entry into the United States, effective today.

Source: Weekly Compilation of Presidential Documents, Jimmy Carter, Vol. 16, no. 15 (Washington: GPO, 1980), 611–15.

DOCUMENT 328: President Carter Decides on Military Rescue Option Following the Collapse of the Jordan-Ghotbzadeh Agreement (11–15 April 1980)

We could no longer afford to depend on diplomacy. I decided to act. On April 11, I called together my top advisers, and we went over the rescue plans again. Because the militants in the compound had threatened to "destroy all the hostages immediately" if any additional moves against them should be launched, we had to plan any action with the utmost care. In the Cabinet Room with me were Vice President Mondale, Secretary Brown, Dr. Brzezinski, Deputy Secretary of State Christopher, Central Intelligence Director Stansfield Turner, General David Jones, Hamilton, and Jody. (Secretary Vance was on a brief and much needed vacation.) Earlier, I had developed a long list of questions for the military leaders. Their answers had become much more satisfactory as the training and preparations for the rescue operation had progressed. David Jones said that the earliest date everything could be ready was April 24. I told everyone that it was time for us to bring our hostages home; their safety and our national honor were at stake. When the meeting adjourned, everyone understood that our plans had to be kept a carefully guarded secret. . . .

When Vance returned, he objected to my decision to rescue the hostages and wanted to present his own views to the NSC group. His primary argument was that we should be patient and not do anything which might endanger their safety. I held the meeting on April 15, but no one changed his mind.

We took every possible step to conceal our preliminary moves in preparation for the hostage rescue mission, encouraging the few people who had to know about airplane and helicopter movements to believe they might be related to the possible laying of mines. On the evening of April 16, we met in the Situation Room for a thorough review of every aspect of the operation. This session lasted two and a half hours, and I was particularly impressed with mission commanders Generals James B. Vaught and Philip C. Gast, and Colonel Charles Beckwith. These were the leaders who, working with the Joint Chiefs of Staff and the Secretary of Defense, would direct the mission after I authorized it to begin.

Source: J. Carter, *Keeping Faith,* 506–7.

DOCUMENT 329: President Carter's Speech Announcing Further Restrictions Against Iran (17 April 1980)

We are beyond the time for gestures. We want our people to be set free. Accordingly, I am today ordering an additional set of actions.

First, I am prohibiting all financial transfers by persons subject to the jurisdiction of the United States to any person or entity in Iran except those directly related to the gathering of news and family remittances. . . .

As of today, any such transaction will become a criminal act.

Second, all imports from Iran to the United States will be barred.

Third, I intend to exercise my statutory authority to protect American citizens abroad by prohibiting travel to Iran, and by prohibiting any transactions between Americans and foreign persons relating to such travel or the presence of Americans in Iran. This authority will not now be used to interfere with the right of the press to gather news.

However, . . . [I] call on American journalists and news-gathering organizations to minimize, as severely as possible, their presence and their activities in Iran.

Fourth, I am ordering that all military equipment previously purchased by the government of Iran, which I had previously impounded, be made available for use by the United States military forces or for sale to other countries.

And finally, I will ask Congress for discretionary authority to pay reparations to the hostages and to their families out of the more than $8 billion in frozen Iranian assets in the United States. These assets will be available to satisfy contract and other commercial claims of American firms against Iranian government entities, and to reimburse claims of the United States for the heavy military and other costs we have incurred because of Iran's illegal actions.

Source: Weekly Compilation of Presidential Documents, Jimmy Carter, Vol. 16, no. 16 (Washington: GPO, 1980), 714–17.

DOCUMENT 330: Secretary of State Vance Decides to Resign (21 April 1980)

Upon his return from an overseas mission, Secretary Vance was informed by Undersecretary Warren Christopher that President Carter had decided to approve the military rescue operation. Stunned and angry that such a momentous decision had been made in his absence, Secretary Vance called upon the president early the next morning (15 April) to spell out again his very strong objections to any rescue mission.

Vance was convinced that even a successful rescue mission would lead to some hostage deaths and further inflame anti-U.S. activity in the Islamic states of the region. He concluded that U.S. national interests in the Persian Gulf would be severely injured by a military raid and that the operation might conceivably force the Iranians into the arms of the Soviets.

> During this forty-five-minute meeting, President Carter asked Sec-
> retary Vance to present his views to the National Security Council later
> that afternoon.

I had disagreed with policy decisions in the past, but accepting that men of forceful views would inevitably disagree from time to time, had acquiesced out of loyalty to the president knowing I could not win every battle. The decision to attempt to extract the hostages by force from the center of a city of over five million, more than six thousand miles from the United States, and which could be reached only by flying over difficult terrain, was different: I was convinced that the decision was wrong and that it carried great risks for the hostages and our national interests. It had to be faced squarely. . . .

I pointed out . . . that the formation of the Majlis, to which Khomeini had given jurisdiction over the hostage crisis, could be a major step toward a functioning government with whom we could negotiate in Iran. As for the hostages, I continued, our intelligence was that they were in no physical danger and were in satisfactory health. We had recently received a report from the Red Cross doctors who had examined them. . . .

No one supported my position and the president reaffirmed his April 11 decision. . . .

On . . . April 21 I sadly wrote out a formal letter of resignation, and delivered it to the president.

Source: Vance, *Hard Choices*, 409–11.

DOCUMENT 331: President Carter's War Powers Report to Congress on the Abortive Hostage Rescue Operation in Iran (26 April 1980)

Dear Mr. Speaker: Dear Mr. President:

. . . Beginning approximately 10:30 A.M. EST on April 24, six U.S. C-130 transport aircraft and eight RH-53 helicopters entered Iran airspace. Their crews were not equipped for combat. Some of the C-130 aircraft carried a force of approximately 90 members of the rescue team equipped for combat, plus various support personnel.

From approximately 2 to 4 P.M. EST the six transports and six of the eight helicopters landed at a remote desert site in Iran approximately 200 miles from Tehran where they disembarked the rescue team, commenced refueling operations and began to prepare for the subsequent phases.

During the flight to the remote desert site, two of the eight helicopters developed operating difficulties. One was forced to return to the carrier *Nimitz*; the second was forced to land in the desert, but its crew was taken aboard another of the helicopters and proceeded on to the landing site. Of the six helicopters which landed at the remote desert site, one developed a serious hydraulic problem and was unable to continue with the mission. The operational plans called for a minimum of six helicopters in good operational condition able to proceed from the desert site. Eight helicopters had been included in the force to provide sufficient redundancy without imposing excessive strains on the refueling and exit requirements of the operation. When the number of helicopters available to continue dropped to five, it was determined that the operation could not proceed as planned. Therefore, on the recommendation of the force commander and my military advisers, I decided to cancel the mission and ordered the United States Armed Forces involved to return from Iran.

During the process of withdrawal, one of the helicopters accidentally collided with one of the C-130 aircraft, which was preparing to take off, resulting in the death of eight personnel and the injury of several others. At this point, the decision was made to load all surviving personnel aboard the remaining C-130 aircraft and to abandon the remaining helicopters at the landing site. Altogether, the United States Armed Forces remained on the ground for a total of approximately three hours. The five remaining aircraft took off about 5:45 P.M. EST and departed from Iran airspace without further incident at about 8:00 P.M. EST on April 24. No United States Armed Forces remain in Iran.

The remote desert area was selected to conceal this phase of the mission from discovery. At no time during the temporary presence of United States Armed Forces in Iran did they encounter Iranian forces of any type. We believe, in fact, that no Iranian military forces were in the desert area, and that the Iranian forces were unaware of the presence of United States Armed Forces until after their departure from Iran. As planned, no hostilities occurred during this phase of the mission—the only phase that was executed.

At one point during the period in which United States Armed Forces elements were on the ground at the desert landing site a bus containing forty-four Iranian civilians happened to pass along a nearby road. The bus was stopped and then disabled. Its occupants were detained by United States Armed Forces until their departure, and then released unharmed. One truck closely followed by a second vehicle also passed by while United States Armed Forces elements were on the ground. These elements stopped the truck by a shot into its headlights. The driver ran to the second vehicle which then escaped across the desert. Neither of these incidents affected the subsequent decision to terminate the mission.

Our rescue team knew, and I knew, that the operation was certain to be dangerous. We were all convinced that if and when the rescue phase of the operation had been commenced, it had an excellent chance of success. They were all volunteers; they were all highly trained. I met with their leaders before they went on this operation. They knew then what hopes of mine and of all Americans they carried with them. I share with the nation the highest respect and appreciation for the ability and bravery of all who participated in the mission.

To the families of those who died and who were injured, I have expressed the admiration I feel for the courage of their loved ones and the sorrow that I feel personally for their sacrifice.

The mission on which they were embarked was a humanitarian mission. It was not directed against Iran. It was not directed against the people of Iran. It caused no Iranian casualties.

This operation was ordered and conducted pursuant to the President's powers under the Constitution as Chief Executive and as Commander-in-Chief of the United States Armed Forces, expressly recognized in Section 8(d)(1) of the War Powers Resolution. In carrying out this operation, the United States was acting wholly within its right in accordance with Article 51 of the United Nations Charter, to protect and rescue its citizens where the government of the territory in which they are located is unable or unwilling to protect them.

Source: Weekly Compilation of Presidential Documents, Jimmy Carter, Vol. 16, no. 18 (Washington: GPO, 1980), 777–80.

DOCUMENT 332: Iranian President Bani-Sadr Contends that Jordan-Ghotbzadeh Agreement for Hostage Release Was Scrubbed after Khomeini-Reagan Contacts (April–October 1980)

Consolidating the mullahs' power was not Khomeini's only reason for entrusting the hostage affair to parliament. There was talk within the government of deals being made prior to the American elections. I have proof of contacts between Khomeini and the supporters of Ronald Reagan as early as the spring of 1980.

Khomeini's justification of a "no show" was the end result of these contacts, the sole purpose of which was to handicap Carter's re-election bid by preventing the hostages' release before the American elections in November 1980. Rafsanjani, Beheshti, and Ahmed Khomeini played a key role in proposing this agreement to the Reagan team. I did everything I could to change Khomeini's mind, but I failed. . . .

Also in the spring of 1980, Khomeini's nephew residing in Spain was contacted by some Americans close to Reagan. They proposed an agreement: not a reconciliation between governments but a secret agreement between leaders. He came to see me and told me that the Americans wanted to establish secret relations with me, and that if I refused, they would make the same offer to Beheshti and Rafsanjani. I categorically refused to become involved in any such scheme. I have never mentioned this until now, because I did not want to cause trouble for this Iranian.

It is no coincidence that everyone who agreed to deal with the Americans—Beheshti, Rafsanjani, Behzad Nabavi, Moshen Rezai—later held important positions in the regime. Except for Beheshti, who was assassinated, they all survived their swindling and their numerous betrayals. . . . It is no coincidence either that their names were all mentioned in connection with Irangate. . . .

When, on October 15, we had completely contained the Iraqi army, I became truly dangerous to the mullahs. They therefore had to act. They knew that my Achilles' heel was the hostage problem. On that day, Rajai, the prime minister, went to the United Nations without consulting Khomeini or me. He apparently learned in New York that Iran was completely isolated because of the hostage affair, which we all knew. On his return trip, during a stopover in Algiers, Algerian diplomats made it clear to him that a solution was urgently needed.

Suddenly, Rajai announced on October 22 that Iran wanted neither American spare parts nor American arms. Rafsanjani repeated the same thing to Eric Rouleau, who published it in *Le Monde* on October 24, 1980. Strange, isn't it?

Everyone knew that we needed spare parts. The enemy was on our territory, we had used all our forces to contain it, and the head of parliament, a member of the Defense Council, was making a statement like this without consulting anyone! It became very clear to me that the Carter solution had been ruled out. Carter was offering the arms we had purchased during the Shah's reign; they were paid for and we desperately needed them. Actually, the mullahs were negotiating secretly with Reagan. To be sure, one of their conditions involved arms, but they could not at any cost be routed through me since they were intended for forces loyal to the mullahs, the Revolutionary Guards in particular.

Reagan's people and the mullahs agreed that the arms would be shipped as soon as Bani-Sadr was out of the picture. This is precisely what happened. The first contract was signed in early March 1981 and the first shipments arrived in July, immediately after my departure. The arrangements had been made around October 22, the day Rajai made that mysterious statement about not wanting American arms. One had to read between the lines.

Source: Bani-Sadr, *My Turn to Speak*, 28–29, 33–34.

DOCUMENT 333: An American Embassy Hostage Recalls Discovering that Air Attacks Against Tehran Were Part of Iran-Iraq War (22 September 1980)

BARRY ROSEN (press attache): From that time on we had blackouts every night. We heard a lot of artillery fire and commotion, and it was hard for us to know who was doing what to whom. Over the course of the next few days, we heard chanting in the prison courtyard where the Iranians gathered for their evening prayers. This was nothing new. They'd been chanting for some time, and the usual fare had been, *"Marg bar Carter! Marg bar Amrika!"* [Death to Carter! Death to America!] But after the bombing raids there was an added attraction. They were chanting something new. . . . I was able to figure it out. I said, "Hey, guys, they're chanting *'Marg bar Sadam Hussein!'* " . . . So immediately we knew that something was going on between Iran and Iraq, and that Iraq was doing the bombing.

Source: Wells, *444 Days*, 389.

REAL BARGAINING AFTER THE 1980 ELECTION, NOVEMBER 1980–JANUARY 1981

Because President Carter chose to assign first priority to saving the hostages' lives, he allowed the United States to suffer humiliation for over a year at the hands of hate-mongering Iranian militants. This national humiliation was translated into his own defeat in the election of 1980. It is significant that even though in the fall of 1980 the Iranian government committed itself to releasing the hostages, it did not finally do so until after the inauguration of Ronald Reagan as president.

DOCUMENT 334: Hostage Barry Rosen Remembers First Anniversary of His Capture (4 November 1980)

Election Day would mark the first anniversary of our capture. The October preceding it was a day-by-day drag, even in comparison to earlier months. Daily topics of conversation had come down to increasing cold in the cell and the old, futile discussion of possibilities and expectations. The sounds of whipping had stopped. From the shortened wait for the toilet and fewer plates of food set out on the corridor floor at meal times—each cell door was opened separately to get them—it was clear that our own numbers were decreasing; and apart from us, the large prison seemed empty. We guessed that heating was the cause. The autumn chill almost froze the air inside the thick stone walls, and guards wore khaki coats over sweaters with hoods indoors.

Early on the morning of November 5, I knocked on the door and flew the ragged toilet flag. Ahmad himself answered.

"What's the news?" I asked.

"Reagan by three to one," he said. "I just heard it on the Voice of America." . . .

Source: Barbara Rosen and Barry Rosen, with George Feifer, *The Destined Hour: The Hostage Crisis and One Family's Ordeal* (Garden City, N.Y.: Doubleday, 1982), 276.

DOCUMENT 335: NSC Adviser Brzezinski Reflects upon the Final Months of the Carter Presidency (November 1980–January 1981)

After the election, the only question facing us was whether we would resolve the hostage issue before leaving office. Not only was this a matter of personal pride for Carter; it also stemmed from the President's desire not to leave the new Administration encumbered by a painful dilemma. During this period Christopher and Cutler continued their effort at negotiations, and I recommended that we send signals that we might be inclined to provide some military aid to the Iraqis if the Iranians were not more forthcoming. . . .

We continued to be worried that at some point the hostages might be put on trial, and this issue was debated at an NSC meeting on December 19, 1980. The President took a hard line: "We mustn't rush into a response, and the fact they are bargaining with us rather than breaking with us publicly indicates that they still may be interested in negotiating. It is hard to tell when they will put any of our hostages on trial. I agree with Zbig that we cannot go out of office with a whimpering situation. We should therefore inform our allies as to what we would do if the trials start. We should recapitulate our plans to them and state the consequences of such trials or of any injury to the hostages."

The logjam in the negotiating process was broken between Christmas and January 20. Our intermediary now was Algeria, and in day-and-night negotiations Christopher and his associates were able to put together a package in which the release of the hostages was a quid pro quo for undoing our punitive sanctions against Iran. There would be no formal apologies, no restitution to Iran of the Shah's alleged fortune, no humiliating one-sided concessions. But even then the Iranians were not to deny themselves one last gesture of human pettiness: they made certain that the hostages were not released while Jimmy Carter was still President of the United States. . . .

It was in these trying months that the moral strength of Jimmy Carter stood out, and that deserves history's acknowledgment. A lesser man, faced with the enormously compelling task of reelection, vilified by the press and by his opponents as weak because of the humiliation inflicted upon us by Iran, might have been tempted to do something dramatic, irrespective of the effect on the lives of the hostages or of geopolitical consequences. Had Carter decided to embark on a series of punitive actions, actions which might have resulted in the death of some or all of the hostages but given the American people relief from their mounting frustration, his electoral chances would have been greatly increased. Instead, he remained steadfast and strong in his view that until we had another practical option, we should persist on the negotiating path. And Jimmy Carter succeeded in preserving both lives and our national interest, but at the cost of his Presidency.

Source: Brzezinski, *Power and Principle,* 506–9.

DOCUMENT 336: Islamic Iran's Terms for Release of the Hostages (2 November 1980)

1. Since, in the past, the American Government has always interfered in various ways in Iran's political and military affairs, she should make

a pledge and a promise that from now on she will in no way interfere, either directly or indirectly, politically or militarily, in the affairs of the Islamic Republic of Iran.

2. Unfreeze all of our assets and to put [*sic*] all these assets and all the assets and capital of Iran which are in America or which are in organizations belonging to America and to American subjects in other countries at the disposal of Iran in such a way that the Government of the Islamic Republic of Iran can use them in any manner it wishes. And that the decree of the American President dated 14 November 1979 and subsequent decrees concerning the blocking of Iranian assets will be declared null and void. . . .

3. Abrogation and cancellation of all economic and financial decisions and measures against the Islamic Republic of Iran and implementation of all the necessary administrative and legal measures with regard to cancellation and abrogation of all claims by the U.S. Government and U.S. companies and institutions against Iran in any form and for any reason. Implementation by the American Government of all necessary administrative and legal measures with regard to not raising any form of new legal or criminal or financial measures by official and unofficial and legal persons. . . .

4. Return of the assets of the cursed Shah, while officially recognizing the measures taken by Iran and their effectiveness in asserting its sovereignty in confiscating the assets of the cursed Shah and his close relatives, whose assets, according to Iranian laws belong to the Iranian nation. . . .

According to this recommendation, the Islamic Republic Government will release all 52 U.S. criminals in return for the fulfillment of these conditions by the U.S. Government. However, should some of these conditions require more time, then when all conditions are accepted by the U.S. Government, with the fulfillment of each condition a number of criminals will be released at the discretion of the Islamic Government.

Source: U.S. Department of State, *American Foreign Policy: Basic Documents, 1977–1980,* Report of Iranian Special Commission, November 2, 1980 (Washington: GPO, 1983), 774–75.

DOCUMENT 337: Declarations and Agreements of Algiers Accords (19–20 January 1981)

The Government of the Democratic and Popular Republic of Algeria, having been requested by the Governments of the Islamic Republic of

Iran and the United States of America to serve as an intermediary in seeking a mutually acceptable resolution of the crisis in their relations arising out of the detention of the 52 United States nationals in Iran, has consulted extensively with the two governments as to the commitments which each is willing to make in order to resolve the crisis within the framework of the four points stated in the Resolution of November 2, 1980, of the Islamic Consultative Assembly of Iran. On the basis of formal adherences received from Iran and the United States, the Government of Algeria now declares that the following interdependent commitments have been made by the two governments:

General Principles

The undertakings reflected in this Declaration are based on the following general principles:

A. Within the framework of and pursuant to the provisions of the two Declarations . . . , the United States will restore the financial position of Iran . . . to that which existed prior to November 14, 1979. In this context, the United States commits itself to ensure the mobility and free transfer of all Iranian assets within its jurisdiction. . . .

B. It is the purpose of both parties . . . to terminate all litigation as between the government of each party and the nationals of the other, and to bring about the settlement and termination of all such claims through binding arbitration. . . .

Point I: Non-Intervention in Iranian Affairs

1. The United States pledges that it is and from now on will be the policy of the United States not to intervene, directly or indirectly, politically or militarily, in Iran's internal affairs.

Points II and III: Return of Iranian Assets and Settlement of U.S. Claims.

2. Iran and the United States (hereafter "the parties") will immediately select a mutually agreeable Central Bank (hereafter "the Central Bank") to act under the instructions of the Government of Algeria (hereafter "the Algerian Central Bank" as depositary arrangements with the Central Bank in accordance with the terms of this Declaration. All funds placed in escrow with the Central Bank pursuant to this Declaration shall be held in an account in the name of the Algerian Central Bank. Certain procedures for implementing the obligations set forth in this Declaration . . . are separately set forth in certain Undertakings of the Governments of the United States and Iran. . . .

3. The depositary arrangements shall provide that, in the event that the Government of Algeria certifies to the Algerian Central Bank that the 52 U.S. nationals have safely departed from Iran, the Algerian Central Bank will thereupon instruct the Central Bank to transfer immediately all monies or other assets in escrow with the Central Bank . . . pro-

vided that at any time prior to the making of such certification by the Government of Algeria, each of the two parties shall have the right on seventy-two hours notice to terminate its commitments under this Declaration. . . .

4. Commencing upon completion of the requisite escrow arrangements with the Central Bank, the United States will bring about the transfer to the Central Bank of all gold bullion which is owned by Iran and which is in the custody of the Federal Reserve Bank of New York.

5. Commencing upon completion of the requisite escrow arrangements with the Central Bank, the United States will bring about the transfer to the Central Bank, to the account of the Algerian Central Bank, of all Iranian deposits and securities which on or after November 14, 1979, stood upon the books of overseas banking offices of U.S. banks, together with interest thereon through December 31, 1980, to be held by the Central Bank, to the account of the Algerian Central Bank, in escrow until such time as their transfer or return is required in accordance with Paragraph 3 of this Declaration. . . .

11. Upon the making by the Government of Algeria of the certification described in Paragraph 3, the United States will promptly withdraw all claims now pending against Iran before the International Court of Justice and will thereafter bar and preclude the prosecution against Iran of any pending or future claim of the United States or a United States national arising out of events occurring before the date of this Declaration related to (A) the seizure of the 52 United States nationals on November 4, 1979, (B) their subsequent detention, (C) injury to the United States property or property of the United States nationals within the United States Embassy compound in Tehran after November 3, 1979, and (D) injury to the United States nationals or their property as a result of popular movements in the course of the Islamic Revolution in Iran which were not an act of the Government of Iran. . . .

   Point IV: Return of the Assets of the Family of the Former Shah

12. Upon the making by the Government of Algeria of the certification described in Paragraph 3, the United States will freeze, and prohibit any transfer of, property and assets in the United States within the control of the estate of the former Shah or of any close relative of the former Shah served as a defendant in U.S. litigation brought by Iran to recover such property and assets as belonging to Iran. . . .

17. If any other dispute arises between the parties as to the interpretation or performance of any provision of this Declaration, either party may submit the dispute to binding arbitration by the tribunal established by, and in accordance with the provisions of, the Claims Settlement Agreement.

Source: U.S. State Department, *Bulletin* 81, no. 2047 (February 1981), 1–15.

ENDGAME: LESSONS FOR PRESIDENTS AND CITIZENS

DOCUMENT 338: A Hostage's Perspective on the Effect of the Crisis on America (1981)

COL. CHARLES SCOTT (Defense Liaison Office in Tehran): I couldn't help but contrast my return from Iran with my return from Vietnam. When I came home from the Vietnam War, there weren't any brass bands and flags. . . .

So I really didn't expect the welcome home that we received. Even though we had been told what to expect, I took it all with a grain of salt. My memories were of a different era. I saw mobs and mobs of Americans cheering, and that did me a whole world of good. I could see that it was a reception that cut across all races and age groups. . . . To see and feel the rejuvenation of the American spirit was an amazing thing.

After all of the downers we've had in American politics since World War II, particularly in the Vietnam and Watergate era, the hostages became an international political issue where the United States was clearly in the right. That was important for our people. We needed it. Instead of being a divisive issue, it brought people together. Everyone felt the same way. So when we were finally released, it gave people a chance to celebrate America, and to celebrate the fact that we were in the right. I looked out at those crowds and crowds of people that welcomed us home and said to myself, "Chuck, they're not celebrating you. They're celebrating themselves. You're only a symbol of something that goes much, much deeper than the release of fifty-two people from a foreign prison."

Source: Wells, *444 Days*, 450–51.

DOCUMENT 339: *New York Times* Columnist Reports that President Carter's Priority Was to "Put the Hostages' Lives First" (1981)

In an interview in Plains after leaving office, Carter remembered that he had experienced, almost immediately, a nightmare vision that would haunt him for months to come. "I could picture the revolutionaries keeping the 72 hostages, or whatever the number was at the time, in the compound," Carter said, "and assassinating one of them every morning at sunrise until the Shah was returned to Iran or until we agreed to some other act in response to their blackmail. It's still a very vivid memory to me." . . .

Jimmy Carter had second thoughts of his own. "I've thought about it a lot," he said. "The first few weeks, or even months, I neither did anything nor had to do anything to keep the issue of burning importance in the minds of the American public. But later, when the press was excluded from Iran, I think the issue would have died down a lot more if I had decided to ignore the fate of the hostages or if I had decided just to stop any statements on the subject. That may have been the best approach."

He paused for a moment, reflecting on what he had said. "But," he continued, as though arguing with himself, "if that had happened, what would the Iranians have done to the hostages to revive the issue? That was always a concern to me."

Carter said he thought both sides had learned bitter lessons from the experience. "Iran suffered horribly," he said. "They became vulnerable and, I think, precipitated the Iraqi invasion." For the United States, it was vivid proof that "there are limits, even on our nation's great strength," he said quietly, his voice trailing off. "It's the same kind of impotence that a powerful person feels when his child is kidnapped."

Source: Terence Smith, "Putting the Hostages' Lives First," in *No Hiding Place: Inside Report on the Hostage Crisis* (New York: Times Books, 1981), 190, 214.

DOCUMENT 340: American Hostage and Chargé d'Affaires to Iran Bruce Laingen Comments on Family Liaison Action Group and the "Yellow Ribbon" Campaign in the United States (1992)

As my wife and as founder of FLAG (Family Liaison Action Group) and the originator of the yellow ribbon campaign, Penne has my special thanks and respect for the role she played in the crisis. . . .

For 444 days, the American public responded with flags, prayer vigils, bell ringing, and—in abundance—with yellow ribbons. And on our return the nation celebrated with us in a remarkable surge of national patriotism. For at least a brief time, Americans felt better about themselves. Perhaps some of that remains a part of our collective national psyche.

The lesson is clear and has been throughout our history. When Americans sense agreement on a cause, we are capable of responding as a community, and we are the stronger for it. Desert Storm is only the most recent example. . . .

My wife Penne's identification with the yellow ribbon as a symbol of caring and remembrance continued throughout the 1980s and especially during Desert Storm. In April 1991, a Washington ceremony saw her present the original "Mother of All Yellow Ribbons," the one she had wrapped around the oak tree in our front yard during the hostage crisis, to the Library of Congress.

Source: Bruce Laingen, *Yellow Ribbon: The Secret Journal of Bruce Laingen* (Washington: Brassey's, 1992), 294.

FURTHER READING

Bill, James A. *The Eagle and the Lion: The Tragedy of American-Iranian Relations* (1988).

Brzezinski, Zbigniew. *Power and Principle: Memoirs of the National Security Adviser, 1977–1981* (1983).

Buhite, Russell D. *Lives at Risk: Hostages and Victims in American Foreign Policy* (1995).

Jordan, Hamilton. *Crisis: The Last Year of the Carter Presidency* (1982).

Kuniholm, Bruce R. *The Origins of the Cold War in the Near East: Great Power Conflict and Diplomacy in Iran, Turkey and Greece* (1980).

Laingen, Bruce. *Yellow Ribbon: The Secret Journal of Bruce Laingen* (1992).

Ledeen, Michael, and William Lewis. *Debacle: The American Failure in Iran* (1981).

McFadden, Robert, Joseph Treaster, and Maurice Carroll. *No Hiding Place: New York Times Inside Report on the Hostage Crisis* (1981).

Rosen, Barbara, and Barry Rosen, with George Feifer. *The Destined Hour: The Hostage Crisis and One Family's Ordeal* (1982).

Sick, Gary. *All Fall Down: America's Tragic Encounter with Iran* (1985).

———. *October Surprise: America's Hostages in Iran and the Election of Ronald Reagan* (1991).

Smith, Gaddis. *Morality, Reason and Power* (1986).

Part VIII

The Persian Gulf War with Iraq, 1990–1991

On 2 August 1990 President Saddam Hussein of Iraq ordered the occupation of neighboring Kuwait with 80,000 Iraqi troops. He had several probable motives for his action: to take territory historically considered a part of Iraq; to punish the Kuwaitis for pumping so much oil that they helped depress the world price of that commodity at a time when Iraq needed oil revenues to retire its large debt from its war with Iran; and as the first step in a move to achieve political and economic domination of the Persian Gulf region. Not incidental in Saddam's calculation was his belief that he could get away with his aggression—largely because the United States had tilted in his favor during the lengthy war with the Islamic Republic of Iran, providing him with nearly $40 billion in credit sales of arms during the 1980s. Within three months, the Iraqis had more than quadrupled their force in Kuwait.

Convinced that Saddam Hussein's control of a major portion of the world's supply of oil would be inimical to American economic interests and those of its allies, President George Bush quickly announced on 8 August that "this aggression will not stand." He also began comparing Saddam to Adolf Hitler as a way of suggesting that the Iraqi move had its antecedent in the violently expansionist behavior of the fascist state of the 1930s and 1940s, Bush's own formative years. As his next political step, the president sent 180,000 American troops to Saudi Arabia as a "shield" to protect that country. He followed this by organizing an international coalition against Iraq that included other Arab states as well as the Soviet Union. In early November he doubled the number of U.S. forces in Saudi Arabia.

In a departure from the behavior of other post–World War II presidents, Bush then went to Congress for an authorization to use force to evict the Iraqis from Kuwait, an authorization that he received after intense congressional debate. What had originally been called Operation Desert Shield to protect Saudi Arabia was about to become Operation Desert Storm. After a month-long bombing attack on targets in Iraq, the U.S.-led coalition forces on 24 February 1991 launched a ground offensive against the Iraqi army. In just 100 hours the Iraqis were defeated, a stunning development given the size and strength of the Iraqi military, which numbered 545,000 men, 5,000 tanks, 500 fighter aircraft, biological and chemical weapons, and hundreds of Soviet-supplied missiles. Even more stunning were the comparative losses: the United States suffered 136 killed; Iraq, 100,000. But while as a result of this war the United States liberated Kuwait and badly bloodied Iraq's military, it did not remove Saddam Hussein from power, a resolution of the conflict that remains even today unpopular with many Americans.

CHRONOLOGY

1985

March. Gorbachev assumes power in USSR

July–August. Arms sales to Iran for U.S. hostages

1986

April 14–15. U.S. bombing raid on Libya

October 11–12. Gorbachev-Reagan summit in Iceland

1987

January–August. Iran-Contra hearings

February 26. Tower Commission (commission created in 1987 by President Ronald Reagan to investigate and report on the Iran-Contra affair) Report released

May 17. Iraqi missile damages U.S. frigate *Stark*, kills 37 sailors

August. U.S. Navy escorting reflagged Kuwaiti oil tankers in Gulf

1988

July. U.S. warship shoots down Iranian passenger jet

November. George Bush elected president

December. Terrorists blow up a Pan Am jet over Scotland

1989

June 4. Chinese repress democracy movement

November 9. Berlin Wall pulled down

December 2. Bush-Gorbachev summit in Malta

December 20. U.S. invasion of Panama

1990

July 25. Ambassador Glaspie meets with Saddam Hussein

August 2. Iraq invades Kuwait

August 8. President Bush declares "This will not stand"

August 23. Alex Molnar's "Open Letter" to President Bush

October 3. Germany unified after 45 years

November 29. Vice President Quayle's Seton Hall address

1991

January 12. Congress authorizes use of force against Iraq

January 15. Iraq ignores UN deadline; air campaign begins

February 24. Gen. Schwarzkopf leads attack against Iraqi forces

February 27. Bush declares Persian Gulf War is over

August 19. Gorbachev survives coup attempt

December. Anderson released by Islamic Jihad after 2,455 days

December 25. Breakup of USSR; Gorbachev resigns

1992

November. Bill Clinton elected president

A BORDER DISPUTE AMONG ARABS, 1932–1990

DOCUMENT 341: Iraqi Prime Minister and Kuwaiti Ruler Reaffirm the Kuwait-Iraq Border Drawn at the 1913 UK-Turkish London Convention (July–August 1932)

Iraqi Prime Minister Nuri Pasha to League of Nations Secretary-General. July 21, 1932.

I think your Excellency will agree that the time has now come when it is desirable to reaffirm the existing frontier between Iraq and Koweit.

I therefore request that the necessary action may be taken to obtain the agreement of the competent authority or authorities in Koweit to the following description of the existing frontier between the two countries:—

From the intersection of the Wadi-el-Audja with the Batin and thence northwards along the Batin to a point just south of the latitude of Safwan;

thence eastwards passing south of Safwan Wells, Jebel Sanam and Um Qasr leaving them to Iraq and so on to the junction of the Khor Zobeir with the Khor Abdullah. The islands of Warbah, Bubiyan, Maskan (or Mashjan), Failakah, Auhah, Kubbar, Qaru, Umm-el-Maradin appertain to Koweit.

* * * * *

Letter from the Ruler of Kuwait to the League of Nations. August 10, 1932.

WITH the hand of pleasure we have received your confidential letter dated the 7th instant (Rabi Thani 1351 [the 9th August, 1932]), and have noted the contents of same, as well as the translation of . . . the letter dated the 21st July, 1932, of his Excellency Nuri Pasha-as-Said, the Iraq Prime Minister, regarding the Iraq-Koweit frontier. We also have noted from Hon. the Political Resident's letter dated the 30th July, 1932, that the frontier proposed by the Iraq Prime Minister is approved of by His Majesty's Government [Iraq/Kuwait were former protectorates of Great Britain]. And, therefore, we beg to inform you that we agree to reaffirm the existing frontier between Iraq and Koweit as described in the Iraq Prime Minister's letter.

Source: John N. Moore, *Crisis in the Gulf: Enforcing the Rule of Law*, Vol. 1, 2nd series, *Terrorism: Documents of International and Local Control* (New York: Oceana Publications, 1992), 609–10.

DOCUMENT 342: Agreed Minutes of Borders Between Kuwait and Iraq (4 October 1963)

In an attempt to resolve their border dispute and gain admission into the World Bank, the Iraqi Prime Minister invited a Kuwaiti delegation to Baghdad. On 4 October 1963 they held a meeting to map out their mutual border and released this joint communiqué.

The talks between the two delegations were conducted in an atmosphere rich in fraternal amity, tenacity to the Arab bond and consciousness of the close ties of neighbourliness and mutual interests. . . .

The two delegations have agreed to the following:

1. The Republic of Iraq recognized the independence and complete sovereignty of the State of Kuwait with its boundaries as specified in the letter of the Prime Minister of Iraq dated 21.7.1932 and which was accepted by the ruler of Kuwait in his letter dated 10.8.1932. . . .

In order to realize all the foregoing objectives, they shall immediately establish diplomatic relations between them at the level of ambassadors.

Source: Moore, *Crisis in the Gulf,* 631–33.

U.S. RESPONDS TO IRAQI INVASION OF KUWAIT WITH DESERT SHIELD, AUGUST–DECEMBER 1990

DOCUMENT 343: Text of the Meeting Between Iraqi President Saddam Hussein and U.S. Ambassador April C. Glaspie, as Released by the Government of Iraq (25 July 1990)

SADDAM HUSSEIN: . . . You know that our relations with the United States were severed [from 1967] until 1984. You are aware of the circumstances of and the reasons for the break in relations. We made it clear to you that the decision to restore ties with the U.S. was actually made in 1980, about two months before the outbreak of the war between us and Iran. But once war had broken out, given the opportunity for misunderstanding, we were careful that our conduct in this and in all-important matters should not be misinterpreted by our counterparts, and we postponed the resumption of relations until the hoped-for day when the war would end. But the war dragged on for a long time. . . . So in affirming our commitment to the principle of nonalignment, we had to restore ties with the U.S. . . . This took place in 1984. . . .

However, the relationship, while still new, suffered a number of traumas as it ran its course. The most important blow to the relationship was in 1986 (two years after the resumption of ties), in the form of what came to be called Irangate. By coincidence, that year Iran occupied the Fao Peninsula. . . .

That was the tenor of our relationship. Nagging suspicions grew after we liberated the Fao Peninsula, propaganda got mixed up with politics, our suspicions surfaced anew, and a big question mark appeared as to what the United States was after, seeing as it wasn't happy with the results of the fighting through which we liberated our territory. . . .

Then we were confronted with the start of a policy that forced down the price of oil. America, which speaks of democracy, began to lose patience with the views of the other side. An information campaign was launched against Saddam Hussein by the official American Information

Center [Voice of America]. The United States thought that Iraq was in a situation similar to that of Poland, Romania, or Czechoslovakia. . . .

Kuwait and the United Arab Emirates were the front for this policy aimed at humiliating Iraq and robbing it of the opportunity for a life of happiness, and yet you know that our relations with the Emirates and with Kuwait used to be good. In addition, while we were busy with the war [with Iran, 1980–1988], the state of Kuwait was expanding at the expense of our territory.

You might say that this is just propaganda, in which case we refer you to a single document, called the "Patrol Line," which is the line of demarcation established by the Arab League, with the intention of keeping any military forces well clear of that line in 1961—that is, away from their side of the line.

Go and check for yourselves, go stand on the Kuwaiti side and see if you can't spot police stations, farms, and oil installations to a considerable depth from this line. All these facilities and installations were set up where none had existed before in order to confront Iraq with a fait accompli. This was going on while the Kuwaiti government enjoyed stability, whereas the government in Iraq kept changing—until well after 1968, for ten years after that date, we were busy with many things— once in the north [Kurdish insurrection], then once again in the 1973 war, and there were many other things too that kept us busy. Then the war with Iran came along ten years ago. . . .

Let me be quite clear on this point: We shall obtain every single one of Iraq's rights mentioned in the memorandum [submitted by Iraq to the Arab League on disputes with Kuwait, 21 July 1990]. This might not take place right away, after one month or even a year, but we will secure them all, because we are not the sort who will forgo our rights. . . . Kuwait and the Emirates have no historic rights, no legitimate basis, and no need to usurp our rights. If they are in need, so are we. . . .

We understand perfectly when America says that it wants to ensure the flow of oil. We understand when America says it wants ties of friendship with states in the region, that it wants to expand the scope of common interests in various fields. But what we cannot understand are the attempts to encourage some to do harm to Iraq. . . .

It is out of the question that we should ask our people to bleed rivers of blood for eight years and then tell them that they now have to accept the aggression of Kuwait, the Emirates, the U.S., or Israel. We do not place all these countries on the same footing. In the first place, it pains us that matters between us, Kuwait, and the Emirates should come to such a point. The solution for it is to be found in the Arab context and through direct bilateral relations. . . .

What does the summoning of the Zionist minister of war [Israeli Defense Minister Moshe Arens met with Defense Secretary Dick Cheney in

Washington on 21 July 1990] at this time to America mean? What do these inflammatory statements that have been coming out of Israel in the past three or four days mean, and the talk of an increasing probability that war is at hand? . . .

You shower the usurper with your economic and political favors, with arms and with praise in the media. I wait for the day when, for every three words of praise for the usurper, you will have just one kind word for the Arabs. When will humanity have its day in the form of a just American decision, which will give the same weight to the human rights of 200 million people as it does to the human rights of three million Jews? . . .

Of course, I do not place all these states on the same footing. Israel has usurped Arab land. America is supporting it. But the Emirates and Kuwait are not. They are Arabs after all. Yet when they insist on weakening Iraq, they are helping our enemies—under those conditions, Iraq has a right to defend itself. . . .

Convey my regards to President Bush.

I hope that he will look into this matter himself, and not leave it in the hands of the clique in the State Department—that does not include the secretary of state and [Assistant Secretary John H.] Kelly. . . .

APRIL C. GLASPIE: I thank you, Mr. President, and it is a great pleasure for a diplomat to meet and talk directly with the president. I clearly understand your message. We studied history at school. They taught us to say freedom or death. I think you know well that we as a people have had our experience with the colonialists.

Mr. President, you mentioned many things during this meeting on which I cannot comment on behalf of my government. But with your permission, I will comment on two points. You spoke of friendship and I believe it was clear from the letters sent by our president to you on the occasion of your National Day that he emphasizes . . . (interrupted)

SADDAM: He was kind and his expressions met with our appreciation and respect. . . .

GLASPIE: I have a direct instruction from the president personally to deepen and expand the scope of relations with Iraq.

SADDAM: But how? We too have this desire. But matters are running contrary to this desire.

GLASPIE: The more we talk, the less likely that becomes. . . . I saw the Diane Sawyer program on ABC [on ethnic genocide and the nuclear program in Iraq]. And what happened in that program was cheap and unjust. It is a true picture of what happens in the American media— even to American politicians themselves. These are the methods the Western media employs. I am pleased that you add your voice to the diplomats who stand up to the media. Because your appearance in the media, even for five minutes, would help us to make the American people understand Iraq. This would increase mutual understanding. If the American president had control of the media, his job would be much easier.

Mr. President, not only do I want to say that President Bush wants better and deeper relations with Iraq, but he also wants "a historic" Iraqi contribution to peace and prosperity in the Middle East. President Bush is an intelligent man. He is not going to declare an economic war against Iraq.

You are right. It is true as you said that we do not want higher prices for oil. But I would ask you to contemplate the desirability of oil not being overpriced. . . .

I admire your extraordinary efforts to rebuild your country. I know you need funds. We understand that and our opinion is that you should have the opportunity to rebuild your country. But we have no opinion on inter-Arab disputes, like your border dispute with Kuwait. [In her testimony before the Senate Foreign Relations Committee on 20 March 1991, Glaspie acknowledged that she made a statement on border disputes, but that she also had said, "But we insist that you settle your disputes with Kuwait nonviolently," emphasizing "that we would insist on settlements being made in a non-violent manner, not by threats, not by intimidation, and certainly not by aggression."]

I served in the American Embassy in Kuwait during the late sixties. Our instructions during this period were that we had nothing to do with this issue and that America had nothing to do with it. James Baker has directed our official spokesman to reemphasize this instruction. We hope you can solve this problem using any suitable methods via [Arab League Secretary Chadli] Klibi or via [Egyptian] President [Hosni] Mubarak. All that we hope is that these issues are solved quickly. [Glaspie claimed she added the word "peacefully" in this exchange.] Nevertheless, may I ask you to see how the issue appears to us?

My assessment after 25 years of service in this area is that your objective must have strong backing from your Arab brothers. I now speak of oil. But you, Mr. President, have fought through a horrific and painful war. Frankly, we cannot help but see that you have deployed large units in the south. Normally that would not be any of our business. But when this is seen in the context of what you said on the anniversary of the Revolution; when we read the details in the two letters of the Foreign Minister; and when we examine the Iraqi point of view that the measures taken by the UAE [United Arab Emirates] and Kuwait are, in the final analysis, tantamount to military aggression against Iraq, then it is reasonable for me at the least to be concerned. And for this reason, I received an instruction to ask you, in the spirit of friendship—not in the spirit of confrontation—about your intentions.

I have simply described the concern of my government. I do not mean that the situation is a simple situation. But our concern is a simple one.

SADDAM: As a country, we have the right to prosper. We have lost so many opportunities. Others should value Iraq's role in protecting them. Even this Iraqi (the president means the interpreter) feels bitter like all other Iraqis. We do not intend to commit aggression but we do not accept aggression from others either. We sent them envoys and hand-written letters. We tried everything. We asked the Custodian of the Two Shrines—King Fahd—to hold a quadripartite summit, but he suggested a meeting at the level of the oil ministers. We agreed. And as you know, the oil ministers [of Iraq, Kuwait, UAE, Qatar, and Saudi Arabia] met in Jiddah. They reached an agreement that fell short of the mark, but we agreed.

Only two days after the meeting, the Kuwaiti oil minister made a statement that contradicted the agreement. We also discussed the issue during the Baghdad summit [of the Arab League in Baghdad on 29–30 May 1990]. After we had finished all the tasks on the agenda, I told the Arab kings and presidents that some brothers were waging an economic war against us, that not all wars are fought with arms, and that we regarded this kind of war as a military action against us. Because if the capabilities of our Army are lowered then, if Iran renewed the war, it could achieve goals that it had been unable to achieve before. And if we lowered the standard of our defenses, then this could encourage Israel to attack us. I said that in front of the Arab kings and presidents. Only I did not mention Kuwait and the UAE by name, because they were my guests. . . .

SADDAM: Brother [Hosni] Mubarak [President of Egypt] told me that the Kuwaitis were scared. They said troops were only 20 kilometers north of the Arab League line (the Kuwaiti border). I said to him that regardless of what is there, whether they are police, border guards, or Army, and regardless of how many are there, and what they are doing, reassure the Kuwaitis. We are not going to do anything from our side until we meet with them. If we see that there is hope when we meet, then nothing will happen. But if we are unable to find a way out, then naturally Iraq will not accept death. . . . And yet wisdom is above every-thing else. There, you now have good news.

TARIQ AZIZ [Iraqi Foreign Minister]: This is a scoop [journalistic ex-clusive].

GLASPIE: I had planned to go to the U.S. next Monday. I hope to meet with President Bush in Washington next week.

Source: Elaine Sciolino, *The Outlaw State: Saddam Hussein's Quest for Power and the Gulf Crisis* (New York: John Wiley and Sons, 1991), 272–84.

DOCUMENT 344: U.S. Ambassador to Kuwait W. Nathaniel Howell Recalls Iraqi Siege of U.S. Embassy (2 August– 13 December 1990)

It was hardly possible to foresee, in those initial moments, that the Embassy would be called upon to hold out against a close Iraqi siege for 110 of the 134 days before our departure on December 13. Had anyone asked then whether we could endure almost four months, with electricity and water cut off and access to the compound tightly controlled by elements of the Iraqi Army, I would have been inclined to say no. . . .

It soon became clear that the crisis would not be solved quickly and that, far from being permitted to depart the war zone, expatriate communities were viewed by Baghdad as hostages against the actions of their governments. As the Kuwaitis demonstrated their rejection of Iraq's pretensions and their commitment to the independence of their country, it likewise became important for embassies to resist Iraqi intimidation, flying their flags as long as possible to demonstrate international opposition to Iraq's illegal activities. Withdrawal was not an option I considered in those circumstances.

. . . With seven other men and women of the Foreign Service, I accepted Washington's charge to hold out as long as possible. I had not doubted that my colleagues, veterans of other Middle East crises, would acquit themselves with distinction. I didn't immediately appreciate, however, our secret weapon—a chance assortment of American civilians who sought refuge in our compound or were snatched from scattered hotels, sometimes moments ahead of Iraqi search parties. . . .

When the opportunity for all expatriates to depart came with unanticipated suddenness in early December, many among us left with mixed emotion. While I understood and accepted the Department's instruction to bring out my staff while leaving the Embassy officially open, a part of me wished it were possible to see the crisis through until Kuwait's liberation.

Source: Ambassador W. Nathaniel Howell, 15 April 1993, in Richard P. Stevens, ed., *The Iraqi Invasion of Kuwait: American Reflections* (Washington: International Education and Communications Group, 1993), 1.

DOCUMENT 345: U.S. Chargé in Baghdad Joseph C. Wilson IV Meets with Saddam Hussein (6 August 1990)

SADDAM: I have been informed about the American position in detail. We understand that up to now, whenever something of this sort happens, whether it is in the Arab world, Europe, Asia, or Latin America, the United States adopts a position. We are not surprised that the United States should condemn an action of this sort, especially as it had no part in it. But I wanted to say that the U.S. should not rush headlong, under the influence of bad advice, into some action that might get it into a tight position.

I say this because it is in our nature, regardless of our convictions or those of the other side, to do what we think is necessary [to prevent] the damage that may result from present or future developments. . . .

I shall talk of the relationship between Iraq and the United States in the light of the developments, and what the future will hold if the U.S. were to take the wrong course of action. . . .

Kuwait was and still is a state with unfixed borders—that is, a state without borders. Until 1961 it was not a state in the opinion of many people. Then certain events took place during the time of Abd al-Karim Qassim, who issued a presidential decree appointing the ruler of Kuwait a provincial governor under Basra, making Kuwait a province of Basra.

Why did this take place in 1961? Abd al-Karim Qassim and all Iraqis knew very well that Kuwait was part of Iraq and that the ruler of Kuwait was really a provincial governor who received a salary from the ruler of Basra in the Ottoman era. That situation continued until 1912. Then World War I came along and a new situation resulted. So, up to now Kuwait was a state but it had no borders. Not to quibble over fine points, the internal developments that took place in Kuwait and Iraq's entry [invasion of Kuwait] should not be taken as a standard for action throughout the Arab world. . . .

. . . [W]e fail to understand the significance of the sudden about-face represented in the statement that the Americans are concerned about Saudi Arabia in light of Iraq's strength and all the talk and the great number of statements that it will be Saudi Arabia's turn after Kuwait. . . .

The Saudis are our brothers; they helped us in the war. At their initiative we secured an oil pipeline, and they gave us financial aid in the form of grants and not loans, some of which we did not even request but which came at their initiative. Things took their natural course. They are our brothers—unless you should spoil things between us and incite them against us—in which case each will have the right to defend its legitimate interests.

Therefore, if you are concerned about Saudi Arabia, there is no objective reason for your concern. If, on the other hand, you are trying to appear to be concerned in order to create anxiety among the Saudis, then that is a different matter. . . .

This leads us to the third point I want to make. There were rumors that Saddam Hussein promised certain Arab officials that he would not resort to force in any way, shape, or form or under any circumstances against Kuwait. We have also learned in one way or another that certain Arab officials have led the Americans to this conclusion. I do not want the Americans to form the impression that we have no regard for our credibility.

I gave no such guarantee to any Arab. What happened is that some officials among our Arab brothers had discussed with me the existence of Iraqi force concentrations toward Kuwait. They told me that the Kuwaitis were anxious and scared. I told them that I would promise not to take any military action before the meeting [of the prime minister of Kuwait and the deputy chairman of the Iraqi Command Council on 31 July–1 August 1990] in Jiddah took place. And that is what happened. . . .

When our vital interests were exposed to certain and premeditated danger and all other means to find a solution failed, we used military force. I address my question here to the president of the United States and to American officials: Where is the danger to American interests, both inside and outside Kuwait?

You know that Iraqi oil has been sold to you ever since we came to power, although relations were severed at the time. The volume of trade increased following the restoration of relations in 1984 and up to the time you decided to embargo Iraqi oil. You were importing about a third of our exports. This came about not at the initiative of the technicians or market preferences but as a result of a political decision.

We are familiar with the declarations that have been made. Your interests are your trade and the continuation of oil supplies to you. What then is the threat that makes you contemplate military action in which you shall be defeated? And I will tell you how you shall be defeated.

You are a great power, and we know that you can hurt us, as I told the ambassador. But you will lose the region afterward. You would not get us to kneel down even if you were to use all your weapons.

You can destroy our scientific, technical, economic, and oil facilities. But the more you destroy, the more difficult it will become for you. After that, we will not hesitate to attack your interests in the region. We even attacked Kuwait once it became clear to us that [we had to choose between] the conspiracy and its dangerous consequences or a proud, peaceful, and capable Iraq. . . .

WILSON: Thank you, Mr. President. I shall certainly relay it to my government. I shall first relay your words by telephone upon my arrival at the embassy, then I shall relay them in writing.

You justly observed that this is a critical period not only for Iraqi-U.S. relations but also for stability in the region and the world.

SADDAM: Why critical to the world?

WILSON: There is anxiety and instability in world markets.

SADDAM: You knew that. We accepted $25 per barrel, and now, had it not been for your embargo, the price would have gone down to $21 per barrel, more or less.

However, when there is a sudden embargo on five million barrels, anxiety arises. We are committed to the OPEC decision of $21 per barrel. . . . Perhaps others, the merchants, will benefit, but not the American people. We have a strong case. A small part of Iraq [Kuwait] instead of respecting greater Iraq and its interests, was encouraged by some to play a conspiratorial role against the economy of Iraq so as to destroy our economy. We defended ourselves without detriment to any other party, such as the United States.

WILSON: . . . In the first part of your message, you mentioned that Kuwait is a part of Iraq.

SADDAM: That is historically accurate. In saying this, we are affirming that Kuwait should have cooperated with Iraq, not conspired against it. Yet Kuwait's paranoia made it conspire against Iraq.

That is the special relationship between Iraq and Kuwait that should have guided its actions. That relationship does not exist with all the other countries, such as Egypt and Saudi Arabia, which have the best of relations with Iraq.

WILSON: It is very important that I understand the precise nature of this relationship.

SADDAM: The nature of this relationship is determined by the relationship between the peoples of the two countries. Neither I nor the Americans nor the Soviets nor anyone else determines them. We are of the opinion that it should be based on shared fraternity and mutual respect.

WILSON: Is that what was missing in the relationship with Kuwait?

SADDAM: Yes, especially in recent months. I kept running after [Kuwaiti Emir Sheik] Jaber [al-Ahmad al-Sabah] so that we could determine where the border should be, and he kept saying, "No, leave it to others." We have documents to substantiate that. We were perplexed by what was happening, then it turned out that he was conspiring against us.

WILSON: Thank you. The second point you raised had to do with your brotherly relations with Saudi Arabia, and you mentioned your nonaggression pact with Saudi Arabia. I wish to convey to you the concern of my government regarding Iraq's intentions now. I feel that you have addressed that concern in a general way, but permit me. . . .

SADDAM: What would it take to put your concerns to rest?

WILSON: I don't know, but I will ask my president. But I do know that you are a clear and frank person. [If] you were to give me your assurances that under current circumstances—as of now we have not witnessed any military action on the part of the United States or Saudi Arabia—under these circumstances I would like to ask for assurances from you that you have no intention of taking any military action against Saudi Arabia.

SADDAM: You may convey my assurances to Saudi Arabia and to everyone in the Middle East. We shall not attack anyone who does not attack us. We shall not harm anyone who does not harm us. Anyone who solicits our friendship shall find us more eager for friendship than he is. This is not an agenda to suit the needs of the hour as some imagine but one due to humanitarian considerations and in the interests of our people. . . .

. . . We would like to know precisely what the legitimate interests of the United States are, and how to reassure the United States about those interests.

I say this not as a tactical ploy because you have imposed an embargo against us—I was careful to wait until after your embargo before I saw you, nor am I trying here and now to get the embargo lifted, or expecting the United States to be in favor of what has taken place—but in order to understand what legitimate U.S. interests are and to advise the United States not to get carried away to the point that it becomes difficult for it to retreat from a position.

WILSON: I shall convey this to my government. I came here with three things on my mind that reflect the concerns of my government. First, there is the nature of the invasion, and you know the position of my government on this point very well. Second, your intentions toward Saudi Arabia, which you have answered. The third point concerns the safety of American citizens, particularly allowing U.S. citizens to leave. You know that Americans are very sensitive about being prevented from leaving. This also concerns Americans in Kuwait, regardless of any withdrawal.

SADDAM: How can you say that there has been no withdrawal, and then say something altogether different?

WILSON: I saw three convoys from Basra, and informed Washington of that.

SADDAM: It took our forces three days to enter Kuwait, so the withdrawal cannot be completed in one day. The withdrawal of forces depends on the international climate. We shall not leave Kuwait a delectable morsel to be swallowed up by anyone, even if we have to fight the whole world.

If the threat to Kuwait increases, we shall double the forces there. The size of our forces will be adapted to fit the size of the threat. When the threat ceases to exist, all forces will be withdrawn. We do not want Kuwait to become another Lebanon. I do not think that it is in [anyone's] interest for Iraqi forces to withdraw in a hurry, which would leave Kuwait to the warring factions.

The provisional government [set up by Iraqi forces on 2 August] was advised to form various militias; we advised them that the Popular Army would suffice.

As to Americans in Kuwait and Iraq, there is a ban on travel that applied to everyone, Iraqis and foreigners, in Iraq and Kuwait. Your sources know that our Army there has been extremely disciplined toward foreigners. Yet the communiqué issued by the Kuwaiti government permits them to travel to Iraq, and over here security clearly reigns.

WILSON: May I ask you directly: When will you allow American citizens, both residents and visitors, to leave?

SADDAM: Rather, when shall we allow foreigners in general to leave?

WILSON: I do not permit myself to talk on behalf of others.

SADDAM: I wanted to make it clear that this restriction does not apply only to the Americans. In due course we will inform you.

WILSON: Please allow me to ask you that you study this question urgently because it is a highly emotional and sensitive issue both for our government and our people.

SADDAM: We understand that and we also understand the humanitarian aspect.

WILSON: Finally, I would like to say two things. You have pointed to the good behavior of Iraqi troops, and your minister and your deputy minister also assured me of this and I think this is expected. Let me draw your attention, and this is an important point, to the fact that last night the house of the counselor of our Embassy in Kuwait was broken into by some Iraqi soldiers. This contradicts the policy that you have stated, and I add that it is also a violation of diplomatic immunity. I would not have said this if you had not brought up the matter.

SADDAM: Yesterday I met with some of our officers and they told me about some elements—Asians, Saudis, and others—who were breaching security in some warehouses. Anyway, if the Iraqi Army had done this, we would acknowledge it and assure you that it was a mistake and we would take measures to punish those involved. This behavior is against our policy.

WILSON: Last point. During these difficult days, especially on the safety of the American citizens. . . .

SADDAM: Do you plan to attack us and for that you want to remove your citizens?

WILSON: No. But it is my duty to give them the freedom to decide to leave. I personally will stay, and I love life here. I would like to say also that during the crisis the doors were always open to me and to my colleagues in the Foreign Ministry from 8 A.M. to 4 P.M. and I appreciate that. I appreciate your wish to meet with me and to reassure me on the fate of our citizens in Kuwait.

Source: Sciolino, *Outlaw State,* 284–93.

DOCUMENT 346: Vice President Dan Quayle Recalls Decision to Begin Operation Desert Shield to Protect Saudi Arabia from Possible Iraqi Invasion (2 August 1990)

I was at home when, at about 9:00, [NSC Assistant Adviser] Bob Gates called with the news. The first thing I did was call [National Security Adviser] Brent Scowcroft to ask if it was necessary to convene the National Security Council that night. Brent was opposed to it and suggested we wait until morning.

That meeting, which was held at 8:00 A.M. seemed routine. The President did allow some reporters in before we got started ("We're not discussing intervention," he said), but once they were gone and we got down to business, there wasn't an overpowering atmosphere of crisis. The various implications of what Saddam had done were calmly assessed, and the normal machinery of government went to work. CIA director Bill Webster said he thought there were now over one hundred thousand Iraqi troops inside Kuwait, and Bob Kimmitt, who was substituting for Jim Baker while the Secretary of State was in the Soviet Union, brought us up to date on what the UN and other diplomatic organizations were doing to condemn the invasion. In terms of punishing Saddam, the only measure really discussed was economic sanctions that would keep his own oil (and now the oil he had captured in Kuwait) off the world markets. The President did not underestimate the seriousness of the situation, and he did say that aggression could not be tolerated, but there was no sudden brainstorming about how we could achieve the military liberation of Kuwait—or even any agreement that that was our objective.

At this point our discussions did not involve pushing Saddam back but rather keeping him from going any further. The real catastrophe everyone feared was an invasion of Saudi Arabia by Iraq, and that's what our military planning was concerned with on that first day. Throughout the 1980s, the United States had wanted Iraq to be strong enough to counter Iran. In doing so, we now realized, we had created a far more dangerous monster.

Just what it might take to protect the Saudis from a move by Saddam was outlined by a general I'd never really noticed before, a man who even that morning seemed like just another briefer from the Pentagon. His name was H. Norman Schwarzkopf, and as he gave us his report he seemed very matter-of-fact and, like all the military brass we saw, very deferential to Colin Powell. By the time the Gulf War was over I would recognize him not just as a good soldier but, like his commanding officer General Powell, a master of the press.

Early Saturday morning I helicoptered from the vice-presidential residence to Camp David, where President Bush wanted his team to gather in the big conference room located in Laurel cabin. This turned out to be the crucial meeting, the one that launched Desert Shield, but as we sat down at the table, two and a half days after the invasion, the essential premise for a response had yet to be decided. What was our goal beyond preventing aggression against the Saudis? To get Saddam out of Kuwait? This most basic question remained unanswered.

I sat between the President and [the President's Chief of Staff John] Sununu. [Secretary of State] Jim Baker, back from the Soviet Union, was across from me. His side of the table included Colin Powell, Scowcroft, and General Schwarzkopf; [Secretary of Defense Richard] Cheney was across from the general, on Bush's right. Bill Webster, the CIA director, was also present; a judicious, competent man, he was forced, like other CIA directors, to be overly solicitous of Congress, because of all the over-sight legislation that existed. He told us just how vulnerable the Saudis were at the moment, how Saddam had positioned himself to overrun their very small defense force at any moment he wanted to. General Schwarzkopf gave us a rundown on the state of the Iraqi army: formidable but not invincible. He outlined two phases of a massive, still hypothetical, military operation. One phase would involve the deployment of up to a quarter of a million troops on the Arabian peninsula. This would be about half the maximum number the United States had at any given time in Vietnam; combined with American air and naval power, Schwarzkopf thought it ought to be enough to repel any move Saddam might make against the Saudis. But dislodging him from Kuwait would require even more in the way of troops, money, and time—it could take a year before everything was in place for a fight that would include a very bloody ground war. An even worse thing to contemplate: Iraq's known possession [of]—and willingness to use—chemical weapons.

By the end of the meeting we were still far from committed to a war that would force Saddam back across his own borders. Although there was general agreement about the need to protect the Saudis, there was no certainty that even the first part of the military scenario Schwarzkopf had outlined could actually be implemented. Would the Saudis, threatened not only by Saddam's army next door but by the convulsions of Islamic fundamentalism throughout the region, really allow a quarter of a million American troops to base themselves in a country that contained the Moslem world's holiest sites? Could they afford the hostility that American protectors might excite among zealots in the region? Would the Saudi royal family be thinking of the price Anwar Sadat had paid for his closeness to the United States, and therefore decide to appease Saddam, letting him content himself with the meal he had just made of Kuwait? By the time the Camp David meeting broke up, the only thing definitely decided was that President Bush would call King Fahd and ask him if the Saudis would be willing to talk about the idea of having American troops on their soil. The King agreed to receive American representatives to discuss the matter, and so the following day, Sunday, Cheney and Powell were on their way to Jidda, seeking permission to lay a massive American shield across the Arabian desert.

Source: Dan Quayle, *Standing Firm: A Vice-Presidential Memoir* (New York: Harper Collins, 1994), 204–7.

DOCUMENT 347: President Bush Announces Decision to Send U.S. Troops to Saudi Arabia, the Guiding Principles to His "This Will Not Stand" Position (8 August 1990)

... Iraq has massed an enormous war machine on the Saudi border, capable of initiating hostilities with little or no additional preparation. Given the Iraqi government's history of aggression against its own citizens as well as its neighbors, to assume that Iraq will not attack again would be unwise and unrealistic. And, therefore, after consulting with King Fahd, I sent Secretary of Defense Dick Cheney to discuss cooperative measures we could take. Following those meetings, the Saudi government requested our help, and I have responded to that request by ordering U.S. ground and air forces to deploy in the kingdom of Saudi Arabia. . . .

The mission of our troops is wholly defensive. Hopefully, they will not be [needed] there long. They will not initiate hostilities, but they will defend themselves, the Kingdom of Saudi Arabia and other friends in the Persian Gulf. . . .

Appeasement does not work. As was the case in the 1930s. . . . Standing up for our principles will not come easy. It may take time and possibly cost a great deal, but . . . America has never wavered when her purpose is driven by principle. . . .

[The Four Principles that] guide our policy. . . .

First, we seek the immediate, unconditional and complete withdrawal of all Iraqi forces from Kuwait. . . .

Second, Kuwait's legitimate government must be restored to replace the puppet regime. . . .

And third, my administration . . . is committed to the security and stability of the Persian Gulf. . . .

And fourth, I am determined to protect the lives of American citizens abroad. . . .

A line has been drawn in the sand. . . . My military objective is to see Saudi Arabia defended. That's the military objective. . . .

Q: Are we at war?

BUSH: We are not at war. We have sent forces to defend Saudi Arabia. . . .

Q: Is this an open ended commitment?

BUSH: Nothing is open ended, but I'm not worried about that at all. I'm worried about getting them there and doing what I indicated in our speech in there as necessary, the defense of Saudi Arabia and trying, through concerted international means, to reverse out this aggression. . . .

Q: Was there any single thing that tipped your hand in deciding to send U.S. troops . . . into Saudi Arabia . . . ?

BUSH: There was no single thing that I can think of. But when King Fahd requested such support we were prompt to respond. . . .

Q: How long will you keep American forces in Saudi Arabia, and why not use them to drive the Iraqi forces out of Kuwait?

BUSH: Well, as you know, from what I said, they're there in a defensive mode right now, and therefore that's not the mission, to drive the Iraqis out of Kuwait.

Source: Text of President Bush's speech and news conference, 13 August 1990, in *Weekly Compilation of Presidential Documents, George Bush, 1990,* Vol. 26, no. 33 (Washington: GPO, August 14, 1990), 1216–18, 1218–23.

DOCUMENT 348: An American Hostage Recalls How He and Other Civilians Were Captured Attempting to Flee Kuwait (August 1990)

At this time the Iraqi government stated that it would not recognize the American Embassy as of August 24 and that those who stayed within the compound could be taken captive. We were given the opportunity by the Embassy to take a limited supply of food and drink, etc. and leave the compound if we chose, depending on the ability of the Kuwaiti Resistance to hide us. Alternatively, we could attempt to hide on our own, attempt an escape or remain inside the Embassy. Mr. [Talmadge] Ledford [Raytheon Co. Supervisor in Kuwait] and I used information given to us by one of the State Department personnel who had debriefed us on our arrival and left the compound around 1:00 P.M. We attempted to escape through the south but were unsuccessful and had to turn back. We decided to go to Mr. Ledford's apartment in Abu Halifa where we were subsequently joined by Mr. and Mrs. Jerry Willis. We immediately began planning a different escape route.

On August 25th, with the Willises in one vehicle and Mr. Ledford and I in another, we left Abu Halifa and headed north hoping to cut across the desert to Saudi. But we were captured and searched at gun point. Mr. Willis, Mr. Ledford and I were ordered into a military vehicle while Mrs. Willis was held behind with the soldiers. Despite our objections we were forced at gun point to leave her and were taken to the Iraqi tank headquarters where, after much insistence, an Iraqi officer sent for Mrs. Willis and the vehicles that we were driving. Upon her arrival Mrs. Willis said that she had been sexually harassed with suggestive remarks and abusive language.

We were interrogated as to where we were going, who we were, who were our employers, where our identification papers were, etc. and after about two hours were loaded back into our vehicles with an Iraqi driver and guard and taken to the Iraqi Embassy in Kuwait City. We had all our personal belongings taken from us and searched. We were again interrogated and told that we would be taken to Iraq. . . .

We were then placed into the custody of a civilian driver and a civilian guard armed with automatic weapons who appeared to know their way around Kuwait. They transported us in our own vehicles to the Regency Palace Hotel in the Rumathia area. After unloading our suitcases they drove away in our vehicles which we were never to see again. . . .

We were then loaded on a bus and taken to the Meridian Hotel where more westerners were being held. They were also picked up and we continued our trip to Baghdad under armed guard. As we traveled through Kuwait City we were able to see the destruction and looting that had taken place. We numbered about forty at this time.

During our trip north we passed truck after truck loaded with looted items. We saw cars with Kuwait tags being driven into Iraq and loads of household items, new and used, and heavy equipment all heading into Iraq. We saw empty trucks coming from Iraq to haul back loads of stolen property.

Source: Guy Olan Seago, in Stevens, *Iraqi Invasion of Kuwait*, 52–53.

DOCUMENT 349: Alex Molnar's "Open Letter" to President Bush in the *New York Times*, and the Formation of the Military Families Support Network (MFSN) (23 August 1990)

Families of servicemen and women in the military were at the forefront of the antiwar movement in the United States. Their involvement, as well as that of other U.S. veterans of previous wars, received national attention when Alex Molnar, the father of a marine then serving, published an open letter ("If My Marine Son Is Killed") to President Bush in the *New York Times* on 23 August. Molnar and others organized a group called the Military Families Support Network (MFSN), which quickly grew to over 3,000 members united against any U.S. military offensive in the Persian Gulf.

Now that we face the prospect of war I intend to support my son and his fellow soldiers by doing everything I can to oppose any offensive American military action in the Persian Gulf. The troops I met deserve far better than the politicians and policies that hold them hostage.

Source: Max Elbaum, "The Storm at Home," in Phyllis Bennis and Michael Moushabeck, eds., *Beyond the Storm: A Gulf Crisis Reader* (New York: Olive Branch Press, 1991), 145–46.

DOCUMENT 350: Iraqi Dissident Kanan Makiya Urges Arab States to Take the Lead Against Saddam Hussein (25 August 1990)

[W]hen I heard that Saddam Husain [*sic*] had just invaded Kuwait, [my] instinctive thought was that he was going to get away with it. The Arab world was in a moribund, fragmented state and Saddam Husain knew his world, however little he may have understood anyone else's. Had he been allowed to get away with the annexation of the whole or part of Kuwait, everything that he stood for in politics would have been projected outward, shaping the Arab world for generations to come. . . .

"Saddam Husain has to be stopped," I wrote that same August. "The major flaw in the American-led effort against him is that the shock troops in the front lines are not Arabs. The old nationalist, anti-imperialist formulas are therefore already being trotted out, to terrible effect. For the sake of the future of the Arab world itself, Arab must be seen to be fighting Arab in the sands of Arabia for the sake of the restoration of the sovereignty of Kuwait and against the principle of violence in human affairs which is what Ba'thi [sic] politics is all about."

Source: Kanan Makiya (alias Samir al-Khalil), Cruelty and Silence: War, Tyranny, Uprising, and the Arab World (New York: Norton, 1993), 15.

DOCUMENT 351: General Colin Powell as the "Reluctant Warrior" (24 September 1990)

On 24 September Chairman of the Joint Chiefs of Staff General Colin Powell spoke with Secretary of Defense Dick Cheney concerning President Bush's repeated questions over the feasibility of getting the Iraqis out of Kuwait with air strikes. Both men understood the President's restlessness. George Bush was investing enormous political capital in Desert Shield, and his administration had come almost to a domestic standstill as the situation in the Gulf overshadowed his daily schedule; he was particularly concerned about holding the international coalition together against Iraq.

During this meeting at the Pentagon, General Powell emphasized to Secretary Cheney that he and the tactical commander of American forces on the Arabian peninsula, U.S. Central Command's General H. Norman Schwarzkopf, had concluded that the U.S. military should not go on the offensive against Iraq until it had a force in place that could guarantee victory. This logistical deployment, Powell argued, would require a massive commitment by U.S. air and naval active duty and reserve units. This "rapid response" mobilization would also require several weeks, perhaps months, to complete.

During their conversation General Powell also expressed his hope that sanctions against Iraq would lead to the withdrawal of Iraqi forces from Kuwait, thereby lessening the threat to Saudi Arabia. Powell requested from from the secretary an opportunity to give President Bush a more complete description of how long-term sanctions would work against Iraq and what advantages and disadvantages this economic strangulation would have for the president as an alternative to going to war. Powell had already discussed such an alternative with Secretary of State Baker and National Security Adviser Brent Scowcroft;

Baker had been interested, but Scowcroft shared Bush's lack of faith in long-term sanctions.

According to General Powell's memoirs of this Pentagon meeting, Secretary Cheney then scheduled a meeting with President Bush for later that afternoon. Powell and Cheney met the president in the Oval Office as he was talking with Scowcroft and Chief of Staff John Sununu. Secretary of State Baker and the other members of the national security team were not present, since this was a spur-of-the-moment gathering and not an NSC decision meeting. Powell perceived that President Bush was preoccupied with other matters, and he was not sure that he and Secretary Cheney had the president's undivided attention. After Cheney's introductory comments, General Powell briefed President Bush.

"You still have two basic options available. The first is the offensive option." I walked him through the mobilization schedule. I also explained the air option we had in place, should Saddam attempt another provocation requiring our instant response. "I still recommend that we continue preparing for a full-scale air, land, and sea campaign," I said. "If you decide to go that route in October, we'll be ready to launch sometime in January."

But there was still the other option, sanctions. I described how we could maintain our defensive posture in Saudi Arabia while keeping sanctions in place. Even if we built up to an offensive force, we could always ratchet it back down to a defensive level. Containing Iraq from further aggression through our defensive strategy and strangling her into withdrawal through sanctions remained a live option. "Of course there is a serious disadvantage," I conceded. Sanctions left the initiative with the Iraqis to decide when they had had enough. . . . I was not advocating either route, war or sanctions, on this day. . . .

When I finished, he said, "Thanks, Colin. That's useful. That's very interesting. It's good to consider all angles. But I really don't think we have time for sanctions to work." With that, the meeting ended.

In his book *The Commanders*, Bob Woodward . . . has me wanting to steer the president toward a less aggressive course in the Gulf, but fearful to press my point hard enough because none of the other advisors present backed me. After his book came out, there was a lot of talk about Powell the "reluctant warrior." Guilty. War is a deadly game; and I do not believe in spending the lives of Americans lightly. My responsibility that day was to lay out all options for the nation's civilian leadership.

Source: Colin L. Powell, with Joseph Persico, *My American Journey* (New York: Random House, 1995), 478–80.

DOCUMENT 352: Vice President Quayle Recalls the Military Options Secretary Cheney and Chairman Powell Offered to "Contain or Defeat" Iraq (August–December 1990)

Throughout Desert Shield and Desert Storm, we had surprisingly little valuable intelligence. Even the Israelis' much vaunted intelligence agency, Mossad, could not penetrate Saddam's inner circle. No one knew for sure what was motivating him, and it is hard in any case to predict what a terrorist and totalitarian will do. I think part of Saddam wanted to be an Arab hero like Nasser—taking on the infidels. There was also the appeal of martyrdom. But he had simpler political motives, too: invading Kuwait was a way of shifting his population's attention from the grave problems they had at home. We could not be sure which motive was paramount.

I was convinced that the President was making the right decision, the only decision, but neither Baker nor I, nor anyone else in the "inner circle," could predict the outcome. Cheney and Powell were out in front of the issue during those weeks when everything was doubtful. At times, Cheney acted like both Secretary of Defense and Secretary of State. If the whole operation went south, we knew the President would never be reelected. People were worried about getting bogged down in the Middle East, and there were always the nagging questions. Should we be committing American lives and prestige in order to save a sheikhdom ruled by a rich oil family that didn't share our democratic values? This was, some pointed out, not Europe, but Kuwait, and Saddam was a bully but not much else. Was it really worth it? Might we do more harm than good by fanning the fires of radical Islamic fundamentalism?

But the principle of self-determination was at stake. . . . What was essential—to the peace of the world—was maintaining the principle that a country cannot simply reach out and gobble up whatever landmass it chooses when the whim strikes. . . . The Gulf War had far more at stake in the strategic and material sense—keeping oil flowing to the industrialized world was part of the serious business we were faced with—but in the end, it was fought more than anything else for principle. The President knew that the entire new world being born, the one taking shape as the Soviet Union shrank back to its own borders and began to wither within them, depended on respect for the idea of self-determination.

Source: Quayle, *Standing Firm,* 208–9.

DOCUMENT 353: An American Captured in Kuwait Used as "Human Shield" in Iraq (September–December 1990)

The Iraqis had called for foreigners to turn themselves in "for our own protection" although none of us were dumb enough to do it. . . .

By the end of August there were so many [Iraqi] soldiers going in and out of the buildings [in Kuwait City] that we knew we would soon be discovered. People had told us that the Iraqis would go into a neighborhood and ask the "hariss" (porter) in each building if there [were] any foreigners within. Sometimes the fear of the "hariss" was so great that he would report to the Iraqis where the foreigners were located; sometimes the Iraqis would offer a bounty and on other occasions they would lie. . . .

I called a Kuwaiti friend to see if he could hide us. Even though the Iraqis said that they would execute Kuwaitis who did this and destroy their homes, he agreed. However, after one day other considerations came into play and he told us we would have to leave. I didn't know what to do and finally started to panic. I called a young Palestinian who said he would find us a safe place. We thought of this first move as temporary and accordingly took only necessities. . . .

The suspense ended the afternoon of September 14. As I looked out of our second story window I could see three truck-loads of [Iraqi] red berets speed up our street and stop in front of our building. They quickly surrounded the building and entered the compound. . . . The door burst open and 12 soldiers with automatic rifles pointed at us entered along with a captain who held an automatic pistol. There was also a man in "dishdasha" (Kuwaiti garb), also with a pistol (presumably he was secret police, the Mukhabarat). It was almost anti-climatic.

. . . We were told to "quickly pack a bag and come." One of the soldiers struck me with his fist above the left eye, breaking my glasses. We went down to the lobby where our Arab friends were standing outside their doors. . . .

We were taken along a circuitous route stopping at several villas where the soldiers repeated their dash t[hrough] the door. . . . The going was slow as there were a number of check points to pass through. Additionally, the Iraqis had placed concrete blocks and other obstacles in the roadway covering half of the paved surface of each street in an alternating pattern so as to make straight travel impossible. I got my first look at the [war] damage. . . .

At last we were on the Sixth Ring Road going west. . . . We ended up in the basement car park. I thought it odd and looked around to see if there were any bullet holes in the walls. After they made us get out of the car, I was certain that this was it; they were going to shoot us. We were told to get back into the car and were taken to a police station where we were interrogated by a handsome colonel who spoke fluent English. From there we were taken to the Regency Palace Hotel, one of the nicest in Kuwait. . . .

Three days later the Iraqis had gathered enough in their nets to make a lorry full and we headed for Baghdad to become "human shields." It was a long trip but I could see just how poor the country side was and how damaged was Basra, Iraq's second largest city, due to the eight years of war with Iran. We arrived in Baghdad at night and were placed in the Monsour Melia Hotel. . . . After three days . . . I was placed with a bus load of other men of mixed nationalities. We headed out of town and I could tell we were headed toward Mosul, Iraq's third largest city. . . . This area, we were told by some of the German engineers with us, was a large chemical/biological warfare complex.

Source: George Charchalis, in Stevens, *Iraqi Invasion of Kuwait*, 5–7.

DOCUMENT 354: Vice President Quayle's Seton Hall Address (29 November 1990)

The Middle East . . . is the source of much of the oil on which the industrialized world and developing nations depend. It is a region of striking contrasts: vast wealth and grinding poverty; secular radicalism and religious fundamentalism; hatred of the West and emulation of the West. Most importantly, perhaps, the Middle East is caught up in a vast process of change, as ancient societies and cultures strive to adapt to the modern world. This process of adaptation, which entails much turmoil and instability, is what makes the Middle East such an interesting place. Unfortunately, it also makes the Middle East a dangerous place.

Since the onset of the Cold War, the United States has had three strategic objectives in the region. The first objective was to contain Soviet expansionism. In 1947, the Soviet threat to one regional state, Turkey, played a role in President Truman's decision to issue the doctrine that bears his name. Thirty-three years later, the threat of Soviet encroachment on another region of the Middle East—the Persian Gulf—led President Carter to proclaim the equivalent of the Truman Doctrine for the Gulf. The Carter Doctrine, which was also reinforced by President Reagan, warned that, "Any attempt by any outside force to gain control of the Persian Gulf region will be regarded as an assault on the vital interests of the United States of America, and such an assault will be repelled by any means necessary, including military force."

But the Cold War is over. And because it is over, because one of America's strategic objectives has been realized, some commentators have assumed that all of our objectives have been realized. They could not be more mistaken. For in addition to containing the Soviets, American foreign policy has traditionally pursued two other strategic objectives in the Middle East. It has sought to prevent any local Middle East power from achieving hegemony over its neighbors; and it has sought to secure the uninterrupted supply of oil at a reasonable price. . . .

So far, I have talked about traditional U.S. strategic objectives in the Middle East. But there is another strategic American objective in the current crisis that is not traditional—that has only emerged, in fact, as a result of the end of the Cold War. This objective might be described as strengthening the foundations of world order. . . .

Iraq's invasion of Kuwait is the first crisis of the post–Cold War world. One way or another, it is bound to set a precedent—either on behalf of greater world order or on behalf of greater chaos. If Saddam Hussein succeeds in his aggression, it is likely that his success will embolden other dictators to emulate his example. But if he fails—and believe me, he will fail—others will draw the lesson that might does not make right and that aggression will not be allowed to succeed.

Source: Quayle, *Standing Firm*, 369–74.

DOCUMENT 355: Saddam Releases American Hostage George Charchalis to Muhammad Ali (November 1990)

In early November 1990, we were allowed to make an overseas telephone call. At last I could talk to my wife and daughters and let them know I was okay. I had no idea that efforts were being made to secure my release. My wife, my cousin in London, U.S. Senator Harry Reid of Nevada, and a ton of publicity in the newspapers in Las Vegas and Reno as well as others. When you are held against your will, incommunicado, you feel alone, worthless, and abandoned.

Each evening we watched the Baghdad News. First a long program in Arabic, then in Farsee, French and then finally in English. Saddam dominated the news. . . . Various peace missions would be interviewed—Ed Heath, Jessie Jackson, Ramsey Clark, etc. The last week of November Mohammed [*sic*] Ali, the great boxing champion, came to Baghdad and was interviewed by Saddam. Saddam was very deferential. At the end of the interview, Saddam stood up and warmly shook Mohammed Ali's hand and said (In translation) "Mohammed Ali, I cannot allow you to return home without taking some of your American friends." . . . At 4:10 P.M. November 28, one of the men came in and said that I was going home that day. Upon his heels came the head guard or "keeper" as they were known and said "quick Mr. George, get ready. After 15 minutes a car comes to take you to Baghdad. You go home with Mohammed Ali." Then I knew it was true. . . . At 6:45, I was in the Monsour Melia Hotel in Baghdad having a beer.

Source: Charchalis, in Stevens, *Iraqi Invasion of Kuwait*, 7–8.

DOCUMENT 356: Synopsis of UN Resolutions Relating to Iraq's Invasion of Kuwait (August–November 1990)

Resolution 660 (August 2, 1990) condemned the invasion of Kuwait; demanded that Iraq immediately and unconditionally withdraw its forces to the positions held on August 1, 1990; called upon Iraq and Kuwait to begin negotiations for the resolution of their differences.

Resolution 661 (August 6, 1990) imposed a trade and financial embargo on Iraq and occupied Kuwait; called upon all member states to take appropriate measures to protect the assets of the legitimate government of Kuwait and not to recognize any regime set up in Kuwait by Iraq; established a committee (the Sanctions Committee) to monitor progress.

Resolution 662 (August 9, 1990) declared Iraq's annexation of Kuwait to be null and void; called upon all member states not to recognize the annexation.

Resolution 664 (August 18, 1990) demanded that Iraq permit the immediate departure from Kuwait and Iraq of the nationals of third countries and grant immediate and continuing access of consular officials to such nationals; demanded also that Iraq rescind its order closing diplomatic and consular missions in Kuwait.

Resolution 665 (August 25, 1990) called upon all member states with ships in the area to enforce the economic sanctions, by inspecting and verifying the cargoes and destinations of all incoming and outgoing shipping.

Resolution 666 (September 13, 1990) reaffirmed that Iraq remained fully responsible for the safety and well-being of foreign nationals in accordance with international humanitarian law, including the Fourth Geneva Convention.

Resolution 667 (September 16, 1990) condemned the aggressive acts per-petrated by Iraq against diplomatic premises and persons in Kuwait, including the abduction of foreign nationals who were present in those premises; demanded the immediate release of all foreign nationals in Iraq.

Resolution 669 (September 24, 1990) entrusted the Sanctions Committee with the responsibility for considering requests for assistance under the provisions of Article 50 of the Charter of the United Nations.

Resolution 670 (September 25, 1990) confirmed that Resolution 661 (1990) applied to all forms of transport, including aircraft; called upon all member states to detain ships of Iraq registry that were being or had been used to violate the economic embargo.

Resolution 674 (October 29, 1990) demanded that the Iraqi authorities cease and desist from taking hostages and mistreating and oppressing Kuwaiti and other foreign nationals; reminded Iraq that under interna-tional law it is liable for any loss, damage, or injury to Kuwait and other states as a result of its illegal invasion and occupation of Kuwait.

Resolution 677 (November 28, 1990) condemned the attempts by Iraq to alter the demographic composition of the population of Kuwait and to destroy the civil records maintained by the government of Kuwait.

Resolution 678 (November 29, 1990) authorized member states to use "all necessary means" after 15 January 1991 to uphold and implement Security Council Resolution 660 (1990) and all subsequent relevant res-olutions and to restore international peace and security in the area.

Source: Dennis Menos, *Arms over Diplomacy: Reflections on the Persian Gulf War* (Westport, Conn.: Praeger, 1992), 143–44.

DOCUMENT 357: Statement by American Council of Churches (21 December 1990)

We are marching toward war. Indeed the stakes are horribly high. Military experts predict casualties in the tens and hundreds of thousands. And it won't end there. War would unleash a chain of human tragedies that will be with us for generations to come.

Our Christmas pilgrimage to the Middle East has utterly convinced us that war is not the answer. We believe the resort to massive violence to resolve the Gulf crisis would be politically and morally indefensible. . . . The unspeakable loss of lives, especially innocent civilians, would be unacceptable on moral grounds. Nations hold in their hands weapons of mass destruction. It is entirely possible that war in the Middle East will destroy everything. No cause will be served, no crisis resolved, no justice secured.

War will not liberate Kuwait, it will destroy it. War will not save us from weapons of mass destruction, it will unleash them. War will not establish regional stability, it will inflame the entire Middle East. . . .

While we do not accept the proposition that the resolution of all conflicts must precede the solution of the Gulf crisis, we do believe that there will be no lasting peace in the region until interrelated issues are dealt with in a comprehensive framework. What is required is not "linkage," but consistency in the implementation of U.S. foreign policy. Our government should support the convening of an international Middle East peace conference by the United Nations. . . .

Having seen the face of the victims and potential victims, we believe that there must be an alternative to war. That alternative is negotiations—serious and substantive negotiations. . . . The United Nations can be the place where the deadly escalation of armaments of mass destruction in the Middle East can be reversed. . . . Our nation must not submit to the inevitability of war.

Source: National Council of Churches, *Pressing for Peace* (New York: National Council of Churches, 1991), 44–45.

DOCUMENT 358: Vice President Quayle Recalls President Bush's Effort to Gain Congressional Support for Operations Desert Shield and Desert Storm (December 1990)

By the end of December the military alliance against Saddam had swelled to twenty-eight nations, but the President was still willing to try diplomacy. There was a standing offer to send Jim Baker to Baghdad to talk with Saddam Hussein. But in the meantime, war preparations had to proceed on every front, and one of those was Capitol Hill. Could the President succeed in getting Congress to endorse military means to dislodge Saddam if he allowed the January 15 deadline to pass without getting out of Kuwait? Just as the President had wanted the international authority for war making that the UN resolution provided, so, too, did he want a resolution from our own Congress approving the use of force. Once more, the object was to avoid the mistakes of Vietnam. What the President wanted was clear approval—in effect, a declaration of war— nothing ambiguous or fragile, like the Gulf of Tonkin resolution, which wound up being used to justify much more than it actually involved.

We weren't sure we had the votes. In fact, Cheney felt we did not, and he argued against seeking congressional approval. "Don't do it," were his words of advice. I myself didn't believe military action required congressional approval, but I thought that it would be politically much more feasible—and much better for the country—if the President went to war with the authorization of Congress. I also thought we could get a resolution through, though I knew it would be difficult. I argued for an early vote: hold Congress's feet to the fire before the Christmas vacation. I did not want to wait for the new Congress, though I knew that either one—the departing 101st or the incoming 102nd—would try to duck responsibility, to look for the opportunity to have it both ways. Politicians always want a win-win situation. Whatever the outcome, they want to be on the winning side. In the end, a decision was reached to put the resolution before the new Congress—just before the January 15 deadline arrived.

Source: Quayle, *Standing Firm*, 217–19.

OPERATION DESERT STORM AND LIVE COVERAGE OF THE AIR-LAND WAR, JANUARY–MARCH 1991

DOCUMENT 359: President Bush's Letter to President Saddam Hussein (5 January 1991)

Mr. President:

We stand today at the brink of war between Iraq and the world. This is a war that began with your invasion of Kuwait; this is a war that can be ended only by Iraq's full and unconditional compliance with UN Security Council Resolution 678.

I am writing you now, directly, because what is at stake demands that no opportunity be lost to avoid what would be a certain calamity for the people of Iraq. I am writing, as well, because it is said by some that you do not understand just how isolated Iraq is and what Iraq faces as a result. I am not in a position to judge whether this impression is correct; what I can do, though, is try in this letter to reinforce what Secretary of State Baker told your Foreign Minister and eliminate any uncertainty or ambiguity that might exist in your mind about where we stand and what we are prepared to do.

The international community is united in its call for Iraq to leave all of Kuwait without condition and without further delay. This is not simply the policy of the United States; it is the position of the world community as expressed in no less than twelve Security Council resolutions.

We prefer a peaceful outcome. However, anything less than full compliance with UN Security Council Resolution 678 and its predecessors is unacceptable. There can be no reward for aggression. Nor will there be any negotiation. Principle cannot be compromised. However, by its full compliance, Iraq will gain the opportunity to rejoin the international community. More immediately, the Iraqi military establishment will escape destruction. But unless you withdraw from Kuwait completely and without condition, you will lose more than Kuwait. What is at issue here is not the future of Kuwait—it will be free, its government will be restored—but rather the future of Iraq. This choice is yours to make.

The United States will not be separated from its coalition partners. Twelve Security Council resolutions, 28 countries providing military units to enforce them, more than one hundred governments complying with sanctions—all highlight the fact that it is not Iraq against the United States, but Iraq against the world. That most Arab and Muslim countries are arrayed against you as well should reinforce what I am saying. Iraq cannot and will not be able to hold on to Kuwait or exact a price for leaving.

You may be tempted to find solace in the diversity of opinion that is American democracy. You should resist any such temptation. Diversity ought not to be confused with division. Nor should you underestimate, as others have before you, America's will.

Iraq is already feeling the effects of the sanctions mandated by the United Nations. Should war come, it will be a far greater tragedy for you and your country. Let me state, too, that the United States will not tolerate the use of chemical or biological weapons or the destruction of Kuwait's oil fields and installations. Further, you will be held directly responsible for terrorist actions against any member of the coalition. The American people would demand the strongest possible response. You and your country will pay a terrible price if you order unconscionable acts of this sort.

I write this letter not to threaten, but to inform. I do so with no sense of satisfaction, for the people of the United States have no quarrel with the people of Iraq. Mr. President, UN Security Council Resolution 678 establishes the period before January 15 of this year as a "pause of good will" so that this crisis may end without further violence. Whether this pause is used as intended, or merely becomes a prelude to further violence, is in your hands, and yours alone. I hope you weigh your choice carefully and choose wisely, for much will depend upon it.

Source: President Bush's Letter to President Saddam Hussein of Iraq, in *Weekly Compilation of Presidential Documents, George Bush, 1991*, Vol. 27, (Washington: GPO, January 12, 1991), 43–44.

DOCUMENT 360: Pentagon's Public Affairs Officer Announces "Ground Rules and Guidelines for Correspondents in the Persian Gulf" (7 January 1991)

The following information should not be reported because its publication or broadcast could jeopardize operations and endanger lives:

(1) For U.S. or coalition units, specific numerical information on troop strength, aircraft, weapons systems, on-hand equipment, or supplies (e.g., artillery tanks, radars, missiles, tracks, water), including amounts of ammunition or fuel moved by or on hand in support and combat units. Unit size may be described in general terms such as "company-size," "multibattalion," "multidivision," "naval task force," and "carrier battle group." Number or amount of equipment and supplies may described in general terms such as "large," "small," or "many."

(2) Any information that reveals details of future plans, operations, or strikes, including postponed or canceled operations.

(3) Information, photography, and imagery that would reveal the specific location of military forces or show the level of security at military installations or encampments. . . .

(4) Rules of engagement details.

(5) Information on intelligence collection activities, including targets, methods, and results.

(6) During an operation, specific information on friendly force troop movements, tactical deployments, and dispositions that would jeopardize operational security or lives. This would include unit designations, names of operations, and size of friendly forces involved, until released by CENTCOM [U.S. Central Command]. . . .

Guidelines for News Media

News media personnel must carry and support any personal and professional gear they take with them, including protective cases for professional equipment, batteries, cables, converters, etc.

Night operations—Light discipline restrictions will be followed. The only approved light source is a flashlight with a red lens. No visible light source, including flash or television lights. . . .

Because of host-nation requirements, you must stay with your [DOD] public affairs escort while on Saudi bases. At other U.S. tactical or field locations and encampments, a public affairs escort may be required because of security, safety, and mission requirements as determined by the host commander.

Casualty information, because of concern of the notification of the next of kin, is extremely sensitive. By executive directive, next of kin of all military fatalities must be notified in person by a uniformed member of the appropriate service. . . . The problem is particularly difficult for visual media. . . .

To the extent that individuals in the news media seek access to the U.S. area of operation, the following rule applies: Prior to or upon commencement of hostilities, media pools will be established to provide initial combat coverage of U.S. forces. U.S. news media personnel present in Saudi Arabia will be given the opportunity to join CENTCOM media pools, providing they agree to pool their products.

News media personnel who are not members of the official CENTCOM media pools will not be permitted into forward areas. Reporters are strongly discouraged from attempting to link up on their own with combat units. U.S. commanders will maintain extremely tight security throughout the operational area and will exclude from the area of operation all unauthorized individuals.

For news media personnel participating in designated CENTCOM media pools:

(1) Upon registering with the JIB [Joint Information Bureau], news media should contact their respective pool coordinator for an explanation of pool operations.

(2) In the event of hostilities, pool products will be subject to review before release to determine if they contain sensitive information about military plans, capabilities, operation, or vulnerabilities (see attached ground rules) that would jeopardize the outcome of an operation or the safety of U.S. or coalition forces. Material will be examined solely for its conformance to the attached ground rules, not for its potential to express criticism or cause embarrassment. The public affairs escort officer on scene will review pool reports, discuss ground rule problems with the reporter, and in the limited circumstances when no agreement can be reached with a reporter about disputed materials, immediately send the disputed materials to JIB Dhahran [Headquarters of U.S. Forces in Saudi Arabia] for review by the JIB Director and the appropriate news media representative. If no agreement can be reached, the issue will be immediately forwarded to OASD (PA) [Office of Special Declassification (Public Affairs)] for review with the appropriate bureau chief. The ultimate decision on publication will be made by the originating reporter's news organization.

(3) Correspondents may not carry a personal weapon.

Alert Procedures for Combat Correspondent Pool Activation

. . . Operational security (OPSEC) considerations are of the utmost concern. JIB personnel, pool coordinators, and pool members need to be especially cognizant of OPSEC. All involved with the activation of the pools need to remain calm and unexcited. Voice inflection, nervous behavior, etc., are all indicators that something extraordinary is underway and could signal that operations are imminent.

Source: Hedrick Smith, ed., *The Media and the Gulf War* (Washington: Seven Locks Press for Johns Hopkins University, 1992), 4–12.

DOCUMENT 361: American Society of Newspaper Editors Protests U.S. Department of Defense's Rules and Guidelines for Journalists (8 January 1991)

The newly revised (January 7) set of ground rules and guidelines for media coverage . . . are a major improvement over the previous proposals. Still, we have concern in two areas.

First, we must strongly protest the use of a "security review" of any type. Even though you have told us that "material will not be withheld just because it is embarrassing or contains criticism" there is no guarantee that on-site commanders will not do what was done in July, 1987, when the commodore in charge during the reflagging of Kuwaiti tankers insisted on censoring material that in no way violated news media ground rules but merely embarrassed him.

In a world where "spin control" of the news has become commonplace, this form of prior restraint is a tool to gain control over what the American public sees or hears from the battlefield. There was no such prior review in Vietnam, and there were few security breaches of any consequence.

Finally, we are concerned that the entire emphasis of your ground rules is on the pool coverage, over which you will assert direct control. Our view of a pool situation is that it should be in effect only as long as it absolutely has to be, say for the first day or so of fighting, because of the logistical difficulty of getting the press in quickly. But as soon as possible the press should be allowed coverage that would be free of many of the pool restraints. We see no evidence of any attempt to prepare for that circumstance.

There are 250 U.S. reporters on site in Saudi Arabia today. The American public would be best served by a system that allows them to do their job as quickly as possible after hostilities break out.

Source: Letter by ASNE President [Burl Osborne] to Department of Defense [Pete Williams], 8 January 1991, in Smith, *Media and the Gulf War*, 13–14.

DOCUMENT 362: P.L. 102-1, Congressional Resolution Authorizing Military Force Against Iraq (12 January 1991)

On 12 January 1991, the U.S. Congress sent to President Bush Public Law 102-1, which formally authorized the president to use American military forces against Iraq pursuant to United Nations Security Council Resolution 678.

WHEREAS the Government of Iraq without provocation invaded and occupied the territory of Kuwait on August 2, 1990; and

WHEREAS both the House of Representatives (in H.J. Res. 658 of the 101st Congress) and the Senate (in S. Con. Res. 147 of the 101st Congress) have condemned Iraq's invasion of Kuwait and declared their support for international action to reverse Iraq's aggression; and

WHEREAS Iraq's conventional, chemical, biological, and nuclear weapons and ballistic missile programs and its demonstrated willingness to use weapons of mass destruction pose a grave threat to world peace; and

WHEREAS the international community has demanded that Iraq withdraw unconditionally and immediately from Kuwait and that Kuwait's independence and legitimate government be restored; and

WHEREAS the U.N. Security Council repeatedly affirmed the inherent right of individual or collective self-defense in response to the armed attack by Iraq against Kuwait in accordance with Article 51 of the U.N. Charter; and

WHEREAS, in the absence of full compliance by Iraq with its resolutions, the U.N. Security in Resolution 678 authorized member states of the United Nations to use all necessary means, after January 15, 1991, to uphold and implement all relevant Security Council resolutions and to restore international peace and security in the area; and

WHEREAS Iraq has persisted in its illegal occupation of, and brutal aggression against Kuwait; Now, therefore, be it

Resolved by the Senate and House of Representatives of the United States of America in Congress assembled.

Section 1. SHORT TITLE

The joint resolution may be cited as the "Authorization for Use of Military Force Against Iraq Resolution."

Section 2. AUTHORIZATION FOR USE OF U.S. ARMED FORCES

(a) AUTHORIZATION—The President is authorized, subject to subsection (b), to use United States Armed Forces pursuant to United

Nations Security Council Resolution 678 (1990) in order to achieve implementation of Security Council Resolutions 660, 661, 662, 664, 665, 666, 667, 669, 670, 674, and 677.

(b) REQUIREMENT FOR DETERMINATION THAT USE OF MILITARY FORCE IS NECESSARY—Before exercising the authority granted in subsection (a), the President shall make available to the Speaker of the House of Representatives and the President pro tempore of the Senate his determination that—

(1) The United States has used all appropriate diplomatic and other peaceful means to obtain compliance by Iraq with the United Nations Security Council resolutions cited in subsection (a); and (2) that those efforts have not been and would not be successful in obtaining such compliance.

(c) WAR POWERS RESOLUTION REQUIREMENTS—

(1) SPECIFIC STATUTORY AUTHORIZATION—Consistent with section 8(a) of the War Powers Resolution, the Congress declares that this section is intended to constitute specific statutory authorization with the meaning of section 5(b) of the War Powers Resolution.

(2) APPLICABILITY OF OTHER REQUIREMENTS—Nothing in this resolution supersedes any requirement of the War Powers Resolution.

Section 3. REPORTS TO CONGRESS

At least once every 60 days, the President shall submit to the Congress a summary on the status of efforts to obtain compliance by Iraq with the resolutions adopted by the United Nations Security Council in response to Iraq's aggression.

Source: Robert J. Spitzer, "The Conflict Between Congress and the President over War," in Marcia Whicker, James Pfiffner, and Raymond Moore, eds., *The Presidency and the Persian Gulf War*, Praeger Series in Presidential Studies (Westport, Conn.: Praeger, 1993), Table 1: 31–32.

DOCUMENT 363: President Bush's Letter to the U.S. Congress (16 January 1991)

I have concluded that:

1. The United States has used all appropriate diplomatic and other peaceful means to obtain compliance by Iraq with U.N. Security Council Resolutions 660, 661, 662, 664, 665, 666, 667, 669, 670, 677, and 678; and

2. These efforts have not been and would not be successful in obtaining such compliance.

Background. For over five and a half months, the international community has sought with unprecedented unity to reverse Iraq's brutal and unprovoked aggression against Kuwait. The United States and the vast majority of governments of the world, working together through the United Nations, have been united both in their determination to compel Iraq's withdrawal from Kuwait and in their strong preference for doing so through peaceful means. Since August 2, we have sought to build maximum diplomatic and economic pressure against Iraq. Regrettably, Iraq has given no sign whatever that it intends to comply with the will of the international community; nor is there any indication that diplomatic and economic means alone would ever compel Iraq to do so. . . .

From the beginning of the Gulf crisis, the United States has consistently pursued four basic objectives: (1) the immediate, complete, and unconditional Iraqi withdrawal from Kuwait; (2) the restoration of the legitimate Government of Kuwait; (3) the protection of U.S. citizens abroad; and (4) the security and stability of a region vital to U.S. national security. In pursuit of these objectives, we have sought and obtained action by the U.N. Security Council, resulting in twelve separate resolutions that have been fully consistent with U.S. objectives. . . .

U.N. Security Council Resolution 678 of 29 November 1990 authorizes U.N. member states to use "all necessary means" to implement Resolution 660 and all subsequent relevant resolutions of the Security Council, and to restore international peace and security in the area, unless Iraq fully implements those resolutions on or before January 15, 1991. . . .

Iraq has taken no steps whatever to fulfill these requirements. Iraq has forcefully stated that it considers the Security Council's resolutions invalid and has no intention of complying with them at any time. Iraqi forces remain in occupation of Kuwait and have been substantially reinforced in recent weeks rather than withdrawn. Iraq has strongly and repeatedly reiterated its annexation of Kuwait and stated its determination that Kuwait will remain permanently a part of Iraq. . . .

In short, the government of Iraq remains completely intransigent in rejecting the U.N. Security Council's demands—despite the exhaustive use by the United States and the United Nations of all appropriate diplomatic, political, and economic measures to persuade or compel Iraq to comply. . . .

The extensive diplomatic and political efforts undertaken by the United States . . . to persuade or compel Iraq to withdraw from Kuwait have not succeeded. The U.N. Security Council and General Assembly have overwhelmingly and repeatedly condemned the Iraqi invasion and demanded Iraq's immediate and unconditional withdrawal from Kuwait. The Security Council has invoked its extraordinary authority under Chapter VII of the U.N. Charter, not only to order comprehensive economic sanctions, but to authorize the use of all other means necessary, including the use of force. . . .

The President, the Secretary of State and other U.S. officials have engaged in an exhaustive process of consultation with other governments and international organizations. The Secretary of State alone has . . . traveled over 125,000 miles in the course of these contacts. . . . This extensive diplomacy . . . has not caused the government of Iraq to withdraw from Kuwait.

More recently, on January 9, the Secretary of State met at length in Geneva with the Iraqi Foreign Minister, who in six and one-half hours of talks demonstrated no readiness whatever to implement the U.N. Security Council resolutions. The Iraqi Foreign Minister even refused to receive a diplomatic communication from the President intended for Saddam Hussein. . . . For our part, the administration made clear that there could be no reward for aggression. . . . Attempts to link resolution of Iraq's aggression against Kuwait with other issues were rejected on the grounds that these issues were unrelated to Iraq's aggression.

Source: Public Papers of the Presidents: George Bush, 1991, Book 1 (Washington: GPO, 1992), 42–44.

DOCUMENT 364: Michael Glennon's "The Gulf War and the Constitution" (1991)

During the January 1991 debate on whether to go to war in the Persian Gulf, many members of Congress were delighted at the legislature's response. . . . After four months of controversy about the allocation of the power to make war, it seemed easy to conclude . . . that "the United States Constitution had prevailed."

Easy, but wrong.

Starting from President Bush's unilateral commitment to defend Saudi Arabia and proceeding to Congress' jury-rigged approval, the episode represented a textbook example of how an audacious executive, acquiescent legislature and deferential judiciary have pushed the Constitution's system of separation of powers steadily backwards toward the monopolistic system of King George III. When President Bush finally requested legislative approval in a letter to Congress January 8, 1991, he never acknowledged that statutory authorization was constitutionally required. In fact, the president said that he still believed he had the authority to act without legislative authorization. "I don't think I need it," he said the next day, and White House aides hinted that the administration had the right to defy any restrictions that Congress might impose.

In addition to raising disturbing constitutional questions, these events highlight anew the fecklessness of the War Powers Resolution and the urgent need for that 1973 law to be repealed or revised.

Source: Michael J. Glennon, "The Gulf War and the Constitution," Foreign Affairs 70, no. 2 (Spring 1991), 84–85.

DOCUMENT 365: Barbara Bush Recalls Public Opinion on the War (17 January 1991)

Congress and the vast majority of the American people supported George, but the protests continued outside. At one point they said we should expect 100,000, but the turnout was much smaller.

Nevertheless, when George talked to our allies, they all asked about the terrible protests taking place in America. George had to explain that they were seeing only the 20 percent who were against and not the 80 percent who were backing him. Incidentally, I want to emphasize that I didn't for one moment question the motives of the protesters. They were doing what they thought was right. However, I was very grateful one day when I heard a great cheer and looked out my office window to see about one hundred supporters of the administration marching. That was refreshing.

Source: Barbara Bush, Barbara Bush: A Memoir (New York: Charles Scribner's Sons, 1994), 389–90.

DOCUMENT 366: CBS News Crew and Reporter Robert Simon Captured by Iraqi Troops Near Saudi-Kuwait Border (21 January 1991)

I had been with CBS News twenty-four years, most of them overseas. I had been posted to London, Vietnam, and Israel. I had reported from sixty-seven countries including every major nation in the Middle East except Iraq. That was about to change.

Our Saudi friend disappeared after the interview. Peter [Bluff, field producer] and I were chatting; Roberto [Alvarez, cameraman] was taking some long shots when suddenly I realized he wasn't there anymore. Then I heard his engine start. Peter and I looked at each other, then down to the road, to see his Land Cruiser speeding off, away from the border. . . .

We decided to get a few shots in the no-man's land, maybe shoot another stand—upper, to flesh out the story. We parked the van behind a building at the border crossing, walked past the closed white gates which, on better days, lifted and fell to let cars pass, and strolled across the border. We figured we'd be away from the van five to ten minutes. Roberto left the key in the ignition. Juan [Caldera, soundman] left six thousand dollars in his bag; a cash advance he had just taken which he didn't want to leave in the hotel. We took no extra camera batteries or cassettes. Without the hint of a curve, the road stretched out in front of us like a thin black ribbon, cutting through the desolate sands.

Aside from a faint, intermittent rustle from the wind, there was no sound in this vast empty lot. But I had grown accustomed to the desert. I found the silence neither strange nor menacing. Later, when I thought about these moments and compared them to other moments in other wars, I could only conclude that I had been exceptionally lucky over the years—that this stroll was no riskier than a hundred other walks I had taken at other times, in other places. Had we made it back to our bureau in Saudi Arabia that night, I would have told my friends about the massive buildup we had seen on our way to the border, about Hafr el-Baten, the deserted desert town where we had spent the night. Our short stroll across the line would have been hardly worth mentioning. It was no big deal and it didn't seem like a big risk. The Iraqis had deserted their border post two miles north of us. Iraqi lines were six miles away. The Saudis had told us that. . . .

The jeep pulled up a few yards from the road. The driver got out and slowly came toward us saying, "Peace." He was not carrying a rifle. His pistol was in its holster. Two other men were getting out of the back of the jeep. Defectors? More defectors? Peter extended his hand to the driver. Roberto was filming the scene. It was television.

The two other Iraqis were out of the jeep, on either side of it now. They had AK-47s, but were not pointing them at us. In fact they joined the "peace" chorus, adding the refrain, "No more war, no more war." Peter was calmly talking to the driver, clearly the man in charge. "We would like to interview you. We work for CBS." He said it slowly: "C-B-S, American television," Peter's way of talking to foreigners. It all seemed so familiar and benign. Peter and the driver were shaking hands.

It was Peter who first realized what was happening when he tried to withdraw his hand and could not. I understood when another hand copped me on the back of the head and shoved me into the jeep. Roberto

do know that Saddam Hussein does not share our value in the sanctity of life. Indeed, time and again he has shown willingness to sacrifice civilian lives and property to further his war aims.

Source: White House Statement by Marlin Fitzwater, "Statement on Bombing of Building in Iraq," 13 February 1991, in *Public Papers of the Presidents: George Bush, 1991,* Book 1 (Wasington: GPO, 1992), 142–43.

DOCUMENT 369: Secretary of Defense Dick Cheney Announces Ground War (24 February 1991)

Just a short time ago, you heard the president announce that coalition forces of Operation Desert Storm have begun a large-scale ground operation against Iraqi forces inside Kuwait. This phase of the combined air, land, and sea campaign has been carefully planned to force Iraq out of Kuwait, with a minimum number of casualties to allied forces.

Up to now, we've been as forthcoming as possible about military operations. But from this point forward, we must limit what we say. We've now undertaken a major military operation. Allied military units are on the move. Their positions, movements, and plans must be carefully safeguarded. We must assume that the enemy is confused about what is happening on the battlefield, and it is absolutely essential that we not do anything inadvertently ourselves to clarify the picture for him.

Everything we say about the operation from this point forward, every detail we offer, would increase the likelihood that the military forces of Iraq could learn more about our operations.

Such information would put military operations at risk, and even the most innocent sounding information could be used directly against the men and women whose lives are on the line carrying out these operations.

We cannot permit the Iraqi forces to know anything about what we're doing. For that reason, I will not say anything tonight about the operation that is currently underway. We will have nothing to say about it for many more hours. When it is safe to begin discussing the operation we will do so in as much detail as we prudently can.

But for now, our regular briefing schedule here at the Pentagon and in Riyadh [Saudi Arabia] is suspended until further notice.

I want to assure all of you that we understand our solemn obligation to the American people to keep them informed of developments. But I am confident that they understand that this policy is necessary to save lives and to reduce American casualties, as well as those of coalition forces.

Source: Secretary Dick Cheney's News Conference, 24 February 1991, Smith, *Media and the Gulf War*, 27–32.

DOCUMENT 370: CBS News Correspondent Walter Cronkite Asks, "What Is There to Hide?" (25 February 1991)

With an arrogance foreign to the democratic system, the US military in Saudi Arabia is trampling on the American people's right to know. It is doing a disservice not only to the home front but also to history and its own best interests. . . .

It is drummed into us, and we take pride in the fact, that these are "our boys (and girls)," "our troops," "our forces" in the gulf. They are, indeed and it is our war. Our elected representatives in Congress gave our elected president permission to wage it. We had better darned well know what they are doing in our name. . . .

The military is acting on a generally discredited Pentagon myth that the Vietnam War was lost because of the uncensored press coverage. . . .

The military also has the responsibility of giving all the information it possibly can to the press, and the press has every right, to the point of insolence, to demand this. . . .

The greatest mistake of our military so far is its attempt to control coverage by assigning a few pool reporters and photographers to be taken to locations determined by the military with supervising officers monitoring all their conversations with the troops in the field. An American citizen is entitled to ask: "What are they trying to hide?" The answer might be casualties from shelling, collapsing morale, disaffection, insurrection, incompetent officers, poorly trained troops, malfunctioning equipment, widespread illness—who knows? But the fact that we don't know, the fact that the military apparently feels there is *something* it must hide, can only lead eventually to a breakdown in home-front confidence and the very echoes from Vietnam that the Pentagon fears the most.

Source: Walter Cronkite, "What Is There to Hide?" *Newsweek*, 25 February 1991, 43.

DOCUMENT 371: Secretary of State Baker and Soviet Foreign Minister Bessmertnykh's Joint Statement Supporting UN Military Action Against Iraq (29 January 1991)

The ministers reiterated the commitment of their countries to the U.N. Security Council resolutions adopted in connection with Iraq's aggression against Kuwait. . . . The military actions authorized by the United Nations have been provoked by the refusal of the Iraqi leadership to comply with the clear and lawful demands of the international community for withdrawal from Kuwait.

Minister of Foreign Affairs Bessmertnykh . . . agreed that Iraq's withdrawal from Kuwait must remain the goal of the international community. Both sides believe that everything possible should be done to avoid further escalation of the war and expansion of its scale.

The ministers continue to believe that a cessation of hostilities would be possible if Iraq would make an unequivocal commitment to withdraw from Kuwait. . . .

In addition, dealing with the causes of instability and the sources of conflict, including the Arab-Israeli conflict, will be especially important. Indeed both ministers agreed that without a meaningful peace process— one which promotes a just peace, security, and real reconciliation for Israel, Arab states and Palestinians—it will not be possible to deal with the sources of conflict and instability in the region. Both ministers, therefore, agreed that in the aftermath of the crisis in the Persian Gulf, mutual U.S./Soviet efforts to promote Arab-Israeli peace and regional stability . . . will be greatly facilitated and enhanced.

Source: U.S. Department of State, *Dispatch* 2, no. 5 (4 February 1991), 71.

DOCUMENT 372: Statement by Iraq's Revolutionary Command Council (15 February 1991)

The Revolutionary Command Council declares the following:

First, Iraq is ready to deal with Security Council Resolution 660 of 1990, with the aim of reaching an honorable and acceptable political solution, including withdrawal. The Iraqi pledge is linked to the following:

a) A total and comprehensive cease-fire on land, air, and sea.

b) Cancellation by the Security Council of resolutions 661, 662, 664, 665, 666, 669, 670, 674, 677, and 678 and of their provisions, including the cancellation of all measures of boycott and embargo directed against Iraq.

c) The United States and other countries participating in the aggression against Iraq to withdraw all their forces, weapons and equipment from the Middle East, including the weapons and equipment provided to Israel under the pretext of the crisis in the Gulf.

d) Israel to withdraw from Palestine and the Arab territories it is occupying in the Golan and southern Lebanon. If Israel fails to do this, the United Nations should then enforce against Israel the same sanctions it has enacted against Iraq.

e) Iraq's historical rights on land and at sea should be guaranteed in full in any peaceful solution.

f) The political arrangements for Kuwait should proceed from the people's will, and in accordance with a genuine democratic practice, and not on the basis of the rights acquired by the Sabah family.

Second, the countries that have participated in the aggression undertake to reconstruct what the aggression has destroyed in Iraq. Iraq should not incur any financial burdens in this regard.

Third, the debts of Iraq and of other countries in the region which were harmed by the aggression should be written off.

Fourth, the Gulf states, including Iran, should be given the task of freely drawing up security arrangements in the region and of organizing relations among them without foreign interference.

Fifth, the Arabian Gulf region should be declared a zone free of foreign military bases.

Source: U.S. Department of State, *Dispatch* 2, no. 7 (18 February 1991), 113.

DOCUMENT 373: President Bush Responds to Iraqi Statement (15 February 1991)

When I first heard that statement, I must say I was happy that Saddam Hussein had seemed to realize that he must now withdraw unconditionally from Kuwait. . . . Regrettably, the Iraq statement now appears to be a cruel hoax, dashing the hopes of the people of Iraq and, indeed around the world. . . .

Not only was the Iraq statement full of unacceptable old conditions, but Saddam Hussein has added several new conditions. . . . Now let me state once again: they must withdraw without condition and there must be full implementation of all Security Council resolutions. And there will be no linkage to other problems in the area, and the legitimate rulers of Kuwait must be returned to Kuwait.

Until a massive withdrawal begins, with those Iraqi troops visibly leaving Kuwait, the coalition forces . . . will continue their efforts to force compliance with all resolutions of the United Nations.

But there's another way for the bloodshed to stop, and that is for the Iraqi military and the Iraqi people to take matters into their own hands, to force Saddam Hussein the dictator to step aside and to comply with the United Nations resolutions and then rejoin the family of peace-loving nations.

Source: "Remarks to the American Association for the Advancement of Science," in *Public Papers of the Presidents: George Bush, 1991*, Book 1 (Washington: GPO, 1992), 145.

DOCUMENT 374: Soviet President Mikhail Gorbachev's Peace Proposal (22 February 1991)

1. Iraq to carry out Resolution 660 of the U.N. Security Council, i.e., withdraw its forces immediately and unconditionally from Kuwait. The troop withdrawal will begin the day after a cease-fire is agreed upon, and be completed within 21 days. Troop withdrawal from Kuwait City will be accomplished within the first four days.

2. Once the Iraqi troops have withdrawn from Kuwait, all U.N. Security Council resolutions against Iraq will be lifted as no longer applicable.

3. All prisoners of war will be freed and repatriated within three days of the cease-fire.

4. The cease-fire and withdrawal of Iraqi troops from Kuwait will be monitored by U.N. designated peacekeeping forces.

Source: U.S. Department of State *Dispatch* 2, no. 10 (11 March 1991), 166–67.

DOCUMENT 375: President Bush's Ultimatum to Saddam Hussein (22 February 1991)

In view of the Soviet initiative, which very frankly we appreciate, we want to set forth this morning the specific criteria that will insure Saddam Hussein complies with the United Nations mandate. . . .

We learned this morning that Saddam has now launched a scorched-earth policy against Kuwait, anticipating perhaps that he will now be forced to leave. He is wantonly setting fires to and destroying the oil wells, the oil tanks, the port terminals and other installations of that small country.

Indeed, they are destroying the entire oil-production system of Kuwait. And at the same time that the Moscow press conference was going on and Iraq's Foreign Minister was talking peace, Saddam Hussein was launching Scud missiles. . . .

The coalition will give Saddam Hussein until noon Saturday to do what he must do—begin his immediate and unconditional withdrawal from Kuwait. We must hear publicly and authoritatively his acceptance of these terms. . . .

1. Iraq must begin large-scale withdrawal from Kuwait by noon New York time, Saturday, February 23 and complete military withdrawal from Kuwait in one week. Kuwait City is to be freed within the first 48 hours so as to allow the prompt return of the legitimate government of Kuwait. Within the one week specified above, Iraq must return all its forces to their positions of August 1 in accordance with Resolution 660.

2. In cooperation with the International Red Cross, Iraq must release all prisoners of war and third-country civilians being held against their will and return the remains of killed and deceased servicemen.

3. Iraq must remove all explosives or booby traps, including those on Kuwaiti oil installations, and provide data on the location and nature of any land or sea mines.

4. Iraq must cease combat air fire, aircraft flights over Iraq and Kuwait, except for transport aircraft carrying troops out of Kuwait. It must cease all destructive actions against Kuwaiti citizens and property and release all Kuwaiti detainees.

Source: "Remarks on the Persian Gulf Conflict," in *Public Papers of the Presidents: George Bush, 1991,* Book 1 (Washington: GPO, 1992), 165–66.

DOCUMENT 376: General Powell Reflects on Possible Iraqi Use of Chemical Weapons (1995)

We knew from CIA estimates that the Iraqis had at least a thousand tons of chemical agents. We knew that Saddam had used both mustard and nerve gases in his war against Iran. We knew that he had used gas on Iraq's rebellious Kurdish minority in 1988, killing or injuring four thousand Kurds. We briefly considered and then rejected sending over

U.S. chemical weapons. The Iraqi chemical threat was manageable. Our troops had protective suits and detection and alarm systems. In battle, we would be fast-moving and in the open desert, not trapped as civilians might be. A chemical attack would be a public relations crisis, but not a battlefield disaster. What to do about Iraq's biological capability, however, remained a more troubling question.

Source: Powell, *My American Journey,* 468.

DOCUMENT 377: General Norman Schwarzkopf Agrees with President Bush's Decision to Cease Offensive Operations in the "Hundred Hour War" (27 February 1991)

Soon [General Colin] Powell called in a relaxed and happy mood and said, "We ought to be talking about a ceasefire. The doves are starting to complain about all the damage we are doing."

"What do you mean?" I said. What had happened, of course, was that journalists had interviewed Air Force pilots who'd been hitting the convoys fleeing Kuwait. A four-lane road northwest of Kuwait City later came to be known as the "Highway of Death"—a scene of utter devastation with the burned-out wreckage of more than a thousand military vehicles and stolen civilian trucks, buses, and cars. "Shooting fish in a barrel" was the way one pilot was quoted describing the bombing, and that's what people heard Tuesday night when they turned on their TV sets. Powell informed me that the White House was getting nervous: "The reports make it sound like wanton killing."

He and I both knew that was not the case. Though many Iraqis in the convoy had died, most had jumped out of their vehicles and run away. I felt irritated—Washington was ready to overreact, as usual, to the slightest ripple in public opinion. I thought, but didn't say, that the best thing the White House could do would be to turn off the TV in the situation room. . . .

. . . I relayed what [General] Yeosock had said he needed to finish off the [Iraqi] Republican Guard. By the end of the day, while we'd be able to declare Iraq no longer militarily capable of threatening its neighbors, there would still be a hell of a lot of military equipment moving in the Basra pocket. "So here's what I propose," I said. "I want the Air Force to keep bombing those convoys backed up at the Euphrates where the bridges are blown. I want to continue the ground attack tomorrow, drive to the sea, and totally destroy everything in our path. That's the way I wrote the plan for Desert Storm, and in one more day we'll be done." I paused: "Do you realize if we stop tomorrow night, the ground campaign will have lasted five days? How does that sound to you: the 'Five-Day War'?"

Powell chuckled. "That has a nice ring to it. I'll pass it along." He added that we would need a media update at the end of the day. I suggested that the briefing be given in Riyadh rather than Washington because our information would be more timely, and he agreed.…

For the remainder of the afternoon I busied myself monitoring the battle. The charts were ready at seven P.M., and I took them upstairs to review them for an hour before heading across the street to the Hyatt Hotel for the media briefing. The presentation came off even better than I'd hoped.…

Powell called again, at 10:30 P.M. "I'm at the White House. We've been batting around your idea about ending the war at five days." He told me that in Washington the controversy over wanton killing had become uncomfortably intense—even the French and the British had begun asking how long we intended to continue the war. "The President is thinking about going on the air tonight at nine o'clock and announcing we're cutting it off. Would you have any problem with that?"

… He waited as I took a minute to think. My gut reaction was that a quick cease-fire would save lives. If we continued to attack through Thursday, more of our troops would get killed, probably not many, but some. What was more, we'd accomplished our mission: I'd just finished telling the American people that there wasn't enough left of Iraq's army for it to be a regional military threat. Of course, Yeosock had asked for another day, and I'd have been happy to keep on destroying the Iraqi military for the next six months. Yet we'd kicked this guy's butt, leaving no doubt in anybody's mind that we'd won decisively, and we'd done it with very few casualties. Why not end it? Why get somebody else killed tomorrow? That made up my mind.

"I don't have any problem with it," I finally answered. "Our objective was the destruction of the enemy forces and for all intents and purposes we've accomplished that objective. I'll check with my commanders, but unless they've hit some snag I don't know about, we can stop."…

A few hours later Powell called to confirm: "We'll cease offensive operations, but there's been a change. The President will make his announcement at nine o'clock, but we won't actually stop until midnight. That makes it a hundred-hour war." I had to hand it to them: they really knew how to package an historic event.

President Bush and Secretary Cheney each came on the line to offer congratulations.

Source: H. Norman Schwarzkopf and Peter Petre, *It Doesn't Take a Hero* (New York: Bantam Books, 1992), 542–45.

DOCUMENT 378: General Powell's "Force Employment" Strategy Against Iraq (January–March 1991)

The Gulf War was a limited-objective war. If it had not been, we would be ruling Baghdad today—at unpardonable expense in terms of money, lives lost and ruined regional relationships.

The Gulf War was also a limited-means war—we did not use every means at our disposal to eject the Iraqi Army from Kuwait. But we did use overwhelming force quickly and decisively. This, I believe, is why some have characterized that war as an "all-out" war. It was strictly speaking no such thing.

To help with the complex issue of the use of "violent" force, some have turned to a set of principles or a when-to-go-to-war doctrine. "Follow these directions and you can't go wrong." There is, however, no fixed set of rules for the use of military force. To set one up is dangerous. First, it destroys the ambiguity we might want to exist in our enemy's mind regarding our intentions. Unless part of our strategy is to destroy that ambiguity, it is usually helpful to keep it intact.

Second, having a fixed set of rules for how you will go to war is like saying you are always going to use the elevator in the event of fire in your apartment building. . . . In short, your plans to escape should be governed by the circumstances of the fire when it starts.

When a "fire" starts that might require committing armed forces, we need to evaluate the circumstances. Relevant questions include: Is the political objective we seek to achieve important, clearly defined and understood? Have all other nonviolent policy means failed? Will military force achieve the objective? At what cost? Have the gains and risks been analyzed? How might the situation that we seek to alter, once it is altered by force, develop further and what might be the consequences?

As an example of this logical process, we can examine the assertions of those who have asked why President Bush did not order our forces on to Baghdad after we had driven the Iraqi army out of Kuwait. We must assume that the political objective of such an order would have been capturing Saddam Hussein. Even if Hussein had waited for us to enter Baghdad, and even if we had been able to capture him, what purpose would it have served? And would serving that purpose have been worth the many more casualties that would have occurred? Would it have been worth the inevitable follow-up: major occupation forces in Iraq for years to come and a very expensive and complex American proconsulship in Baghdad? Fortunately for America, reasonable people at the time thought not. They still do.

Source: Colin L. Powell, "U.S. Forces: Challenges Ahead," *Foreign Affairs* 71, no. 5 (Winter 1992–93), 36–37.

DOCUMENT 379: General Schwarzkopf Concludes Cease-fire with Iraqi Generals at Safwan Airfield (3 March 1991)

I climbed aboard my airplane for . . . Safwan. . . . I gazed out the window thinking about the upcoming negotiation. I wanted the meeting to be a straightforward military discussion with no crowing, no posturing, and no humiliation of the Iraqis. But by the same token, I didn't want them thinking we'd just forgive and forget. . . .

We took off and flew north along the so-called Highway of Death. In every direction we could see the burnt wrecks of military and civilian vehicles that the Iraqis had used to try to flee with their booty from Kuwait City. . . . It was all down there on the ground, totally destroyed.

About ten miles north of Kuwait City we came clear of the smoke and the sky was blue again. But burning oil wells remained visible on the horizon. Suddenly I was overtaken with anger. This was an ecological disaster that the Iraqis had perpetrated, not just on Kuwait but on the entire region. . . . I'd left Riyadh determined to conduct the cease-fire talks in a calm, levelheaded, professional way. But by the time we set down at Safwan, I was just plain mad. . . .

We made it to the search tent seconds before the Iraqis. Their escort convoy raced onto the airfield—two MlAl tanks, two Bradley Fighting Vehicles, then eight humvees, each driven by an American soldier with an Iraqi in the passenger seat. A pair of Apache helicopters, flying just ten feet off the ground, brought up the rear.

I stood at the door of the search tent and watched the Iraqis walk up. I'd worn my battle-dress fatigues and a field cap; they had on their green dress uniforms and black berets. General Ahmad, the leader, was a stocky fellow with a heavy Saddam-style mustache. I recognized him with a start. . . . He now looked extremely uptight. . . .

We entered the meeting tent and I showed the Iraqis where to sit. The press was allowed in briefly to photograph us facing each other across the table. Ahmad wore an uncertain little smile, probably thinking this was the beginning of a public show trial. But before starting the meeting, we cleared out the photographers and reporters.

I opened by reminding the Iraqis that our purpose was to lay out the military conditions for a cease-fire and informed them that we would tape the conversation so that each side would have a permanent record. . . .

I expected the Iraqis would pretty much take notes from this point on—any agreement, we all figured, would come only after they'd had a chance to confer with Saddam. "The first thing that we would like to discuss is prisoners of war," I said. I made my first request—that the Red Cross be allowed immediate access to POWs held by Iraqis—and Ahmad promptly declared, "This will be accomplished." . . .

"That's good." Next I said that we wanted to discuss the release of prisoners of war. He immediately asserted, "We are ready to return all POWs at once, in any way convenient for the Red Cross."

Ahmad had clearly been given authority to come to terms on the spot. I proceeded to work my way down the conditions—the identification of coalition MIAs, the return of bodily remains, the disclosure of minefields and unconventional-weapons bunkers in Kuwait, and so on. The Iraqis agreed to all. . . .

Finally I raised the issue of drawing a cease-fire line. "We had an unfortunate incident yesterday where our troops got in one more battle that we did not need," I began. Ahmad bristled and demanded to know why we had destroyed the Iraqi armored column in the Euphrates valley. "The ones you shot were drawing back," he claimed. . . .

I knew what was on Ahmad's mind: he had been ordered not to concede any territory, and the cease-fire line we were proposing was deep within Iraq's borders. The atmosphere had become tense. When I said we had prepared a map, he interrupted: "We have agreed that this is not a permanent line?"

[I reassured him] "It is absolutely not a permanent line. . . . It has nothing to do with borders. It is only a safety measure. We have no intention of leaving our forces permanently in Iraqi territory once the cease-fire is signed."

But Ahmad wasn't finished. He wanted to know why the coalition had launched ground forces into his country in the first place, "after we had withdrawn from Kuwait and announced it on the television and radio."

. . . There was a brief silence. At last he seemed ready to continue the discussions, and regarding measures to prevent further fighting between our forces, he said, "In this matter we will cooperate."

Now that we had covered the coalition's main points, we had a brief discussion of how vehicles in the cease-fire zone would fly orange flags to signal peaceful intent. Then I asked, "Are there any other matters the general would like to discuss?"

"We have one point," he said. "You know the situation of our roads and bridges and communications." I nodded, thinking of the overwhelming damage our bombing had done. "We would like to fly helicopters to carry officials of our government in areas where roads and bridges are out. This has nothing to do with the front line. This is inside Iraq."

It appeared to me to be a legitimate request. And given that the Iraqis had agreed to all our requests, I didn't feel it was unreasonable to grant one of theirs: "As long as it is not over the part we are in, that is absolutely no problem. So we will let the helicopters fly. That is a very important point, and I want to make sure it's recorded, that military helicopters can fly over Iraq. Not fighters, not bombers."

Then Ahmad said something that should have given me pause. "So you mean even helicopters that are armed can fly in Iraqi skies but not the fighters?" . . .

"Yeah. I will instruct the Air Force not to shoot at any helicopters flying over the territory of Iraq where our troops are not located."

In the following weeks, we discovered what the son of a bitch had really in mind: using helicopter gunships to suppress rebellions in Basra and other cities. By that time it was up to the White House to decide how much the United States wanted to intervene in the internal politics of Iraq. . . .

After that, there was only one moment at which Ahmad showed any emotion. He presented an accounting of coalition prisoners of war held by Iraq. "We have forty-one in all," he said. I made notes as he read them off:

17 Americans . . . 2 Italians . . . 12 British . . . 1 Kuwaiti . . . 9 Saudis

This left a number of people unaccounted for, and I quickly brought out our list of MIAs, but he stopped me. "And we would like to have the numbers of the POWs on our side as well."

"As of last night, sixty thousand," I replied. "Or sixty thousand plus, because it is difficult to count them completely." His face went completely pale: he had had no concept of the magnitude of their defeat.

When the meeting adjourned, we had to wait a few minutes [to give] the Iraqis their set [of audiotapes] and escorted them outside. The convoy was waiting. . . .

When Ahmad reached the humvee he turned, stood at attention, and saluted. I returned the salute. He stuck out his hand. I shook it and wished him a safe journey. He looked at me and replied, "As an Arab, I hold no hate in my heart." . . .

For the first time, I had a sense, not of triumph, not of glory, but of relief. I . . . told . . . myself again and again, "It really is over."

Source: Schwarzkopf and Petre, *It Doesn't Take a Hero,* 557–69.

THE AFTERMATH OF ARMS OVER DIPLOMACY, 1991–1993

DOCUMENT 380: President Bush's Address Before Joint Session of Congress (6 March 1991)

From the moment Operation Desert Storm commenced on January 16 until the time the guns fell silent at midnight one week ago, this nation has watched its sons and daughters with pride—watched over them with prayer. As Commander in Chief, I can report to you that our armed forces fought with honor and valor. And as President, I can report to the nation that aggression is defeated. The war is over.

This is a victory for every nation in the coalition; for the United Nations; a victory for unprecedented international cooperation. . . . It is a victory for the rule of law and for what is right. . . .

The recent challenge could not have been clearer. Saddam Hussein was the villain; Kuwait the victim. To the aid of this small country came the nations of North America and Europe, from Asia and South America, from Africa and the Arab world. . . . Tonight in Iraq, Saddam walks amidst ruin. His war machine is crushed. The ability to threaten mass destruction is itself destroyed. . . . And when his defeated legions come home, all Iraqis will see and feel the havoc he has wrought. For all that Saddam has done to his own people, to the Kuwaitis, and to the entire world, Saddam and those around him are accountable.

Source: "Address Before a Joint Session of Congress," 6 March 1991, in *Public Papers of the Presidents: George Bush, 1991*, Book 1 (Washington: GPO, 1992), 218–22.

DOCUMENT 381: Synopsis of UN Resolutions Relating to Iraq's Defeat by UN Coalition of Forces (March–September 1991)

Resolution 686 (2 March) demanded that Iraq rescind its actions purporting to annex Kuwait; cease hostile or provocative actions by Iraqi forces against all Member states, including missile attacks and flights of combat aircraft; identify Iraqi chemical and biological weapons and material in Kuwait and Iraq.

Resolution 687 (3 April) calls upon Secretary General to lend assistance to Iraq and Kuwait to demarcate the boundary between Iraq and Kuwait according to the "Agreed Minutes Between the State of Kuwait and the Republic of Iraq Regarding the Restoration of Friendly Relations, Recognition and Related Matters" signed by them in the exercise of their sovereignty at Baghdad on 4 October 1963.

Resolution 688 (5 April) condemned the repression of the Iraqi civilian population in the Kurdish region of Iraq and insisted that Iraq allow international humanitarian access to the Kurdish population.

Resolution 689 (9 April) in accordance with Resolution 687 (1991) the Security Council authorized the Iraq-Kuwait Observation Mission to operate for six months.

Resolution 692 (20 May) established a UN Compensation Fund to which Iraq will pay reparations for the direct loss, damage, including environmental damage and the depletion of natural resources, or injury to foreign Governments, nationals and corporations, as a result of Iraq's unlawful invasion and occupation of Kuwait.

Resolution 699 (17 June) confirmed that the International Atomic Energy Agency (IAEA) had the authority to destroy, remove, or render harmless materials associated with the production of nuclear, chemical or biological weapons.

Resolution 700 (17 June) continued the monitoring of prohibitions of arms sales to Iraq and maintained economic sanctions against Iraq.

Resolution 705 (15 August) allowed Iraq to export 30 percent of the annual value of its exports of petroleum for humanitarian requirements within Iraq.

Resolution 706 (15 August) authorized Member States to purchase Iraqi petroleum through an UN escrow account to meet the humanitarian needs of the Iraqi population.

Resolution 707 (15 August) demanded that Iraq provide full disclosure of all aspects of its programmes to develop weapons of mass destruction and ballistic missiles with range greater than 150 km; make available to UN Special Commission, and the IAEA Inspection Teams immediate access to denied areas, including permission to conduct both fixed wing and helicopter flights throughout Iraq for inspection, surveillance, and aerial surveys.

Resolution 712 (19 September) decided that all revenues from Iraqi petroleum and petroleum products were immune from legal proceedings and that all monies obtained by the sale of Iraqi oil be deposited in UN escrow account to provide Iraqi population with foodstuffs, medicines or other humanitarian necessities of life.

Source: Moore, *Crisis in the Gulf,* Vol. 1, 421–55.

DOCUMENT 382: Findings of U.S. Army Report on Iraqi War Crimes (8 January 1992)

Beginning on 3 August 1990, the Office of the Judge Advocate General of the U.S. Army began an investigation of Iraqi war crimes during its invasion of Kuwait. Media reports indicated that U.S. citizens in Kuwait had been taken hostage by Iraqi forces and forcibly deported to Iraq, constituting grave breaches under the Geneva Conventions. The investigation's final report was released on 8 January 1992.

2. Iraqi Treatment of U.S. Prisoners of War

A total of forty-seven U.S. military personnel were initially listed as either prisoners of war or missing in action during the Gulf War. Since then, twenty-six have been officially listed as having been killed in action. Twenty-one individuals were captured and held as prisoners of war by Iraq. They were repatriated between 3–9 March 1991.

All of the prisoners war were the victims of war crimes committed by Iraq. Although unable to identify the individuals who abused U.S. prisoners of war, the Center has accumulated extensive circumstantial evidence to support a *prima facie* case that the mistreatment of U.S. prisoners of war occurred with at least the acquiescence, and probably at the direction, of the Iraqi leadership.

3. Iraqi Treatment of U.S. Hostages

Records of the Department of State and Defense Intelligence Agency document Iraq's unlawful taking of U.S. civilians as hostages, the forced removal of U.S. civilians as hostages, the forced removal of U.S. hostages from Kuwait, and the use of U.S. hostages as "human shields" around Iraqi strategic sites. Each of these actions is a violation of the Fourth Geneva Convention. The Center has evidence of over 4,900 U.S. hostages taken by Iraq, 106 of whom were used by Iraq as "human shields." The files and documents gathered by the Department of State establish a *prima facie* case of grave breaches of the Fourth Geneva Convention committed against U.S. citizens by Iraq. . . .

C. Findings

1. Iraqi War Crimes

The term "war crime" is the technical expression for a violation of the law of war, and every violation of the law of war is a war crime. The Army's investigation makes it clear that Iraqi violations of the law of war were widespread and premeditated. They included taking hostages, torture and murder of civilians, looting civilian property, looting cultural property, indiscriminate attacks on noncombatants by the launching of SCUD missiles against cities rather than specific military objectives, illegal employment of sea mines, mistreatment of prisoners of war, and unnecessary destruction of property, as evidenced by the release of oil into the Persian Gulf and the destruction of hundreds of Kuwaiti oil wells.

Specific Iraqi war crimes, which have been extensively documented by the War Crimes Documentation Center, include the following:

a. The taking of Kuwaiti nationals as hostages, and their individual and mass forcible deportation to Iraq, in violation of Articles 34, and 147, Geneva Convention (GC).

b. The taking of third country nationals in Kuwait as hostages, and their individual and mass forcible deportation to Iraq, in violation of Articles 34, 49, and 147, GC.

c. The taking of third country nationals in Iraq as hostages, and their individual and mass forcible transfer within Iraq, in violation of Articles 34 and 147, GC.

d. Compelling Kuwaiti and other foreign nationals to serve in the armed forces of Iraq, in violation of Articles 51 and 147, GC.

e. Use of Kuwaiti and third country nationals as human shields in violation of Articles 28, and 38(4), GC.

f. Inhumane treatment of Kuwaiti and third country civilians, to include rape and willful killing, in violation of Articles 27, 32, and 147, GC.

g. The transfer of Iraq's civilian population into occupied Kuwait, in violation of Article 49, GC.

h. Torture and other inhumane treatment of Coalition and U.S. prisoners of war, in violation of Articles 13, 17, 22, 25, 26, 27, and 130, General Principles of Warfare (GPW).

i. Using coalition prisoners of war as human shields to render military objectives immune from military operations, in violation of Article 23, GPW.

j. Unnecessary destruction of Kuwaiti private and public property, in violation of Article 23(g), Annex to Hague IV.

k. Pillage, in violation of Article 47, Annex to Hague IV.

l. Illegal confiscation/inadequate safeguarding of Kuwaiti public property in violation of Article 55, Annex to Hague IV, and Article 147, GC.

m. Pillage of Kuwaiti civilian hospitals, in violation of Articles 55, 56, 57, and 147, GC.

n. Indiscriminate SCUD missile attacks against the noncombatant civilians of Saudi Arabia and Israel (the latter a neutral to the conflict), unnecessary destruction in violation of Article 23(g), Annex to Hague IV.

o. Intentional release of oil into the Persian Gulf and its sabotage of the Al-Burgan and Rumalia oil fields in Kuwait, unnecessary destruction in violation of Articles 23(g) and 55, Annex to Hague IV, and Articles 53 and 147, GC.

p. Employment of unanchored naval mines and mines lacking devices for their self-neutralization in the event of their breaking loose from their moorings, in violation of Article 1, Hague VIII. . . .

D. Conclusion

. . . The national command authorities of Iraq, as well as individual Iraqi officials, perpetrated numerous war crimes against both military and civilian personnel of the United States and Kuwait. The War Crimes Documentation Center has assembled the evidence to prove it.

Source: Stevens, *Iraqi Invasion of Kuwait*, 63–69.

FURTHER READING

Baker, James A, III. *The Politics of Diplomacy: Revolution, War and Peace, 1989–1992* (1995).

Bennis, Phyllis, and Michael Moushabeck, eds. *Beyond the Storm: A Gulf Crisis Reader* (1991).

Brune, Lester H. *America and the Iraqi Crisis, 1990–1992: Origins and Aftermath* (1993).

Dunnigan, James F., and Austin Bay. *From Shield to Storm: High-Tech Weapons, Military Strategy, and Coalition Warfare in the Persian Gulf* (1992).

Freedman, Lawrence, and Efraim Karsh. *The Gulf Conflict, 1990–1991: Diplomacy and War in the New World Order* (1993).

Friedman, Norman. *Desert Victory: The War for Kuwait* (1992).

Hilsman, Roger. *George Bush vs. Saddam Hussein: Military Success! Political Failure?* (1992).

Jervis, Robert, and Seweryn Bailer. *Soviet-American Relations after the Cold War* (1991).

Mazarr, Michael, Don M. Snider, and James A. Blackwell, Jr. *Desert Storm: The Gulf War and What We Learned* (1993).

Palmer, Michael A. *Guardians of the Gulf: A History of America's Expanding Role in the Persian Gulf, 1833–1992* (1992).

Powell, Colin, with Joseph Persico. *My American Journey* (1995).

Schwarzkopf, H. Norman, and Peter Petre. *It Doesn't Take a Hero* (1992).

Smith, Jean Edward. *George Bush's War* (1992).

Sultan, Khaled Bin, with Patrick Seale. *Desert Warrior* (1994).

Woodward, Bob. *The Commanders* (1991).

Index

About the Editor

RUSSELL D. BUHITE is Professor of History and Head of the Department of History at the University of Tennessee. He is the author of eight books and numerous articles in the field of American foreign relations.